FOR THE TEMPORARY
ACCOMMODATION
OF SETTLERS

FOR THE TEMPORARY ACCOMMODATION OF SETTLERS

Architecture and
Immigrant Reception
in Canada, 1870–1930

DAVID MONTEYNE

McGill-Queen's University Press
Montreal & Kingston | London | Chicago

ISBN 978-0-2280-0638-1 (cloth)
ISBN 978-0-2280-0755-5 (ePDF)

Legal deposit fourth quarter 2021
Bibliothèque nationale du Québec

Printed in Canada on acid-free paper that is 100% ancient forest
free (100% post-consumer recycled), processed chlorine free

This book has been published with the help of a grant from the
Canadian Federation for the Humanities and Social Sciences,
through the Awards to Scholarly Publications Program, using funds
provided by the Social Sciences and Humanities Research Council
of Canada.

We acknowledge the support of the Canada Council for the Arts.

Nous remercions le Conseil des arts du Canada de son soutien.

Library and Archives Canada Cataloguing in Publication

Title: For the temporary accommodation of settlers : architecture
    and immigrant reception in Canada, 1870-1930 / David
    Monteyne.
Other titles: Architecture and immigrant reception in Canada,
    1870–1930
Names: Monteyne, David, author.
Description: Includes bibliographical references and index.
Identifiers: Canadiana (print) 20210145552 | Canadiana
    (ebook) 20210163852 | ISBN 9780228006381 (hardcover) |
    ISBN 9780228007555 (PDF)
Subjects: LCSH: Architecture and society—Canada—History—
    19th century. | LCSH: Architecture and society—Canada—
    History—20th century. | LCSH: Architecture and state—
    Canada—History—19th century. | LCSH: Architecture and
    state—Canada—History—20th century. | LCSH: Immigrants—
    Canada—History—19th century. | LCSH: Immigrants—Canada—
    History—20th century. | LCSH: Canada—Emigration and
    immigration—History—19th century. | LCSH: Canada—
    Emigration and immigration—History—20th century.
Classification: LCC NA2543.S6 M66 2021 | DDC 720.1/030971—dc23

Set in 11.5/14.5 Emigre Filosofia with Linotype Trade Gothic Std
Book design & typesetting by Garet Markvoort, zijn digital

FOR THOSE WHO MIGRATE, AND
THOSE WHO HELP THEM

CONTENTS

ACKNOWLEDGMENTS

The first discoveries that eventually led to the publication of this book occurred when I was beginning work on a remotely related research idea as visiting scholar at the Canadian Centre for Architecture (CCA) in Montreal, on the invitation of Alexis Sornin. During that time, I was doing some research in the Canadian Pacific Railway archives in Windsor Station. At lunch, I took a stroll in the vicinity of the station and stumbled upon a boarded-up and well-graffitied building on Saint-Antoine Street. Peering through the overgrown shrubbery obscuring the side entrance of the building, I could discern the word "Immigration" carved over the door. The next morning, I found the full set of original architectural drawings in the Ross & MacFarlane fonds at the CCA collection. It seemed serendipitous: from that point forward, I focused on government immigration buildings and the experiences of the immigrants that passed through them.

During my next sabbatical, I explored some of the theory and historiography for my project as a visiting fellow at the University of Cambridge's Clare Hall and The Centre for Research in the Arts, Social Sciences, and Humanities (CRASSH), where I was hosted by Simon Goldhill and Dana Arnold. Research leaves, research assistants, and research trips to Libraries and Archives Canada have been funded by a series of small grants from the University of Calgary and the School of Architecture, Planning, and Landscape.

My editor at McGill-Queen's University Press, Jonathan Crago, recruited the project before it was a project, when it was a vague proposal at the CCA. He has stuck with it for a decade, as I figured out what the book would be about. His advice and responses to my writing have been invaluable.

I have had a group of excellent student research assistants over the long course of this project. Shannon Murray was there right from the start, before this even became about immigrants, and she continued to contribute for many years thereafter. She did much more than literature reviews and archival research, helping me understand the historiographic debates and, importantly, how "real historians" think. Jonathan Weller came along later and dug up material in various archives that made the book's narrative richer. Other former students who made important contributions for research and graphics include Stuart Barnard, Sandy Barron, Sarah Bramley, and Kendra Kusick.

A long list of archivists and historians have provided valued sources, information, and direction over the years. Among those who stand out for particular thanks are Larisa Sembaliuk Cheladyn, Gareth Evans, Donald Luxton, Rebecca Mancuso, Forrest Pass, and Richard White. Steve Schwinghamer of the Canadian Museum of Immigration at Pier 21 was exceedingly helpful on early research visits. Harry Sanders, Calgary's first "historian laureate," was a continuous source of anecdotes and nineteenth-century news clippings.

Others demonstrated to me the worth of my project through invited lectures, conversations, and encouragement at the right times. These include Annmarie Adams, Victoria Baster, Catherine Boland Erkkila, Marta Gutman, Mary McLeod, and Jane Rendell. Kate Solomonson, who was my PhD supervisor and then series editor when I published my previous book, *Fallout Shelter*, has continued to be my most valued mentor. Nowadays, our research has much more in common than when I was writing about Cold War civil defence.

My family migrated with me to provide support on three sabbaticals during the research and writing of this book. Although we got to live in a lot of different places, they will be glad to see it finally finished.

FOR THE TEMPORARY
ACCOMMODATION
OF SETTLERS

INTRODUCTION

"For the Temporary Accommodation of Settlers"

In order to make Canada more attractive to "desirable" immigrants, the Dominion government built a network of immigration buildings to provide newcomers with shelter, services, and state support. "Immigration sheds" — where transoceanic liners would dock and immigrants would be processed — were complemented by a wide range of facilities in receiving areas. In this book, I document and analyze the architecture and the spatial practices manifested along the immigration journey in Canada between 1870 and the mid-1930s, when this network was built and most heavily used. I consider the arrival, processing, and transfer of global migrants at Canadian piers; the accommodation and advising of new arrivals at Prairie reception halls; and also the incarceration at quarantine stations and immigrant detention hospitals of those deemed unfit or "undesirable." The extent of this Canadian network, and the range of building types that comprised it, seem to have been unique among immigrant-receiving nations in this period.

The central premise of the book addresses a broad issue in architectural history: how people experience, navigate, transform, and produce meaning in the built environments that they encounter. Canadian immigration architecture provides a rich area of research for exploring this problem, because it allows us to appreciate how spaces designed by the government to achieve certain long-term policy goals were occupied by migrants to achieve immediate personal objectives upon their arrival in the country. In turn, government representatives often found themselves reinterpreting policy and reshaping immigration architectures to accommodate or attempt to control what immigrants were doing in its buildings. In each of the following chapters, I answer two specific questions: what were the intentions of the Canadian government in designing, erecting, and operating immigrant reception buildings on quarantine islands, in ports, and in Prairie towns, and how did new arrivals negotiate and use these government buildings to satisfy their basic needs, to ensure safe journeys for their families, to learn of land and job opportunities, and ultimately to arrive at their Canadian destinations?[1]

No source survives describing a single migrant's experiences in all these types of government buildings and spatial situations. Moreover, many of their experiences necessarily remained of the moment, never recorded on the written page for historians to discover. But a great number of sources exist in Canadian archives and libraries which touch on different aspects of migrants' journeys, arrivals, and first impressions. Alongside

I.1 Exterior view of the 1887 Dominion government immigration building, Quebec, c. 1905.

architectural plans, official correspondence, and policy statements, this book plumbs these varied first-person sources to explore and understand the practices and encounters of migrants with officials, volunteers, interpreters, and others within government immigration architecture. Throughout, I interpret official, governmental intentions evidenced by immigration architecture, but foreground the unofficial, informal practices of people who occupied, used, and were processed through these spaces.

We can comprehend something of architectural intentions and spatial practices through two photographs and one plan of the Dominion

government pier building in Quebec City from around 1910. In a contextual view (Figure I.1), a long, one- and two-storey structure, with a series of cross-gables, is sandwiched between busy rail lines, a road, a grain elevator, and other structures; the harbour waters can be glimpsed in the background. The eave of the deep veranda aligns closely with the top edge of the waiting passenger cars. The sheer length and complex roofline of the building suggest a layered architectural program, while the tall fence and shed-roof gate structure at the lower right represent controlled access from the public street. This historic photo hints at clear intentions behind the design: for example, that the building would interface with the transportation infrastructure of the port, affording the fluid transfer of immigrants and baggage from ship to train; and that this facility would cater to all the basic needs of immigrants upon their arrival, from food and shelter to tickets and advice, all in a safe space separate from the public. A hand-sketched plan of the ground floor, from immigration-branch correspondence with architects in the Department of Public Works, confirms these intentions (Figure I.2). A large waiting room is complemented by railway and government offices, a kitchen, immigrant dining room, and restaurant, plus bath and wash rooms. Unlabelled spaces also included a government-run store and rooms for religious and other charitable organizations that supported immigrants. Upstairs were doctors' offices and men's and women's dormitories. The toilets were a short walk down the pier.

After long ocean voyages in steerage-class accommodations, one basic need of the new arrivals was an opportunity to wash up. In an intimate interior view, two migrant women work at deep laundry sinks in the morning light from a window opened to the harbour (Figure I.3). Their spatial practices conform to the government's intent in providing these washing-up rooms, which were architecturally emphasized in their own wing of the Quebec building. Spaces for bathing and laundering were always available to newcomers stopping in immigration buildings at each stage of their Canadian journeys. A 1911 description of a similar scene in the laundry room at the government immigration hall in Winnipeg further confirms that the immigrants made good use of them: "a number of women immigrants, up to their elbows in lather, were rejoicing in the opportunity of getting a lot of washing done at nothing but the cost of the soap."[2]

I.2 A ground-floor plan of the 1887 Quebec immigration building, hand-sketched in 1907.

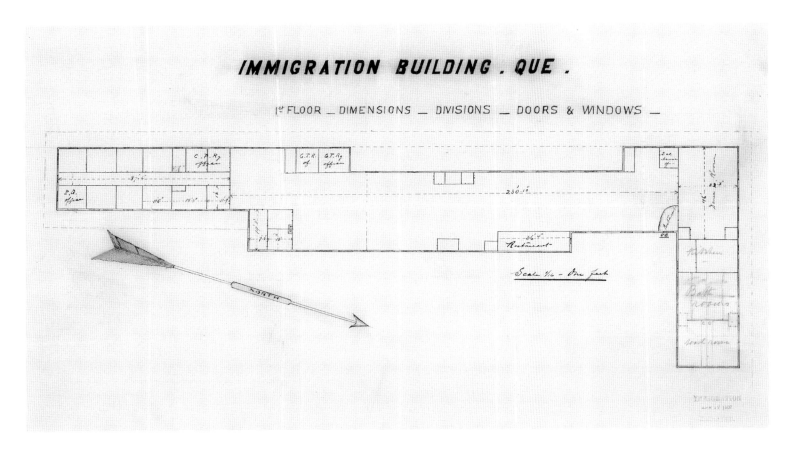

IMMIGRATION BUILDING . QUE .

1st FLOOR _ DIMENSIONS _ DIVISIONS _ DOORS & WINDOWS _

I.3 Quebec immigration building of 1887, laundry room for immigrants (the Wash Room on the plan), c. 1911.

I.4 New arrivals on the front steps of the Dominion government immigration hall in Winnipeg; this building served from 1890 into the 1910s.

The government's commitment to hygiene drew on age-old beliefs that immigrants were unclean, and the onus seemed to be on the migrants to prove otherwise. The famed "Canadian Immigration Representative to the Austro-Hungarian Empire," Joseph Oleskiw, advised migrants that Canadian immigration buildings were "clean, as is generally the British custom." More personally, he warned that those who "hope to succeed in a new country" would have to "get used to keeping their body and clothes extremely clean and maintain this standard throughout the trip." North Americans, he claimed, "never sit down to eat without washing before the meal and they all wash with soap at least three times a day."[3] Oleskiw's rather exaggerated distinction between Canadians and the eastern Europeans that he addresses as "our peasants" is a cardinal instance of what post-colonial scholar Ann Laura Stoler terms "prescriptions for comportment" that "graded the distinctions of privilege and class" among the inhabitants of European colonies.[4] The pre-eminence of cleaning practices in Dominion government immigration architecture reinforced these distinctions. In the photograph, the women are dressed in simple and demure floor-length print dresses, their well-used work aprons attesting to their industriousness as a class of desirable immigrants suitable to populate a new nation.

Performing the perceived duties of personal cleanliness was a way for newcomers to fit in with the spatial practices of a new home. Yet, the littered floors and filthy walls around the sinks call into question the government's ability to manage fully the comportment of so many immigrants passing through its buildings. Officials complained that "the walls in the wash room are somewhat disfigured with pencil marks and it would consequently be well to have them painted … and any future scribbling readily erased."[5] They saw these marks and graffiti as dirt out of place, but it is difficult to know whether the migrants themselves would have agreed. Looking back, we can appreciate these inscriptions as recorded evidence of the migrants' presence in a new space, as traces of ephemeral spatial practices that nevertheless reverberate back through official correspondence and are ultimately reflected materially in specifications for maintenance and new construction.

The early post-Confederation years in Canada saw the promotion of immigration as one of the key themes of a nationalization policy. The Dominion government sought ways to attract and keep immigrants, in competition with the United States and other countries. One result, as seen in the architecture of port and Prairie reception facilities, was an attempt to render Canada the kinder, gentler immigrant destination (Figure I.4). At the same time, Canada would protect her population from real or perceived Old World epidemics through the modernization and extension of coastal quarantine stations. The infrastructural network begun in the 1870s became much more important and extensive when immigrant numbers finally rose to significant levels around 1900. Before the First World War, the network peaked at over sixty different sites, some with multiple buildings, and stretched from Halifax to Prince Rupert, from William Head to Lawlor's Island.

Although all this architecture was meant to promote the welcome and welfare of immigrants, it also supported selectivity and sorting. Throughout

I.5 Side elevation of the Montreal immigrant detention building, Ross & MacFarlane Architects, 1912–14. Note the screened verandas attached to the rear.

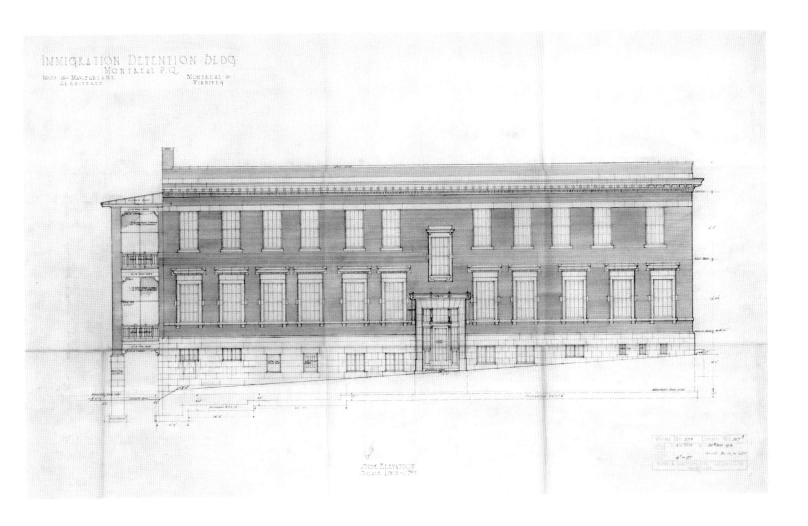

the period of this book, immigrants were classified as more or less desirable by government policies and public sentiment. While the exact classifications could change over time, driven by the economic need for specific types of labour, they were fundamentally racial and occupational. Farmers and female domestic servants of British and northern-European stock topped the hierarchy; mechanics, clerks, unskilled labourers, "foreigners," and Asians were typically deemed undesirable, but often were allowed entry anyway. Thus, to sort these different classes of arrivals, inspection and detention joined reception as key functions of certain immigration buildings of the early-twentieth century. In particular, "immigrant detention hospitals" appeared as an architecture designed both to effect deportations on the east coast, and to control Asian migration to Canada's west coast (Figure I.5).

The First World War slowed immigration, and the buildings were used as barracks and convalescent hospitals for troop deployments and demobilization. A resurgence of immigration activity in the mid-1920s came with attendant construction of facilities at eastern ports and certain transportation hubs on the Prairies, even as the need for quarantine stations waned. One of the new port buildings of this era was Halifax's well-known Pier 21 (now the Canadian Museum of Immigration), which opened just before the onset of the Great Depression. The Depression years, followed by war, curtailed the need for reception facilities, so Pier 21 mainly hosted deportees in its early years — other Canadian immigration buildings also served this seemingly contradictory purpose. This book ends with these return journeys that were forced on some immigrants. By the end of the Second World War, the nature of immigration had changed: migrants were healthier, they arrived less and less by ocean ports, a smaller proportion were destined for small Prairie towns, and those Prairie towns now had hotels and established ethnic

support networks. These changes rendered the government's immigration infrastructure obsolete, and it is now long forgotten.

METHODOLOGY AND HISTORIOGRAPHY

To explore the Canadian architecture of immigrant reception, I analyze and interpret archival documents from federal government immigration and building agencies, and mobilize immigrant stories as recorded in first-person sources, such as memoirs and letters. While immigration historians have long used immigrant voices to narrate experience and illustrate arguments, in this project I ask new questions about the spaces that these subjects passed through — and reflected upon. The immigration process often is seen as "placeless," as a period characterized by movement and in-betweenness. However, all these migratory moments are emplaced; immigrants in transit engage in activities that occur in architectural space. Insights from this study of social space can inform and modify immigration history, as much as they do architectural history.

This book contends that to achieve a comprehensive understanding of the history of Canada's immigration architecture — or of architecture anywhere — it is necessary to study both the formal strategies of governments, institutions, or other organizations, *and* the informal individual and group tactics for shaping space. The framework for my research on immigration architecture developed out of my appreciation of cultural theorist Henri Lefebvre's *The Production of Space*. Lefebvre calls for a history of "social space" encompassing the study of three elements: the spaces conceived and constructed by architects and their clients; the cumulative lived experience of people in these spaces; and the ongoing, ephemeral spatial practices of people. What Lefebvre calls "lived experience" can be understood as a layered storehouse of spatial memory and knowledge to draw on in everyday life. Lived experience allows individuals or social groups to negotiate, understand, and make use of cities, buildings, and other built environments. It is this ongoing negotiation, interpretation, and use of space that constitutes "spatial practice": a mode of bodily action that is framed within existing built environments, and conditioned by previous lived experience, but not dictated by either of these. People's spatial practices can be habitual or conform to given paths, but they may also be improvised or resistant within the material possibilities of a particular space.[6] Always though, spatial practices are informed by individual and group histories inflected through identity markers such as race, gender, sexuality, or citizenship. Because the presence of the migrant rarely lasted more than a few hours or days – or, in the case of detention, a few weeks – in any one building, their uses of these spaces never became habitual, making immigration architecture an advantageous site for researching temporary spatial practices.

Of Lefebvre's three elements of social space, it is the architecture of professional designers and powerful patrons that has been the traditional focus of architectural historians. As a corrective, in recent decades vernacular-architecture historians have become increasingly sophisticated at researching the lived experience of everyday spaces.[7] Spatial practices, however, have eluded historians, few of whom have attempted to research this often unchoreographed and unrecorded element of Lefebvre's triad. Due to the difficulty of finding sources that describe spatial practices, those who have taken on the challenge of discovering and analyzing them have often researched deviant activities documented in police records, local bylaws, or other sources that must be read "against the grain." Other historians have mapped and interpreted the more normative spatial practices recorded in subjective first-person sources, such as memoirs, diaries, and oral histories.[8] Both of

these streams of research have provided models for the present inquiry into the spatial practices of Canadian immigrants. For example, government correspondence often records migrants' stories in its concern to manage immigrants who were singled out as problematic, for political, racial, medical, or other reasons. Meanwhile, immigrants themselves have recounted the spatial practices that were required to "get by" in their new country.

Canadian immigration historians Lisa Chilton and Yukari Takai have argued recently that official government sources, when read mindfully, with an understanding of their limitations, can be "useful for gaining insight into the actual experiences of immigrants or the socio-cultural contexts within which those experiences were produced." Although we are unlikely to find explicit statements of the thoughts and feelings of immigrants in government sources, we can find evidence of bureaucratic, legislative, and executive reactions to, and anticipations of, immigrant practices.[9] It is necessary to try to hear migrant voices in conversation with government sources. Many migrants reflected in written form on their journeys, a period during which they were especially alert to spatial change. Social historians have noted that first-person accounts proliferate in relation to unusual circumstances such as immigration, especially when compared to recordings of daily life.[10] When migrant writers portray Canadian buildings and sites, recalling how they negotiated new and unfamiliar terrain, historical spatial practices can be delineated, described, and analyzed.

First-person sources are inevitably subjective, misremembered, and edited; they may lack detail and contradict official accounts. But their subjective nature is no reason to discard them. Historians can be just as analytic with first-person sources as they are with more formal archival statements; the latter are just as partial in their recording of history. Without migrants' intellectual and sensual perceptions, it is impossible to comprehend anything but a top-down view of government architecture. Historian of migration Dirk Hoerder has realized the most exhaustive mining of Canadian first-person sources in his compelling book *Creating Societies: Immigrant Lives in Canada*. Contemplating their subjectivity, Hoerder declares that, certainly, the sources he uses "reflect a perceived society and a specific social space within it, not an objective one. But men and women act on the basis of their perceptions … These subjective processes are as important as detached scholarly analysis."[11] There will be gaps in any one migrant's story, so the history of immigration architecture will have to be assembled from many stories of spatial practices. From migrants' depictions of brief or seemingly unimportant encounters in government space, from their asides and hazily remembered emotions, I strive in this book to compose a narrative and draw conclusions about architectural history.

However, the influential architectural historian Dell Upton cautions us about using sources produced by people outside professional design discourse, be they patrons, users, or observers. With these kinds of informants, he has found that space "was narrated more often than it was analyzed … that architecture was rarely discussed or criticized as a discrete object … [and that] it was most often treated as an actor in narratives of real or potential human interaction."[12] People encounter space as limiting or facilitating their needs, and sometimes as landmarks or meaningful sites, and they adjust their spatial practices accordingly. We cannot expect to find migrants or government officials communicating in the specialized language of architects and describing buildings in the manner of an architectural historian. Rather, to help us imaginatively reconstruct spaces long gone, we need to supplement these voices with other sources, such as historic photographs and architectural drawings.

Thus, the official preparations for immigrants, and the perceptions of the migrants, still tell only a fragmented story of their practices in space, because the spaces themselves were designed and constructed with intent. As government architecture, immigration buildings were representations of space as ordered, categorical, hierarchical, and processual. Government correspondence among branches and ministries reveals intent, sometimes in explicit statements, and sometimes in statements that must be read against the grain. Other official sources used in this book include the annual reports of ministries, House of Commons debates, and, of course, architectural drawings, especially plans. Building elevations, like photographs, can indicate the importance of a structure by exhibiting its style, facade composition, and level of detail. But by demonstrating the relationship of spaces to one another, plans can show how people in space circulated, were sorted, connected, or separated, or were differently abled to achieve their ends. Plans can be read as statements of intent, even if actual spatial practices did not always follow the lines laid down on blueprints by designers and patrons. In this book, then, the appearance of architecture takes an analytic back seat to its social effects. The goal of understanding historical spatial practice will thus be attained by interpreting the words of immigrants, comparing them with stated intentions of government officials, and situating these forms of knowledge within documented architectural space. All historical sources are partial; by examining stories through multiple lenses and archives, the historian can hope to make some sense of them.

Despite these efforts at triangulation, the argument of the book necessarily has limitations. I foreground the moment of the migrant's encounter with designed space; analysis of Lefebvre's third element of social space, lived experience, remains speculative in this book. That is, the questions of how the migrant's past lived experience in the "old country" shaped their spatial practices in Canadian immigration architecture, or how their practices of space in government quarantine stations, pier buildings, and so on, was then crystallized in their lived experience going forward, are beyond the possibilities of this study. There is no doubt that, as the American immigration scholar Sucheng Chan wrote many years ago, "immigrants have often drawn on skills developed in 'Old World' societies which were more hierarchical and more rigidly bound by age-old status prescriptions. Although the nature of the restrictions in the 'New World' differed, the existence of limitations per se was something with which immigrants were quite familiar … [and they were able] to insure their own survival in an unfamiliar environment."[13] By studying spatial practices, I hope to demonstrate the ways that immigrants enacted some of those learned survival skills in negotiating the formal architectures of arrival and passage.

It has been the tendency of Canadian immigration historians to tell the story of immigrant reception as one of absorption into urban ethnic enclaves or group settlements. In particular, historians have been interested in the desires of social reformers, labour organizers, and the state to penetrate and dilute those ethnic enclaves to assimilate immigrants to an image of Anglo-Canadian respectability, and in the acquiescence or resistance of those ethnic groups to Canadianization.[14] Both the history of government-managed reception, and of multicultural experiences, have been neglected by comparison.[15] The present volume therefore is not a study of ethnic settlements and their hybrid architecture, push-and-pull factors, assimilation, or policy, subjects which form the core of many histories of immigration. In addition, I have limited my purview in this book to government and migrant voices and actions. The wide array of non-governmental actors and supporters of immigrants have been largely excluded for the sake of containing the research and the argument. That is, the transportation companies — always major players in this period of Canadian history — the colonization societies, immigrant-assistance programs, and religious and ethnic organizations, all of which became involved with migrants in some way, are not addressed in this book, except where they directly impact or comment on architectural space and spatial practices. Although this limitation promotes clarity, it runs the risk of reifying a binary relationship between state and subject, when the reality was more diffuse and negotiated among multiple actors.

I see in the interaction between government architecture and migrants' spatial practices illustrative instances of Michel Foucault's theorizing about the micropolitics of governance. According to this line of reasoning, the governance of society in modern liberal states is a negotiation between coercion and co-operation. Social-welfare movements, public-health campaigns, immigrant selection and assimilation programs, these were supported by multiple actors, state and non-state, and required the "buy-in" of the individuals and groups that were their subjects. In the biopolitical contract, individuals hoped for better health and security in exchange for their consent to be counted, monitored, examined, and restricted in their activities. The carceral institutions, such as prisons, that Foucault studied in his early works remain vestigial in the biopolitical institutions, such as quarantine stations, that developed in the late-nineteenth century. But subjects were now formed less by subjection to power, than by their participation with it.[16] We need new interpretations of our sources to produce research on these modes of power, according to Stoler: "Treating governance through the microphysics of daily lives has redirected historians to new readings of familiar archives … [and] has changed how we read — for discrepant tone, tacit knowledge, stray emotions, extravagant details, 'minor' events."[17] As the sources used in the subsequent chapters will demonstrate, the Dominion government's immigrant-reception architecture was a built manifestation of this model of governance, dedicated as it was to the protection and improvement of the immigrants; the management of their movements, emotions, and impressions of the country; the control of their individual impact on the public health; and the local ordering of Canadian society.

Recent histories of migration and of immigration policy have mobilized the insights of governmentality research, analyzing how migrants resisted, exploited, conformed to, and helped to produce state procedures that increasingly aimed to identify, categorize, and control mobilities. In the midst of massive nineteenth-century movements of people, according to historian Adam McKeown, national borders and bordering procedures emerged "to facilitate and block certain kinds of mobility." Grounded in "extensive mechanisms to distinguish individual identities," migrants thus were sorted in transnational space.[18] These developments required a new architecture for borders, such as the renowned complex on New York's Ellis Island, and other facilities in immigrant-receiving nations like Australia and Argentina. In Canada, the protection and control manifest at the Dominion government's dockside immigrant-reception buildings were extended deep into the interior via its managed network of hostels, hospitals, and detention centres.

Historians of immigration in the United States and Canada have in recent years studied migration as individual and group mobilities in negotiation with bordering processes. The practices of identifying, sorting, and producing desirable and undesirable immigrants in these countries have assumed historiographic significance alongside more traditional studies of policy, ethnic enclaves, and assimilation. An early stimulus to my research was Dorothee Schneider's compelling approach to the US story, *Crossing Borders*, the title of which is a spatial metaphor for each step of the migrant's journey, from gathering information, choosing a destination, and leaving home, to the arrival process, settlement, naturalization, and partial assimilation.[19] Similarly, Hoerder's extensive survey of autobiographical sources emphasizes the experiences of migrants in multiple sites. His overall implication that state and other institutions were relatively minor players in immigrant lives is tempered by the top-down, policy-oriented studies of other Canadianists.[20] The insights of race and gender theory have contributed significantly to this scholarly shift to mobilities and bordering processes, emphasizing the differential treatment of migrants depending on their perceived essential characteristics. For example, in both the United States and Canada, the racialized differences between immigrant reception on the east and west coasts of North America are seen spatially in contrasting port facilities and policy implementation. San Francisco's Angel Island has been analyzed in this way, but there has been little scholarship recognizing the way Canadian government spaces discriminated among migrant groups.[21] In many ways this scholarship addresses the interactions among migrants, government officials, and others, and considers space at the transnational scale — but it has less to say about the architectural scale.[22] By setting its drama in the immigration buildings, our story contrasts policy with local contingency; I try to avoid generalizing migrant experience, while still offering the possibility of synthetic understandings of policy and practice.

In the theoretical frame proposed here, architectural history can make innovative contributions to the historiography of immigration and transnational mobilities. I further an approach that takes seriously the social production of space and subjects. In particular, architectural histories of institutions inform this project through their analysis of the sorting of people in space, showing how institutions implement policy, but are equally shaped by spatial practices.[23] Catherine Boland Erkkila takes this tack to some extent in her excellent dissertation on US immigration architecture, in which she studies the designs of port and railroad facilities, the social discriminations they betray, and the resulting experiences of migrants. Additionally, she shows that, while the railroad companies occasionally erected immigrant hostelries to promote the purchase and settlement of their lands, the US government came late to the game, establishing Ellis Island only in the 1890s. Other than quarantine stations, Ellis Island remained the sole purpose-built US government immigration facility until after 1910.[24] We can conclude from this that the range and extent of Canadian federal immigration infrastructure was unique in North America.

For the most part, though, architectural historians who study North American topics have not addressed the immigration process. This may be due to a number of reasons related to the buildings: they often were ephemeral and short-lived; were of an undefined type; were designed by anonymous government architects; and were typically plain and aesthetically undistinguished. Architectural historians have tended to focus on the permanent and monumental, great or beautiful, buildings designed by known architects according to aesthetic and typological conventions. But even the history of the monumental Main Building at Ellis Island, which conforms to many of these criteria, has largely been left to social historians and cultural theorists. By looking at Canadian government immigration infrastructure, this book foregrounds less-common, sometimes short-lived, but socially and politically significant, building types. It examines buildings designed within government bureaucracies, rather than by famous firms. It is attentive to standardization, rather than uniqueness in architectural design, although some of the buildings included in the following chapters were indeed one-offs.[25]

Architects rarely appear in this book. Most of the government immigrant-reception buildings that I study were designed and maintained by the Chief Architect's Branch in the Dominion's Department of Public Works. Its history has been explored in detail by Parks Canada historian Janet Wright, who concludes that immigration "was one of the Chief Architect's Branch's most important and least troublesome clients." She explains that, during the period covered by the present study, the Chief Architect's Branch preferred to design buildings in-house, to control costs and to be better able to satisfy the needs of different government ministries. Although individual chief architects sometimes brought an aesthetic design sensibility to the position, Public Works architecture in general aimed for a conservative uniformity. The branch intended its buildings to be easily recognizable as icons of a federal presence, and they often had to be designed and built quickly to serve the burgeoning settlements of the new nation. Moreover, Wright emphasizes that the Chief Architect's Branch did not operate like a private design firm, because it was also responsible for improvements and maintenance to existing buildings.[26] Thus, acting in the context of their civil-service positions, these architects were not associated with an oeuvre of masterpieces, but rather with the consistent and cost-effective production and management of the government's large building stock. Studying the work of an agency like the Chief Architect's Branch allows an architectural historian to follow the use of buildings over time, as social spaces and not merely as static objects of an individual architect's design intent.

Complementing Wright's study, I call attention to one of the patrons of Public Works architecture: the various ministries, branches, and officials responsible for immigration in the decades from Confederation to the Great Depression.[27] Sometimes, when in need of a new building, immigration agents or officials provided preliminary drawings that the Chief Architect's Branch could choose to develop or ignore. More typically, the government architects designed from fairly minimal textual briefs provided by the deputy minister in charge of immigration. For the architects, there was room for invention in space planning, as the branch was tasked with designing new building types for immigration by drawing on their knowledge of existing institutions. After the initial construction of a building, continued extensive correspondence between the two branches — regarding renovations, furnishings, utilities, and other mundane subjects — further elaborated architectural intentions.

Wright's book, combined with her colleagues' heritage inventories and historic sites reports, constitute the bulk of the research on immigration architecture in Canada. Beyond these architectural sources, immigration buildings occasionally appear in immigration histories to illustrate particular arguments.[28] In all these works, immigration architecture is seen to represent public policy, national aspirations, and state formation, but rarely are buildings analyzed as designed, functional spaces where bureaucrats and citizens interacted. Policies certainly are reflected in government architecture, but it is more than that: without the buildings, there is no implementation, and the architecture shapes the implementation of policy. In taking an architectural perspective, I offer a fresh assessment in this book of previous historical understandings of migrant experience and government immigration programs.

THE ORGANIZATION OF THE BOOK

The present volume is therefore the first sustained approach to Canadian immigration through its essentially spatial and architectural character. I seek to understand architecture as an element of a broader social terrain, formed from the accumulation of physical infrastructure — here, commissioned and designed by the federal government — and also by the interactions, memories, desires, and activities of ordinary people in their occupation of spaces. To guide us on our journey, the book is organized chronologically

and typologically. Chronologically, the book is divided into two parts, corresponding to two eras: the first, a gestation period from Confederation to the early-twentieth century, when the Dominion government established its first policies, procedures, and building types for receiving immigrants, is covered in chapters 1 to 3; the second, a span between the early-twentieth century and the mid-1930s, during which practices and architectures were modified, modernized, and newly conceived, is the subject of chapters 4 and 5. The periodization of the book's two parts is inexact, because it is characterized by the long duration of certain building types, the invention of others, the extension of some old ones into newly settled territories, and the fluctuation of requirements with waves of immigration. Both parts examine pier, Prairie, and detention buildings. Each chapter addresses a different building type, or typological grouping of buildings, according to their function within the immigrant-reception context.

During the period of history under focus in this book, immigrants' first architectural experience of Canada normally occurred in pier buildings designed and constructed by the federal government. Apart from a few earlier structures erected by colonial or municipal governments, the first of these was built in Quebec City in 1870, and this site serves as the primary case study for chapter 1. By the 1890s, similar buildings stood in Halifax and Saint John. Often referred to as "immigration sheds," these pier buildings ultimately incorporated on one site most of the immigrant-reception functions that would be provided by the Dominion government. (As we will see in subsequent chapters, some functions received specialized treatment in other building types.) At the pier buildings, migrants would be welcomed and inspected by immigration officials in large waiting rooms; they could eat and sleep and bathe; gather information, tickets, and supplies for their continued journey; and, in later years, they could be sent to small hospital wards or detention cells. These institutions addressed the basic needs of migrants while, in parallel, satisfying the federal government's desires to both control and ameliorate the process of arrival in Canada and distribution to distant destinations. In practice, within the pier buildings this resulted in spatial negotiations, as reflected in bureaucratic correspondence and migrants' first-person sources.

Quarantine facilities predate any other architectures of immigrant reception in Canada; they follow pier buildings in the second chapter only because a smaller portion of new arrivals ever stayed in quarantine structures. Quarantine was a response to epidemic diseases prevalent in the mid-nineteenth century. Early facilities in Toronto and Montreal were shed-like structures for containing sick immigrants and keeping them separate from city residents. An insular dimension was added when the quarantine station on Grosse-Île was established in the 1830s downstream from Quebec City. As procedures became formalized in the decades following Confederation, all incoming ships would be met by the facility's doctor: any shipboard symptoms resulted in the entire crew and passengers being quarantined on the island for some period of time. Quarantine stations – at Grosse-Île and also near Halifax, Saint John, Victoria, and other smaller ports – consisted of collections of buildings to accommodate the needs and expectations, medical care, and decontamination of different classes of passengers from the ships. As isolated sites, the stations also served as permanent residences for staff and their families, with attendant institutions, structures, and interactions.

The medical and carceral intentions behind the quarantine facilities stand in contrast to the impetus for Prairie immigration halls, explored in chapters 3 and 4, bridging parts one and two of the book. Immigration halls were distributed across the towns and transfer points of the Prairie provinces. Inspired by the temporary accommodations offered at pier buildings, the Prairie immigration halls provided free shelter, information, and sometimes food for immigrants in transit, and for those searching locally for land, jobs, and homes. The architectural characteristics of the immigration halls remained largely consistent over six decades, with variation occurring in scale across different locales. Small, one-storey dormitories at the end of steel in rural Alberta and Saskatchewan offered rudimentary support for new arrivals, whereas a complex of three multi-storey halls (plus a hospital) ultimately housed immigrants and a stable of federal officials in Winnipeg during the decade preceding the First World War. Migrants remember their experiences in Prairie immigration halls, sometimes with gratitude, and sometimes with disgust due to vermin, overcrowding, or unwanted social mixing . Caretakers and land agents gave advice and represented the federal government in communities remote from Ottawa; their memories reflect senses of wonder and sympathy and sometimes disgust at immigrants' precarious journeys. Numerically the most prevalent building type produced for immigrant reception, the Prairie immigration halls form two chapters at the core of the book. In tracing their history over the entire period of the study, we see an increasing bureaucratization and centralization of functions, as well as an expansion of the role of immigration buildings more generally, which is manifested by the typologies examined in the final chapter of the book.

In chapter 5, we first return to the piers for an update on the procedures and spaces of immigrant debarkation. During the first few years of the twentieth century, existing pier buildings in Quebec City and other eastern ports were required to evolve to accommodate new policies and practices related to immigrant inspection and selection. Officials were increasingly on the lookout for undesirable immigrants, as defined by race, unemployment, perceived indigence, bad health, or radical political orientation. One result was a new building type – the so-called "immigrant detention hospital," the main iteration of which appeared in Montreal just before the First World War, though precedents had been built on both the east and west coasts. Detention hospitals helped to cure recent arrivals who had taken ill on the way to Canada. But they also included prison cells for the incarceration of regulated minorities, mental cases, and communists. If one compares the detention buildings of Halifax or Quebec City with those in Victoria and Vancouver, striking differences can be seen, architecturally, as well as in policy, practice, and the resulting experiences of migrants. If the eastern pier buildings and hospitals were designed largely to support the welfare of immigrants and their rapid processing and forwarding to settlement sites, the Pacific-coast buildings were effectively detention centres. As the Dominion government sometimes admitted, the contrast was racial, with "undesirable" Asian immigrants being the predominant clientele in British Columbia ports. Paradoxically, the west-coast buildings were more "architectural" than other port buildings, in the sense of formal facade composition, stylistic detailing, and the use of more enduring materials. Records of bureaucratic infighting contrast with narratives of incarceration and of daring escapes from these institutions, illuminating a range of spatial practices. Finally, starting in the 1910s, but peaking during the Depression of the early 1930s, the detention hospitals, along with the pier buildings and even the Prairie immigration halls, took on essential roles in facilitating a massive increase in deportations,

sometimes of people who had been resident in Canada for many years.

An epilogue concludes the discussion of Canada's network of immigration architecture, as well as briefly describing some of its social and architectural legacies after the 1930s and up to the pandemic of 2020. Few of the buildings are extant: wood-frame Prairie dormitories have long disappeared, while urban and port development have taken the others. Exceptions include Halifax's Pier 21 and buildings of the quarantine station on Grosse-Île, which serve as museums, and a scattering of other survivors that have been converted to new uses. While these surviving buildings provide a material connection to the history of migration to Canada, the present book fills the gaps left by the disappearance of most immigrant-reception (and detention) architecture. Immigration facilities were often the first Canadian government buildings in their towns, thus establishing a federal presence. They were the subject of local pride as well as political controversies, and the sites of cultural interaction. In the end, it seems that immigrant-reception infrastructure before the Depression represented a kind of proto-welfare-state program in its paternalistic concern to give people a leg-up, while simultaneously keeping an eye on them. Migrant first-person sources provide some sense of the ambivalence with which this governmental intervention was experienced and remembered by newcomers of diverse backgrounds. Viewing immigration history through the lens of architecture and spatial practices thus offers an original mode for synthesizing immigrant experience, while recognizing the contingency of migrants' (and officials') spatial practices.

CHAPTER 1

Dominion Government Pier Buildings: Immigrants Arrive in Canadian Ports

The debarkation of migrants in a North American port during the nineteenth century was typically a riotous affair. On the piers there was a heady mingling of passengers and baggage, stevedores and freight, locals offering jobs and opportunities, and others hoping to fleece naive newcomers. As a result, governments in Canada strove to provide institutional infrastructure that could sort immigrants, support them, and get them safely on their way to inland destinations. Among the new Confederation government's early achievements in the immigration portfolio was the erection of buildings in Quebec City and a few other places to shelter and feed travellers and provide them a place to gather strength and information before continuing their journeys.

Constructed in 1870, the new pier building in Quebec City was a small, two-and-a-half-storey rectangular structure with clapboard siding and dormer windows. It had two floors of lodgings above a ground-floor mess hall. *Canadian Illustrated News* published a series of somewhat romanticized views of this building not long after it opened, though they lacked the throngs of people and baggage that often crowded the pier (Figure 1.1). The exterior view (top left) depicts the narrow end of the structure, with a broad ramp for rolling baggage wagons up from the waterfront,

a perspective that would have been viewed by the passengers on ships approaching upriver. A wide entrance gives a welcoming face to the building. Shed roofs project from the two long sides, similar to a railway station, and close to one side, the baggage shed has a similar canopy, creating an almost fully covered outdoor space to shelter immigrants waiting for help or transportation. Several other small buildings complete the scene.

We are conducted into the building courtesy of the *Canadian Illustrated News*. In a view of the dining hall (top right), three long tables recede into the distance, the perspectival effect emphasized by the regularity of the windows and ceiling beams. The dining hall is depicted as a model of order, which may belie the actual behaviour of diners so recently released from the confines of steerage. Each spot at table is taken by a primly seated immigrant, in an image reminiscent of those produced to demonstrate to patrons the institutional tranquility and effectiveness of nineteenth-century schools.[1] The main impression is of the spatial containment and organization of this large group of people, banqueting in the muted light of late afternoon.

Later on, one floor up in the Women's "Bed Room," we see the nighttime preparations for sleep (bottom right). Children are tended to,

GENERAL VIEW OF THE SHEDS.

DINING ROOM.

MEN'S WASH ROOM.

WOMEN'S BED ROOM.

1.1 Quebec – The Immigration Sheds, from the *Canadian Illustrated News*, 12 July 1873.

prayers are said, and we sense a feeling of quietude and relief for being on terra firma. The interior finishing itself is rustic, as we see the inside of the clapboards behind the braced timber frame. Since immigration through Quebec City closed in the fall, robust winter insulation was unnecessary; more typically, immigrants complained of the heat. The final image in the quadriptych shows the morning toilet in the Men's "Wash Room" (bottom

left). In various states of deshabille, men shave, rinse, and dry themselves on a shared towel roll. Glowing light shines through the window from the east, heralding a new day and a bright future for these pilgrims. One man, fully dressed, his toilet complete, consults a sheet of information gathered from the agent during the brief stay in the Quebec immigration building. These four etchings from the *Canadian Illustrated News*, read clockwise, present us with a kind of architectural day-in-the-life of this early institution, beginning with our first sight of the building, dockside, to our preparations for departure the following morning. In doing so, they reveal the core functions of immigration architecture, in the government's paired aims of controlling the comportment of the immigrants and attending to their protection and welfare.

The 1870 immigration building in Quebec City served solely for the feeding and overnight accommodation of needy steerage passengers, and only if they had to wait for local boats or trains. It was an early version of a building type that would soon incorporate a more complex program. Organized stevedoring and luggage transfer; customs, identity, and medical inspections; nurseries and shops and ticket windows — all functions that would soon characterize immigrant reception buildings in ports all over the world — were as yet unheard of. This would change by 1887, with the opening of a more modern immigration building in Quebec City, Canada's principal port of arrival. Now immigrants would be received and processed, protected and controlled, and forwarded to their destinations in an efficient manner, all under one roof. Similar buildings would soon appear in other east-coast North American ports.

The various iterations of the Quebec City pier building seen over several decades serve as a case study in this chapter to introduce the intentions of the Dominion government in developing immigration architecture, and to explore some of the ways that migrants, government officials, and others practised space to achieve their diverse goals. First, to help understand the motivations behind Canadian immigration infrastructure, I study the architectural and policy precedents inherited by the new national government in 1867, which comprised a number of existing buildings, and immigration agents, in several places. I then compare and contrast these precedents with descriptions of the successive Dominion government pier buildings at Quebec and other ports. In this chapter, we observe in some detail the processing of immigrants and their baggage through the official spaces of the immigration buildings, and how changes to reception practices reflected and transformed the architecture.

LOCAL PRACTICES AND PRECEDENTS FOR IMMIGRATION ARCHITECTURE

Prior to the age of steam, migration into Canada from Europe was seasonal and fraught with dangers. The crossing of the Atlantic was long, and the St Lawrence River, by which one accessed the interior of the British North American colonies, froze up in the winter. There were year-round ports in Halifax and Saint John, but these received only a trickle of immigrants destined for those localities. Most early-nineteenth-century migrants hoped to arrive as far upriver as possible, and by the 1830s Quebec City had become the principal port of entry north of New York. At Quebec, they could transfer to canal and lake boats or wagon trains taking them to the United States, Upper Canada, or, later, the Canadian Northwest. Weather, destination, and rumoured or real opportunities could all affect the journey. If migrants arrived too early in the spring, they could be delayed by frozen lakes and impassable roads. Arriving too late in the fall might mean a lean winter for a farmer or farm labourer. The changing availability of jobs and land could strand a migrant; or the offer of a situation along the way might truncate their journey.

Changes in immigration policy and transportation technologies caused ongoing recalculations of the routes that migrants followed. For instance, the establishment of quarantine requirements below Quebec City in the 1830s redirected many apprehensive migrants to New York, even if they were destined for Canadian colonies. They also complained that the St Lawrence boats were slower and more crowded. By the late 1840s, there was a reversal, as migrants tried to avoid New York's head taxes by taking the Laurentian route to access the Great Lakes and the Midwest. Before the end of that decade, railroads also connected Quebec City – or more specifically, Pointe-Lévy on the south side of the St Lawrence – to the New England states. Many migrants took advantage of these connections, and, until the late 1870s, most passengers coming through the port of Quebec were destined for the United States.[2] The completion of the Canadian Pacific Railway (CPR) in the following decade again changed travel patterns, as it established direct connections from Quebec City to the far western reaches of the nation.

Sailing ships could take many weeks to cross the Atlantic Ocean; crowded steerage quarters below decks – where most migrants travelled – were less than salubrious, and many arrived ill from the voyage and unable to continue past their port of entry. Even if they arrived healthy, immigrants were often penniless and stranded after paying their passage. Great burdens were placed on local communities to succour these destitute arrivals, most of whom were merely transients. At every stop and transfer along the way, migrants could be delayed for a multitude of reasons. Towns rarely had sufficient lodgings, cafeterias, hospitals, or other spaces necessary to accommodate the seasonal waves of immigration. More importantly, town residents wanted to contain immigrants in one place. For one thing, it was thought that the separation of newcomers from healthy local residents could prevent epidemics. Even though, as Geoffrey Bilson argued in his comprehensive study of cholera in Canada, little evidence actually connected immigrants to this water-borne disease, and most cases originated in poor neighbourhoods rather than at the wharves, immigrants became associated strongly with contagion in the public imagination, and would remain so throughout the century. "At the end of the tale, as at the beginning," Bilson wrote, "cholera and the immigrant were linked."[3] Though epidemics of cholera,

and later typhus, did not arrive with every season of navigation, the principle of separating immigrants in specialized institutions – if these early sheds justify that designation – for the sake of public health and safety, was founded. Containment of immigrants would protect local citizens.

As a result, government immigration infrastructure first began to appear in the Canadian colonies during the early 1830s. The major Laurentian ports of Quebec and Montreal were the first to erect shelters near the waterfront for sick or destitute immigrants. Other towns on the coast and further inland soon followed suit. Although many of these early buildings appeared in response to fears of epidemic disease entering the colonies along with poor European immigrants, they were not quarantine stations, as we will examine in chapter 2. Rather, these were urban institutions to shield locals from floods of outsiders.

Little is known about the architecture of these early immigration buildings, which typically were wood-frame, shed-like structures, often on minimal foundations. Because they were seen as temporary and expedient, they were not professionally designed or built to last. Immigration was seasonal, restricted to the summer months; epidemics came and went quickly, and were soon forgotten; and the numbers of immigrants in need fluctuated widely, as they followed upon various push-and-pull factors, the weather, and the effects of these conditions on transportation schedules. Temporary immigration buildings would rot, burn, be repurposed, abandoned, or shuttered in between seasons of need. One exception to this rule was the Quebec Marine Hospital, used for sick sailors and immigrants alike: built to monumental scale and with classical detailing of cut stone, it was begun during the cholera epidemics of the early 1830s, and served through several disease events of the coming decades. This structure was an adjunct to the general hospital, well away from the port, and it was regularly supplemented with temporary "fever sheds" for immigrants, but it was not an immigration building per se.[4]

The mass migration of the Irish-famine years, especially 1847, brought about a significant expansion of immigration architecture in Canadian towns. At this time, Quebec, Montreal, and Saint John all had a number of fever sheds built for those suffering from the cholera, and dormitory sheds for those accompanying them. Some of these facilities encompassed extensive building stock, such as at Montreal, where a Confederation-era inventory listed no less than twenty-seven hospital-ward buildings for a total of more than ninety thousand square feet of ward space. Associated outbuildings including "surgeries," wash and cook houses, stables, a "grave-digger's" residence, and two "coffin-houses."[5] According to Parks Canada historian Norman Anick, in addition to the infrastructure in Lower Canada, new immigrant lodgings appeared in Bytown, Toronto, Hamilton, and Kingston during the early 1840s. A government-appointed agent reported from the latter town that the immigrants' need for accommodations depended on the schedule of departures for their various destinations, and he rarely had to provision them for more than a day or two.[6] In some places, though, the numbers and durations of stay could be much greater.

Municipalities were motivated to erect buildings by more than the fear of disease: their streets and waterfronts were often thronged with indigent immigrants who had no place to stay. Particularly in transfer points, migrants waiting for connections, or drained of the money to pay for the next leg of their journey, had little choice but to squat. One eyewitness of this early period wrote of "the emptying of a newly-arrived cargo of emigrants on the unknown shore … Each pours forth with a load to carry or care for, like the busy population on an ant-hill, and group after group sit or watch by their slender store." Once debarked with their baggage, many "hang helplessly around it, the children

tumbling on it."[7] Where would these anxious newcomers shelter for the night? An 1830s report from the inspecting physician at Quebec City provides an answer:

They commonly established themselves along the wharfs and at the different landing-places, crowding into any place of shelter they could obtain, where they subsisted principally upon the charity of the inhabitants … I have known the shores of the river along Quebec, for about a mile and a half, crowded with these unfortunate people, the places of those who might have moved off being constantly supplied by new arrivals … Those who were not absolutely without money got into low taverns and boarding-houses and cellars, where they congregated in immense numbers."[8]

Under desperate circumstances, these migrants shaped the spaces of the piers, the undeveloped shorelines, and the existing building stock to satisfy their most basic needs.

However, the newcomers were constrained in where and how they could shape space. Stigmatization of immigrants as diseased precluded their sheltering in many neighbourhoods and towns. An account of the upcountry journey of one migrant family that had members sick with the cholera contributes details that evoke expedient spatial practices at stopping points in colonial Canada. "I enquired for a room at all the Inns, but they all refused. I then inquired if there was any outhouse in the Place, they all said no," wrote one man in his 1832 diary. "We were obliged at last to go out on the Wharf and get on the underside of the store-house." His younger cousin, in her later memoir, remembered it with slight differences: "we was not allowed even a shed. Everyone was afraid of us, would not open there [sic] doors … & as a last resort our dying father was laid on the wharf on a bed with no shelter but a cart turned over." That night the children hid from a storm in a pitching boat tied to the dock. Later, in another town, they "slept in a Barn here for several nights," where one more family member passed away.[9] These narrations of the plights of new arrivals reveal that the process of immigration to Canada in the middle decades of the nineteenth century was often a frightful experience for migrants and a great inconvenience to individual residents and towns along the way. Port towns in particular felt the burden of the sick and indigent, even though many migrants were merely passing through on their way to rural Ontario or the United States. Thus, there were significant incentives for ports and other transfer points to develop immigration infrastructure, though this continued to be achieved in an ad hoc manner prior to Confederation.

In parallel with the first sheds of the early 1830s, immigration agents were appointed to manage arrivals in Quebec City and Toronto, and to advise and forward immigrants who were passing through to other stops.[10] The role of these agents had less to do with public health and more with the protection and care of the immigrants, ensuring that shipping companies and other interested parties obeyed the laws in place. Agents would receive immigrants as they debarked in order to record their arrival and give them advice regarding accommodations, employment, and transportation. Sick and indigent immigrants were directed to the sheds, or sometimes a local hospital, while more independent arrivals could be shown to a café or hotel. The activities of these colonial civil servants established precedents for the roles later played by Dominion government officials at the ports, managing the expectations of immigrants, their behaviours, and their interactions with locals. This role would expand, as both the scope of government and the magnitude of immigration grew in the late-nineteenth century.

In the early 1830s, the newly appointed agent at Quebec issued a travel advisory for immigrants that was a combination of practical tips, health superstitions, and remonstrations about comportment. Keep your baggage and possessions "in a small compass" at all times, he counselled. Don't bring "old dirty clothing ... and other useless articles." Overdressing would cause fevers. "Avoid night dews" and "ardent spirits of any kind." Keep "your hair short, and wash daily." And don't risk drowning by rushing off the boat before the right tide. The travel advisory continued, admonishing immigrants "not to loiter their valuable time at the port of landing; but to proceed to obtain settlement or employment ... in Upper or Lower Canada" – and definitely not in the "aguish swamps" of the Midwestern United States.[11] This recommendation reflected two aspirations on the part of colonial governments: to relieve port towns from responsibility for the welfare of transients, by forwarding them upcountry; and to keep them in the British colonies, an imperative that would increase in importance later in the century. Single men were directed by the immigration agent to job opportunities in the bigger cities, and large families to the unsettled farming country of Ontario and the Eastern Townships.

Thus began a long line of pamphlets, books, and newspaper articles describing the process of arrival and attempting to control the conduct of the immigrant. Distributed both by government bodies and commercial presses, these publications reveal that the protection of immigrants was as important as protecting local residents when developing the infrastructure of immigrant reception. In her well-known 1854 publication, *The Female Emigrant's Guide*, Canadian author Catherine Parr Traill quoted at length one philanthropist's advice to new arrivals to North America. Again, migrants "should not linger about ... but go at once into the interior." There were temptations in port towns:

"Intoxicating drinks are unfortunately very cheap in America and Canada. They are a great curse to the emigrant," and may result in them "spending their time and their little means, often refusing work when it is offered them, till their last penny is spent, when the trunks and other property are seized to pay for lodging."[12] Immigrants seemingly needed protection from their own propensities, though that hardly justified government infrastructure.

More significantly, immigrants required "protection from the clutches of the unprincipled 'runners' who infested the wharves," in the words of historian Edwin Guillet, who reported that "the chief items of advice in guidebooks" were to avoid liquor and swindlers. He quotes one observer of the time, who reported that the piers of Quebec City were home to "the lowest of the low, who are aptly, though not elegantly, designated 'land-sharks,' and to such demons in human form the loitering stranger is almost certain of becoming a prey."[13] Comparably, a Norwegian arrival of the 1860s warned his fellow countrymen that no "truth-loving person can deny that for many years Quebec has been and still remains the worst den of robbers an emigrant may be trapped in."[14] The bribing of ship captains to steer innocent passengers to unscrupulous vendors, the luring of migrants with misrepresented opportunities, and of course, their fleecing by devious innkeepers, restauranteurs, or money changers, were common perils. The agents and facilities put in place by colonial and municipal governments in the first half of the nineteenth century were meant to bring order to the chaos attendant on arrival. Immigration facilities on or near the piers were places to gather and contain the immigrants – to keep them apart from unscrupulous local residents, to help them recover from long and unhygienic journeys, and hopefully see them on their way to final destinations.

Historian Lisa Chilton finds that, in the decades leading up to Confederation, "disease control" slowly gave way to a broader concept of immigrant welfare and "nation-building strategies" as the motivations behind immigration infrastructure. Her main case study is Toronto, where she traces the steps taken by municipal, colonial, provincial, and Dominion governments to control and protect immigrants. For disease containment, temporary isolation sheds on the hospital grounds served newcomers from the 1840s to the 1860s. The growing concern for immigrant welfare, and the intervention of the national government, would result in a more permanent and multi-faceted institutional approach. A new immigration depot for Toronto was completed by the Dominion government in 1870, the same year it erected the new building on the pier in Quebec City that opened this chapter. In Toronto, after much local debate over an acceptable site – specifically, resistance from potential neighbours, which reflected the traditional stigmatization of immigrants as diseased – the Dominion government settled on a large plot of land that it appropriated at the meeting point of several railways. A grouping of buildings provided office space for the Dominion government agent, baggage storage, dormitories, and a large mess hall, where meals were provided by the provincial government, which also took responsibility for other forms of immigrant welfare, such as medical care and transportation subsidies.[15] As we will explore further below, the basic form and functions of the 1870 Toronto and Quebec depots are analogous to the Prairie immigration halls that the Dominion government would begin to build that decade (see Figure 3.1).

The Toronto example suggests that, in the early years after Confederation, responsibility for the welfare of immigrants was partly shared and subject to negotiation among different levels of government. Eventually, all responsibility for immigrants and immigration facilities would devolve to the federal level, though inflected by occasional provincial or municipal attempts to attract settlers or workers to certain regions. Chilton argues that the control of immigrants by different levels of government "during the middle decades of the nineteenth century established the groundwork for the more overtly coercive policies and practices that would become central to immigration management."[16] True, policies began to grow more restrictive after 1885, and border procedures more so after the turn of the century, but intertwined with coercion was co-operation. Canada needed immigrants. To get them, many Canadians felt the country should make sure that new arrivals were taken care of and content to stay, and this led to increasing state support of immigrant reception. What was developing in the decades before and after Confederation were new institutions of immigrant reception and, with them, new building types designed to achieve the aims of the state. These places and practices were shaped by concerns over both public health and the welfare of newcomers.

1.2 Quebec Immigration Shed of 1880, shown in a sketch plan made ten years later.

EXPANSION IN THE PORT OF QUEBEC: THE 1880 IMMIGRATION BUILDING AND AFTER

In 1867, the new Dominion government inherited the old wooden immigration buildings in several cities, many of which had seen little use since the mid-1850s. Perhaps the newest structure that the youthful government inherited was an 1863 immigrant shed on the old Customs House wharf below the Citadel in Quebec City; this structure had replaced an 1847 shed — built at the crisis moment of the Irish Famine migration — that was lost in a fire. The 1863 shed was available for feeding and sheltering those who had just arrived, but it was not located where most passenger ships docked. It was replaced by the Dominion government in 1870 with the immigration building on the pier, described at the outset of this chapter. By the early 1880s, though, the 1870 shed proved too small, and did not accommodate all the functions increasingly required of such an institution, so a new, more substantial immigration building was designed and built by the Chief Architect's Branch. It was a long, narrow structure which ran parallel to the river for some four hundred feet (Figure 1.2). The kitchen and mess hall at its eastern end were connected to a large baggage room, and that to a suite of offices, all comprising

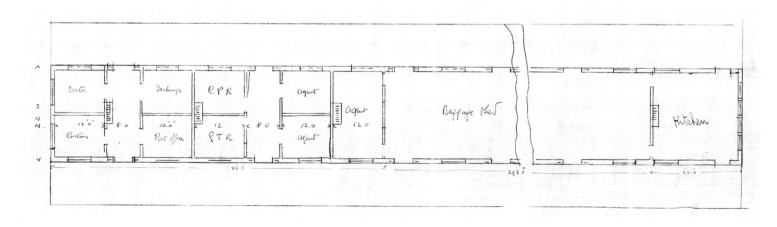

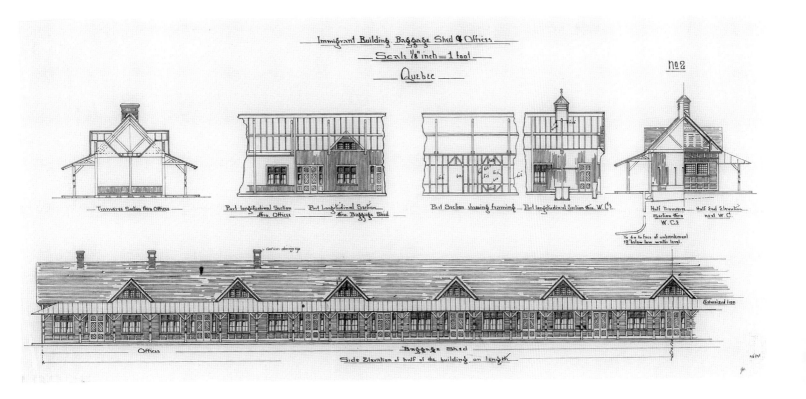

Immigrant Building Baggage Shed & Offices

Scale ⅛" inch = 1 foot

Quebec

no 2

Transverse Section thro Offices

Part longitudinal Section thro. Offices

Part Longitudinal Section thro. Baggage Shed

Part Section shewing framing

Part longitudinal Section thro. W.C.ˢ

Half Transverse Section thro W.C.ˢ

Half End Elevation next W.C.

To ₐ₀ to face of embankment 12' below low water level.

Galvanized iron

Offices

Baggage Shed

Side Elevation of half of the building on length

a single architectural form. An attic storey, with repeating dormer windows, held common rooms and sleeping areas. Compared to the 1870 shed, this early 1880s iteration accumulated some of the functions of a modern immigration building, such as ticket offices and place for a port physician. However, it still lacked the kinds of processual spaces and waiting rooms that this building type soon would encompass.

Aesthetically, this new structure was a step above the basic and rough finishes of the earlier immigration sheds. The long facade parallel to the waterfront presents a thoughtfully designed rhythm, established by the consistent pattern of veranda posts and brackets, doors and windows, battens, and dormers (Figure 1.3). There is no figurative or classical decoration on the building, but the variegated patterns of horizontal and vertical siding, the multi-pane windows, lively door treatments, and recurrent peaks of the dormers give

1.3 Immigration Building, Baggage Shed, and Offices, Quebec, 1880. Seen here in a Department of Public Works drawing sheet of 1888.

it a picturesque appearance. Its aesthetic seems to draw upon the Stick Style, just then becoming popular in the northeastern and midwestern United States for houses and small-scale public structures, such as train stations. The architecture of this new immigration facility thus brings a new level of sophistication to Dominion government pier buildings, which reflects a broader development in the quality of design coming out of the Chief Architect's Branch in this era.[17] It confirms a desire to appear current, to produce facilities consistent with North America's burgeoning transportation infrastructure, and to present a welcoming – even a domestic – appearance to migrants hanging over the ship's railing in anticipation of landing in the New World. This particular building, however, would serve its original function for only a short time.

The Dominion government's fundamental goals of protection and control were partly satisfied by the immigration architecture of the first years after Confederation. The modest pier buildings in Quebec City, complemented by half a dozen inland agencies, were seen as sufficient for the numbers of destitute or ill immigrants staying in Canada, or just passing through. For decades, Quebec City had been a "port of passage" for immigrants en route to the central United States. As historians Ninette Kelley and Michael Trebilcock note, "the first thirty years of the new Dominion are commonly considered a disappointing period for immigration … [as] more people left Canada than arrived."[18] Yet, by the late 1880s, the government began to make preparations for an expected large increase in immigration, both in response to and in anticipation of technological changes and geographic opportunities.

There were always were calls upon the government to do more to recruit and secure immigrants, and to convince them to stay, and immigrant reception architecture was one response. From the start, the Dominion government also employed recruiting agents overseas, sometimes assisted passage for certain types of workers, and enacted legislation to make the journey more bearable.[19] In the context of global competition for immigrants, and especially compared with the giant to its south, Canada's early efforts were ineffectual. A full-page editorial cartoon from an 1880 cover of the *Canadian Illustrated News* illustrates several of the key issues (Figure 1.4). Taking as its occasion the recent arrival of "no less than three steamers" full of immigrants destined directly for the Canadian Northwest, the caption urges that still more "Come to Stay." A voluptuous allegorical figure of Canada, leaning on a shield bearing the arms of the provinces, gestures toward the interior. She welcomes a throng of immigrants of different ages

1.4 "Come to Stay," from the *Canadian Illustrated News,* 14 August 1880.

and sexes who disembark from a large steamship in the background. At the front of the crowd is a young family: a robust-looking working-class man, carrying his bundles, seems poised to step forward; his demure spouse stands a little behind, holding an infant; his son, a miniature version of him, stands abreast. Here we have a present and future for the country. And yet, this vision remains anticipatory. Though stepping forward, the patriarch retains a skeptical look on his face. The son, whose clothing and features are drawn to an exceptional level of detail compared to the other immigrants, stands rooted to the spot, hands stuffed in his pockets in a noncommittal manner. Across the foreground of the image is an invisible boundary that these immigrants have yet to traverse.

The accompanying editorial expresses its hope that the ships full of settlers for Canada "will be steadily followed" by more, for here in the new "western world, which is only a few days' sail from 'home,' they will find British laws, British institutions, British customs … homestead rights, equality in all relations … unhampered by any details of rank and station." Above all, though, the editorial is addressed to the "Ottawa authorities," who, it is hoped, "will be equal to the occasion" and do their utmost to encourage immigrants to remain north of the border. How would Canada skim off its share of the immigrants who might otherwise be bound for the American Midwest? One way was to emphasize Canada's Britishness in contrast to the United States. Another was to emphasize the modernity of the country's infrastructure. Indeed, a separate article on the same page describes the scene at the construction site for an "immense" new pier in Quebec City. There, amidst "streamers of flags of all nations, with the royal ensign as the central flag … Her Royal Highness the Princess Louise spread the cement under the tablet stone, which bore her name."[20] This issue of the *Canadian Illustrated News* thus encapsulates many of the issues and changes at play on either side of 1880.

The Louise Embankment, as it became known, was built to maintain Quebec's prominence as a port in the age of steam. New piers and other infrastructure were necessary to land the larger cargoes – both freight and human – disgorged from bigger ships with steel hulls and screw propellers. Increasingly, European immigrants expected fluid transfers to long-distance rail routes from their port of entry. Consequently, several competing steamship companies and railways wanted streamlined access to immigrant and baggage transfer in the port. The larger, corporately organized, transportation concerns of the steam era wanted to transfer hundreds, or even thousands, of passengers at once, and adhered more closely to set schedules of arrival and departure. Although Canada still struggled to attract settlers, the numbers of immigrants arriving at one time – regardless of their final destination – continued to grow exponentially. These technological and geographic developments required the modernization

of the pier infrastructure at Quebec, which grew up around the 1880 immigration building, which quickly began to seem inadequate.

The driving of the Last Spike in 1885 signalled the completion of Canada's first transcontinental rail route, the CPR, some fifteen years after the analogous accomplishment south of the border. Since the United States had a significant head start populating its western regions, this meant that much of the best land there was already settled by the time Canada's Prairies and west coast became easily accessible. Frederick Jackson Turner announced the closing of the US frontier in his famous essay of 1893, but Canadian officials had been anticipating the event for some years, seeing it as an opportunity for immigration. "Free grant lands are a thing of the past in the United States," wrote a travelling immigration inspector in 1889. "In many of the leading countries of Europe the emigration movement seems to be increasing rather than diminishing and … our greatest rival is no longer able to absorb the people landing by thousands on her shores." It seemed "inevitable" to this Canadian official that many of these immigrants would "be diverted to our domain."[21] He felt that Canada was well-positioned to receive them – partly because its immigration architecture accommodated more supportive policies and procedures than did the US facilities.

This inspector had been sent to investigate how immigrants were received at New York City's Castle Garden facility. On the southern tip of Manhattan, Castle Garden was a former amusement hall that had been turned into an immigrant receiving station by the State of New York in 1855. It was the main point of arrival in the United States until the federal government opened the first Ellis Island facility in 1890, just after the Canadian inspector's visit.[22] In his report, this inspector describes the process of arrival at Castle Garden in appreciative detail. Sick immigrants were diverted to an infirmary within the facility or, if stricken with a contagious disease, sent to the quarantine station on Ward's Island. Meanwhile, "inside of the circular landing depot, the immigrants are obliged to pass through narrow passageways," where each one is questioned and their admissibility determined. A "complete," but privately run, baggage-handling system, labour bureau, and money exchange rounded out the "Castle Garden Conveniences." Upon admission to the country, however, the immigrant was turned over to the railway companies, private lodging houses, and ethnic welfare societies.

The inspector concluded that the process at Castle Garden was "satisfactory," but lacked social-welfare supports. Free meals at the station, poor relief, and assisted passage inland for the destitute were things of the past. In 1889, "no such evidences of liberality are found. It would really seem as if the United States were about to take active steps toward *discouraging* immigration into that country, rather than by special assistance and facilities … to encourage it." Beyond the brief interactions with officials at the station, "each immigrant must look after himself." There was no "organized means" of distributing immigrants around the country, and "no system of affording the newcomer information." Overall, the reception in New York did not "compare favourably with the facilities … provided by the Canadian government at Quebec," and at other locations where the infrastructure "for handling an enormous volume of immigration are at hand and in operation." In Canada, an "immigrant and his family may be carried from the seaboard to a homestead in less than a week, a fact which stands out in marvellous and happy contrast with the tedious, painful and ofttimes dangerous course" that the settlers experienced in the United States. "In this respect," crowed the travelling inspector, "the Canadian system again seems superior to the American."[23]

The Canadian system, of course, had to be superior in order to attract immigrants who otherwise may have chosen to go elsewhere. Competition was fierce, write Kelley and Trebilcock, and "Canada simply was not well known" in comparison to its "formidable rivals in the quest for settlers."[24] To make Canada a more attractive destination, immigrants would be guided each step of the way by agents of the government. If they needed sustenance or accommodations, they were given them at the pier buildings, inland agencies, and — increasingly by the late 1880s — at Prairie immigration halls. If they needed information, it was available from Canadian officials stationed in Europe, travelling on the boats and trains, and waiting in the immigration buildings.

The comparably extensive development of architectural and policy infrastructure to support newcomers to Canada was based on the belief that it was crucial for immigrants to receive a favourable first impression. Many migrants would send letters home immediately upon arrival, describing their journey, welcome, and prospects. As former western commissioner of immigration and member of parliament William McCreary said in the House of Commons some years later, the immigration authorities needed "to see that every one upon arriving will be able to write a letter back home saying that he has been well treated."[25] These letters were an abiding concern of lawmakers and officials and would impact the material culture of the immigration buildings. In the late 1880s, when she commenced working at the immigration building on the Louise Embankment, the government matron arranged with "the authorities" to have a postbox installed near the store that sold provisions. Initially, she had been carrying bundles of letters into town and posting them herself, after immigrant correspondents had been hurried onto trains or boats. Henceforth, wrote the matron, "upon the arrival of each steamer, I stood at the counter with a supply of paper, envelopes, post cards, stamps, &c and the immigrants could stand there, write their letters and post them, themselves, which was a great satisfaction to them." If the immigrants were illiterate, she would write for them. She claimed, in requesting reimbursement for stationery and postage, that on average sixty-five letters were sent home with the arrival of every steamship.[26] A mailbox, and sometimes even a post office, became a standard feature of Canadian immigration buildings.

Thus, further to the benefits associated with managing the process of immigration, in developing its network of immigration architecture the Canadian government also strove for the management of affect. It wanted each person to feel good about their arrival in the country. This was used explicitly to justify requests for new construction. In the 1889 annual report written by the Montreal agent, he asserted that, "for some years past," there had been an increase in the number of immigrants debarking in that city rather than in Quebec. But Montreal had no facilities to receive them. "First impressions count for a great deal, especially with immigrants in a new country … they are either favorably or unfavorably impressed with the reception tendered them, upon landing. In order therefore that a good first impression be made, it would be desirable that an Immigration Depôt be provided … at this port." The Montreal agent's reasoning was sound, but unsuccessful. Notably, in summarizing his agents' reports for the minister's annual presentation to parliament, the superintendent of immigration neglected to mention the need for a new building in Montreal.[27] In fact, with the recent completion of a new pier building at Quebec City, the Dominion government made the decision to require all immigrants be landed in that port; henceforth, Montreal would be merely a way station on the rail route to the west.

THE 1887 PIER BUILDING IN QUEBEC CITY

In his comparison of the US and Canadian systems of immigrant reception, the travelling inspector specifically mentioned the brand-new pier building in Quebec City as an example of his country's readiness for a large influx of new arrivals. It was opened during the immigration season of 1887, and the architecture of the new building represented a significant leap forward for the branches of government responsible. Not only was it a much larger structure than the one built less than a decade earlier, it was designed with the efficiency of the arrival process in mind. The protection and control of immigrants remained fundamental purposes of the pier building, but these goals would now be achieved through more modern, almost industrial, means, which attempted to ensure immigrants were not unavoidably delayed or discomfited.

1.5 In a site plan of 1890, the new, L-shaped immigration building is at the top of the image, and the 1880 shed is to the right, along the pier. Note the two separate toilet structures, one for each building, placed on the edges of the pier.

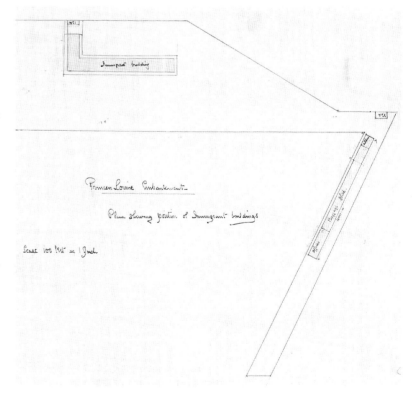

29

1.6 Quebec Immigration Building of 1887, shown in a photograph from 1905. This image gives some sense of the industrial environs of the building; immigrant ships would dock several hundred feet to the left of the frame. The smaller, gable-roofed structure to the right is the United States pre-clearance building erected shortly before the time of the photo.

1.7 (*opposite*) Quebec Immigration Building of 1887, plans and elevations.

The new Quebec building of 1887 incorporated some fifteen thousand square feet of interior space on the ground floor, about twice that of the earlier structure it replaced (Figure 1.5). However, much of the earlier building had been occupied by a huge baggage room, whereas that function was now relegated to outbuildings. Situated between the water and newly laid railroad tracks, the new building was another long, narrow structure, but with an ell containing the cafeteria and wash rooms. A broad gable roof sloped down over wide verandas that wrapped the entire building (Figures 1.6 and 1.7). The main mass rose up through this lower roof to establish a second storey and attic capped by a series of five cross gables, with the appearance of full-size dormers. This vertical bump-out differentiated the sleeping quarters above from the more bureaucratic functions of the substantial ground floor.

As architectural historian Janet Wright points out, the design of this pier building (like the one before it) "borrowed some features, such as the wide bracketed canopy, from those of railway stations." Many stations by this time were finished in a picturesque manner, characterized here by the cross gables, bracketed cornices, sculptural

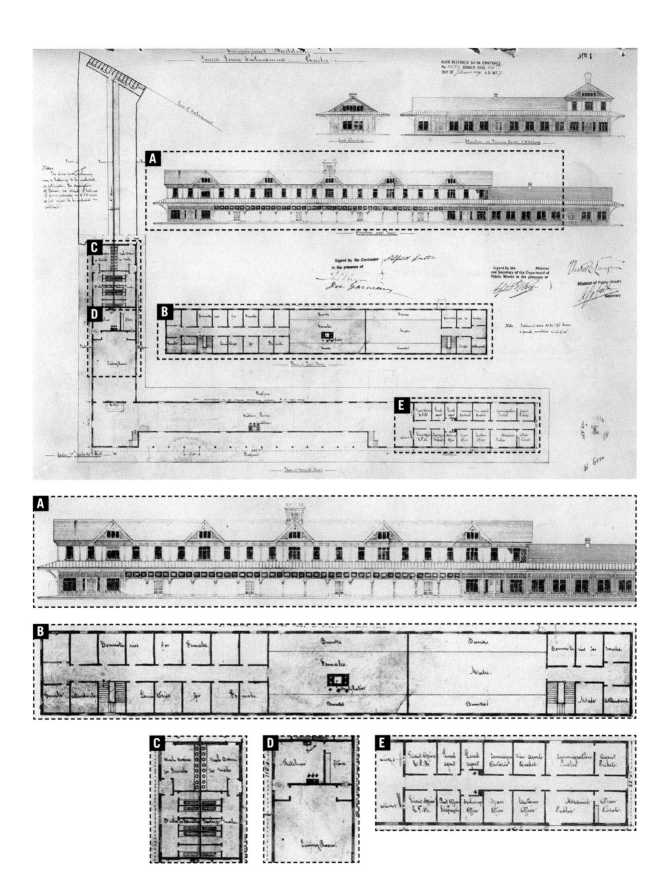

chimney, and by what Wright describes as the "decorative treatment of the woodwork, defined by a pattern of horizontal and diagonal planks, [and] varied patterns of shingling."[28] The Stick Style of the early 1880s pier building, and the similar Shingle Style of this new one, were borrowings from US architecture, recontextualized as manifestations of the Queen Anne taste in Canada. The association of the two buildings with other transportation infrastructure and with popular international architectural styles consciously played to migrant expectations of global travel.

The Department of Agriculture was proud of its new flagship architecture at Quebec, and its 1889 *Annual Report* includes the most detailed account of any Canadian immigration building of the nineteenth century:

> The Immigration Hall erected by the Dominion Government in 1887, is a good two story building 400 feet long, with a wide veranda all around, and fixed seats where people are secure from sun and rain. It is admirably situated, almost surrounded by flowing water, pure fresh air in abundance, and plenty of spare ground adjoining. During the two years it has been in use, all who have passed through have given free expression to their satisfaction with the building and conveniences provided for the weary passenger, after spending ten or twelve days in the limited space available for air and exercise on board ship.
>
> On the ground floor at one end, are sufficient double and single offices to accommodate all the officers connected with the various branches of Immigration Service, viz.: Dominion and Provincial Agents, Port Physician, Customs, Ticket, Telegraph and Telephone Offices, all easy of access to any person either in or outside the buildings [i.e., the offices opened to the veranda as well].
>
> The Main Hall, about 250 feet long, has ample room for 1,000 passengers with their hand baggage, is well lighted by large windows, and many wide doors afford easy means of communication with the verandah. In this hall is a long counter and shop, kept by a person appointed by the Government, where immigrants can procure provisions for the journey at moderate rates. For the guidance and information of immigrants, price lists of articles for sale, and tables of the Canadian currency value of foreign money, are posted up in the several parts of the hall; these are printed in French, German, Scandinavian, Russian and other foreign languages …
>
> At the [north] end is a dining-room, seating 200 at once. As tea, coffee or milk with bread and butter costs 10 cents and a full hot meal of meat and vegetables, 25 cents, everyone can be satisfactorily accommodated. A large kitchen, supplied with a new modern range, adjoins the dining room.
>
> The wing is divided into two apartments (male and female, entirely separate). Each contains six bath-rooms and a number of wash-basins and always furnished with soap and towels.
>
> On the second flat, are two large rooms, that can accommodate 300 people each: fixed seats [or "bunks," as per Figure 1.7] run all around these rooms, and they will be found useful in case of over crowding from any cause. On the female end there are 15 bedrooms and quarters for a matron and assistant. On the men's end there are 4 bed-rooms. These may be used by people who wish to rest a day or more before starting on a long rail journey, or those awaiting remittances from friends, &c., &c.
>
> The building is supplied with the very purest water from a well in the rear, sunk

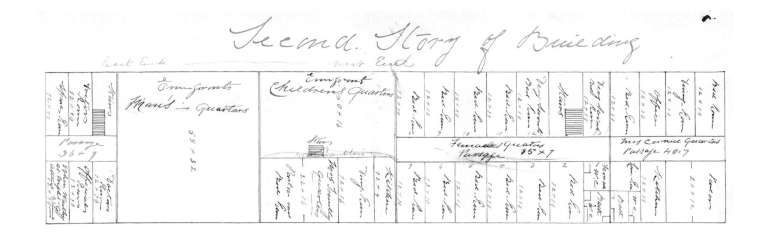

below the river bed; it is pumped by steam into cisterns in the attic, whence every part is supplied freely with pure cold water. The drinking taps in the Main Hall are fitted with hose couplings and sufficient hose is always at hand to reach any part of the building, either for washing, or in case of fire.[29]

There are numerous takeaways from this lengthy description. First, the tone of the passage suggests that the building is open and available to all who may "wish" to use it – not only the poorest immigrants in need of shelter. Its services are affordable, explained in multiple languages, and even state-regulated. As well, the building is portrayed as being particularly healthful for the arriving immigrant, with purity, freshness, and light emphasized as a respite from the ocean voyage. We can imagine in particular the exuberance of the children among the immigrants as they regained access to open space and exercise. The description ends by referring to the risk of fire, which reminds us that this was a large wooden building, often packed with people at all hours of the day and night. Cooking was done with fire and illumination provided by oil lamps.

Most importantly, this long passage from the *Annual Report* provides a description of the various

1.8 Quebec Immigration Building of 1887, second storey, in a sketch plan of 1903. From left to right: the doctor's office with waiting and examining rooms, and an office; the men's dormitory; the children's dormitory and common room, alongside the assistant matron's room; a series of bedrooms for single female or family use; and the matron's apartment.

offices and officers, services and spaces made available in the Quebec building, an arrangement that would become the model for other pier buildings, and, in parts, for other typologies of Canadian immigration architecture. It was a spatial arrangement that would evolve over time. A 1903 sketch plan of the second storey reveals the specification of uses by that date (Figure 1.8). The quarters of the matron and assistant matron are marked clearly, their separate lodging rooms – including parlours and kitchens – are situated at either end of the women's dormitories, thus maximizing their supervision of the immigrants. Adjacent to the assistant matron's quarters, one of the large waiting rooms is devoted to immigrant children, most likely the "home children" sent to Canada as farm labour by British poor-relief societies. Finally, the plan shows, at the end next to the men's quarters, that the four bedrooms mentioned in the *Annual Report* are no longer for immigrant use. Three have been converted to a doctor's and other offices to support medical and civil inspections that were introduced just before the sketch was made (see chapter 5). The fourth, charmingly hand-labelled "When Waiting at Night," allowed inspectors to catch up on their sleep while keeping an eye out for incoming vessels through the window in this well-placed room.

A series of photographs from 1911, late in the building's life, help provide a sense of the Quebec immigration building's interior spaces. The "Main Hall" was a long open space, interrupted by a row of timber columns, innumerable wooden benches, and various counters (Figures 1.9 and 1.10). Gleaming white walls, floors, and ceiling gather some of the extensive daylight alluded to in the official description. Walls and columns are hung with notices, posters, and framed images. The latter likely depicted scenes familiar from Canadian immigration promotional materials: the happy homesteading family; stretches of land covered in yellow wheat; a steam engine rounding a curve in the Rocky Mountains. These provided the migrants with something to daydream about while waiting, which was the primary activity in the pier buildings. Immigrants awaited interviews with government officials, who would briefly check their documentation, destinations, and financial situations, but above all would provide advice and other support. Although the waiting rooms of government agencies are typically arranged to

1.9 Quebec Immigration Building of 1887, main hall with store, c. 1911. Note the mailbox at front left.

emphasize state power over the subject, we see these hierarchies only in immigration buildings erected after the introduction of medical and civil inspections. There is little evidence of this kind of spatial arrangement in nineteenth-century immigration buildings, which were modelled more closely on railway stations. In the open plan of the waiting rooms shown in these images, government agents would have mingled freely with new arrivals, almost all of whom were considered admissible. In general, waiting rooms would have been everyday public spaces to which immigrants were accustomed.[30] Finding themselves in a new country, but in a seemingly familiar situation, where much still seemed to ride on their comportment, adult migrants likely would have behaved diffidently in such waiting rooms. Children, less layered and moulded by these types of lived experience, and with days of pent-up, shipboard energy to expend, brought different, perhaps unruly or disruptive, practices into these spaces. Unfortunately, the interior photos show the waiting rooms empty, devoid of the human relations, excitement, and anxieties that would have enlivened their use.

In these photos one can sense some of the functional arrangements of the Main Hall. Steel poles and chain-link fencing delineate the location of railway ticket wickets and other services for

1.11 Quebec Immigration Building of 1887, a posed photograph of the steerage-class dining hall, c. 1911.

1.12 Dining at the immigration shed, from the *Canadian Illustrated News*, 28 June 1879. Note that the same tables and benches are seen at use in Figure 1.11, a photograph taken thirty-two years later.

the immigrants. The kiosk for selling provisions extends into the space, its wooden cabinetry, with a diagonal pattern surmounted by glass and wire mesh, running to the ceiling. Goods can be seen stacked and hanging from above – not only food, but picnic baskets and even mattresses for use in the dormitories or on the colonist cars. These luxuries were for "those who wish to travel in comfort," according to one commentator.[31] Large roof brackets stretch out over the store, indicating that this was once an outdoor space. Several portions of the veranda were enclosed at different moments to make space for new functions or to expand old ones – for example, there were continual requests from corporate and philanthropic organizations for office accommodations.

At the far end of the waiting and processing area was the dining hall for steerage passengers (Figure 1.11). Long, sturdy wood tables and benches filled the space. So would the hubbub of babies crying, children being rambunctious, and many languages recounting departures and voyages, arrivals, and hopes for the future. For comparison, an 1879 image of the dining hall in the earliest Dominion government pier building at Quebec offers a feeling for the spatial practices of the dining hall (Figure 1.12). Women prepare and serve food in the background. Family groups and single travellers crowd the benches around a large table, on which is turned out a simple meal and a pot of tea. Four children of about the same age are clustered tightly around the father, as he seems to remonstrate them for their bickering. The mother is to the side, pouring milk for the infant in her lap. Out the door is seen the smoking funnel of a train engine, reminding the migrants to hurry up. Other than the somewhat neoclassical, turned-wood table legs, the steerage-class dining halls were thoroughly spartan. At some point, a separate dining room was added in a covered portion of the veranda for the use of officials and the higher classes of passenger. This latter restaurant boasted sheer floral curtains, fine table linens, china and glass crockery, and a bell to summon service, thus standing in clear contrast to the spatial qualities in the rest of the building (Figure 1.13).

Upstairs, the sleeping accommodations were austere. By the time of these 1911 photographs, the men's dormitory shows signs of heavy use, with marked-up walls and exposed, iron plumbing (Figures 1.14 and 1.15). Originally there would have been rough wooden communal bunks and straw ticks. The steel-pole framework of quadruple bunks – some with thin mattresses – represents a modernization, as these efficiently stacked beds were needed to accommodate increased immigration after the turn of the century. There was no privacy in the dormitories, but compared to the conditions in steerage compartments, this would have been no surprise to the migrants, nor would they have had middle-class expectations of private rooms. The women's dormitories were smaller, with fewer beds, but no more private. These smaller rooms would have been made available to family groups when possible – a practice evident in Prairie immigration halls as well. Overall, the interior finishes of the Quebec immigration building were utilitarian, almost industrial, in character (see also Figure I.3). In the ideal view, immigrant masses would be serviced efficiently, fed and watered and scrubbed in a staged, assembly-line

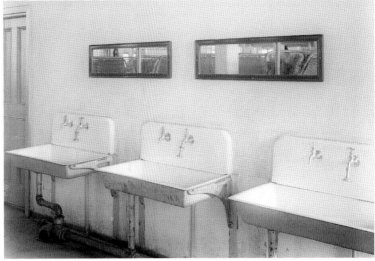

1.13 Quebec Immigration Building of 1887, restaurant-class dining room, c. 1911.

1.14 Quebec Immigration Building of 1887, men's dormitory sinks, c. 1911.

1.15 Quebec Immigration Building of 1887, men's dormitory, c. 1911.

process managed by government officials from gangplank to colonist car, through the designed spaces of the building.

QUEBEC'S STATUS AND BUILDINGS FOR THE OTHER EASTERN PORTS

By the early 1890s, the Dominion government's strategies for immigrant reception began to coalesce into a nationwide network of facilities that punctuated each stage of the journey. Because Quebec City remained a destination limited to the warm seasons, the government needed immigration buildings in the winter ports of Halifax and Saint John. Fewer immigrants arrived in the winter months, but some did arrive. However, the Maritimes port buildings would always be developed to lower standards, since Quebec remained the primary destination for steerage passengers. As a travelling inspector wrote about Quebec, the "arrangement of the building and its appointments are a long way in advance of those of the other Agencies visited."[32]

The first building for processing arrivals in Halifax opened in 1890, sandwiched between two railroad tracks that ran along the edges of the wharf. Compared to the Quebec building there were few services in this one-storey structure: an open plan is simply marked "shed," with the only interior partitions marking three small offices for the agent, baggage handlers, and ticketing. An existing warehouse of about a thousand square feet was connected to the shed and converted into dining and sleeping accommodations (two small dormitories and half a dozen family bedrooms), with staff rooms in the attic. These facilities seem on par with the situation at Quebec some twenty or thirty years earlier. A fire destroyed the site, occasioning a new immigration building for Halifax, which was completed in 1897.

This later project was built to a more detailed program, incorporating all the functions seen

concurrently at Quebec. It was an L-shaped building, with one of the wings topped by a second storey for sleeping accommodations (Figures 1.16 and 1.17). The ground floor is organized carefully, with areas delineated for baggage, waiting, provisioning, and dining. A new function appearing here for the first time is the "Disinfecting Room" for baggage and clothing. Even though Halifax had its own quarantine station, which was where disinfection typically occurred, it was deemed necessary to include the apparatus here too, perhaps because the island station opened only in times of need. As will be discussed in chapter 2, the rising prominence of disinfection practices at this time indicates the waxing of germ theory, and the belief that sulphuric steam would thoroughly clean articles being imported.

In this building there is also a more careful arrangement of male and female quarters, services, and circulation. On the second storey of the ell, dormitories are arranged along the outside walls, wrapping around two sex-specific sitting areas. Married and unmarried men's dormitories occupy the north end of the ell, with the matron's quarters supervising a section of smaller bedrooms for women and children. This women's area is accessed from the south stairway: adjacent to the ground-floor waiting room is a lobby fronting the agents' offices, from which these stairs ascend to a vestibule outside of the matron's quarters. Thus, female immigrants and their rooms would be under surveillance at all times. In contrast, the north stairway rises directly from an exterior door next to the railroad tracks, and accesses the men's dormitories without intervening surveillance. Men's toilets and bath rooms are on the ground floor, easily accessible from the wharf and baggage room, while the women's are found only in the domestic areas of the top floor. The government's paternalistic concern for the protection of women and child travellers is made manifest by these architectural plans.

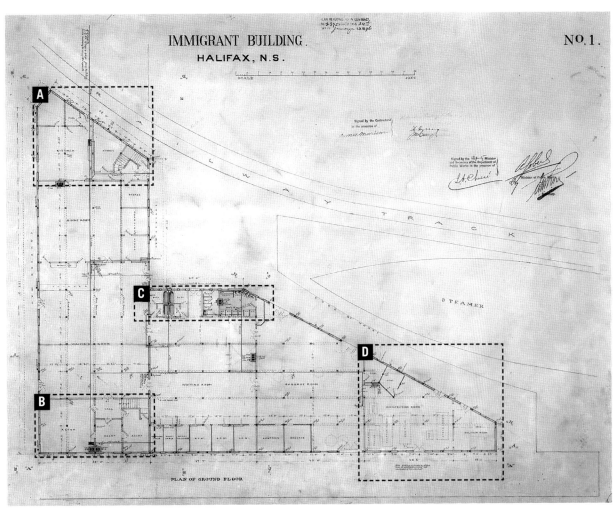

1.16 Immigrant Building,
Halifax, Department of
Public Works ground-
floor plan of 1896.

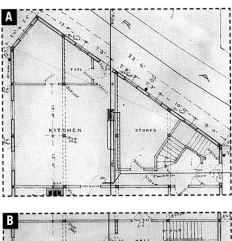

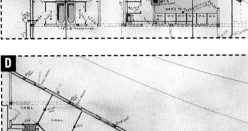

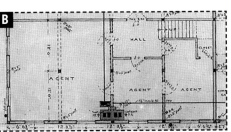

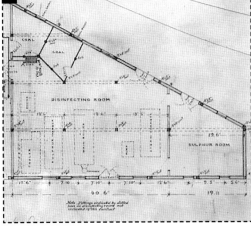

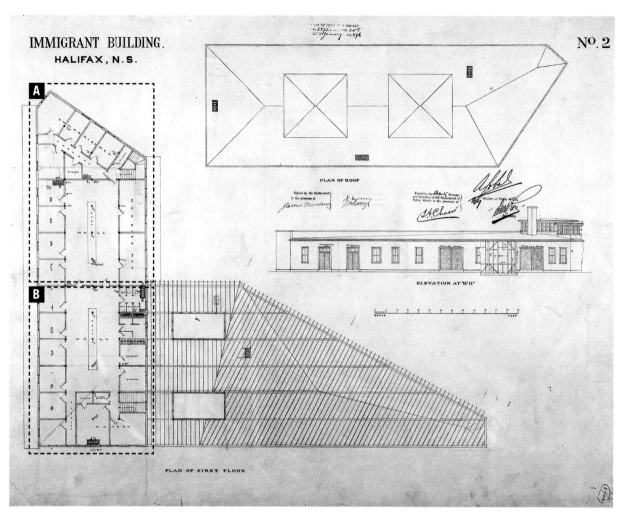

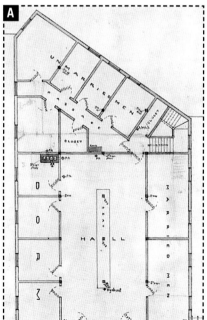

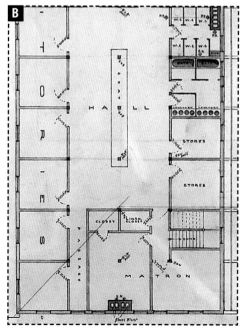

1.17 Immigrant Building, Halifax, Department of Public Works first-floor plan, roof plan, and partial elevation, 1896.

No photographs survive of the first two Dominion government immigration buildings in Halifax. Only a partial elevation of the facade facing the water indicates the aesthetic of the 1897 structure, which is exceedingly plain. These buildings did not aspire, architecturally, to appear as anything other than industrial sheds. There are no sculptural gables animating the roofline or indications of a decorative facade treatment, as seen on the two most recent immigration buildings on the pier at Quebec City. This may be a reflection of what Wright called "the central Canadian focus of the Chief Architect's Branch," a bias that no doubt affected the decisions of the immigration branch as well.[33]

Immigration architecture in the other east-coast winter port received slightly more aesthetic consideration. Saint John, which had become the Maritimes terminus of the CPR, invested heavily in port development around the turn of the century. The Dominion government opened its first immigration building there for the winter season of 1901–02. It offered the same services as the other two pier buildings, but was smaller; later, the government would rent additional space in an adjacent warehouse. The Saint John pier building exhibited a third aesthetic, with coloured shingle siding contrasting with heavy white trim, perhaps in a nod to local vernacular traditions (Figure 1.18). The constricted site in Saint John, following the curve of the railroad tracks, required a series of bump-outs and shed-roofed adjuncts to

1.18 Immigration Building of 1902, Saint John, New Brunswick. The date of the photo is unknown.

the building, with the overall effect of a rambling Victorian residence or hotel.

Despite the development of these seasonal facilities in the Maritimes, during the last decade of the nineteenth century, the Dominion government took steps to solidify the position of Quebec City as the principal Laurentian port for immigrants to Canada. In 1893, it decreed that all summer steerage passengers would debark at its pier building on the Louise Embankment. This decision caused a significant amount of controversy with one of the shipping lines and with immigrant-aid societies that had become accustomed to bringing assisted immigrants all the way to Montreal, where many had their head offices and hostels. The immigrant-aid societies expressed their "dismay" and begged to "enter a most earnest protest against this regulation," which, they claimed, would deal such a "fatal blow" that "the respectable class of people we help will not consent to undertake emigration to Canada at all." For its part, the shipping line argued that debarking immigrants at its own dock and shed in Montreal worked perfectly well, and that the government should mind its own business. Moreover, by taking them upriver to Montreal, the shipping company claimed to be saving immigrants money. Debarking in Quebec City, changing to a train, and buying food made the journey cost more, "especially to incoming travellers, of the poorer class, whose ignorance of the Country and its people is apt to involve them in greater expense." The company could ensure that these naive passengers were "kept apart" from locals. Meanwhile, it would be happy to allow access to its sheds for "a representative of the government" to interview and inform the immigrants, as at Quebec.[34]

The Dominion government was unimpressed by these protestations. The other shipping lines concurred with the intent of landing all steerage passengers in Quebec, where the government had existing facilities and staff. It was also pointed out that immigrants, if they transferred to trains in Quebec, would be well past Montreal before their steamship even arrived at that city. Ultimately, the government felt strongly enough about centralizing the process of immigrant reception that it had the Governor General issue a Royal Proclamation asserting its power to control where and when passengers would debark. The place, henceforth, would be Quebec City, where, the memo to the Governor General reasoned, "comfortable and commodious buildings have been erected" for this exact purpose. The time would be from 6 a.m. to 6 p.m., or daylight hours, when there was staff available and they could see what they were doing.[35]

As the 1887 building in Quebec was being finished, the Dominion government had worked to convince the south-shore railways and their shipping partners to abandon the practice of debarking steerage passengers across the river at Pointe-Lévy. At that time, the government shared space in a building there with the Grand Trunk Railway, as its own shed had burned down. An 1886 plan for a new immigration shed at Pointe-Lévy never came to fruition, for the same reasons that none was built in Montreal: rather than duplicating its facilities and staff, the government would compel the companies to bring immigrants to the Louise Embankment. Finally, the Canadian Pacific Railway was not uninterested in this issue and seems to have influenced the government to require debarkation on the north side of the St Lawrence, where the trains of that company ran. As the vice-president of the CPR acknowledged in an 1888 letter: "We have had a long struggle to get the steamships to our side of the river and we must not give them any excuse for going back."[36] In these years, the Dominion government still relied heavily on the CPR to deliver immigrants to the Prairie provinces, and the company often exercised its influence over decision-making.

SPATIAL PRACTICES AT THE NINETEENTH-CENTURY PIER BUILDINGS

The Welch family of nine, arriving in Quebec City in 1881, was taken aback by the chaos of arrivals, spectators, and cargo, and struggled to escape the wharf with all their children and possessions. The father of the family chronicled the "bustle and noise in getting onshore, and then the trouble of getting all our boxes together among the thousands that are hurried onto the quay." It was "a heavy piece of work … and the sun was quite a scorcher." He also helped a widow with two children gather her baggage. Welch wanted to nail tags onto the widow's boxes, "but could not find a stone anywhere, its wood, wood, everywhere, this indeed must be a woody country if this is a specimen." Indeed, these were new spaces to negotiate. Welch chronicled better luck with the customs officials, who "passed all my boxes without opening one." Upon application, the immigration officials gave him tickets for free passage onwards to the family's Ontario destination. Then he was able to purchase food for the train, "some milk and an apple or two for the children, poor dears." Meanwhile, several "ladies and gentlemen are on the lookout for servant girls … Annie, Kate and Bessie might have had a situation there and then," but the family did not want to separate. Less than nine hours after mooring, the Welches were on the train rolling out of Quebec City.[37] Despite the seeming chaos, the immigrant reception system seemed to have worked.

When all went well, the debarkation of immigrants at the modern Dominion government pier buildings of the late-nineteenth century could be an ordered affair. A newspaper reporter observed the processes and people involved in the 1902 reception of the largest passenger vessel to dock in Halifax to date. On board were almost 2,700 immigrant arrivals, 1,700 of them for destinations in Canada – including some 450 children. The remainder were headed for the United States. The passengers were of "all nationalities – Galicians, Italians, Jews, and Germans … huddled together near the bow of the steamer as she drew into the wharf this morning, all straining their eyes to catch a glimpse of the landing point of their future home." Debarked, the passengers "were pleased to step once more on terra firma." The reporter judged that these immigrants were of a "superior" stock than previous arrivals, "much cleaner and neater looking, there being but very few sheepskins among them." After this racist aside, the reporter continued his narrative: "Inside the immigration shed a busy scene was presented, all the rooms were occupied, the ticket offices were surrounded by hundreds eager for information and buying tickets, some slept on chairs or on the floor, while in the dining-room many others were enjoying lunch … The manner in which such a large number of people were attended to reflects much credit on the immigration, railway and customs officers."[38] This outsider's view provides an understanding of the general excitement of the arrivals, and of the occupation of space when the immigration pier buildings were in operation, but offers minimal insight into individual experiences or practices.

Despite the more formal organization of the immigrant's journey by government architecture and bureaucratic procedures, migrants still experienced arrival as an anxious and trying event. One Icelandic immigrant recalled:

We arrived in Quebec, August 7, 1893, to face another ordeal. Immigrants' baggage was loaded on the dock and the head of each family told to keep an eye on it, until the wagons came to load it up to take it to the trains.

There was no shelter on the docks and no refreshment was offered. The 90 [degree] heat was almost too much for people used to the cool of Iceland. They waited until near five o'clock in the afternoon, many took sick and near sunstroke.[39]

Often, as may have been the case here, the simultaneous berthing of several steamships overtaxed the immigration facility and staff in Quebec. Presumably, this group could not crowd onto the shady veranda or into the building's common spaces to wait and to take advantage of its cafeteria and other amenities. As described, this seems little different from steerage arrivals sixty years earlier, when the colonial immigration agents were first hired. For that matter, it was little different a dozen years later. In 1906, for example, the Harbour Commissioners at Quebec City laid out similar problems in detail for the minister of the interior: one of the two baggage sheds (which were surviving portions of the 1880 immigration hall) had just been demolished, and the other "reduced in size, having its overhanging roof taken away, consequently, the provision for shelter to passengers and luggage is worse than formerly, and the number of passengers has very materially increased." So as not to "discourage them on their arrival in the country," new provision for shelter was desperately needed, especially since, as "the season advances, the probability of heavy rain storms largely increases."[40] Protection from Canada's climate extremes was necessary to ensure immigrants received good first impressions.

In addition to inclement weather, the preceding quotations allude to the need for immigrants to keep an eye on their possessions. The protection of immigrants from thieving locals remained a serious problem for officials in the late-nineteenth century. One memoirist related her mother-in-law's landing at the Halifax pier building in 1893. "She had a sickly boy, a little girl, and the baggage. A man who had a horse and rig came up to her and said, 'You give me your baggage checks and I'll look

after your baggage for you.' That was the last she saw of it. That was her introduction to the country."[41] This harried mother probably did not post an encouraging letter home from the pier building. Reflecting events like this, an 1897 Dominion government handbook for prospective immigrants went into great detail describing a system of baggage checks, with which European migrants were evidently unfamiliar. According to the handbook, this North American "custom has great safety as well as convenience."[42]

Dominion government agents strove to keep immigrants isolated, but nevertheless were inundated with locals. Notices in local newspapers let everyone know the date that the immigration building would open each season, and regularly listed the projected number of immigrants on scheduled arrivals, often along with their ethnicities and occupations.[43] Like other nineteenth-century institutions, the immigration buildings attracted journalists, philanthropists, and rubberneckers, along with the requisite swindlers. A Ukrainian migrant remembered with some horror her debarkation at the Halifax pier building:

On the shore, a crowd of people stared at us, some out of curiosity, and some out of contempt. Our men, particularly those from Galicia, were dressed like gentlemen for the voyage, but the women and children travelled in their everyday peasant costumes. The older men from Bukovyna attracted attention to themselves by their waist-length hair greased with reeking lard and by their smelly sheepskin coats. Perhaps that was the reason why the English people stopped their noses and glued their eyes upon us, a strange spectacle, indeed.[44]

This recollection may have received added colour from the image, developed over several decades in the early-twentieth century, of Ukrainian migrants as "men in sheepskin coats." But the emotions attendant to debarking in a strange land are manifest here. The woman describes spatial practices that establish relationships of power across an invisible boundary: the vulnerability of the migrants facing the dominant gaze of the "English" natives. At the end of the passage, by appending the word "indeed," this woman took ownership retrospectively of her other-ness, having survived the gauntlet in place at her arrival.

Government facilities and procedures were modified continually in attempts to protect immigrants from different sorts of imposition, both human and environmental. The issue of fencing at the Quebec pier building comes up repeatedly in immigration-branch correspondence. In the early 1890s, letters from several civil servants

associated with the Quebec agency prompted the Department of Public Works to erect a fence and gate on "the city side of the shed … [to] exclude outsiders during the debarkation of passengers." The Scandinavian interpreter employed at the pier building argued that, with a barrier, the work of processing the passengers would be easier and "the immigrants would be safe from being robbed by possible sharpers or from being induced to stroll into Quebec for one purpose or other."[45] A fence indeed was erected at this time (Figure 1.19; see also Figure 1.6), but it was ineffective without enforcement. Later that decade, the mayor of the

1.19 Galician immigrants at Immigration Sheds, Quebec, c. 1908. This family group stands in front of the gate into the building; the fence is to the right, tracks in foreground.

city telegrammed Ottawa to ask that its agent in Quebec "refuse admission to strangers to come within the fence." Similarly, the money changer stationed in the building described "the large crowds that constantly *infest* the place." They were "a great nuisance to all concerned in handling the immigration work there," and policies and procedures should "forbid, any person to enter, or interfere without a pass or permit."[46] In response, the immigration branch merely admonished the head agent to enforce already-existing rules at the Quebec building.

Fencing also was required on the water side of the shed to marshal immigrants from ship to building without them getting hit by baggage lorries or shunting rail cars. In this matter, the CPR was concerned about both liability and efficiency when loading and unloading people and baggage. Writing in 1903 of the need for more fencing, the general passenger agent expressed the company's desire to "absolutely control the immigrants," who currently were able to "wander unrestrained on the railway track." The port continually was being modernized and altered for various reasons, so the paths taken by arrivals shifted. As one concerned party noted in 1905, "we have to lead passengers from the Macadamized Roadway between the baggage platform and the freight shed on which vehicles are constantly passing and re-passing and which is in a muddy condition." Throughout the building's history, migrants were obliged to carry their hand baggage on a "long and slow passage from the Ship to the Building." The CPR agent helpfully suggested that a roof over this sidewalk would protect immigrants from a "wetting" in poor weather.[47] Later these problems of controlling and protecting the immigrants on the wharf would be solved with extensive aerial gangways.

When a train sat on the tracks, it could block access to the building and other parts of the wharf (see Figure I.1). As late as 1910, the port physician was exercised about the troubles "caused by freight cars being left on the railway track immediately in front of the immigrant verandah." Reminding the engineer of the Harbour Commission how "essentially important it is to keep outsiders from intermingling with the immigrants," he proceeded to detail the dangerous characters in the vicinity: "there is nothing to prevent sailors from the different ships, or in fact any other class, from getting on the [freight] cars from the outside and stepping over the protecting fence ... Furthermore, the cars when empty provide very acceptable sleeping apartments for whatever loafer who happens around, and they not only lounge but very often smoke in them, thereby ... threatening the Buildings with fire." Although the railway companies downplayed the issue, the commission's wharfinger was sent to ensure that boxcars would not stand on those sidings. Through spatial modifications, and the practices of officials and others, the immigration building was fitfully defined as a space apart.

These examples remind us that the spatial practices of migrants took place in the bustling, dangerous, and sometimes deviant environs of wharves, rail yards, and industrial zones (Figure 1.20). Even the buildings themselves needed protection from port denizens. When it closed to immigrant traffic in the winter months, the Quebec facility had to maintain a full-time security detail. For example, back in 1889, soon after the opening of the new building, the older immigration building was decommissioned and slated for conversion to a cargo shed. The Public Works architect tasked with the renovations found that, after a couple of years lying idle, the old building was in a "disgraceful state completely left to the access of those who wish to make it their abode." Doors had been "broken through," hardware removed, and most of the windows smashed. The architect was affronted by the interior of the building, which was "fearfully dirty and used for improper purposes ... the bad smell making it very

unhealthy."[48] The image of order, safety, and appropriate welcome that the government wished to project were continually jeopardized by the press of everyday life in a port.

Finally, there was the shit. For all three Dominion government pier buildings erected in Quebec City between 1870 and 1887, toilets were placed in outbuildings on the edge of the wharf, projecting over the water for direct disposal of waste, which could be swept down the river (see Figure 1.5). Unfortunately, this did not always work so well. The agent at Quebec described the problem in the summer of 1897: the "closets were always an eyesore and wrongly placed within about 50 feet from

1.20 This 1911 aerial view of the immigration pier building on the Louise Embankment in Quebec City provides a good sense of the crowded and chaotic spaces of circulation into which migrants debarked.

the Kitchen and Dining Room, and at low tide the odor is very offensive." A plan was made to shift them further down the wharf over deeper water, but the contractor showed up to disassemble them at the height of immigration season – which would have left the agency without toilets for thousands of arrivals. Then the issue seems to have been neglected by the Department of Public Works. The need for new biffies resurfaced in letters dated

1901 and 1903, when the local immigration agent again prioritized this project over all others. But the Public Works architect brushed him off, assuring his superiors in Ottawa that the water closets were "good" enough where they were, and merely needed "proper maintenance."[49] The outhouses were never moved, until a railroad track realignment required it some years later.

The environs of the immigration pier buildings may not have signalled an auspicious beginning to newcomers, though they likely were accustomed to the smell of human feces — and perhaps to urban-industrial dangers as well. In contrast, the migrants might have been pleasantly surprised by the typically friendly treatment they received from government officials. The guide to immigrants from the Austro-Hungarian empire, Joseph Oleskiw, anticipated that rural migrants would be unaccustomed to helpful authorities. In Eastern Europe, he wrote, "even the most miserable village clerk expects the peasants to bow to him." Not so in North America: "an official is there a worker like everyone else and … [people] keep their hats on in an office, even in a Ministry, and walk into the office freely, without bowing and bending their backs."[50] A Dominion of Canada *Handbook* was less sensationalist, but equally reassuring to the mystified migrant, promising that "he may always rely on the perfect honesty of any statement made to him by any Government agent." Moreover, the money exchange, railway ticket wickets, grocery, and cafeteria were under the eyes of "Government officials supervising everything under rules."[51] Interactions within the spaces of Dominion immigration buildings would reinforce the migrant's perception of a "new world" of egalitarianism and order.

Although they were in a position of relative power, government officials, railway employees, and other locals often acted with sympathy for the immigrant arrivals, and the latter recognized this with gratitude. The first government-paid matron

for immigration proudly appended to her annual report letters of thanks received from single female immigrants she had helped during their time in those places. The single women who were "under the particular care of the lady agent, were retained at the 'Building' until suitable situations were provided for them" by the immigrant-aid societies. "I thank you very much indeed," one woman wrote to the matron from Toronto, "for your kind help and assistance to me when I landed in Quebec. I felt such a stranger in the City, but when you asked me had I anyone to meet me I felt so thankful … to our Father, for all His goodness to me."[52] In her book about women's immigration societies, *Agents of Empire*, Lisa Chilton carefully deploys this sort of thank-you letter. Even though immigrant women said what the "lady agents" who helped them wanted to hear, Chilton argues that this "should not completely undermine their value as emigrant-authored texts."[53] In this case, the letter to the matron affectively evokes the bewilderment of a woman immigrant so far from her familiar spaces. How would she practice space with such a lack of context? The authority of the matron, and her Lord, helped her negotiate that new space.

Even though the policy was that immigration pier buildings were reserved for brief stays upon arrival, there are many indications that officials allowed longer-term inhabitation, and sometimes even return stays for recent arrivals who lost their jobs, were between situations, or waiting for better weather. A European visitor felt that providing a "quiet and safe shelter" for people who had "been in Canada for some time" was a sign of bureaucratic benevolence: "The officials, from the highest to the lowest, distinguish themselves for their kindness and for their readiness to help the immigrants."[54] Not everyone saw this as a good thing. A representative of the Allan Lines steamship company visited the Quebec building early in 1905 to check on its readiness for the coming immigration season, and he "found the place pretty well littered up with dirt and a large number of Russian Jews housed there." He had two steamships of immigrants on the way to that port, and he chided the superintendent of immigration in Ottawa: "We understood these people would be all removed before the Building was required for its legitimate purposes … and it will be very unfortunate, and indeed dangerous, if the place has not been cleared out, thoroughly cleansed and ventilated before the passengers arrive."[55] The underlying racism of these comments emphasizes the long association of immigrants with uncleanliness and threats to health, while simultaneously trying to delegitimize the use of the building for anything other than immediate immigrant processing and distribution.

The housing and supervision of single female immigrants, and the long-term stays of others reminds us that, although most migrants passed through the pier buildings in a matter of hours, for some they became a temporary home. Certain members of the staff too, such as the caterers, the matron, the assistant matron, and even their children, made the immigration buildings their permanent homes. Requisitions for domestic supplies, such as area rugs, blinds, and kitchen utensils are jarring inclusions in reams of bureaucratic correspondence about policy, procedure, and personnel. Without these "indispensable articles necessitated for life," an assistant matron complained to Ottawa in 1901, she would not feel as if she was being "treated like a civilized woman."[56] The Department of Public Works was consistent in stating that its responsibilities ended with basic furnishings for the function of the building: desks and chairs, waiting-room benches, and beds. Everything else would have to come from the budget of the immigration branch.

In the 1890s, the sole government matron shuttled seasonally between the immigration buildings in Quebec and Halifax. By the early 1900s, the Halifax office had hired its own matron, and an assistant had been taken on in Quebec.[57]

By the 1910s, the matron and assistant matron had grown so accustomed to free lodgings in the Quebec building that the agent – with the insistent urging of his superiors in Ottawa – had to evict them when the building was shuttered each winter. The now-elderly matron, for whom the immigration building was practically a rest home, typically went to stay with her son in Montreal during the off-season. The Quebec agent, a medical doctor, wrote that she "required to be attended to on account of her advanced age and rapidly failing memory as well as her marked inclination to sickness." Meanwhile, a generous disbursement to the assistant matron for renting an apartment in town for the winter did not hasten her to relocate her family. Just before Christmas in 1911, the women remained "the only obstacle preventing the closing of this Building for the winter" and shutting off the water and heat. The agent in Quebec was exercised that the assistant matron had "added a new card to her hand to play her usual game," by influencing the doddering matron to stay put.[58] Future correspondence regarding the seasonal closure of the building suggests that the men in charge ultimately prevailed with the temporary evictions. Nevertheless, this domestic layer confirms the diversity of spatial practices that characterized immigration buildings. The space of immigration architecture was produced through a complex layering of interactions among migrants, officials, and residents, vendors, helpers, and hangers-on.

CONCLUSIONS

The historian Dirk Hoerder has argued that in Canada "no collective memory, no myth about the ports of arrival, developed in any way comparable to the Statue of Liberty–Ellis Island myth in the United States."[59] This lack of mythology is partly due to the immigration buildings in eastern-Canadian ports, which tended to be less impressive than their New York counterparts, first at Castle

Garden and then at Ellis Island after 1890. There certainly were parallels: Canadian pier buildings shared the complex institutional layers of the busier New York sites, and both federal architectures of immigration were concerned with the management of bodies and affect. But as an island, the Ellis facility in particular was unmistakably a space apart from the bustle of the piers and waterfronts and rooming houses — and totally detached from the mainland United States. As others have noted, its island situation contributed significantly to its understanding as a heterotopia where immigrants endured a rite of passage that contributed to national myth-making.[60]

Ellis Island's Main Building clearly represented the idea of arriving at a significant border crossing. Immigrants for processing would transfer from their ocean liners to a ferry that would deposit them on the island. Set back from the slip to emphasize a formal, axial approach, the Main Building's front steps rise through arches framed by classical and nationalist symbols carved in masonry, before ultimately depositing an immigrant in the impressive great hall, a vaulted basilica-like interior festooned with American flags. We might assume that a Canadian government architecture designed for a similar purpose and forming a symbolic entry point for thousands of arriving immigrants would put forth a correspondingly consistent and monumental representation of space. But no, in contrast, steamships would slip up directly alongside the anonymous facades of baggage sheds, and immigrants would trudge along boardwalks or gangways amid railroad tracks. The Dominion government's pier buildings partook of the gritty and industrial everyday atmosphere of the port. Along with the differing aesthetics of the New York and the Canadian facilities, the spatial arrangements of arrival communicated qualities and meanings of both architectural and national spaces. For instance, at what particular point did a migrant step across the border into Canada and become an immigrant? This spatial process was markedly more clear in the Ellis Island case, and in fact was later discussed as a problem in Canadian pier buildings.[61]

Architectural trappings, such as the different Victorian styles adopted on pier buildings in Quebec and Saint John, were largely lost amid the chaotic and constantly encroaching built fabric of the working waterfronts that these facilities occupied. But if no immigrants were lost in this chaos, the architecture was performing its duties. The same sentiment does not apply to the quarantine stations that we turn to in the next chapter. Although most migrants survived quarantine, it was, at least in its early years of development in Canada, a place where many thousands were lost to epidemic diseases and other maladies of poverty and overcrowding.

CHAPTER 2

Coastal Quarantine Stations and Defence against Disease

Catherine Parr Traill immigrated to Canada in 1832, at the height of a terrible cholera epidemic raging across Europe and eastern North America. The ship she sailed on was detained for three days at the newly established quarantine station at Grosse-Île, in the middle of the St Lawrence River, downstream from Quebec City. As a cabin passenger, Traill was not expected – nay, was forbidden by the quarantine doctor – to debark and experience the process of quarantine first-hand. However, the view through "the captain's glass" permitted her to write detailed descriptions of the station and the spatial practices occurring there. "We reached Gros Isle yesterday evening," she recorded:

> It is a beautiful rocky island, covered in groves of beech, birch, ash, and fir-trees. There are several vessels lying at anchor close to the shore … When any infectious complaint appears on board, the yellow flag is hoisted, and the invalids conveyed to the cholera-hospital or wooden building, that has been erected on a rising bank above the shore. It is surrounded with palisadoes and a guard of soldiers … who are there to enforce the quarantine rules. These rules are considered as very defective, and in some respects quite absurd, and are

productive of many severe evils to the unfortunate emigrants.

If the quarantine doctor confirmed the presence of a contagious illness on board a ship, then all the crew and steerage passengers had to "go on shore, taking with them their bedding and clothes, which are all spread out on the shore, to be washed, aired, and fumigated, giving the healthy every chance of taking the infection from the invalids." Worse, the sheds provided for accommodation of the healthy immigrants were "in the same area as the hospital" (Figure 2.1). She concludes that quarantine seemed designed to "wantonly sacrifice" healthy immigrants to protect the "colony at large."

At the same time, Traill's description evokes how the healthy migrants occupied the space and time of quarantine, with everyday tasks and a certain festive feeling at having survived the voyage:

> You may imagine yourself looking on a fair or crowded market, clothes waving in the wind or spread out upon the earth, chests, bundles, baskets, men, women, and children, asleep or basking in the sun, some in motion busied with their goods, the women employed in washing or cooking in the open air, beside the wood fires on the beach; while parties of

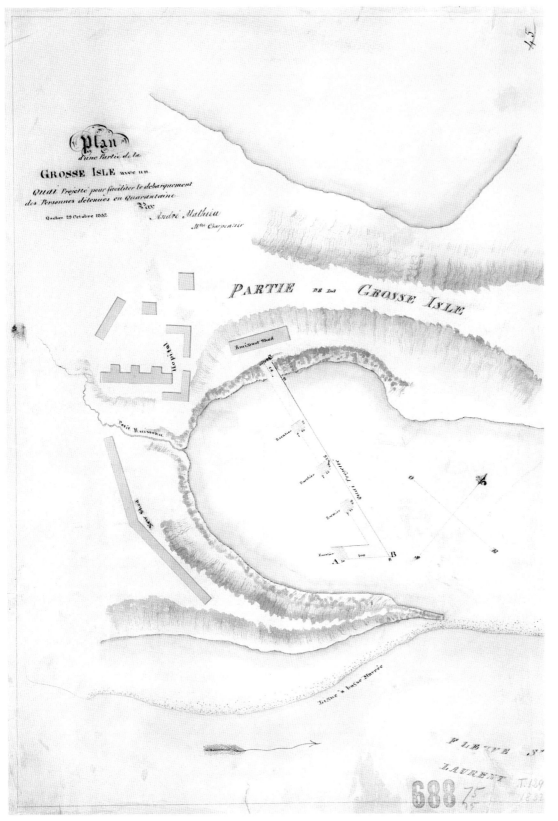

2.1 An 1832 site plan of the quarantine station on Grosse-Île, showing the E-shaped hospital and associated structures, and the immigrant shed at the head of the quay. The long, V-shaped building marked "New Shed" was erected at the conclusion of the 1832 immigration season, after the worst of that summer's overcrowding.

children are pursuing each other in wanton glee rejoicing in their newly-acquired liberty. Mixed with these you see the stately form and gay trappings of the sentinels.

An officer from the detachment assured Traill and her husband that "distance lends enchantment to the view," that, close up, they would have seen "human misery in its most disgusting and saddening form." Indeed, although she found the delay "annoying," class privilege allowed Traill's family to avoid the worst aspects of the island station.[1]

Traill's narrative touches on most of the descriptive motifs and key issues that would characterize writings about Canadian quarantine stations for the next century. To begin with, her limited experience is of waiting in quarantine, and not of isolation in a hospital ward. There are no first-person sources describing a writer's hospitalization. Like many subsequent commentators, Traill opens by emphasizing the picturesque qualities of the island. All the major Canadian quarantine stations boasted beautiful wilderness settings, which stood in stark contrast with the horrors that some experienced in them. She mentions several times the military presence, which was there to enforce the quarantine rules. As quarantine became more accepted and the necessity for martial law receded, the authority over the stations would reside in their head doctors, who came to play lead roles in immigrants' portrayals. Traill describes in some detail the process of cleaning and defumigation undertaken by the migrants. As the century progressed, the basic principle of bathing and laundering each immigrant and their possessions remained the same; however, this process increasingly became industrialized through the introduction of chemicals, machine-generated cleaning power, and a kind of assembly line. All of this occurred in specific architectures of quarantine: hospitals for the ill; sheds, and later hotels, for the well; and an assortment of attendant structures to support it all, including barracks and staff housing, schools and churches, bakeries, stores, wharves, disinfection chambers, and laboratories.

Finally, Traill's critique of quarantine's threat to the very health of the migrants presages a litany of attacks on its policies and practices. Over the coming decades, travellers, politicians, and doctors questioned the efficacy and made suggestions for the improvement of quarantine. But the primary criticism was always economic. For a ship's captain or a large transportation company, every delay cost money. The length of detention, from a few days to a month, was never standardized, and depended on the disease, the current medical theory, the overcrowding of the stations, and the pressure exerted for release by the transportation companies or by the inmates (especially the cabin-class inmates). The result was a continual negotiation among interested parties over the length of quarantine, and the quest for ever-more-efficient processes to discriminate between the sick and the healthy.

The purpose of nineteenth-century maritime quarantine was to control perceived vectors of disease, including ships, cargo, baggage, and passengers. Infectious diseases that concerned Canadian quarantine officials — such as cholera, typhus, and smallpox — often did not reveal their symptoms until immigrants were well beyond the government surveillance and aid established at borders and ports of entry. As historian Geoffrey Bilson explains, the intent of government officials was simply to protect the public "by providing for a quarantine that would bar the sick from entering Canada until they had recovered."[2] In theory, the sick would be isolated in hospital buildings, to ensure they did not infect others; the well would be quarantined and observed for a period of time, to see that they did not develop symptoms. In the meantime, ships, baggage, and clothing could be cleaned or disinfected. Residents of Canada would be protected from contagions imported from the

Old World; the immigrants would be protected from the risk of finding themselves incapacitated in a new country, unable to work and support their families. Without quarantine, recent arrivals who took ill would be thrust upon the charity of local communities who did not know them; with a quarantine system in place, those communities would be protected from the danger and expense of caring for transients.

Human quarantine in the nineteenth century was organized according to class and racial categories. In the early years of its implementation, cabin passengers such as Traill were exempt, though their servants might be sent ashore to wash the clothes and bedding. More-affluent travellers were assumed to be healthier than poor migrants, and even if the former did take ill, they had the means to support themselves while convalescing. In addition, they were rarely considered "immigrants," even if they were prospective settlers.[3] Steerage-class passengers were considered to be immigrants, and were thereby stigmatized as more likely to be malnourished, dirty, and exposed to infections in the crowded, miasmic spaces of a ship's hold. If they were Irish – or, later in the century, southern and eastern Europeans, Chinese, and other Asian migrants – the stigmatization was supported by stereotypical racial hierarchies. The controls of quarantine would include all classes of passenger, but with strictly distinguished facilities and expectations for the different classes and races.

Quarantine exemplifies the recurring themes of protection and control that were central to the history of Canadian immigration architectures. Historian of science Alison Bashford has written that, annexed to ports all over the world, "quarantine islands could quickly invert" from forcible detention to "accommodation and benevolent care."[4] But it is imprecise to refer to these two aspects of quarantine as inverse operations. In the spirit of Foucault, the practices of incarceration

and reform, of government surveillance and social welfare, are simultaneous and mutually constitutive. Sick migrants had to submit to examination and detention to access the benefits of their new country. But quarantine stations were intended as much – or more – for detaining and housing healthy immigrants, and healthy immigrants fit uneasily into common categories of institutional inmate. As historian Krista Maglen observes, these subjects "were not considered mentally or physically ill, nor were they classed as criminals, yet their personal liberty was greatly restricted at the discretion of the government, and their economic autonomy frozen."[5] They remained under the control of the authorities, for their own protection and the protection of the population.

By the early 1870s, trenchant criticism of quarantine led to the implementation in Britain of a new system of port health control that largely eschewed the detention of ships, cargo, and passengers. In what Maglen calls "the English system," ships were inspected and defumigated in port, and the sick were hospitalized there, but healthy passengers would be sent on their way if they were willing to be monitored for emergent symptoms by local public-health authorities at their final destination. This new system tracked and distinguished among individuals, rather than effecting a blanket ban on entire ships and their contingents.[6] However, quarantine remained a key policy and practice in the colonies long after it was abandoned in the metropole. In the late 1880s, Canadian officials developed a kind of hybrid approach, which combined inspection, isolation, and disinfection regimes of "maritime sanitation" similar to those practised in British ports, with the traditional concept of extended detention for "suspects." All these practices would take place before ships entered Canadian ports, at the permanent and expensive facilities of quarantine stations.[7]

Maglen argues that, in the colonies, quarantine practices were sustained due to a lack of public-health and sanitary infrastructure in the urban and rural areas that were the destinations of immigrants; the inconsistency of vaccination practices; and a desire to preserve the new world as virgin land, unsullied by old-world diseases.[8] Canada developed public-health measures and overcame resistance to vaccination only at the end of the nineteenth century. In the meantime, the country would enforce a cordon sanitaire through a series of quarantine stations along its coasts. A range of historians have argued that quarantine policy was of special interest to new-world nations anxious to assert their independence, as forays into the development of state power and national sovereignty. In an era of both massive global migration and nation-state formation, the control and protection of immigrants allowed countries to work on defining their borders and identities.[9]

The extent of quarantine infrastructure peaked at about twelve sites along the coastal boundaries of Canada, but the principal stations were Grosse-Île in the east and William Head in the west, and these two quarantine stations serve as the main case studies in this chapter.[10] Because Grosse-Île operated for over a century, and was the station where each new technology or practice was implemented by government officials, its history provides an overall framework. I begin by describing the spaces and spatial practices associated with the great epidemics of the 1830s and 1840s. Then, as we examine the modernization of Grosse-Île after 1880, the story of William Head is inaugurated in parallel. These modernizations reflected changes in the medical theory of contagion, the ascendance of steam travel, the exponential rise in the number of immigrants and other travellers, and the development of public health as an aim of the Dominion government. Over time, the quarantine stations took on village-like characteristics, with facilities for resident staff as well as for immigrants. Quarantine stations contained a heady blend of incarceration, hygienic intervention,

tourist hospitality, and daily life. Here, memoirs of permanent residents complement those of immigrants, and interface with official records to offer an understanding of these complex and contested environments.

THE EARLY YEARS OF CANADIAN QUARANTINE STATIONS

Recurring epidemics in the first half of the nineteenth century resulted in the intermittent, crisis-driven development of a quarantine system in Canada. The first government structure that was purpose-built for immigrants was a temporary fever hospital that appeared in Quebec City in 1824. No analogous structure existed in Halifax three years later, when both typhus and smallpox "spread throughout the town" after arriving on transatlantic vessels. More than 7 per cent of the town's population perished that year, and the epidemic touched other Maritimes ports as well.[11] By the early 1830s, therefore, when cholera threatened Canadian residents almost annually, municipalities took a more proactive role and began to "experiment with local quarantine and travel restrictions."[12] As seen in the previous chapter, towns began to build immigrant sheds to segregate new arrivals from residents. In 1832, Halifax, in memory of its recent epidemic, erected three isolation hospitals in different parts of the town. The same year, a volunteer committee of citizens had "cholera sheds" built in Montreal, despite strenuous objections from the residents of the adjacent neighbourhood. In Quebec City, to pre-empt protests from neighbours, the governor attempted to rent extra hospital space prior to the summer season of immigration and sickness. Across the river in Pointe-Lévy, a small quarantine building had existed since 1830, but its proximity to inhabitants was considered too dangerous.[13] Urban institutions were often unsuccessful at segregating immigrants from local populations, who continued to nurse and feed the sick before returning home to their families. The spatial politics of these local solution soon pointed the way toward isolated sites, typically islands. The first dedicated quarantine sites in Canada were Partridge Island in Saint John harbour, established in 1830, and then Grosse-Île in 1832. This quarantine infrastructure, represented as the first line of defence against disease, would be funded by per-capita taxes on immigrant arrivals, legislated in colonial legislation of 1832.[14]

The beginnings of Canadian quarantine were far from auspicious. Bilson sets the scene: "Grosse Isle, a small, hilly island thirty miles below Quebec, was chosen, over the objections of its resident farmer and his seigneur, to be the site of the station. Despite its unsafe landing and limited facilities, the island was to be the first landfall in Canada for tens of thousands of immigrants in this and many future years."[15] Parks Canada historian André Sévigny carefully inventoried the built fabric on Grosse-Île during each stage of its development, from expedient beginnings to mid-century neglect, and eventual modernization after the 1880s. When Traill viewed the station in the summer of 1832, its first season of operation, the infrastructure included a hospital, a shed-like shelter, a dispensary, apothecary, wash house, kitchen, toilets, some staff housing, and a morgue (see Figure 2.1). Basically E-shaped in plan, the forty-eight-bed hospital seems to have been comprised of a single-loaded corridor or veranda, with three wards projecting perpendicularly. The crude wooden shelter, really a lean-to or loggia, provided cover for only about three hundred healthy immigrants, and stood at the head of the wharf near the hospital. A much larger, and properly enclosed, shelter was erected later that fall, but would only be available for future immigration seasons. In the central part of the island were barracks, houses for administrators and military officers, a signal mast or semaphore, and a battery of guns to require

ships' captains to heave to for inspection. At the far end of the island were some eighteenth-century stone farm buildings that the military had appropriated.[16] The new quarantine buildings were all of wood, and erected on stilts, allowing rapid construction, but also indicating that they were assumed to be temporary.

We know little else about the appearance of these early buildings, though one pioneer recalled his perceptions of them: "Those immigrants who had not been attacked [by the fever] were held in quarantine in great barn-like structures. The sick were housed in buildings of like construction and with little more by way of comfort."[17] A highly critical report from a Montreal health committee similarly emphasized that the sheds on Grosse-Île seemed fit to serve only as shelters for farm animals:

> Without wishing to attribute or attach blame to any person in particular your committee considers it a duty to express their conviction that this establishment has been in reality not a safeguard against the epidemic but, on the contrary, its fosterer and propagator ... The sheds erected there do not in size or structure appear to have been intended for the protection of human beings. Indeed the emigrant possessed of self-respect, often preferred remaining on the bare rock, exposed to the inclemency of the weather rather than sleep among the congregated hundreds under the shed lest he should thereby hasten the approach of the disease that was hurrying on every side his fellow passengers to eternity.

Many of the "detained were housed in tents," according to historian of medicine John Heagerty, who concluded that the infrastructure at Grosse-Île during the crisis of 1832 was "quite inadequate."[18] In fact, during peak years of quarantine, when a large number of immigrant ships coincided with a high incidence of disease, the hospitals and accommodations would never have enough space for everyone.

The overcrowding of Grosse-Île forced many migrants to ride out their quarantine shipboard, in the same — or sometimes in worse — conditions as they experienced during their difficult ocean crossing. One ship's captain was exercised about the treatment of his poor passengers during the quarantine. On the ship's arrival, forty passengers were admitted to the forty-eight-bed hospital, making the total number of patients there seventy-eight. The remainder of the ship's passengers, the healthy ones, waited two days before there was space on the island to debark and wash themselves. They spent four nights on the island (he does not describe their accommodations there) while the captain "got the vessel cleaned and fumigated." In the process, the straw mattresses and bedding used by steerage passengers on the crossing were thrown overboard. Thus, as they waited out the rest of their quarantine back on the ship, the immigrants were "obliged to lie on the boards, without a covering," sleeping in their clothes "to prevent the boards from cutting their hips. There are mothers and their children in this state. It is inconsistent with reason to expect them to remain healthy." The authorities were not forthcoming with new straw or other supplies, and the captain was forced "to victual the passengers" at his own expense while they waited at anchor for a clean bill of health from the quarantine doctor.[19]

For most migrants, the experience of quarantine was one of waiting. Once they had cleansed themselves and their possessions, migrants had little to occupy their time at the stations. Though some returned to newly scrubbed ship's quarters, many crowded together in the sheds and inhabited the beaches and wooded areas of the island. An elderly labourer, Benjamin Freure, who was detained for ten days on Grosse-Île when smallpox was detected on his ship in the summer of 1836, reflected in his diary the experiences of his family. Things had started rather poorly as they were debarked at "the foot of a rock of solid stone, in very rough state. We had then to remove our luggage up the rocks about two hundred yards, which was no easy task. However we set about it huskily." The Freure family's experience was not unusual; wharfage at Grosse-Île remained inadequate and dangerous until the 1890s. They were happy enough with their accommodations in the shed, which Freure states was "by no means an uncomfortable place." It was built for about a hundred people arranged in a double row of bunks, and there would have been less crowding than during the crisis years of 1832 and 1834. Freure also felt that the structure was attractive, with the sides and the slate-covered roof painted white.[20] This is perhaps the only surviving aesthetic assessment made by an immigrant regarding a Canadian government immigration building, which were usually judged on the basis of their function and cleanliness.

Once the family had performed their ablutions, it was mostly waiting. As someone who had worked all his life, Freure found idleness difficult; on the ocean crossing, he had written that the "time sometimes seem[ed] rather irksome and heavy," even though he had good health, books to read, and plenty of liberty. But enforced idleness continued in quarantine. On the island, they were "guarded night and day by two soldiers and an officer in almost constant attendance." The quarantined were "not allowed to go any where further than the front of the house [which] extends down to the foot of the rock at the waters edge," writes Freure, and "I shall be very glad when we get our freedom. Because the mind is kept continually in suspense." Still, he was able to find some enjoyment in detention. The island was picturesque, with its thick forest growing out of the stone, and he identified familiar plants. On Sunday morning, Freure and his son "went on the rocks and read the service for the day with the psalms and lessons; nothing could be pleasanter than it was. The morning very fine and water gently washing against the rock at our feet." They also carved their names on a tree. Inscribing graffiti was an exceedingly common spatial practice among immigrants and other travellers, to record their presence while detained at quarantine stations or waiting in other immigration buildings.[21]

The elderly Freure was a pious and contemplative fellow. For other healthy detainees, however, Grosse-Île took on a carnival atmosphere. Just released from long and trying ocean voyages, provisioned by ship's masters, and with no regular work available, migrants occupied the island's spaces and produced their own entertainments with gusto. Some of these are described by the author Susanna Moodie, who immigrated to Canada just a few weeks after her sister, Catherine Parr Traill. From the ship's rail, Moodie perceived the island through a picturesque filter, much as her sister had. Over several pages, including eighteen stanzas of rhyming poetry, she describes the "surpassing grandeur of the scene that rose majestically before me … The rocky isle in front, with its neat farmhouses at the eastern point, and its high bluff at the western extremity, crowned with the telegraph – the middle space occupied by tents and sheds for the cholera patients, and its wooded shores dotted over with motley groups – added greatly to the picturesque effect of the land."[22] Unlike her sister, Moodie managed to convince the authorities to let her and her husband tour the island for their own amusement, the way London asylums were visited by upper-class observers. When she took "the glorious privilege of once more standing firmly on the earth," Moodie was shocked and disgusted by what she saw of the immigrants:

Never shall I forget the extraordinary spectacle that met our sight the moment we passed the low range of bushes which formed a screen in front of the river. A crowd of many hundred Irish emigrants had been landed during the present and former day; and all this motley crew – men, women, and children, who were not confined by sickness to the sheds (which greatly resembled cattle-pens) – were employed in washing clothes, or spreading them out on the rocks and bushes to dry. The men and boys were in the water, while the women, with their scanty garments tucked above their knees, were trampling their bedding in tubs, or in holes in the rocks, which the retiring tide had left half full of water. Those who did not possess washing-tubs, pails, or iron pots, or could not obtain access to a hole in the rocks, were running to and fro, screaming and scolding in no measured terms. The confusion of Babel was among them. All talkers and no hearers – each shouting and yelling in his or her uncouth dialect … I shrank, with feelings almost akin to fear, from the hard-featured, sun-burnt harpies, as they elbowed rudely past me … The people who covered the island appeared perfectly destitute of shame, or even of a sense of common decency. Many were almost naked, still more but partially clothed. We turned in disgust from the revolting scene.

Moodie and her husband were driven to seek shelter in a bower along the shore, "out of sight, but, alas! not out of hearing of the noisy, riotous crowd. Could we have shut out the profane sounds which came to us on every breeze, how deeply should we have enjoyed an hour amid the tranquil beauties of that retired and lovely spot!" A sergeant of the garrison waited on them there, bringing Moodie some fresh-picked plums and hazelnuts, along with his own, oft-quoted impressions of the immigrant inmates: "our night scenes far exceed those of the day. You would think they were incarnate devils; singing, drinking, dancing, shouting, and cutting antics that would surprise the leader of a circus. They have no shame – are under no restraint – nobody knows them here … The healthy actually run the risk of taking the cholera by robbing the sick … We could, perhaps, manage the men; but the women, sir! – the women! Oh, sir!"[23]

Moodie's depiction of the quarantine scene, seasoned with class, ethnic, and gendered judgments, presents a vibrant collection of spatial practices and sensory experiences. The conversion of tidal pools and shrubbery for washing and drying clothes exemplifies the tacit knowledge and improvisations necessary to migrants' survival in unfamiliar terrains and situations. Meanwhile, Moodie wonderfully evokes a sense of place, from the picturesque views to the noisome squeals and shouts and songs and the bronzed texture on the rough elbows of Irish matrons. We can almost feel the cold water of the St Lawrence flowing around our calves. The history of quarantine in Canada and elsewhere is rife with images of a sombre and mortal nature, with the rending of families foremost among them. But Moodie's recollections of these racialized others remind us that most of the quarantined were relatively healthy and spiritually whole. In that vein, they made use of their period of enforced idleness, on a beautiful island in the summertime, by occupying the space with music and movement, bonfires and ballyhoo. Overall, surviving first-person accounts from the first years of Grosse-Île's operation present mixed feelings about the quarantine station and the range of spatial practices observed there. Certainly, it was the migrants themselves who were compelled to shape space for their own survival, with minimal infrastructural support.

QUARANTINE STATIONS DURING AND AFTER THE IRISH FAMINE

Epidemics came and went irregularly, and it was more than a decade before Grosse-Île or Partridge Island were occupied again as intensely as in the early 1830s. The Irish Famine migration of 1847 presented scenes of desperation that far exceeded those of earlier years on the quarantine islands. The stations were unprepared for the great resurgence of need from those struck with typhus fever, and other illnesses such as dysentery and measles. When a head tax was instituted at the port of New York early that year, over five hundred ships full of destitute Irish immigrants sailed for Quebec and the Maritimes. The "fever fleet," in the words of Heagarty, was affected by "disease in its worst type superinduced by the extremity of famine and misery."[24] In previous years, a certain amount of new construction had been done on the islands. Sévigny reports that, between 1832 and 1846, the number of buildings at the Grosse-Île station doubled. These buildings must have appeared after 1842, because a surviving plan of the station from that year shows only two small structures that had not been present ten years earlier: Protestant and Roman Catholic chapels. The 1842 transfer of authority, from the military officer in charge to a dedicated medical superintendent, likely prompted the new construction of those years. The additions up to 1847 brought the station to a total of two hundred hospital beds and accommodations for eight hundred healthy immigrants under observation.[25]

During the first month of navigation in the spring of 1847, more than five hundred were admitted to hospital on Grosse-Île. Over the ensuing summer, the number would reach almost nine thousand, more than twice the number of patients hospitalized at the station in its first fifteen years of existence. The sick were placed in quarantine sheds meant for the well; the well stayed aboard their ships or transferred onto steamers for Quebec City and Montreal. Historian of the Irish Famine Cecil Woodham-Smith wrote that, by mid-summer, "quarantine had virtually been abandoned," because as many as twenty-five thousand suspect immigrants and crew would have had to be detained and observed, which was "physically impossible" according to the station doctor. Many who passed the island quarantine station appeared well, but were already infected; in 1847, three times as many immigrants died in Canadian towns as did on Grosse-Île.

Temporary wards were built hastily in Quebec City, again "in the face of opposition from citizens in the district, who threw down the first sheds." The Marine Hospital there was overflowing. In Montreal, the downtown site of the 1832 fever sheds proved too small and lacked fresh water. Moreover, a great number of rubberneckers would hang around the gates; according to the local newspaper, "[b]etween four and five in the afternoon is the favourite hour of promenade." A new compound was soon built on the river's edge in Point St Charles; a large number of sheds for the purportedly healthy formed around a grand courtyard "where the coffins were piled, some empty waiting for the dead, some full awaiting burial."[26] The architectural order achieved at the new suburban site could not overcome the disorder of the epidemic. As noted in chapter 1, the new Dominion government would inherit this compound twenty years later.

Back on Grosse-Île, authorities strove to respond with a zealous building campaign. Fifty buildings were erected on the island in the summer of 1847, some prefabricated in Quebec City. The total included twenty-two large structures for use as hospital wards and quarantine sheds, plus kitchens, wash houses, and other outbuildings (Figure 2.2). By the end of the year, there was built accommodation, however temporary or shoddy, for 2,000 sick and 3,500 well. Hundreds of tents were also used. Unlike the case in the 1830s, a first attempt was made to segregate the sick from the well, with the construction of a dozen huge fever sheds on the eastern part of the island, well away from the cove where the original grouping

of buildings served the rest of the quarantined (Figure 2.3). Most of this construction, though, was completed after the peak of the disaster.[27]

One migrant's memories of arrival at Grosse-Île registered an attempt on the part of quarantine officials to bring spatial order to the process of debarking shiploads of suspect passengers:

Bad as it was on board, it became infinitely worse when we reached quarantine. On our arrival at the dock, ropes were stretched across the deck so as to leave a passage in the middle. A doctor was stationed on each side of this passage and only one person was allowed through at a time. All those who showed any symptoms of the disease were forced to go into quarantine [sic], while others were sent ashore ... I am an old man now, but not for a moment have I forgotten the scene as parents left children, brothers were parted from sisters, or wives and husbands were separated not knowing whether they should ever meet again.[28]

Similar lineups were conducted before immigrants were allowed to leave the island at the completion of their quarantine period. The process described here foreshadows the notorious medical gauntlet at Ellis Island in New York City, where immigrants climbed stairs or walked a short distance while being observed briefly by doctors who marked them down as healthy or suspect — which could lead to further examination, and perhaps detention or rejection at the border. In Canada, the early-twentieth-century development of medical inspection by immigration-branch doctors stationed in the pier buildings (to be discussed in chapter 5) would be modelled on these earlier examples.

The quarantine station in Saint John also was overburdened in 1847. Although it received only about one-third the number of immigrants as

Grosse-Île, Partridge Island "contributed more than its share to the misery of long-suffering humanity," in the words of historian Edwin Guillet.[29] Several new sheds were built there that summer, but these did not suffice. The New Brunswick immigration commissioners reported that the hospital sheds were packed with patients, "the floors of every ward being completely covered to the very doors." The structures were only twenty feet wide, and

so narrow that there was hardly any space between the beds of the crowded wards. Patients suffering from different stages of fever, and many in a dying state, were often

2.2 One of the 1847 immigrant sheds at the east end of the Grosse-Île quarantine station, now much restored as part of the National Historic Site. Parks Canada declares that this building was one of the prefabricated structures sent down from Quebec City. Open dormitory spaces are interspersed with vestibules marked by cross gables. After its erection, this building was quickly converted from healthy accommodations into a "fever shed," as part of the station's "Sick Division" seen in Figure 2.3.

jammed together with convalescents. Usually, they slept on the floor, males and females in the same room; with their chests, boxes, and other personal effects scattered around them; congesting the main passageways. One of the buildings had no covering on the outer walls,

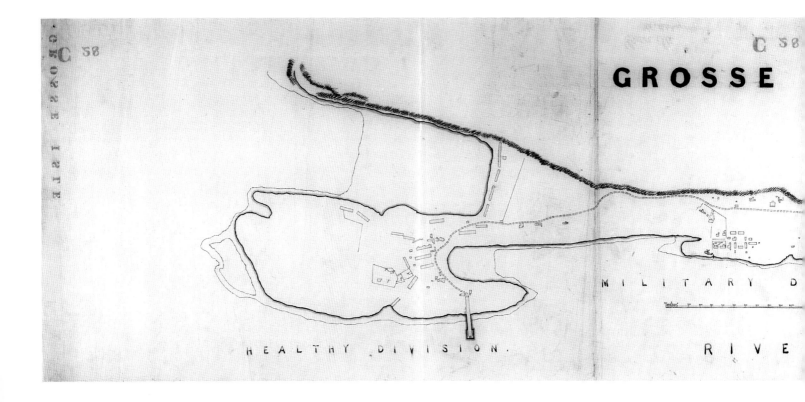

GROSSE

HEALTHY DIVISION.

MILITARY D

RIVE

2.3 An 1847 site plan of the quarantine station on Grosse-Île. This is the moment when the island is laid out into zones for the healthy and sick, with the staff quarters in the middle (denoted as the "Military Division"). Evidence of a significant amount of new construction extends away from the cove at the west end, as well as in the hospital buildings, lined up barracks-like, in the new "Sick Division."

and it was impossible to hire carpenters to complete it due to their fear of the disease.

Tents were deployed; lean-tos were formed from a few boards; borrowed sails, spars, and rigging from the quarantined ships were fashioned into expedient shelter.[30] Even so, as the investigatory committee reported at the time of their visit, "many of the emigrants have slept all night in the open air upon the damp ground, with no other covering except their wearing apparel. We found patients suffering from fever and dysentery in this destitute and neglected condition." The "impurities upon the island" included, among other things, "the filthy condition of the tents, the filthy habits of the people, and the exhalations from the burying ground," where mass graves were covered insufficiently. Offensive odours arose from corpses, trash, and excrement. Compounding these issues was a "deplorable lack" of hospital supplies and food, fuel, and water.[31] For example, the well water was polluted, the island's spring exhausted, and water delivered from town would be delayed by bad weather. For warmth, immigrants burned the fences from the grounds of the lighthouse and a supply of wooden bedsteads destined for the sheds.[32]

One advantage on Grosse-Île was the supply of food and firewood there. As in earlier years, the bakery and shops on the island could provision crews and passengers after the long ocean crossing

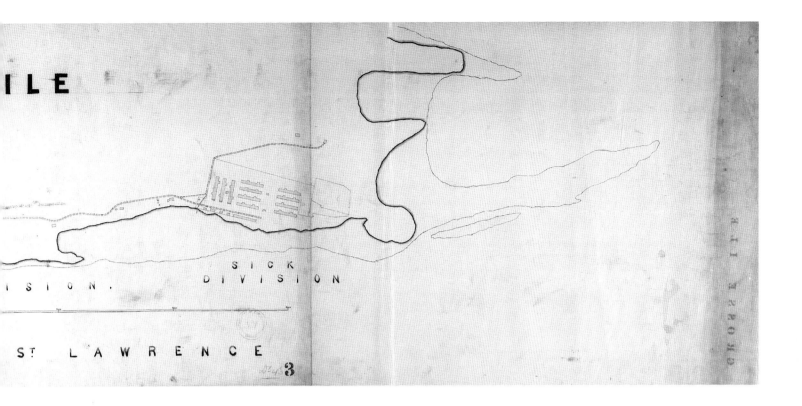

and during their quarantine. One cabin passenger, Robert Whyte, who was quarantined at Grosse-Île in 1847, gave a somewhat mixed review of "the store licensed to sell provisions upon the island. It was well stocked with various commodities, among which were carrion beef and cattish mutton, bread, flour, cheese, &c … there was a vast concourse of mates, stewards, seamen, and boys, [each] buying his different articles and stowing them away in their boats. The demand for bread was very great; and several batches were yielded from a large oven while we remained."[33] The bread was fresh, though it seems that the meat left something to be desired. Even the cabin passengers welcomed fresh bread after its lack of availability on the voyage.

Period accounts of the quarantine stations in 1847 echo the themes of the early 1830s. Whyte published an account of his voyage in the tradition of Traill and Moodie. His descriptions of the island oscillate between appreciation of the picturesque

beauty and contrasting revulsion, often in the same sentence:

> After a long pull through a heavy swell, we landed on the Isle of Pestilence; and climbing over the rocks passed through the little town and by the hospitals behind which were piles upon piles of unsightly coffins. A little further on, at the edge of a beautiful sandy beach, were several tents, into one of which I looked, but had no desire to see the interior of any others. We pursued our way, by a road cut through a romantic grove of firs, birch, beech, and ash, beneath the shade of which blossomed charming wild flowers, while the most curious fungi vegetated upon odd, decayed stumps. The path led us into a cleared lawn, passing through which we arrived in front of the superintendent physician's cottage.[34]

The untold horrors he witnessed in the tent are set against the exquisite detail of botanical cataloguing. Not surprisingly, even in the chaos of the Irish Famine year, the grounds of the chief quarantine officer are neatly kept, thus effecting the distinctions between nature and culture, and between steerage class and ruling class. In effect, Whyte's narrative, like those of the two sisters some fifteen years earlier, represents a kind of dark tourism. Each writer could retreat to their cabin when the island's realities became overwhelming.

Steerage passengers did not have that option. They could, however, celebrate their enforced idleness and return to terra firma, as seen in Moodie's horrified narrative. Whyte relates a similar tale of revelry, wondering how the immigrants could be so insouciant in quarantine:

> Hearing the music of a fiddle accompanied by the stamping of feet in time with the tune, I walked up to the shed from which it issued. There were two men dancing a jig; one of them a Canadian, the other a sailor — both fine fellows, who were evidently pitted against each other in a trial of skill … The fiddler … stood upon a barrel; and around the dancers was a circle of "habitans" and sailors, who encouraged them by repeated "bravos." I did not remain long, nor could I enjoy the amusement in such a place.[35]

While government officials struggled to order space — at the scale of both island and nation — immigrants and inhabitants strove to invert and remake it, however temporarily, as a site of cultural interaction and expression.

Meanwhile, ships' crews had work to do during their delay, scrubbing decks and holds, ferrying passengers back and forth to the island, and gathering provisions. But they too were subject to quarantine and hospitalization. The first mate on Whyte's brig took ill, and the writer went along

with the captain to visit him in the hospital. The mate "was lying with his clothes on, upon a bed; the next one to which contained a figure writhing in torture … the sailor who, but the evening but one before was dancing with the Canadian. When the mate perceived us, he rose from the bed, and taking the captain by one arm, and me by the other, walked us both out of the hospital, to the porch; saying that we had no business there, as there was fever upon all sides of us." Indeed, the first mate had resisted the transfer ashore to the hospital building and, even in his feverish delusion, he assured the captain he was well and ready to return to duty. This attitude reflects the reputation of nineteenth-century hospitals, and certainly contagious disease hospitals, as charitable institutions where one went to die. Not until the modernization of the quarantine stations after the 1880s was serious consideration given to curing patients, as opposed to just terminal care.

The hospital for crew members, appropriately, was one of the chapels, converted for use as such. Whyte reports that it was "exceedingly clean and well ventilated, the large windows were all open, causing a draught of air that was agreeable."[36] The miasmic theory of disease implied that lots of fresh air would reduce further contagion, and perhaps help manage fevers. As Maglen explains, "miasma" was "an ambiguous term generally meaning disease poisons found in the noxious air associated with overcrowding, dampness, lack of ventilation and drainage, and emanating from all kinds of filth."[37] In effect, the concept of miasma obscured the general lack of scientific knowledge about the cause of disease. At the quarantine stations of the nineteenth century, this ignorance led to the warehousing of the sick in ventilated wards, with minimal medical or hygienic intervention.

As Guillet concluded, during the worst of "the plague years the congestion and suffering at Grosse Isle made the performance of quarantine an ordeal of great severity."[38] One gets the impression that quarantine – when it was even possible – was indeed a kind of performance. The authorities had to appear to be doing something to prevent the next epidemic from descending upon the residents of Quebec or Montreal. They would choreograph the poor immigrants in a pantomime of health preservation; ritualistic purification would provide symbolic assurance that the audience was safe to pursue their everyday lives. Similarly, hospitalization allowed government representatives, doctors, and others to act as if they could do some good for the sick. Beyond its purely functional character – and it was minimally functional at that – the architecture of the early quarantine stations served to set the scenes for these dramas. In years when the performance was less imperative, the stages were quiet.

After the typhus of 1847, cholera returned with immigrant fleets several times in the early 1850s, and fears of it were regularly renewed in the 1860s and 1870s following smaller local incidents or reports of epidemics in distant international ports. As a result, the symbolic importance of the quarantine islands in signifying a cordon sanitaire retained its place in the public imagination. However, when there was no news of epidemics afoot, inspection of immigrants could be more cursory. As a Norwegian migrant described his 1854 quarantine experience: "In the afternoon of June 1 we reached an island where a doctor lived. We anchored at this point, and at nine in the morning of the second the doctor came on board. Fifteen minutes after eleven that evening we anchored at Quebec Harbor."[39] Another doctor inspected them there. For this migrant, as for many new arrivals, quarantine rated hardly a mention.

Epidemics never again hit Canadian immigrant destinations like they did in the earlier decades.[40] In between incidents or scares, the infrastructure of quarantine sat idle and, made of wood, went to ruin. The facilities at Grosse-Île and Partridge Island had expanded rapidly during the crisis of 1847, so, of course, the buildings had been constructed quickly and cheaply, and sometimes were left unfinished. In subsequent years, when there were fewer immigrants, and even fewer sick ones, there was far too much infrastructure to be maintained efficiently. The island quarantine stations were generally underused during the decade after 1854, and their building stocks reduced. Of about one hundred buildings at Grosse-Île, twenty-five were demolished in 1860 due to a downturn in immigration.[41] One exception to this tendency toward attrition was a new laundry building, erected in the mid-1850s, which provided an interior space where immigrants' clothing could be washed in large cauldrons heated over wood fires (Figure 2.4). This new structure represented a technological innovation rather than an increase in the capacity of the station.

2.4 The waterfront laundry shed of the 1850s on Grosse-Île. According to Parks Canada, the dormers were added later.

On the eve of Confederation, a typhus scare mobilized the full reoccupation of Grosse-Île and the renovation of some of its structures. According to Sévigny, the churches, residences, stores, and laundries all required urgent repairs by this time, while the hospitals and hostels were dilapidated or in ruins. A new wharf and an isolation building were built in 1865.[42] New quarantine regulations were proclaimed the following year, which, as historian Bruce Curtis writes, "attempted to close loopholes in past practice." In particular, enforcement of ship inspections and quarantine had become lax. The regulations now would require most ships from foreign ports to be conducted by the river pilots to anchor at Grosse-Île — though exceptions, and evasions, endured. New forms of medical examination and record-keeping were also instituted, and the powers that quarantine personnel held over ships and passengers were clarified. The steamship companies were not pleased with the delays caused by this renewal of inspection and quarantine, especially when no epidemics arose, but from this point forward quarantine practices began to be regularized.[43] Rather than being a form of emergency triage reserved for plague years, health inspections and the quarantines that sometimes resulted became routine and expected adjuncts to ocean voyages. To accommodate and to represent this new bureaucratization of health checks for all arrivals, and to assert sovereignty over its borders, the Dominion government undertook to modernize and systematize the facilities and procedures at the quarantine stations that it inherited with Confederation, and at the ones that it built thereafter.

QUARANTINE STATIONS IN THE FIRST DECADES AFTER CONFEDERATION

Assuming responsibility for quarantine sites was one of the Dominion government's first actions related to immigration. Based on the Immigration Acts of 1869 and 1872, it took charge of Grosse-Île and Partridge Island and began developing a new quarantine station on Lawlor's Island in Halifax harbour. At this time, the largest station, Grosse-Île, consisted of twenty immigrant sheds in various states of repair, staff houses, support buildings, and two chapels in need of replacement (Figure 2.5); Partridge Island had only a few sheds and a residence for the doctor; and on Lawlor's, the Dominion government built three sheds for isolation and quarantine. All these structures were of wood, with wood shingles and siding, usually clapboard. If they did not rest directly on the ground, they sat on natural stone piers or foundation walls.[44] One new building at Grosse-Île which received slightly more care and consideration was a Protestant chapel of the late 1870s, which survives today. Janet Wright describes how its "board and batten siding, gothic windows, and decorative wooden buttresses represent a toy-like example of the Carpenter Gothic style." But the unadorned plans from Ottawa included none of those decorative elements. She concludes that "the local builders or staff took it upon themselves to dress up the building with the added detailing."[45] The extra effort taken with this chapel, which sits on cut stone piers, suggests that staff and station were beginning to take on a permanent character.

This indeed was the case. Among various permanent staff in residence on the islands, medical superintendents were appointed by the early 1870s at all the east-coast quarantine stations. A medical superintendent was also appointed in Victoria, though on the west coast no station would be established until the end of the following decade. These men, reporting to Ottawa and imbued with the science of late-nineteenth-century medical professionalization, brought modern practices to quarantine. Throughout this period, the germ theory of disease gradually replaced the miasmic theory, partly undermining the medical justification for quarantine. Cholera, it turned out,

was not passed on due to bad air in close quarters; it was not even contagious, although other contagious diseases remained of concern, including measles and tuberculosis. The architecture of the stations would need upgrading to accommodate the latest medical knowledge and technologies regarding disease transmission and cure. Two significant advances were vaccination and bacteriology. Vaccination could be performed anywhere, in quarantine or aboard ships. Bacteriology required laboratories, and small structures dedicated to this purpose would appear at the stations beginning in the early 1890s.

In parallel, the stations needed to allow for new scales and speed of transport. It was 1878 when the last sailing ship quarantined at Grosse-Île. Steamships carried more passengers of all classes, in healthier settings, with better food and medical care. Importantly, they crossed the ocean much more quickly, reducing the opportunity for contagion or debilitation among passengers and crew. Steamship companies, increasingly large corporations, could be induced to check passenger health

2.5 This later photograph, from around the turn of the century, gives some sense of what Grosse-Île looked like when most of the buildings were shed dormitories such as these. Many of the mid-nineteenth-century sheds continued to be used into the twentieth.

prior to embarkation, and to have ship's surgeons monitor it during the voyage. Ships were big enough that it was possible to isolate a patient on board as soon as symptoms of a contagious disease were detected. Ultimately, epidemics became less common, thanks to these advances in medicine, technology, and service, and also due to sanitary improvements in ports and other cities of the old and new worlds.

Quarantine, though, remained a significant way for Canada to manage its borders. The doctors retained their powers, and the stations their facilities, to isolate and quarantine immigrants. As quarantine events became relatively less common than earlier in the century, the stations took on new roles in the examination of immigrants and their convalescence from a wide range of ailments and illnesses. That is, quarantine processes became foundational to the development of public-health policies and practices at the national level. According to Bilson, throughout the century, each disease scare "exposed the shortcomings of the Canadian medical profession," of the public services provided by towns, and of the preparation and ability of governments to protect inhabitants. Each "epidemic left some residue" in the form of architecture, policy, and the professional organization of public health.[46] Quarantine stations became less about arbitrary incarceration and more about the biological monitoring of populations – for instance, ensuring that all passengers were vaccinated prior to entering the country. Quarantine officers became respected leaders in the national discourse around public health. In fact, the superintendent of Grosse-Île from 1869, Dr Frederick Montizambert, became the director general and deputy minister of public health in 1899, a post he then held for some twenty years. Montizambert began lobbying for the compulsory vaccination of all passengers and crew as early as 1871. Though he was initially unsuccessful, the Dominion government finally required it in 1886, and vaccination became one of the most important services provided at Grosse-Île.[47]

There was relatively little building activity at quarantine stations during the 1870s, which were years of recession, with low numbers of immigrant arrivals. They also were "unusually healthy" years according to Montizambert.[48] Still, he worried in his annual reports that too many ships circumvented medical inspection by passing Grosse-Île at night, and that established fines were insufficient to deter ships' captains from ignoring regulations or concealing sickness on board. Other vessels were exempt because they carried mail for the Dominion government, or if there were no diseases reported at their point of origin. Not until 1887 did new regulations eliminate exceptions and better enforce the inspection of every vessel.[49]

In these same years, Montizambert worked to establish an efficient process for examining large shiploads of passengers at all the stations. All this being achieved, though, the records indicate that few immigrants were hospitalized or quarantined between the 1870s and the early 1890s: immigration numbers remained low, epidemics became less frequent, diagnosis improved, and the health of new arrivals was generally better.[50]

Even though these were slow decades at the quarantine stations, Bilson argues that they also saw "the revival of the traditional fear of immigrants as carriers of disease." The social justification for the performance of quarantine remained just as powerful as ever. As he concluded: "Whatever the medical arguments about contagion, no government wanted to release hordes of 'filthy immigrants' onto the domestic population without some sort of inspection." These fears took on new cultural and political connotations. In addition to carrying diseases, immigrants were now condemned for genetic deficiencies that would dilute and debilitate the British, French, and other northern European, white ethnicities, which were seen as the originators of the new Dominion.[51] That is, in the eugenics-inspired view of many Canadians, southern and eastern Europeans, and all non-Europeans, were not only potentially contagious, they also would undermine the strains of the dominant culture. Thus, quarantine practices continued to offer social reassurance, and significant federal resources were poured into improvements at the stations. To preserve the health of the body politic, an inspection would be performed on all entrants before they were deemed suitable to land in Canada. In reality, these inspections were a performance directed at residents of the country; few new arrivals were rejected for any reason in this period, and almost none for medical reasons. Eventually, more restrictive procedures comprising medical and civil inspections at Dominion government pier buildings would be developed to control which immigrants were admissible, but for the time being contagious disease checks at the quarantine stations remained the only real entry test.

It is in this context of protecting the perceived purity of the body politic that we can understand the establishment of the first west-coast quarantine station on Vancouver Island, where there were relatively few arrivals. Those who did arrive on this coast were typically of undesirable races, according to nativists. A short-lived station was opened at Albert Head, near Victoria, in 1885, with a wood-frame hospital building that was never properly finished or furnished. There were few other amenities. By 1892, the local newspaper was forced to conclude that this was a quarantine station in "name and very little more."[52] During a minor smallpox epidemic that summer, both nurses and patients were required to stay in tents, and there were neither fresh water nor cooking facilities available at this isolated site. A series of reports, rebuttals, and patient testimonials brought to light absurdly awful conditions at the station, while revealing utter confusion regarding the jurisdiction of the three levels of government over quarantine – and, more broadly, over public health. Both the Province and the City of Victoria found themselves intervening in the operation of the smallpox quarantine, expending money and staff where the Dominion government ought to have been fully responsible. Due to numerous shortcomings at the Albert Head site – and no doubt some embarrassment arising from this – the Dominion government soon replaced it with a new station situated at William Head, a peninsula that had more access to fresh water and better moorage for ocean-going vessels.

A hospital, a house for the medical superintendent, a disinfecting shed, first-class quarantine lodging, and large "Japanese and Chinese suspect" dormitories were all were erected quickly at William Head in the summer of 1893 – too quickly, as

we will see. Regardless, after many years of lobbying the Dominion government for proper facilities on the west coast, locals were ecstatic about "how complete and convenient the new quarantine station" seemed to be. The newspaper enthused that the "excellent arrangement of the buildings, the selection of the site, and the designing of the buildings are a credit to the Public Works Department." The paper was assured that "no germ or microbe survives this experience." The superintendent of west-coast quarantine, now with a proper headquarters for the first time, agreed: "With the new station fully equipped, as it ought to bc, and will be, the Williams [sic] Head quarantine will be one of the bulwarks of Canada so far as public health is concerned, and it will be hard lines if any disease is allowed to come into British Columbia, or into any part of the Dominion, from the Orient."[53] In the 1889 *Annual Report* from the immigration agent in Vancouver, he similarly had emphasized the need for an operational quarantine station to deal with the increasing number of "direct shipping connections" from Asia, and the fear of importing contagious diseases.[54] Direct steamships required the control of incoming diseases and persons, but also enabled it, because they could be legally bound to dock for inspection at William Head. The implication was clear: national space would be protected from Asian and other undesirable contaminations.

MODERNIZATION AND ITS EFFECTS AT THE EAST-COAST QUARANTINE STATIONS

It would not be until the 1890s that campaigns of modernization reconfigured the spaces of Dominion government quarantine stations. The first glimmerings appeared, however, with a new hospital building completed on Grosse-Île in 1882 (Figure 2.6). This two-storey hospital had two wings, for a total of four twenty-bed wards, flanking a central administrative and service block in

2.6 New hospital building on Grosse-Île, completed in 1882.

a T-shaped plan. The structure boasted cut stone foundations and was built of load-bearing brick — a materiality that heralded the new sense of permanence at the quarantine station, and endowed it with legitimacy as a national institution. This time, the moderate decorative detailing of the architecture emanated from the Ottawa offices of the Chief Architect's Branch.[55] Symmetrical facades of six bays, and windows with stone lintels topped by segmental arches of brick, gave the ward blocks a Renaissance-palazzo effect in conformity with other public buildings of the period. The centre block assumed a more local, Québécois appearance, with a steep mansard roof descending below the bottom of the second storey and extending out over the veranda. The mansard is pierced by round-arched dormers in low relief. Coterminous with the Stick Style pier building on the Louise Embankment in Quebec City, this hospital bestowed for the first time a representation of formal architectural order upon immigrant reception at Grosse-Île.

Montizambert consulted with the Public Works architects on the plans of the hospital. This form of collaboration was common in the design of hospital architecture during this period, as these buildings became complex programs over which doctors would preside as scientific professionals.[56] The result on Grosse-Île conformed to standards established in the 1860s for pavilion-plan hospitals, in which wards would be separated in their own architectural volumes to maximize their access to light and air, and to allow for the sorting of patients. As architectural historian Annmarie Adams writes, the "hallmark of the plan type was the open ward, in which ... beds were arranged regularly against the outside walls, which in turn were punctuated by a regular rhythm of large windows. The premise was that copious amounts of fresh air circulating between patients would mitigate the chances of contagion." As the beds were arranged around the outside of the ward, "a single nurse could supervise a large group of patients," catering to their needs but also ensuring that they followed the rubrics of their cure.[57] This efficiency of surveillance was well suited to the quarantine-station hospitals, which were remote, seldom used, and had limited staff. All the hospitals built at Canadian quarantine stations in the next couple of decades would adopt variations on the pavilion ward plan.

The concern with fenestration and air circulation was a typical architectural response to the miasmic theory of disease. Even though germ theory was ascendant in the medical profession, hospital historian Jeanne Kisacky shows how, for numerous reasons, this did not immediately affect the pavilion ward system, which continued to be used for new buildings well into the twentieth century. However, the notion that micro-organisms, rather than bad air, cause disease, did result in new approaches to contagion and the care of the sick, even if hospital architecture was slow to change.[58] Germs could be identified and killed, so scientific diagnosis and antisepsis became fundamental characteristics of both hospital management and quarantine procedures. Fresh air in fever sheds, and beating clothes and bedding on the rocks, no longer sufficed. New architecture appeared on the quarantine islands in the form of laboratories for testing samples taken from immigrants, and of defumigation and shower buildings, where scientific cleansing could be monitored by officials.

These new facilities would allow Canadian stations to conform to standards of New World quarantine. Facilities in the United States were an important point of comparison, as they had been with the pier buildings. In 1889, Montizambert made a study tour of the New York City quarantine station on Hoffman and Swinburne islands and sent a meticulous report to his superiors in Ottawa. On Hoffman Island, which was designated solely for the quarantine of healthy passengers, his group "had pointed out to us the new and commodious dock, the new boiler house, kitchen, lavatories, dining room, dormitories, etc., and the – as yet unfinished – rooms for disinfecting by super-heated steam." Similarly, modern facilities were in place or under construction at Charleston, New Orleans, and other US ports, ensuring the near totality of that country's cordon sanitaire. Even if the Dominion government spent half as much money on Grosse-Île as had gone into the New York station, concluded Montizambert, it could achieve "a similar assurance as to the St. Lawrence" for detecting and preventing the entry of disease. The doctor allowed some frustration to creep into his entreaties that the government appropriate funds for modernization:

as I have been reporting in season and out of season for the last twenty years ... [t]he great deficiency and requirement of the Quarantine Station of Grosse Isle continues to be that of a deep water wharf. A wharf to which infected vessels could be brought to land their passengers and effects for disinfection; and on which could be placed the steel cylinders for the prompt and scientifically approved disinfection of clothing and effects by superheated steam, the elevated tanks for drenching with the mercuric chloride solution, and the steam fans, furnaces, etc., for changing the atmosphere in the holds and storages and replacing it by one charged with

2.7 Disinfection building at the head of the wharf, Grosse-Île. This photo from about 1900 depicts the rails and rail cars that would carry baggage and clothing into the disinfection chambers. The chimney exhausts the burning of fuel for the steam retorts.

sulphur dioxide … Until that is supplied, and fully equipped as above, the service cannot be depended upon, nor be expected, to protect the country from the invasion of epidemic disease.[59]

In his closing statements, Montizambert emphasized the economic argument: that large steamships were being delayed on their schedules because they could not dock at the station. All the shuttling back and forth of doctors, passengers, crew, and defumigation equipment between Grosse-Île and these ships was subject to every change in the weather, and largely limited to daylight hours.

Eventually, Montizambert got his wish, as a new deep-water wharf was built in 1893, with the attendant cleaning apparatus for use on ships. The

rinsing of ships with mercuric chloride, and their defumigation with sulphur dioxide, was meant to kill micro-organisms causing infections – as well as their carriers, especially rats. Additionally, at the head of the wharf stood what Wright describes as an "irregular-shaped" structure, somewhat industrial in appearance and in function (Figure 2.7). It contained disinfection chambers for baggage and showers for passengers. The clothing and possessions of the immigrants would be packed into wire-mesh lockers on rail cars that could be wheeled into huge airtight cylinders for high-temperature steam cleaning (Figures 2.8 and 2.9). Meanwhile, on another level of the building, the immigrants themselves, stripped naked, were required to take hot showers laced with disinfectants such as kerosene, thought to kill lice and other parasites (Figure 2.10). Combined with the portable disinfection equipment on the station's boarding launch, Grosse-Île became "un véritable complexe de stérilisation," in the words of Sévigny.[60] Similar structures would soon appear at the other quarantine stations.

First-person descriptions of how immigrants perceived and responded to these invasive procedures are rare. There are, however, accounts from writers close to the process which illuminate some of the spatial practices of immigrants and officials. In 1899, for example, two large, Dominion-government-sponsored groups of about two thousand Doukhobors were each quarantined – one group in the summer on Grosse-Île, one in the winter on Lawlor's Island. Both groups of these Russian religious and political dissenters were detained for about three weeks due to cases of smallpox found on board their ships. A Russian physician who helped escort the first group penned her observations of Grosse-Île for a newspaper back home:

the main activity of the quarantine doctors was, of course, the disinfection of all the

2.8 Sealable doors of the disinfection chambers, Grosse-Île. This image clearly aestheticizes the industrial nature of the modern disinfection process.

2.9 Open-door view of a disinfection chamber, with rail car in use, Grosse-Île. Note the multilingual signage explaining the process to immigrants.

2.10 Reconstructed waiting room in the disinfection building at Grosse-Île. The showers can be seen up the stairs. This is likely what the space would have been like by the 1920s, as the building was renovated several times just before and during the First World War.

baggage and the ship itself. They really had a lot of trouble doing this. Those accompanying the ship were also obliged to expend no little energy convincing the Doukhobors that this was essential, and that without disinfection of their baggage they would not be allowed to leave the island. Our party had brought a fair number of possessions with them, including

reminders of their previous days of wealth, and the Doukhobors greatly feared that this would all be spoilt by the disinfection. There were many doubts, questions and negotiations at first, but then little by little the matter was resolved, the Doukhobors became convinced that everything would remain safe and unharmed … In fairness to the quarantine personnel, it must be said that they were actually very attentive and careful with the Doukhobors' baggage.[61]

Within the coercive and ordered industrial cleaning process, immigrants negotiated their well-being in conjunction with the government's demands.

The letters and diary of Sergey Tolstoy, the chaperone for the Lawlor's Island group of detained Doukhobors, adds further details to the overall experience of quarantine, and of the cleansing ordeal. "First of all the quarantine boat approaches, and our doctor calls out: 'One case of smallpox!' – other boats approach but immediately turn back; all others are sent away, and two doctors [Montizambert and the local medical superintendent] come on board with expressionless, clean shaven faces, and we sail into quarantine." We learn of the ship captain's disappointment at being "detained in quarantine as no extra payment … is foreseen for such a circumstance, while there are many extra expenses." Over the next several days, the Doukhobors would debark into several different buildings. About one thousand went into the huge steerage-class dormitory that was designed for – and had beds for – half that many. Not until the tenth day would the bulk of the remaining immigrants move from the ship into a just-completed dormitory that lacked enough stoves, furniture, and insulation. Government workers would add a few layers of cardboard to the inside of the walls a few days later. The carpenters who had built the new dormitory had been staying in the first-class hotel while they finished their contract; they now were quickly evicted so that the last few hundred Doukhobors could occupy these quarantine accommodations. In the description of the diarist, this latter hotel had been "designed for a 'purer' class of people," and built to a higher level of quality, with individual rooms and corridors, as opposed to large open dormitories. Even after the Doukhobors were all "quartered on the island," Tolstoy describes how "they continue to live the life of Robinson Crusoe — cooking in outdoor cauldrons, doing their laundry at the seashore and so forth." Despite two decades of modernization at east-coast quarantine stations, the daily experience of the Doukhobors seems little different from that of healthy suspects in the 1830s and 1840s.

Handwashing of laundry and swabbing the decks was no longer considered sufficient, however. For the Doukhobors on Lawlor's Island, defumigation of clothing, baggage, and ship took many days, interrupted when steam pumps burst because of the frigid February weather. It was decided that their sheepskin coats might be ruined by the steam treatment, and so these were specially disinfected with formalin. The first-class cabins on the ship also got this special treatment, while the rest of the ship was gassed with sulphur dioxide. As for the disinfection of the humans, Tolstoy writes that the "procedure is as follows: in a wooden barn with thin, creviced walls, and which is barely heated by an iron stove, people strip naked and sit in large tubs of warm water ... until their clothes are brought back to them. It is quite cool in the barn, especially since the door opens directly to the outside." Highly critical of the whole process, and of the lack of preparedness at this seasonal station, Tolstoy is also particularly perceptive about the politics of performance on the quarantine stage. "Indeed," he writes,

> to disinfect two thousand people with their things is virtually impossible. For example,

there is no way now of ensuring that the fumigated things will not get mixed in with those which have not yet been fumigated ... Montizambert is acting properly under the terms of his obligations, but it is impossible to ignore the fact that much is being done for show — so that the newspapers will not say that the quarantine was not strict enough.

Sect-based group migrations endorsed by the Dominion government always caused political controversy, as critics questioned whether these were desirable immigrants. Quarantine for these groups offered an opportunity to present them to the Canadian public as clean and respectable agriculturalists. In fact, at the close of the quarantine, Tolstoy notes sardonically, "everyone was allowed to come" and view the spectacle of the Doukhobors, "reporters, travelling salesmen, photographers, the curious."

Their ordeal in the spaces of quarantine complete, the Doukhobors proceeded to Saint John to board a Canadian Pacific Railway (CPR) train for Winnipeg. In Saint John as well, "a crowd had assembled on the dock; the Canadians greeted the Doukhobors most warmly: ladies gave out candy to the children, and many shook hands," asked questions, and complimented the newcomers. Tolstoy was even asked to "autograph the wooden spoons which the ladies were buying from the Doukhobors," souvenirs of the momentous arrival of this exotic group, and perhaps a sign that some of the stigma attached to them had been scrubbed off on Lawlor's Island.[62]

WILLIAM HEAD STATION AND THE CLASSES OF QUARANTINE

The most comprehensive explanation of the antiseptic procedures of late-nineteenth-century Canadian quarantine comes from the medical superintendent of the west-coast station at William Head. Dr A.T. Watt was appointed to the post late in 1896, a few years after the station opened. At that moment, despite earlier optimistic statements, many of the buildings remained incomplete and unfurnished, reminiscent of the earlier station at Albert Head. The Dominion government seems to have forgotten about its west-coast quarantine station and the buildings it placed there in 1893. Worse, minimal thought or detailing had been put into their initial construction. In his first report to Ottawa the following spring, Watt itemized the material and design deficiencies of the station as he found it. First of all, he was concerned that many of the buildings at the station were of rough wood, and lacked proper ventilation and drainage, making them "almost impossible" to disinfect and defumigate. In the disinfection shed itself, "rough scantling and rafters make all sorts of recesses and surfaces where infection may lodge. All the walls [and ceiling] require boarding with T. and G. lumber." According to Watt, a similar intervention with smooth-finish, tongue-and-groove sheathing was also needed in the dormitories.

Meanwhile, in the hospital, the plaster was cracked due to settling, none of the doors fit properly, and in fact there were no doors at all separating the central administrative block from the wards, so "that when sulphur is burned in the ward it makes its way through all the rest of the building." As Watt added, it "is not necessary to say that the different divisions of an infectious disease hospital should be such as can be completely isolated. The present arrangement of the hospital is a serious defect."[63] Dr Watt points to what were by then well-established hospital design standards for promoting antisepsis. In particular, as Kisacky documents, with the ascendance of germ theory, porous materials like plaster and wood "fell into disfavor" for use in hospital buildings, to be replaced by "harder and smoother" finishes that could be disinfected.[64] It is noteworthy that, although the William Head hospital took the same

form as the 1882 building on Grosse-Île – a central block with two flanking wards – the west-coast edition was only a single-storey, wood-frame structure, with unadorned clapboard siding on the outside and lathe and plaster within (Figure 2.11). Grosse-Île clearly was the Dominion government's flagship station, but the Chief Architect's Branch had failed to achieve even the minimal requirements of the building type in its specifications for the hospital at William Head.

Continuing his report, Watt provides a critical, but evocative, description of disinfection and cleaning at William Head. "The station when I took charge," he writes, "was lacking some of the most essential requisites of a quarantine station, particularly were the appliances for disinfection wanting or not working properly." The "sulphur blast" for defumigating ships had been overheated and severely damaged due to improper firing. The "steam sterilizer" for the clothing and baggage had been manufactured poorly by a local company that did not understand the technical requirements. As a result, it could disinfect "only by steaming steam, not by superheated steam." Regardless, there were no thermometers provided to monitor these levels. Watt also maintained that, due to the cycles of loading and unloading, heating, cooling, and drying, there was an insufficient number of rail cars to process the baggage of a large ocean liner without causing long delays to shipping.

The large rectangular structure housing the steam retorts was "the worst feature of the whole station." It was an industrial shed with a single, unpartitioned volume. As a result, believed Watt: "Infected clothing brought in to go through the retort infects the whole place before entering the retort and consequently when it is brought out clean, it becomes immediately re-infected." This shed also offered the only space for bathing passengers, so the same problem occurred with people: they ran the risk of being re-infected after their corporal disinfection, which, according to

2.11 Hospital building, William Head, BC.

Watt, had "actually occurred."[65] Here, at the architectural scale, Watt was encountering the same problem of segregating the sick from the healthy — or, more specifically, the possibly contagious from the presumed clean — that characterized the early years on Grosse-Île. Furthermore, there were no showers available and no partitions to make space for change rooms. Plans were afoot for renovations that would solve these problems. Watt envisioned an addition at one end to include "a large disrobing room which will house about a hundred persons at a time," the number whose clothes could fit in the retorts during one steam cycle. Along one side of the building, ten showers would be "placed in a row." At the other end of the shed, another addition would provide a dressing room, where disinfected immigrants would be issued "blanket wraps" while they waited for the return of their steam-cleaned clothing. These changes would result in a processual series of spaces, from one end of the shed to the other, through which immigrants would pass in a kind of disinfection assembly line. A few years later, Watt reported that, with some modifications to the wharf, the process of disinfection had been perfected further, such that "those who have passed through the same may

COASTAL QUARANTINE STATIONS

be kept completely separated from those who are waiting their turn." With these last improvements, "people will pass on in a sort of circle going one way and returning by another."[66] At the quarantine stations, antisepsis would be mass-produced.

Of course, the assembly-line process applied only to steerage passengers. On the opposite side of the building from the steerage-class showers, yet another addition would be reserved exclusively for cabin passengers from infected ships. This addition comprised four private bathing facilities that each accommodated the steps of disrobing, cleansing, and dressing in clean clothes.[67] Although everyone was subject to the disinfection regime, distinct spaces would ensure the continued segregation of the classes at the quarantine station.

All the improvements to the process came too late to preclude serious passenger complaints about the incommodious procedures at William Head. Far away from the site, Ottawa had been slow to approve the requested renovations to the shoddily built station. In the meantime, Watt was forced to deploy expedient measures to accomplish his mandate. With the sulphur blast broken, to defumigate ships he resorted to burning that element in "pans and ash buckets" placed in the holds and cabins. With no bathing facilities, Watt had the plumbers jury-rig a water tank that could be heated from the steam retorts. As he described to his superiors, by "means of a hose leading from this tank I was able to hose down the suspects with a disinfectant solution" while they stood in a couple of "wooden wash tubs."[68] These were not the bathing facilities that cabin-class passengers were accustomed to.

Unfortunately for Watt, a large steamship of the CPR line arrived in 1897 with smallpox on board, and he was obliged to detain everyone while the station still lacked the essentials he described. The first-class passengers, who included a Chinese ambassador and "men of influence of many

nationalities," formed a committee of protest and fired off furious telegrams to members of parliament and seething missives to the local newspapers. Beyond the financial losses they would incur during their detention, the disinfection process was a deeply felt insult to their dignity – indeed, to their racial and class privilege. "We were to be taken out of our comfortable cabins in batches of a dozen or so at the time; stripped naked and subjected to a foul chemical bath; our clothes taken from us to be fumigated and baked, we sitting meanwhile in a shed, clad in an old blanket gown and pair of slippers, which had previously been used to cover the nakedness of no one knows how many Chinese." This letter to the editor counted the Chinese ambassador as one of the first-class "European passengers" and not "amongst the Asiatics, where infectious disease will make its appearance." Class could trump race in the perception of quarantine procedures. Until the complainants received replies to their telegrams, the letter concluded, "no attention [was] being paid" to the orders of the quarantine superintendent.[69]

The CPR was also quick to criticize the treatment of its customers at William Head. The company's local superintendent wrote a long and angry letter for his bosses to share with government officials in Ottawa, "protesting" how the indignities of quarantine would do "unnecessary damage to our trade." Questioning Watt's suitability for the position of medical superintendent, the writer pilloried the doctor for his "absolute want of tact in dealing with first class passengers." The letter expresses empathy with the steerage class too, condemning "the danger to which passengers were exposed, and the suffering of some, by the indiscriminate use in the hands of ignorant people ... of disinfectants which produced irritation and eruption" on the skin. As well, the "liberal use of sulphur" burning caused one case of lung hemorrhage. The CPR man explains that "in face of the want of proper accommodation ashore the Saloon and Intermediate passengers refused to land and take up their quarters in the house supposed to be available for this purpose," because it lacked enough private rooms "and had not a stick of furniture in it." Being white or wealthy, these passengers had the power to flout the orders of the government's quarantine superintendent, negotiating to remain in their cabins on the ship and taking a "medicated bath" there. Later, after much heated debate with Watt, they went ashore and "submitted to the bathing and disinfection a second time," once the station's cleaning apparatus had become operational. After this concession to Watt's demands, the cabin passengers were allowed to proceed on their journeys after seven days' delay at William Head.

The Chinese steerage-class passengers had no such power to negotiate or refuse, and they were typically faced with a much longer stay at William Head – in this case, they were detained more than three weeks. The Chinese migrants immediately debarked to large dormitory buildings where, since these were no more fully furnished than the other accommodations, they "were sleeping on the bare floor." From the opening of the William Head station, segregated dormitories had been provided for Chinese, Japanese, and European steerage-class detainees. It was believed that these different racial groups would not want to bunk together. In reality, there were few European steerage-class immigrants passing through William Head. To some extent, Asian immigrants arriving on trans-Pacific steamers were treated in a manner similar to steerage-class immigrants on the east coast of Canada – especially those denigrated steerage travellers from eastern and southern Europe, who likewise stayed in overcrowded dormitories at quarantine stations. And yet, the administration of Asian travellers was different in some ways. Of particular note, according to the CPR man, was the "inhuman treatment of Chinese passengers in this

and previous cases, where they have been cruelly exposed naked ashore, in inclement weather, after hot baths." Moreover, there had been "damage to their effects when exposed for disinfection." The writer believed that "the deliberate destruction of handsome silk garments in the presence of their Chinese owners would, but for the interposition of the [ship's captain] and his men, have cost Dr Watt severe injury and perhaps his life."[70]

Asian immigrants were regularly victims of bizarre and invasive procedures at William Head. Early-twentieth-century annual reports from the station record aspects of the hygienic and medical procedures that were made standard for Asians, but were seen only in special cases at Grosse-Île. In eastern-Canadian quarantine stations, the defumigation and disinfection regime for ships and people was instituted only when contagious disease was found on board. By about 1902, officials at William Head began the "routine disinfection of all steerage passengers from China and Japan and of the Asiatic members of crew," regardless of whether infection was discovered on their ship. In addition, all "Asiatics" were subject to "a special examination of glandular regions."[71] The glandular exam remained in effect during subsequent decades, and was supplemented by urine, stool, or sputum tests, depending on the diseases being reported at Asian ports of origin. On the east coast, these kinds of tests were deployed on an individual basis only in response to specific symptoms.

It is clear that racism and racial hierarchies provided a context in which west-coast quarantine operated. The denigration of Asians as filthy, devious, and uncivilized was a pan-Pacific practice which upheld the boundaries of whiteness in settler colonial nations.[72] In chapter 5 we will witness how, in Victoria and Vancouver, racially based immigrant reception practices resulted in a federal immigration architecture different from that found in eastern-Canadian ports. At the quarantine stations there was initially little difference between east and west: a shed is a shed, and these were meant for steerage-class passengers whatever their ethnicity. In subsequent years, though, the basic lodgings for Asian immigrants at William Head received minimal upgrades, even as accommodations for steerage-class Europeans at east-coast stations were newly built or improved on a regular basis. Though mattresses eventually were provided, at William Head the same racially designated, wood-frame dormitories would remain in use throughout the history of the station.

The description of the 1897 incident at William Head demonstrates the differential privileges received by various classes of passenger, and how race intersected with class to determine the treatment of suspected cases. As the stations modernized, the results of class distinctions changed. In some ways they levelled out. For example, now all passengers from an infected ship – regardless of what they paid for their ticket – would be debarked and put through the cleaning process. And if a ship was quarantined for a longer period, the cabin passengers were almost as likely to be detained as the steerage class. Therefore, the Dominion government was obliged to provide at the quarantine stations class-segregated accommodations in parallel with those found on the steamships. As Maglen argued regarding Australian quarantine practices, "the maintenance of class structures and boundaries that had existed on board ship was central to the compliance of passengers during their incarceration at the quarantine station … Healthy passengers appeared to cope better with the restrictions of quarantine if it was perceived within the framework of the voyage … [and] a continuation of shipboard limitations to which passengers had already adjusted."[73] To avoid complaints from rich and influential inmates, such as those who resisted Watt's injunctions, the Dominion government would build hotels. By the early 1890s, all the Canadian quarantine stations had fairly new hospital buildings, even if they were

of differing quality; for the next two decades, most new construction was of hotel accommodations. The most important architecture at the stations was now housing for healthy inmates.

First-class quarantine hotels comprised a centre block with symmetrical wings, a form not unlike the quarantine hospitals. But the similarities ended there. The wings of the first-class hotel built on Grosse-Île in 1893 each contained fifteen private rooms per floor, plus bathrooms and toilets (Figure 2.12). The centre block included an elegant dining room on the ground floor, with a large hall above for entertainments and pastimes, each with a fireplace. A veranda ran across the front facade, allowing the leisured class to enjoy afternoon tea with a lovely view of the waterfront. Only a single storey, the first-class hotel at William Head was a scaled-down version of the one at Grosse-Île, but it occupied a gorgeous site nestled in the woods and overlooking a small lake (Figure 2.13). As Wright puts it, these first-class hotels "could almost be mistaken for summer resorts."[74] The goal was to model them on shipboard accommodations: according to the local newspaper, the hotel at William Head had guest rooms "in design very much like the first class cabins on a ship, except for the fine, large window in each"; the dining room was fitted up "the same as the dining saloon of a vessel."[75] That said, until the 1910s these hotels continued to be relatively unadorned, inexpensively built, wood-frame structures.

The other class of detention hotel, notes Wright, "offered fewer amenities and less spacious accommodation."[76] Until the early twentieth century, steerage-class detainees would continue to reside in sheds, though these seem to have been improved compared to earlier eras. By 1894, all the sheds on Grosse-Île had electric lighting; one had running water. Later buildings included common rooms at the end of each floor, while huge dormitories ultimately gave way to smaller shared rooms, each with a few bunks – just as mass

2.12 First-class detention hotel, Grosse-Île, built in 1893 and photographed when still being used as such.

2.13 First-class detention hotel, William Head, begun in 1893, completed in 1897.

2.14 Third-class detention hotel, Grosse-Île, completed in 1914. The repetitive facade elevation is enlivened by three false fronts similar to those found on the contemporaneous pier building in Quebec (see Figure 5.7). In the left foreground can be seen the early-twentieth-century bakery, and in the right foreground an 1893 summer kitchen for second-class passengers.

transit in steerage was replaced by shared berths. The third-class detention hotel on Grosse-Île exemplifies these advances (Figure 2.14): a two-storey, reinforced-concrete structure, it had a facade patterned by pairs of double-hung windows separated by pilasters. Noticeably, in comparison to the other classes of quarantine hotel, there are no verandas or even a front stoop on this building, from which steerage-class immigrants might have enjoyed the view of the St Lawrence River and the Quebec countryside (see Figure 2.17). This simple-but-modern structure represents the lodgings provided for European immigrants who arrived at east-coast quarantine stations just

prior to the First World War; as we have seen, shed dormitories endured as the standard for Asian immigrants to Canada's west coast.

EVERYDAY LIFE AT THE QUARANTINE STATIONS

In addition to accommodations, immigrants had to have their other needs met in quarantine: food, drink, warmth, and social life. First-class guests were catered to: for example, if the dining room of the quarantine hotel was not in operation, or did not meet expected standards, ships' stewards would deliver meals from the galley to the passengers on the station. Steerage-class detainees fended for themselves. Returning to the 1897 controversy at William Head, the CPR man castigated Watt for "his ignorance of the Chinese and their ways," noting that this large group of quarantined immigrants felt keenly the "absence of means for cooking rice and other Chinese food."[77] Watt soon learned from this experience and arranged to provide appropriate cooking appliances. He was also known to provide Asian steerage passengers with occasional eggs, chicken, and geese of his own produce. The immigrants supplemented these with forage from the forested peninsula.[78] Many years later, in 1916, a new "Oriental kitchen with steam cookers" was erected between the Chinese and Japanese dormitories. Four new flush toilets installed that year would be shared among all the Asian steerage and European second-class passengers.[79]

Our Russian physician, who experienced quarantine on Grosse-Île with the Doukhobors, supplies an excellent description of quotidian spatial practices at the station. Even in 1899, two-thirds of a century after Traill and Moodie, the physician's narrative conformed to many of the early established motifs. On arrival at Grosse-Île: "What a paradise it seemed to us after the ship! Even before disembarking we admired the picturesque group of Doukhobor women and children who had gone to the island first and who had spread themselves out along the shore to wash all their clothing and underwear in the water – finally, fresh water! The little children took great delight in playing and running through the grass around their mothers." Had she been reading Traill's published letters during the transatlantic voyage? The physician continues in fine detail:

Part of the island, about a kilometre square, had been sectioned off for the ship's passengers. At the other end of the island was a general hospital and the smallpox dormitory. Most of the island was covered with a splendid forest. In the middle of it stood the employees' houses and the house of the quarantine director... At our end of the island were eight large, bright dormitories and a fairly spacious old kitchen ... [and] a new kitchen with well-appointed stoves and pantries. Besides the kitchen, the Doukhobors could use the bakery to make bread and

in one of the dormitories there was even tap water, and bath-tubs.

Those escorting the party and the ship's crew were housed in a splendid large building called an *hôtel*, which was divided, like the ship, into first and second classes, with rooms appointed in the fashion of ship's cabins ...

About twenty paces from the hotel were the quarters of the sergeant who ran this part of the island, and next door to them was a small room where smallpox vaccinations were administered. Next came the disinfection chambers.

Those put in isolation at the hospital communicated with their healthy relatives in quarantine by writing "cheerful" letters, stating that "their needs were being well looked after and the food was splendid."[80] Referring to all types of detainees, this invaluable narrative of Grosse-Île during a quarantine gives us an understanding of how the spaces were organized, the people were sorted, and how they coped.

The spatial practices of the Doukhobors allowed them to convert Grosse-Île from a space of fear and governmental authority into one of everyday life. These subaltern claims on space sometimes had unforeseen consequences. Before we bid adieu to the Russian physician, she relates a curious incident in which the spaces of quarantine were haunted by the legacy of past practices:

not far from two dormitories which stood some distance off to one side, was an old blocked-off well, alongside a huge abandoned cemetery containing the graves of some 3500 people who died on this island from cholera and smallpox [in 1847] ... To avoid going further afield – i.e., to the river – the Doukhobors in these dormitories unblocked the well without telling anyone and began drawing drinking water from it. The quarantine guards noticed it two days later, but the dysentery had already managed to infect almost all the residents of these dormitories and spread even further.[81]

The quarantined often felt compelled to shape the space of the station in order to meet their needs, but their self-sufficiency could backfire.

During the quarantine of the other Doukhobor group on Lawlor's Island, the immigrants had a lot of work to do settling into everyday activities. They helped finish the new dormitory, chopped firewood, and whittled cutlery, then cooked their own meals, baked bread, and washed clothes in the frigid harbour waters. On Sundays, they managed to "put on their best clothes and [go] out on the wharf to hold their service – that is, singing psalms and exchanging bows and kisses. The English looked on in amazement, but also with a certain respect," writes Tolstoy.[82] Indeed, as we will see in the next chapter, with their hard work and piety, the Doukhobors won fans at Canadian immigration buildings all along their journeys.

For first- and second-class detainees, quarantine spatial practices were a little less rustic. Reading, letter-writing, and parlour games could pass the time in the lounge spaces provided for these passengers. According to a Montreal sanitarian reporting to the Provincial Board of Health in 1893, the first-class accommodations at Grosse-Île were so comfortable that "many of the passengers delayed there have left the island with regret."[83] At William Head station, Watt developed picturesque walking paths in the woods, viewpoints, playing fields, and golf links for the use of the inmates.[84] The Victoria *Daily Colonist* had an abiding curiosity about activities at William Head; in 1900 it published an exposé by a journalist quarantined there. What the article mainly exposed was the pleasant time had by the cabin-class passengers, who enjoyed a range of recreational activities,

including a weekly baseball game. Once, a boat came out from Victoria to serenade the inmates on the shore of the peninsula. Having the run of the park-like setting, the cabin-class detainees gave pet names to their favourite landscape features: a tongue-in-cheek colonial gesture mimicking early explorers who claimed space by naming it. On a separate note, the reporter humorously recounts the escape of a German man the night before he was scheduled for the disinfection process; inspired, the cabin-class quarantined considered founding an "Escape Club, with one victim a day," but in the end, they could not conceive why anyone "would ever think of leaving here unless the business pressure, elsewhere, was enormous." Although he perhaps overstates the case, these stories unambiguously establish the distinction between leisured detainees and the hewers of wood and beaters of clothing. Watt did not take so lightly the escape, and the subsequent talk of escape. The number of guards was increased, while the boarding steamer "kept up a constant patrol" of the waters surrounding the peninsula.[85] Escapes from quarantine were rare, not least due to the remote locations of the stations. However, we will read more about daring breakouts from Canadian immigration buildings in chapter 5.

Finally, there were a number of people who remained at a quarantine station after a ship received its clean bill of health. These were the permanent staff and their families. The medical superintendent of each station was a full-time resident, at least in season, as were the seamen who ran the inspection boats, interpreters, attendants, guards, and caretakers who could operate the defumigation and disinfection equipment. Additional doctors, nurses, and other staff might be permanent or seasonal.

The surviving pages of a diary written in 1902 by a young woman living on Partridge Island offers a sense of everyday life for families in these places. Nellie McGowan's father was a long-serving caretaker at the quarantine station there, her brothers provided needed labour on the island, and her sister was the nurse at the isolation hospital. During quarantines, Nellie helped out at home with her mother: "Everyone else is kept busy all the time as the clothes have to be disinfected and the men have to bring all the provisions down, pump water and carry coal." Her sister would stay at the hospital throughout the quarantine period, to ensure there was no cross-contagion to their home. That year there were several serious smallpox cases, and Nellie movingly describes the attendance of island family members at two burials, one of a crewman and veteran of the Boer War, the other of a two-year-old boy. Not all was tragedy during the quarantine, though. The medical superintendent's family hosted healthy detainees, such as a ship's captain and officers, for dinner and entertainments, which Nellie and her family were invited to attend. She regales her readers with a record of "all the songs and speeches made at the table," and the singing that went late into the evening, accompanied by the doctor on his organ. Meanwhile, the diversions of Saint John were tantalizingly close; Nellie always hopes to get there, but she is thwarted on numerous occasions, even on the Sabbath. As she sums it up, the "trouble is Sunday is usually quite as busy a day in quarantine work as any other and the plans are very likely to fall through on that account." The work similarly limited the family's ability to attend weddings and funerals off-island. With the passing of Nellie's father, the family moved into Saint John, "for of course we cannot stay on the Island now." Her sister continued to commute to the quarantine hospital when needed, but her brothers' roles as labourers seem to have been dependent on her father's official position with the government.[86]

The decade prior to the First World War saw the largest number of inhabitants at the stations. Staff grew as the work grew: not so much the work of quarantine, since the detention of ships and passengers became relatively rarer, but the work of ship inspection, vaccination, and hospitalization for various ailments. Some staff just needed to be on hand in case a quarantine situation arose. William Head, which operated all year, by 1900 was home to twenty full-time staff and their families, including sixteen children. A one-room school was inaugurated at the station in 1909.[87] At the other end of the country, Grosse-Île took on the appearance of a village, with its school, staff houses, churches, and presbyteries (Figure 2.15). A dozen families lived on Grosse-Île permanently, but the resident population spiked to about 250 during the summer months of the immigration season.

Some sense of everyday life on Grosse-Île is found in a moving memoir by Jeanette Vekeman Masson, the daughter of a government interpreter, who spent a dozen years of her childhood living year-round at the quarantine station, and enjoying its forests, fields, and shorelines. Due to her age, Vekeman Masson did not interact with immigrants in official spaces, such as hospitals or hotels; rather, she and the other children and spouses of staff met immigrants across the divide between full-time and short-term residents. She describes how sick immigrants were landed at the wharf and transported to the 1882 hospital in a horse-drawn ambulance with a foot-rung bell — not to warn other traffic, as there was none, but to alert the doctors and nurses of their approach. Some of the staff housing, including the "lower row," where she lived, was close to the smallpox isolation building, so, she writes, "we were able to make friends with some of the immigrants" because the children "often came to chat with us" through the fence.

Other immigrants detained simply for observation had more freedom to move around on the island, and had more meaningful exchanges with the residents. Vekeman Masson relates a tale in which her family's kitchen and garden flooded during one of the full-moon tides that came in the fall, and all their firewood was scattered and

2.15 Staff residence on Grosse-Île, photographed in the first few years of the twentieth century. The fence carves off private space from the institutional space of the island quarantine station.

frozen to the ground. When some quarantined immigrant women "saw us gathering our firewood, they came to help ... They had guessed it was our supply for the winter ... Theirs was a spontaneous gesture which ... warmed our hearts." What can be witnessed in these stories are small-town spatial practices that layer into the official representations of space intended at government facilities. As always, children found common cause with others their age, despite the barriers in their way, and neighbours helped each other out, even when some of them were transient.

On another occasion, Vekeman Masson's parents intervened when some eastern-European immigrants at the station threw their first meal on the ground and broke some windows in protest at their incarceration. Despite the language barriers, her father shared tobacco and conversation with the men, her mother candies and concern with the women and children, helping to defuse the situation. As her father explained to the medical superintendent: "You must understand these people. They have suffered. They fled to Canada, looking for a country where they could live in peace, and as soon as they arrived, they were submitted to checks and confined to an island. During the night, they kicked around in protest." The immigrants' resistance to their detention caused consternation among the residents of Grosse-Île, who shared the small space of the island with the inmates; the global politics of quarantine played out as a local negotiation of spatial practices.

Even for the children who animated the quarantine stations, though, the spectre of detention haunts their recollections. Vekeman Masson recounts the incarceration of a Russian man as he awaited deportation for an entire winter in one of the isolation sheds on Grosse-Île. This would have been an unusual situation, since deportees typically did not pass through the quarantine stations. He escaped the building once and nearly drowned in the frozen river. The man was bored and lonely; from his window he could see only the river and the children on their way to school. "He sometimes waved at us," she writes.[88] The residents of the station understood the boundary between their everyday space and the space of containment. As with so many accounts of Canadian stations, the idyllic nature of an island community stood in contrast to the realities of isolation and detention.

THE BEGINNING OF THE END FOR QUARANTINE

These contrasts are perhaps most stark in the tragic story of the demise of Dr Watt, superintendent of William Head. For Watt, the peninsula was his place of work, but it also was the home of his family and his sheep ranch, almost akin to a country estate for most of the year. Yet, when the occasional ship was quarantined, the station transformed into a strange kind of carceral institution for several hundred inmates, only a few of whom required admission to hospital. The strangest group in this context was the first-class passengers, who were unaccustomed to restraints on their movement. This class of detainee caused Watt problems in 1897, as we have seen, and again in 1902.[89] In the subsequent decade or so, the facilities at William Head had improved considerably. However, these changes did not prevent a similar, more drastic, incident of class-privilege protest in 1913, during the sole quarantine event of that year.

Historian Linda Ambrose, who has analyzed the episode, expresses mild surprise that, even though three-quarters of those detained during this incident were Chinese steerage travellers destined to spend the quarantine period crowded into hundred-bed dormitories, "it was the inadequacy of the facilities and the service provided to the white first-class passengers that proved to be the central concern."[90] By this time, first-class cabins on transoceanic liners were exceedingly luxurious. Meanwhile, the creaky, wood-frame, first-class hotel at William Head was twenty years old, and its tiny rooms, with bunk beds and wash basins, marked with age, did not meet the expectations of its intended guests. In fact, the hotel and other parts of the station were under renovation at the time of the incident, since Watt and his superiors had recognized the shortcomings of the original buildings. The hotel was getting new bathrooms and laundry, hot-water heating, and even servants' quarters for those attendants travelling with the guests.[91]

When a first "indignation meeting" occurred, Watt joined the first-class passengers to discuss the letter they were preparing to send to Ottawa. As Ambrose notes, Watt "was led to believe that it would be signed by all the passengers and that its purpose was to impress upon the authorities that better accommodations were required at William Head, something that he would have welcomed if it meant that more resources would be put toward the improvements that were underway."[92] Instead, letters sent to Ottawa and to local newspapers from a select group of highly privileged and politically connected passengers amounted to a personal attack on Watt and his administration of the quarantine, in conjunction with criticisms of the facilities. The eventual result was a Royal Commission of Inquiry, during which Watt was raked over the coals. The stress of the proceeding drove Watt to commit suicide before the findings – which exonerated him – were released. As historian Peter Johnson shows, the unequivocal conclusion of Victoria citizens and newspapers, was that Watt was hounded to death by uppity first-class inmates.[93]

2.16 First-class detention hotel, William Head, begun in 1913, completed in 1915.

If, in the 1830s and 1840s, the lack of proper and sufficient quarantine infrastructure contributed to the deaths of so many steerage passengers, here we have the converse situation, where the architectural qualities of William Head led to the demise of its medical superintendent.

In fact, during the last few years prior to the First World War, all the main quarantine stations received new first-class hotels – the one at William Head was completed during the winter of 1914–15 (Figure 2.16). Watt's successor as medical superintendent reported that a groundsman from the Government Experimental Station at Sidney "laid out new lawns, shrubberies, etc., round the First Class Detention Building … and the Station should in the future be even more beautiful than before."[94] At Grosse-Île, an identical building, originally meant to serve as a modern second-class hotel, had been completed two years earlier. It was immediately converted for use by first-class

passengers, probably due to pressures exerted on government officials by the steamship companies; the old first-class hotel became the new second-class lodging (Figure 2.17).[95] As Wright explains, in plan and program the new buildings were similar to the twenty-year-old hotels that they replaced, with centre blocks again containing dining rooms and lounges, and symmetrical wings, each with two storeys of private chambers and broad verandas. But now the private rooms were larger, with more modern conveniences, and inhabitable attic space up in the gables of the centre block suggest the presence of servants' quarters. The new structures were built entirely of reinforced concrete, a material then gaining favour with the Department of Public Works. The new hotels also received a little more decorative detail: the picturesque twin gables of their centre blocks were half-timbered in the Tudor-revival manner, in a nod to British domesticity.[96]

During this same period, a grand, new 250-bed hospital building was planned for Grosse-Île and

2.17 Approach to the wharf at Grosse-Île. From left to right, the 1913 first-class hotel on the rise, the 1850s wash house below that, the 1913 third-class hotel in the background behind the original 1893 first-class hotel on the waterfront (later converted for second-class use). This image provides a good sense of the extent of development at the station prior to the First World War.

approved in the federal budget. Throughout the decade of mass immigration prior to 1913, quarantine staff had struggled to fit all the patients in the original hospital of 1882. Although the proportion of sick plummeted, the total number of arrivals had increased exponentially, and therefore, the total number needing hospitalization had grown. Tents and other temporary shelters were regularly used for hospital patients, writes Sévigny, just as they had been during the worst hours of the previous century's epidemics. The new brick-and-concrete hospital was to consist of a central block for doctors and administration, around which a hemicycle of five pavilion wards would radiate. The foundations for the building were dug but, because of the war, construction was suspended.[97] It never resumed.

After the war, quarantine superintendents were increasingly unable to convince decision-makers in Ottawa that new construction or renovation at the stations was necessary. One exception was the 1922 completion of a first-class hotel on Partridge Island, suggesting that the fear of reprisal from privileged guests remained a keen concern less than a decade after the William Head incident. Regardless, the establishment of a federal Department of Health in 1919 changed the political landscape. The new department was responsible for the administration of quarantine, but its provisions for public health were mostly internal to the nation rather than along the borders. Since the turn of the century, the number of ships actually quarantined had been small.[98] Increasingly, vaccinations were given by ships' doctors or in migrants' countries of origin. And although hospitalizations continued for a variety of ailments, many illnesses could be treated in the immigrant detention hospitals built in Canadian ports prior to the First World War (see chapter 5). In a 1925 House of Commons budget debate, the minister of health admitted that "not a single major case disembarked at Grosse Isle during last season" and that shipping companies were lobbying to eliminate the inspections there. Still, he advocated for the continued operation of the quarantine station: often it "is quite idle, but it is a necessity … if we did not have the facilities for handling these cases the reputation of the whole country would suffer."[99] As always, the quarantine stations remained more important as stages for the performance of border surveillance than as actual hospital complexes. Eventually, even that symbolic power waned. Grosse-Île quarantine station closed just over a decade later, in 1937. Perhaps due to racist fears of Asian contagion, William Head survived on into the late 1950s before it was finally converted into a federal prison. Watt's golf course

remains to provide a recreational opportunity for the minimum-security inmates there.[100]

CONCLUSIONS

Immigration to Canada was cyclical, both seasonal and subject to economic and geopolitical factors. Because of that, the immigration branch of the Canadian government was given to producing infrastructure that responded to present crises or seemingly urgent future situations, infrastructure which then sat idle most of the time. The quarantine stations are the primary examples of this architecture of panic. In its early years, Grosse-Île typically received capital investment only in the face of an epidemic; new buildings that were erected might not be put to full use for many years, if ever. Much construction at the quarantine stations, especially of modern detention hotels and staff sectors, was completed in the twentieth century, when the medical and social justifications for quarantine had largely disappeared due to improved public health and medical inspections abroad. The staff housing was always full, but the dormitories and hotels typically sat empty. Ironically, the hospitals were used regularly for minor ailments well into the twentieth century, and often were overcrowded, but were never replaced with modern steel-and-concrete buildings incorporating the latest hospital-design theories. Paradoxically, then, quarantine stations always seemed to be both overbuilt and inadequate for their purpose, as the prevalence of contagious diseases decreased, while the size of steamers and their passenger contingents continued to grow.

Upholding the cordon sanitaire was so important, though, that even the smallest ports might receive stations whose existence can only be considered symbolic. Maritimes harbours like Chatham or Sydney received virtually no immigration traffic, but had minor Dominion government quarantine stations. On the west coast in 1911, the

brand-new town of Prince Rupert, designed and built as the terminus of the Grand Trunk Pacific Railway, got its own island quarantine station (Figure 2.18). This immigration infrastructure was created in anticipation of the trans-Pacific steamship service promised by the railway company at this new port of entry to compete with the CPR and other lines sailing into Victoria and Vancouver.[101] The anticipated traffic never came, and the Prince Rupert station never received patients or suspects. It was closed as early as 1922.

The practice of quarantine thus necessitated significant investments by the Dominion government in rarely used infrastructure. But the government desired this architectural presence

2.18 Quarantine hospital, Dodge Island (formerly Hospital Island), near Prince Rupert, BC. Built in 1911–12, the hospital was never used. The lower portion on the right had residential and office space for medical staff; the two-and-a-half-storey wing on the left held two stacked wards. The eclectic architecture of the building presents a domestic appearance.

on the coastlines in order to assert its sovereignty over border crossing. Historians Alison Bashford and Carolyn Strange write: "Geographically and coercively separating the 'clean' from the 'unclean' in pursuit of the greater health of nations was one formative site where emerging liberal states practised their new and sometimes effectively disputed powers of detention."[102] Canadian quarantine measures were disputed by shipping companies, which decried the delays and loss of revenue, as well as the treatment of their customers in the clutches of the civil servants. It was disputed by those passengers too, who were stripped naked in cold shower rooms and suffered other indignities. Quarantine came with controversies, in particular among the cabin-class passengers detained at these stations, who felt that privilege should trump pestilence. For them, the development of public-health measures such as quarantine were fine for "the public," but they did not perceive themselves as a part of that group, any more than those cabin passengers were considered "immigrants." And quarantine was resisted by many ships' crews and immigrants who attempted to evade the authorities, who petitioned for quick release or more humane treatment, or who "kicked around" in umbrage at being detained as suspects, despite no wrongdoing or symptoms.

There are limits to what we can know about how the experiences of hospitalized and quarantined immigrants, and the spatial practices that ensured their daily needs, were met at the stations. As Merna Foster concluded in her thesis about Grosse-Île in the 1830s, the "immigrant impressions recorded, as well as those not recorded, do however indicate that for many immigrants quarantine was not of sufficient note to merit more than a brief mention — if it was written about at all ... Frequently the immigrants wrote matter-of-factly of quarantine in a few sentences, though short descriptions were not necessarily due to short stays."[103] Still, by compiling many of those "short descriptions" over three-quarters of a century, we have been able to stitch together a textured and sensory understanding of quarantine space.

CHAPTER 3

Heading West: Early Immigration Halls

At the opening of the immigration season in spring 1881, the Dominion immigration agent stationed in Winnipeg received an admonishing letter from his superiors in Ottawa. The secretary to the department under which the immigration branch operated at the time wrote that "information has reached [the minister] from several quarters, including paragraphs in newspapers," that immigrants were not being met or advised by officials on their arrival in Winnipeg. This included a party who arrived on a Saturday night and had to sleep on the floor of the Canadian Pacific Railway (CPR) station until Monday morning: "The women and children especially suffering severe and cruel hardships in the absence of fires, or any other provision for their comfort." The minister, wrote the secretary, "finds it quite intolerable."[1]

The agent's reply to the minister has not come down to us, but surely in his defence he referred to the new immigration shed just then being completed in Winnipeg as a solution to the very problem. Opened that summer, then replaced, relocated, and augmented several times over the coming decades, the sheds provided rudimentary accommodations for newly arriving immigrants, who could receive free room and board there for several days while they decided where to homestead, purchased supplies, or looked for work in

the towns and farms of western Canada. Dominion government immigration agents and land guides operated out of these buildings, offering advice and touring newcomers around the region. To serve these functions, in the next fifty years the federal government would construct some fifty such immigration buildings across the Prairies, rent others, and even resort to "canvas accommodation," its euphemism for tents. By 1906, the immigration-branch western headquarters at Winnipeg would expand to a complex of three large structures, one of them a hospital, the other two providing separate accommodations for British and "foreign" transients, as well as substantial offices, waiting rooms, and service counters where officials met immigrants. Thousands of immigrants each year would avail themselves of free government lodgings like these, along with advice and other support, at rail termini and transportation hubs across the Prairie provinces.

What ultimately became known as "immigration halls" were typically co-located with new train stations, and thus form an architectural meeting point between two tenets of the National Policy introduced by multiple-term Prime Minister John A. Macdonald in the late 1870s. Government-sponsored railway construction, and the promotion of immigration to Canada's west, provide the context for understanding the development of this key federal infrastructure on the Prairies. From 1872, the Dominion government offered homesteading grants to prospective immigrants from Europe or the United States. Agriculturalists could claim this free land in exchange for improving it, by building a house and clearing the ground for farming. In parallel with the opening up of land for immigrant settlers, the Dominion government was closing it to aboriginal peoples, who were increasingly confined to reserves, a practice which undergirded the National Policy.

Despite these nationalization and settlement strategies, until the late 1890s immigration numbers remained low, immigration-reception practices were relatively ad hoc, and reception architecture on the Prairies was relatively sparse. Still, through this period the Dominion government was experimenting with its designs for immigration halls, and developing bureaucratic structures and practices that would serve it well when immigration numbers began to increase rapidly before the turn of the century. The new Laurier government of 1896, and its minister of the interior, Clifford Sifton, inaugurated more-aggressive and wider-reaching policies to promote immigration to western Canada. In particular, Sifton became known – reviled, in some quarters – for encouraging and welcoming eastern and other continental European peasants in much greater quantities than before. While British and American farmers were still preferred, immigrants from southern and eastern Europe were recruited for their agricultural experience.[2] Critics of Sifton's open-door policy wanted only British immigration to support an Anglo-Canadian national identity. As many historians have shown, Ukrainian immigrants were often the targets of these criticisms, though any non-English-speaking arrivals were labelled as "foreign."[3] Aspects of the debate over desirable and undesirable settlers play out in our story of Prairie immigration halls. At a minimum,

the large group migrations beginning in the late 1890s spurred the development of more infrastructure on the Prairies, just as it did at ports and quarantine stations.

Prairie immigration halls were developed to aid "homesteaders seeking free land" made available by the Dominion government. According to officials, this class of immigrants was unable to afford hotels, if such businesses even existed at their destinations.[4] The immigration halls, then, were prototypical social-welfare institutions, modern and networked versions of nineteenth-century charitable hospices for the poor, and the organization and use of these spaces reflected the nation's ideals of class, racial, and gender differentiation. That said, a wide range of migrants used these buildings under different circumstances. Beyond their service to immigrants, the halls were important institutions within the communities where they stood. Often they were the only secular public buildings, and the only buildings with large interior spaces, in small Prairie towns. During the winter, when they typically stood empty of immigrants, and in later years when the tide of arrivals in a particular region receded, authorities received continual requests to borrow or buy their buildings to accommodate other uses.

This chapter provides a survey of immigration architecture across the Prairies from about 1880 to 1905, first establishing the historical context and official justifications for the halls. Architectural precedents for these light institutional buildings are explored, in the course of developing a typological description and interpretation. Using both archival accounts and first-person sources, the chapter recovers some of the social milieu of the immigration buildings, as places of encounter between authorities, locals, and immigrants, between the experienced and the inexperienced settler, the British and the "foreign." As architectural historian Dell Upton writes, every "structure contains several different buildings as imagined by different segments of its public."[5] From the intentionality of the government and its architects, to the spatial practices of migrants and the demands of local residents, immigration halls took on multiple meanings during their lifespans. The immigration hall was a significant institution in early Prairie towns, even if these structures have largely disappeared from cultural landscapes and cultural memory. Despite the ephemerality of most of these buildings, they established a federal presence in remote Prairie territories and in the local lives of settlers.

HISTORICAL CONTEXT OF THE FIRST INLAND IMMIGRATION HALLS

In the first decade after Confederation, the Dominion government began to assume a more activist role in the provision of institutions and accommodations for immigrants all along their journeys. Once they had passed through quarantine, if necessary, and landed through a Dominion government pier building, migrants might still have many miles to travel, and towns to pass through, prior to reaching their destinations. These overland journeys – by boat, wagon, railroad, or a combination of modes – often took several days and nights, due to timetables, transfers, and delays. Migrants with little means of their own needed places where they could eat and sleep cheaply. Inland from the ports, the government increasingly recognized the need to lodge immigrants at important transfer and distribution points, such as Montreal, Toronto, and Winnipeg, where new buildings were erected during the 1870s.

As mentioned in chapter 1, a substantial Toronto immigration depot was completed in 1870, with large dormitories, well-appointed cooking facilities, and offices for the agent. A rare depiction of this early immigration depot, from the marginalia of an 1870s map, shows a large, two-storey, twelve-bay structure, supplemented with a few small

outbuildings, all in clapboard siding (Figure 3.1). The main building is symmetrical, with an entrance on the long side flanked by regularly spaced windows. The single, centrally placed chimney suggests that the interior would have had fewer and larger rooms; this was the dormitory building, with a common room on the ground floor. A covered porch on the gable end of this building allows access to what is likely the baggage shed. Numerous people are shown, standing around, chatting, or moving bundles to the platform. These migrants might have been staying a few days, awaiting trains or boats, or hoping to find a situation in Toronto.

While the Toronto depot was a compound meant to house immigrants for several days while they awaited transfers or searched for work, an example of a more modest sort of immigrant way station could be found in Montreal, where a purportedly temporary shed was put up in 1873 at the "Tanneries" junction, where several railroads met. The location outside of central Montreal would isolate the immigrants from the temptations of the city, ensuring their continued voyage to the west. A one-storey, wood-frame building, it fronted the tracks. Behind it, a short boardwalk led to an outhouse with sex-segregated toilet stalls (Figure 3.2). While there were small bunkrooms for men and women, the main space in the building was the dining hall, or "refreshment room," where immigrants could dine and rest for a short break from their journeys, while their trains refuelled. A series of etchings from the *Canadian Illustrated News* depicts the Tanneries building in action (Figure 3.3). Across the top of the page, a train arrives at the shed. In the kitchen, a large cookstove is shown, with the preparations for a meal under way; an aproned woman with a spatula lifts the lid and leans over a pot to check its progress – just as the government was attentive to the progress of the immigrants. A spic-and-span dormitory with sloping communal bunks awaits tired travellers; a water tank and hose feeds sinks where immigrants

3.1 Immigration Depot, Toronto, detail from "Map of the part of the Province of Ontario for emigration purposes," c. 1877.

3.2 (*opposite*) Immigration shed at the "Tanneries," Montreal, 1873, showing the proximity to the rail line at the top of the plan. The shed sat on pilings to allow for a platform matching the height of the train cars, as at a railroad depot.

could scrub themselves. In the dining hall, a blazing potbelly stove is flanked by long tables, where perfect rows of immigrants sit quietly while a man in a suit supervises the scene. At the top left and right of the page, a vignette presents an immigrant family "Before Starting" and "A Year After." In the first image, a destitute couple in ragged clothing, the woman clutching an infant, the man slumped with exhaustion, are seen in front of a smoking shack, unable to afford even a proper chimney. In the second image we see a profound transformation: the same couple, presumably, are shown in Canada, in clean clothes, with a second baby being tossed joyfully by its mother, while the toddler reaches for an embrace from the father, the latter now dressed like a wealthy, top-hatted industrialist, even though the background is a farm scene with bountiful livestock. The message seems clear: in Canada, we will take care of you within a well-organized immigration infrastructure, and that will allow you to prosper immediately. Nevertheless, even though the *News* showed the Tanneries as a place of order, by 1877 the building had achieved notoriety for its repugnant condition. At that time, it received improvements that gave it a more permanent aspect, and it operated for another decade.[6]

As Lisa Chilton has noted, during the 1870s, immigration "agents working at communities far smaller than Toronto also clamoured for sheds."[7] Small Ontario towns such as Bracebridge, Gravenhurst, and Rosseau, closely co-located, had short-lived immigration hostels in this decade. A depot

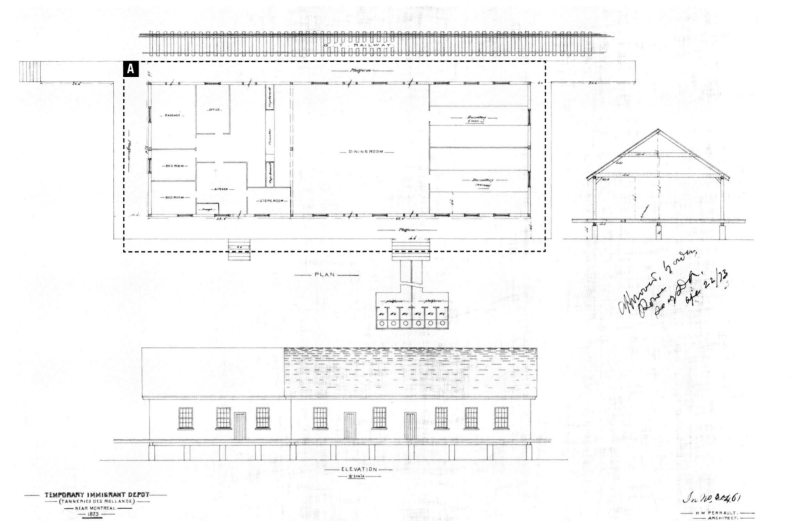

PLAN

ELEVATION

TEMPORARY IMMIGRANT DEPOT
(TANNERIES DES ROLLANDS)
NEAR MONTREAL
1873

H. M. PERRAULT.
ARCHITECT.

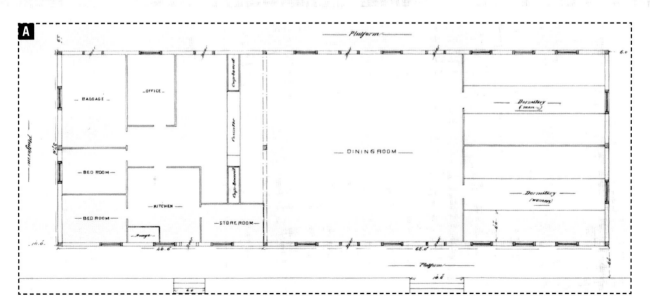

The Station

Before Starting.

At Year after.

At meals, on arrival of a train.

One of the Dormitories.

The Kitchen.

J. P. Pranishnikoff

3.3 Immigration shed at the "Tanneries," as depicted in the *Canadian Illustrated News*, 27 March 1875.

similar to Toronto's appeared at London; a smaller version was built in 1878 at Emerson, where the rail line from Minnesota crossed the border before arriving at Winnipeg. As railroad construction proceeded west, immigration buildings appeared at key points, only to be quickly superceded. Around 1880, Port Arthur became an important transfer point for a brief moment; it had an

immigration building by 1883, the year when the CPR reached Winnipeg, and Port Arthur immediately lost its role as a transportation hub. Within five years, all distribution centres west of Quebec City were eclipsed by Winnipeg, which by then had rail connections from coast to coast, south to the United States, and by branch lines into the interior of Manitoba and the Northwest Territories.

Before 1883, the design of the buildings in each place was idiosyncratic; each was designed by a local architect, seemingly without specific direction from the still-new Chief Architect's Branch in the Department of Public Works.[8] That year, immigration halls began to appear at railway sidings between Winnipeg and the Rocky Mountains: first at Brandon and Qu'Appelle, and then at Calgary, Moose Jaw, Medicine Hat, Whitewood, and Regina by the end of the decade. Starting with these halls on the Prairies, and at least until the 1910s, all immigration buildings would be designed in-house by government architects.

With the completion of the CPR's main line north of the Great Lakes in 1885, Toronto ceased to be an important transfer point, and the agent there dealt mostly in employment advice. By 1888, the Toronto depot was so thoroughly neglected by the Dominion government that it had achieved local notoriety, according to one resident, as "a dumping hole for emigrants, who are flocking there daily in shoals of seven or eight hundred. When they get into what is known as the sheds … they have no money, no fire is allowed, and they have nothing to eat … no bedding or blankets of any kind are furnished." A newspaper article described the dormitory as "reeking with scents and crammed with strangers in a strange land … angry men, the screams and cries of children and the pitiful wailing of infants."[9] While the halls were typically well-appointed, with firewood, furniture, and bedding – and sometimes free meals, as at the Tanneries junction – they also might be absolutely spartan or dilapidated, depending on the year, the demand, the agent, or the responsiveness of Ottawa bureaucrats. The inland immigration halls could be needed desperately in one year, and then abandoned the next when available land ran out or the main immigration routes changed.

The early transfer-point structures established the basic elements that would characterize the Prairie immigration halls as shelters for the indigent and transient, and as reception centres where immigrants could be registered, tracked, protected from imposition, and steered toward available land

and jobs. An important hub like Winnipeg would receive depot buildings similar to the one found in Toronto, while smaller, terminal destinations would get more modest structures, like that at the Tanneries. A first immigrant shed was erected in Winnipeg in 1872, down at the Forks, where immigrants arrived by boat on the Red River. This structure seems to have been the first Dominion government building in the Prairie provinces. Locals had been lobbying for a shed as new arrivals were "enduring much discomfort, if not indeed positive hardship, for the lack of shelter." While it had promised to remedy the situation, Ottawa had been dragging its heels that summer, and the Winnipeg newspaper decried the situation, pointing out that "the immigration season will be far advanced, if not well nigh closed, before the shed can possibly be finished."[10] What was built late that year, and indeed only became available for the following summer's immigration season, was a long, rectangular, one-storey wood structure, finished with board-and-batten siding (Figure 3.4). The building seems to have been bisected longitudinally, with a file of fifteen "apartments" on either side of the line of symmetry. For each side there were small, detached, cookhouse and latrine structures. A twin immigrant shed was built later that summer, doubling the shelter capacity. These sheds lacked insulation and foundations, and flooded every spring, so their usefulness was limited to the summer months. They were, nonetheless, "a great boon to immigrants on their arrival," according to the annual report of the local agent.[11] All these Winnipeg structures had pavilion roofs reminiscent of the Toronto depot. The plan of the apartments, however, was unlike those seen in other immigration sheds of the period, confirming that the design was the responsibility of a local architect or contractor. At this time, there was no standardization of immigration architecture, and Public Works had yet to establish itself as a nationalizing influence.

3.4 The first immigration shed in Winnipeg, built
at the Forks in 1872, and possibly the first Dominion
government building west of Ontario. The cook shack and
latrine are to the right. Three large braces and an uneven
eave line perhaps attest to the lack of foundations in the
building. Demolished in 1884.

When the transcontinental railroad arrived
in Winnipeg in 1881, the sheds at the Forks were
rendered obsolete, and they would be demolished
a few years later. What the minister had identified
in the opening narrative of this chapter marked a
brief gap between the completion of the new CPR
station and the construction of a new immigration building nearby. In the siting of immigration
buildings, proximity to the transportation hub
was everything, as migrants arrived on piers and
platforms with families in tow and all their worldly
possessions in trunks and crates. In Winnipeg,
the sites of Dominion immigration halls shifted

several times, in 1881, 1882, and 1887, as officials
came to understand the importance of proximity. The government then moved all the existing
buildings to another new site, and added a new
one, between 1904 and 1906, in order to maintain
a location adjacent to another newly constructed
CPR station.[12]

Prairie immigration halls offered a base for the
local immigration agent. This figure met incoming
trains to guide immigrants to the building, hosted
them there, and provided information and assistance. The immigration agent in his immigration
hall assumed a role previously performed by the
chief factor at Hudson's Bay Company trading
posts across Rupert's Land, which "served as relay
stations and hostels" prior to "the advent of regular
governmental institutions." As historian Dirk
Hoerder writes: "Knowledgeable factors ruled and
gave advice, their presence gave comfort."[13] Often,
interpreters and land guides were also employed at

the immigration halls. The agent could arrange for new arrivals, potential immigrants, or representatives of group migrations, to be taken out by the land guide on tours of the surrounding area so they could investigate the quality and location of free land open to claims. Rather than career bureaucrats, the immigration agents – and, even more so, the land guides – were local settlers already familiar with the pioneer life and the nature of the surrounding landscape. Indeed, government correspondence regularly emphasized the importance of the tacit knowledge held by its agents, who, on behalf of the state, could impart it to greenhorn settlers. As one Dauphin lumberman and politician wrote to the deputy minister, there was "no use in sending outside men, who have no knowledge of the locality, to act in the capacity of land guide."[14] In addition, after about 1890, the immigration halls typically had resident matrons or caretakers to stoke the fires, manage the space, and maintain the physical plant. Having a caretaker on site was practical, to welcome and supervise the immigrants, and also to protect the government's investment in infrastructure from careless users or vandals. By the late 1890s, the plans for immigration halls began to include a small office for the agent, and sometimes quarters for the caretaker. In the older halls, the caretaker just occupied one of the family rooms, or slept in the kitchen. After 1892, all these civil servants were overseen by a western commissioner located in Winnipeg, at which location there were gathered numerous agents, interpreters, and guides. Encounters with these various people in official roles would have been vital to the futures of incoming immigrants, especially those with minimal capital and little experience on the land in North America. These figures were representatives of the state advising immigrants and their families on the long road toward shaping themselves as Canadian citizens.

The late-nineteenth century was the era of assisted-settlement and group-migration schemes. Charitable institutions, elite sponsors, or well-organized communities would assemble large groups of indigent or peasant families, often victims of industrialization, persecution, or natural disaster, and support their immigration to Canada with funding and guidance. These groups – including Icelanders and Mennonites in the 1870s, Russian Jews in the 1880s, various Scandinavians in the 1890s, and thereafter the Ukrainians and the Doukhobors we encountered in chapter 2 – were often destined for large blocks of government land, where they could establish a colony together.[15] The need to manage these large groups en route and in remote regions spurred the development of Prairie immigration infrastructure.

In addition to its network of immigration halls, in peak years the immigration branch sometimes resorted to renting hotels or to converting large interior spaces for immigrant accommodations. For about two decades, roughly from 1890 to 1910, it also maintained a collection of canvas bell tents that could be shipped around to different Prairie sidings as land became available and immigrants began to arrive (Figure 3.5). There was always a certain air of the ad hoc to providing accommodations for newcomers to the Prairies. Despite all the preparations, some immigrants were left out in the cold if they arrived before halls were built, or if the halls were oversubscribed. Even in Winnipeg, where the western headquarters of the immigration bureaucracy was based, there was no official immigration hall available for about three years after an 1887 fire, and for another year in the early 1890s when the hall was quarantined due to an occurrence of contagious disease among the immigrants. When government halls and tents were unavailable, pioneers describe a range of temporary accommodation options that they took up on arrival: living in tents or shacks in town, rooming with town residents, working for their beds on nearby farms, and sleeping on the floor of the "section house" or under the shadow of the

3.5 Saskatoon in 1903. The two-storey building to the left is the immigration hall, opened that summer. The tents are government-issued "canvas accommodation," supplementary to the hall.

grain elevator. One couple who arrived in Winnipeg about 1880 found they immediately had to purchase a tent to live in, and be taught how to light a campfire by their First Nations neighbour.[16] While the immigration branch tried to build immigration halls in anticipation of new arrivals, based on the completion of rail lines or the opening of land through new surveys, the Dominion government was limited in its ability to operate efficiently in remote, underpopulated regions. Many years, at the opening of the immigration season, agents wrote of unanticipated rushes, begging for more accommodation to be made available immediately by new construction or tents. For instance, in 1902, the Winnipeg commissioner of immigration, J. Obed Smith, wrote to his superiors in Ottawa that there were regular requests for "canvas

accommodation" from railway sidings across the Prairies. Each immigration season, he itemized every location where buildings were owned or operated, and should be newly built or rented.[17] These reactive endeavours by the Dominion government reveal the difficulty of planning comprehensively across a territory represented by few members of parliament, with scattered civil servants, great distances, and slow correspondence.

Because Winnipeg was the hub of Prairie transportation, almost every immigrant to western Canada either stayed at the halls there or visited them for guidance. While an immigration hall in a regional hub like Calgary or Edmonton would host several hundred newcomers each year, mostly in the summer, the annual number of guests staying at the Winnipeg halls in the late-nineteenth century was often between ten and fifteen thousand.[18] During the decade before the First World War, the annual numbers were much higher: up to five thousand would stay in the regional hubs, now also including immigration halls in towns like Saskatoon and Regina, whereas Winnipeg would host as many as thirty thousand immigrants. Based on the records kept by agents and caretakers through these decades, between 15 and 20 per cent of new arrivals stayed overnight in Dominion government immigration halls near their Prairie destinations, with many more dropping in for information and advice. The lower numbers of overnighters at the regional and terminal halls does not indicate that these sites were unimportant nodes in the network of Dominion government immigration architecture. Many migrants stopped for only a few hours in towns with immigration halls, passing through briefly; many were met at the train station or siding by relatives, friends, or employers, and therefore had no need to stay in the halls. Some migrants may have actively avoided staying in the halls due to a perceived stigma around receiving charity, or to a fear of government institutions. This possibility is signalled by the English journalist Arthur Copping, who travelled with and interviewed immigrants for a 1911 book. "I was destined to meet, in the streets of Winnipeg," he wrote, "other new-comers who, little dreaming of the opportunities afforded by the Immigration Hall, had deliberately held aloof from it. After undergoing … a searching inquisition, in the Immigration Hall at Quebec, they were indisposed to visit another institution of the same name."[19] His suggestion was to rename the two building types to distinguish between the supportive reception work done on the Prairies, and the inspection processes – only introduced after the turn of the century – on the piers. However, I found no other intimations of this kind of reaction or resistance in official sources or first-person recollections. A migrant's decision whether to stay in an immigration hall seemed to reside in their ability to pay for other lodgings, and the availability of such; their desire to save money for homesteading and other expenses; the accessibility of local transportation to take them out of town; and in other individual and local contingencies. There were strong incentives for a migrant to stay at an immigration hall, but the Dominion government's coverage of the territory always remained partial.

Migrants could receive room and board in Prairie immigration halls for a few days, a week, or sometimes as long as several months, in unusual cases of inclement weather, impassable roads, illness, injury, or family separation. Large group migrations – such as the Russian Jews, or the Doukhobors – often overwintered in the halls while getting themselves organized to establish their settlements. Large groups could be distributed across several buildings in Winnipeg and along the routes toward their ultimate destinations in the following spring. Although various correspondents – government officials, reporters, and immigrants themselves – indicate different periods as the maximum allowable stay in an immigration hall, there was never a policy to establish this. When questioned in the House of Commons in 1891 about the limit of time immigrants were allowed to stay in the halls, the minister of the interior remarked casually: "If they are there for a week or two, there is no objection. We do not keep them; they keep themselves; but they have the use of a stove and the building."[20] Local agents had to exercise their own judgment deciding when new arrivals had worn out their welcome. Weather, the availability of local guides and transportation, the poverty level, gender, and ethnicity of the immigrant guests, and the impending arrival of another batch of newcomers in need of accommodation all played a part in the duration of the halls' occupancy. Even the western commissioner had to contend with this ambiguity at the Winnipeg hall. In 1903, he wrote to his superiors that "in practically every room in the building there is a printed statement that seven days is all that the Department can allow by the way of free accommodation … When the seven days is up and people have nowhere else to go, I must either continue the accommodation or put them out on the street, which I think is a very dangerous proceeding to take."[21] Since the deputy minister had not sent "any further or fresh instructions in this connection," the commissioner was forced to rely on his own discrimination, empathy, and interpretation of the government's intentions with this social-welfare program.

MOTIVATIONS BEHIND THE NETWORK OF PRAIRIE IMMIGRATION HALLS

From the Dominion government's point of view, it had powerful motivations to develop a network of immigration architecture – motivations that were competitive, paternal, and, of course, pragmatic. In chapter 1, we witnessed how Canadian officials compared their immigrant-reception practices at the ports with those of the United States, concluding that their own were different and better: more supportive to the immigrants, more organized, with more infrastructure. The primary example of this competition to provide better services than their colleagues south of the border was the construction and operation of immigration halls across the Prairie provinces. While immigrants to the United States might be lucky to find commercial "settlement hotels" at their frontier destination, arrivals on the Canadian Prairies would be treated to free shelter. As the historian and former immigration official Robert Vineberg has written, the Prairie halls were "the tangible symbol of Canada's commitment to its immigrants." The government "invested heavily in expanding [these] facilities to help immigrants settle successfully in Canada, in contrast to the American approach of largely leaving immigrants to their own devices."[22] The Dominion government knew it lost most potential settlers to its great competitor to the south, and it endeavoured to be the kinder, gentler immigration destination. The civil servants who

administered immigrant-reception infrastructure posited the competitive advantage it afforded. The 1889 report of a Canadian immigration official sent to research US facilities concluded simply "that settlement will follow in the most inviting groove." Given the better infrastructure north of the border, "a vast stream of immigration must soon flow into the great basin of the Canadian North West."[23] This attitude prevailed throughout the period covered in this chapter. "A large part of our success with immigration matters," the responsible deputy minister noted confidently in one 1902 dispatch, "is that we properly look after the accommodation for the immigrants."[24]

The Dominion government believed that immigrants, especially those of the free-homesteads class, needed to be looked after. As early as 1871, immigrants were being grouped together for their journeys, so that an agent of the government could travel with them to extend protection and control in between brick-and-mortar government facilities. Similar to the port towns, inland destinations were seen by the authorities as sites where naive newcomers could be taken advantage of by unscrupulous locals, often those locals who shared a place of origin or spoke the language of the newcomer. An 1888 CPR guidebook to homesteading, though, assured the prospective immigrant that the "new comer need not fear that when he reaches Winnipeg he will fall into the hands of thieves, impostors, or unfriendly people. If he follows the directions of this pamphlet, he will put himself in the hands of real friends, who will look after him. At Winnipeg, the Government have erected a commodious barracks, which is kept in a tidy and healthful condition." Travellers would be met upon arrival "by the agents of the Government" and of the railroad, "who take charge of immigrants and give them all the assistance and advice they need in a strange land."[25] Because the Dominion government had the best information regarding the availability and quality of remaining free land, and the location of different ethnic settlements, it worked to keep the most vulnerable homesteaders corralled in the immigration buildings, from where they could be steered to appropriate regions and plots. However, as historian John Lehr notes, immigration officials "had no legal authority to require immigrants of any nationality to homestead in any specific location." Instead, they used the arts of persuasion, along with up-to-date information, and sometimes incentives such as free feed or seed, to convince immigrants to go to specific regions. Lehr asserts that, in combination with the "availability of surveyed land" and the number of homesteaders already sent to a particular area, the number of available beds in a local immigration hall was a key basis for directing immigrants to a destination.[26]

When large group migrations to the Prairies began, the Dominion government found it beneficial to house them together in immigration halls, or in expediently rented large spaces. There officials could manage the groups and provide them with information through interpreters and chaperones or other community leaders, rather than trying to communicate individually with each immigrant. These large groups could then be directed to railroad or industry work gangs, or to large blocks of land where they could stay together as a community and have their progress monitored by the government. The congregation of a large group of immigrants in one place might itself be used to lobby for the construction of an immigration hall. Count Esterhazy, the sponsor of several Hungarian colonies started in rural Saskatchewan in the mid-1880s, petitioned the Dominion government in 1902 for the construction of a hall, because recently arrived women and children were encamped "without a roof over their heads, exposed to wind and rain." Eventually, by 1905, the government did rent accommodations in

a couple of these villages, but it was not inclined to build an immigration hall.[27] Even though Hungarian immigration continued at that time, there was an expectation that the established community would support new arrivals. In general, the Dominion government in this period admitted to some responsibility for the welfare of immigrants up to one year after their arrival in Canada – for example, occasionally providing emergency food. Officially, though, it strove to restrict the use of the free accommodations it provided to those persons just off the boat and train, and to those without family, friends, or ethnic connections who could offer shelter. Paternalism had its limits and, as with all early social-welfare programs, officials were at great pains to discourage recidivism.

The Dominion government was interested in monitoring the provenance, quality, whereabouts, and successes of new arrivals. Group migration was often the target of criticism by opposition members of parliament and their supporting newspapers. The immigration agents stationed at the halls gathered qualitative evidence – that is, stories – that the government's paternalistic policies, promotional activities, and processes were working. The halls also served as checkpoints and centres for the collection of quantitative data. Each hall across the Prairies kept a register of guests that recorded names, origins, family size, capital, and ultimate destinations. Statistics compiled from these registers were regularly used to make arguments about the importance of the immigration-architecture program and the need for new halls; alternatively, dwindling numbers of guests would justify closing a hall in a place where all the jobs and land had been taken up. As checkpoints, the halls sometimes caught out fraudulent booking agents or "return men," who claimed bonuses on each immigrant they recruited and delivered to destinations in the Canadian west. One such recruiter telegrammed to Winnipeg officials in 1897 that he had dozens of immigrants en route to the government immigration hall and to several hotels in that city. Suspicions were aroused when the promised newcomers never showed up at the hall. Upon investigation, it was found that almost the entire group was a fabrication. Just as bad, the half-dozen or so bona fide immigrants sent by this recruiter turned out to be enervated urban dwellers, and not the healthy agriculturalists that Canadian policy claimed to prefer. Although they were of the preferred ethnicity, English immigrants who were not from agricultural backgrounds were often compared unfavourably to stalwart eastern-European peasants by immigration officials in charge of implementing Sifton's liberal recruitment policy. In this particular example, his observations of the character of these new arrivals staying in the immigration hall led the Winnipeg commissioner to argue vigorously against the bonus system that encouraged these booking agents.[28]

During the early years of immigration into Winnipeg, and at all times in small towns west of there, the basic, pragmatic needs of shelter and food became paramount prior to migrants establishing their own households. Often, where migrants detrained there was little or no infrastructure of any kind. After having arrived in Regina in the early 1880s, two brides-to-be later reminisced about the nature of their welcome in what was then called "Pile-of-Bones." It was "a dirty little town consisting of a one-roomed station, a few stores, and several shacks." There were no accommodations, so everyone slept at the depot, "on the floor, men, women, and children, rich and poor, side by side"; and they all woke up "stiff and sore."[29] The uncomfortable experience of these brides was not unique among the earliest immigrants to the Prairie provinces. A lack of shelter and services was typical of brand-new towns laid out along railway lines, rivers, and mud roads, and this would hold true well into the twentieth century. In a reminiscing letter, one Saskatchewan townsman recalled his 1901 arrival in one of these instant settlements:

Craik was not a cross-road village at that time; just one road and that was the railroad ... A few trails led out into the vast Prairies ... There was no place where one could get anything to eat, except at the railway station ... Sleeping accommodations were scarce. The Waldorf Hotel was being constructed and a few bedrooms were partially finished, beds installed and as many as three or four frequently tried to sleep in one bed. The waiting room and dining room at the depot were frequently so full that the people could not use the cots or even lie down on the floor, but had to sit up all night.[30]

In response to stories of insalubrious reception sent back to Ottawa by members of parliament, reporters, guides, and settlers themselves, the Dominion government set out to make the immigrant experience in Canada more welcoming. By 1890, there was a government immigration hall in Regina (see Figure 3.12), where brides and other arrivals could lay their heads, and receive sustenance and guidance, prior to embarking on their new lives. Similarly, an immigration hall was erected in Craik shortly after the gentleman's experience described above. Still, a photograph of Craik from about three years after his arrival exemplifies the state of urban development often awaiting immigrants to the Prairies (Figure 3.6). The principal landmarks are the railway depot and the aforementioned Waldorf Hotel, which are directly connected by a short boardwalk. A grouping of three large, attached structures appear in the background, likely the premises of a feed and equipment dealer. Only a single residence is visible, and most of the town lots are empty.

Although the Dominion government strove to get out ahead of settlement and have an immigra-

3.6 Craik, Saskatchewan, c. 1904. The hotel is on the far left of the image, and the railroad depot in the centre.

tion hall awaiting the earliest arrivals, one farmer later recalled for the local newspaper how he arrived in 1902 in their small town, only about thirty kilometres down the road from Craik: "I took the train and landed at the supposed Davidson. When I stepped off the train, I stumbled into the ditch. There was nothing to be seen except a signboard … a tent [for the land agent] … and a building in the course of erection as an immigration hall. The rest was all scenery." The halls in these small settlements were welcome additions, even if their accommodations might remain rather primitive. Another settler recalled his stay as a young man in Davidson's immigration hall in 1906, when the dormitories there were supplemented by as many as twenty-five tents. The hall "was kind of a plain looking big house, more of a house than a hall … It had different sections in it and places to cook. You had to supply your own food. Mostly you slept on the floor – at least that's where I slept."[31] Overcrowding, a lack of furniture, and the fear of vermin in the bunks resulted in some newcomers bedding down on the floors of the immigration halls.

Even if some enterprising pioneer had established a hotel at their destination, many settlers could not afford to spend their last dollars on room and board when there were so many homesteading expenses to consider, such as traction and tools, feed and seed. The promoter of Ukrainian immigration, Joseph Oleskiw, advised that, in Winnipeg and points west, the "family frequently stays behind in the Immigration Hall, while the head of the family takes off to look for a suitable place." Although there were free excursion tickets available – from the government or from the railways themselves – so that men could inspect potential homestead sites, "the trip is nevertheless expensive, because there are no cheap inns or restaurants in these places. There are only hotels with dining rooms, where one is expected behave like a 'gentleman.' The Immigration Halls available at each station … are the places, where a colonist usually stops."[32] Oleskiw's advice hints at another aspect of the class dimension that deterred some from staying at hotels. Hotels were American institutions patronized by travellers with ready cash and broad experience with the sort of class mixing that characterized cities in modern democracies. Likely, Ukrainian peasants and other rural migrants would have been uncomfortable in these spaces, even if frontier hotels – their grand monikers aside – were significantly less opulent than many of those found in North American cities.[33]

Finally, migrants and immigration officials had to contend with Canada's four seasons. Summer was the principal season when most immigrants passed through the halls, when insects, heat, and Prairie thunderstorms necessitated shelter from the elements. Fall and winter were slower. As an Edmonton newspaper updated its readers in a rhyming couplet one December: "Winter days are quiet days at Immigration Hall. The number of immigrants arriving is very small."[34] However, sometimes recent arrivals tried, and were allowed, to overwinter in the immigration halls, if they had been seasonally employed or if they had not had enough time to plant and harvest their first crops. In the spring, when immigrants began to arrive again, washed-out bridges, boggy roads, snow-covered fields, and buried section posts delayed going onto the land, and meant crowded immigration halls. Although frosty midwinter months, the snow pack, and the late spring, were little different from the conditions faced on the northern Great Plains of the United States, Canada's special climate was mentioned often as a justification for its Prairie immigration infrastructure.

The government's three motivations blended and justified each other: without adequate paternal protection and pragmatic support, potential immigrants could be scared off and head for the United States or other competing settler colonies in the southern hemisphere. Government immigration agents feared that without adequate accommodations, "we shall have these people turning back

home on the first train they can."[35] Even worse, they might write home and scare off family members and others. Two years before he became minister responsible for immigration, Frank Oliver spoke of the urgent need for the halls in terms of chain migration: "should the weather become inclement there would necessarily be an immense amount of hardship amongst the new arrivals which would unquestionably have a serious effect not only upon them, but on their friends at home, who would thereby be discouraged from coming because of the danger of undergoing the same experiences."[36] Here again the climate of Canada seems to offer a special rationale for the Dominion government's competitive, paternal, and pragmatic immigrant welfare program.

ARCHITECTURE OF THE EARLY PRAIRIE IMMIGRATION HALLS

In 1883, the Dominion government undertook construction of more-or-less-similar immigration halls in Winnipeg, Brandon, and Qu'Appelle (Figures 3.7 and 3.8). Unlike in the previous decade, it seems that the Chief Architect's Branch had begun to effect some level of standardization. As will be seen, though, any standardization was short-lived. The three 1883 halls were long, narrow, wooden balloon-frame structures that sat on rocks just above grade. They had gable roofs with ten bays of repeating windows and a vertical board-and-batten siding treatment like the earlier London and Winnipeg buildings. The symmetry and repetition of these facades presents an image of power and order, and by orienting these structures with their entrances on the broad side, the government ensured an imposing presence in the wide spaces of the Prairies, where there was minimal built fabric. A central chimney with a kind of witch's-hat roof additionally emphasized the landmark character of these early public buildings, which were easily distinguishable from the train depots and

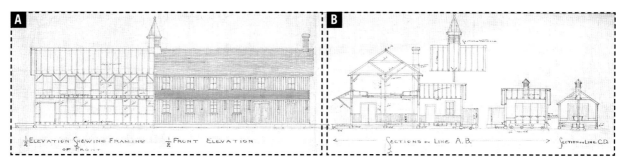

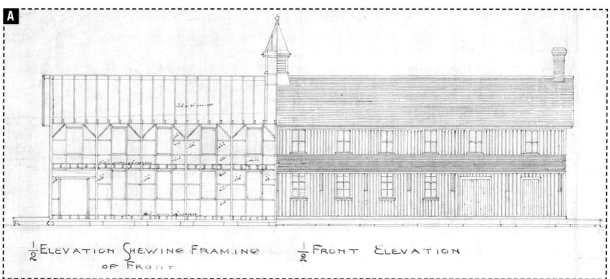

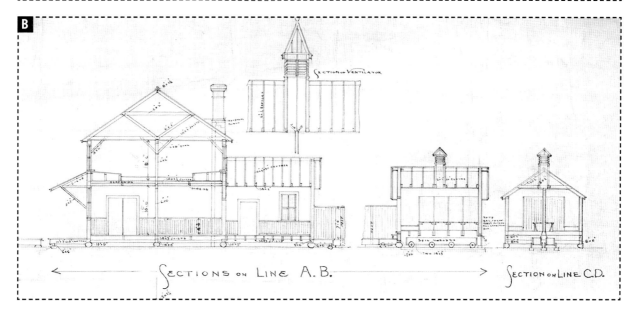

3.7 Qu'Appelle immigration hall, elevation and sections, designed in 1882, built and burned down in 1883, rebuilt in 1884. Compared with the Brandon hall seen in Figure 3.8, the Qu'Appelle hall was appended with an extra bay on the right end, providing two private, separately heated offices, at least one of which seem to have been for the Dominion land agent.

IMMIGRATION SHED
FOR BRANDON
SCALE 1/16" = 1 FOOT

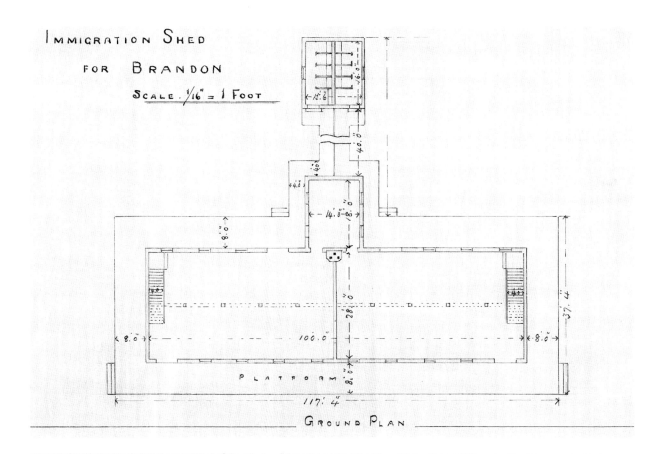

GROUND PLAN

IMMIGRATION SHED
FOR BRANDON
SCALE 1/16" = 1 FOOT

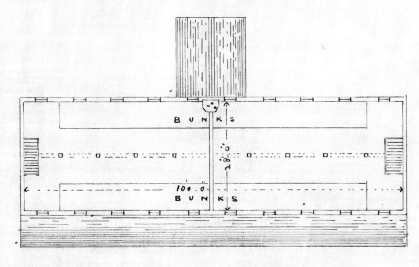

FIRST FLOOR PLAN

other commercial architecture of frontier towns. Typically, these early immigration halls, like those that followed them, stood very close to the railroad tracks, often on CPR land, making them especially easy to find and access when tired migrants stepped off the train (Figure 3.9).

Two entrances were found in the farthest bays to the left and right on the front facades of these buildings. These opened into common rooms separated by sex, also used as mess halls. Each common area had a staircase leading up to the men's or the women's dormitory, respectively, and these two large spaces entirely comprised the upper floor. In the dormitories, the plan indicates continuous built-in bunks against each long wall — a standard feature in immigration architecture of the 1870s and 1880s. Seen in section, from a set of drawings of the London immigration hall, these sloping platforms provided shared, and likely uncomfortable, sleeping arrangements for indigent travellers (Figure 3.10). A considerate design detail is the headrest achieved with a butt joint and a rounded corner, but not all the bunks found in immigration halls featured these supports. The back doors from the ground-floor common rooms accessed a veranda, which wrapped around the gabled kitchen bump-out to access the toilets. A barrier dividing the boardwalk between the kitchen and the latrines maintained the sex

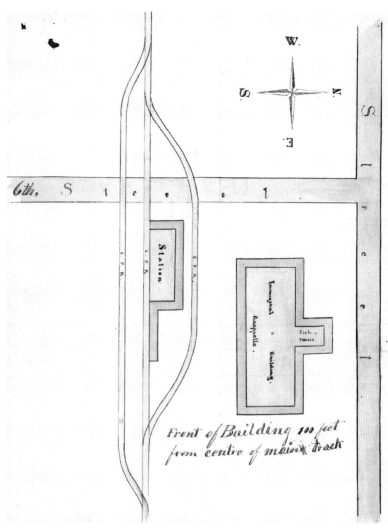

Front of Building 100 feet from centre of main track

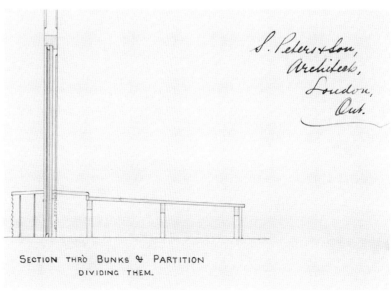

S. Peters + Son, Architects, London, Ont.

SECTION THRO BUNKS & PARTITION DIVIDING THEM.

3.8 (*opposite*) Immigration shed for Brandon, 1883. The plan of the building in Figure 3.7 was identical, except for the extra bay added on the Qu'Appelle building.

3.9 Site plan, immigration hall in Qu'Appelle, showing the proximity between the hall, the CPR station, and the principal streets of the town.

3.10 Section drawing through group bunks, London, Ontario, immigration hall, 1875, like those seen on the first-floor plan in Figure 3.8. By the 1890s, this type of built-in began to be replaced in the halls by mass-manufactured, and movable, bed frames, although see the built-ins indicated on Figure 3.15.

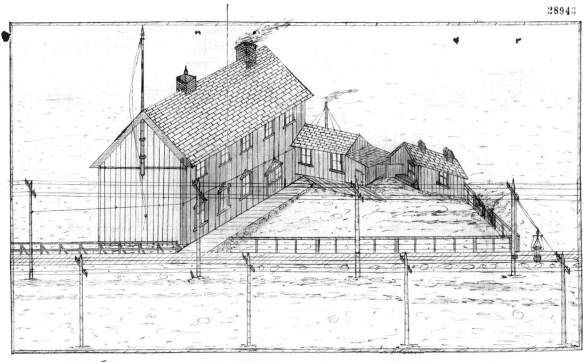

28943

Imengranten Bilding tu Calgary • *von this help yyif-it*

FOR THE TEMPORARY ACCOMMODATION OF SETTLERS

3.11 An immigrant's late-1890s sketch of the immigration hall at Calgary, which was built in 1885 and used until 1913. The Canadian Pacific Railway station stood one block to the left. The immigrant presented this sketch to the local agent in 1896, who forwarded it to his superiors in Ottawa.

separation of the interior spaces. Against the white background of the architectural drawing, the plan effects an ideal segregation. On the ground in the emergent frontier towns, where this design was used, the buildings would have been surrounded by freely accessible open space – undifferentiated grass and dirt plots not subject to governmental control. Once a migrant stepped off the veranda, strict spatial sorting became impossible.

By 1885, a modification of the design appeared in the Calgary immigration hall, which

was a truncated version of the 1883 buildings (Figure 3.11). Still a rectangular, two-storey, gable-roofed, wood structure with board-and-batten siding, the Calgary design was reduced to five bays wide. The sole entrance is placed in the penultimate bay, while a one-storey kitchen building was attached to the final bay. No plan survives of the building, but it is unlikely that the single entrance precluded the sex separation of spaces on the ground and upper floors of this structure. On the Calgary hall, there is a slight hint of decoration in the board pediments placed over ground-floor openings. Perhaps this is a flourish added by the frontier carpenter who contracted the building, since nothing like this appears on architectural drawings produced by Public Works for the immigration branch in this period. The exact details

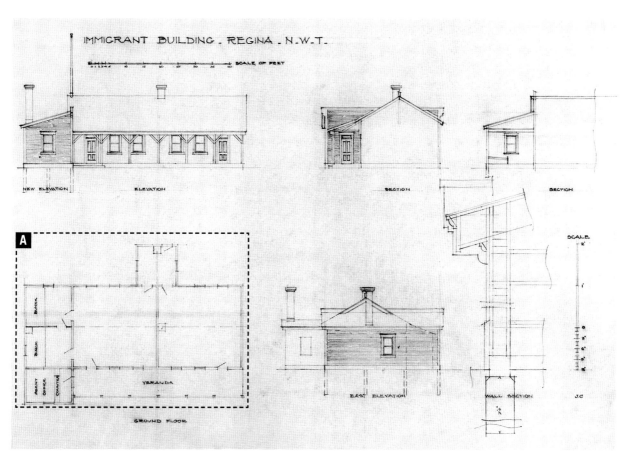

IMMIGRANT BUILDING . REGINA . N.W.T.

SCALE OF FEET

NEW ELEVATION   ELEVATION   SECTION   SECTION

SCALE

A

BUNCK

BUNCK

AGENT OFFICE COUNTER

VERANDA

GROUND FLOOR

EAST ELEVATION   WALL SECTION   J.C

3.12 Architectural drawing sheet for the 1890 immigration hall in Regina, also used in Strathcona two years later.

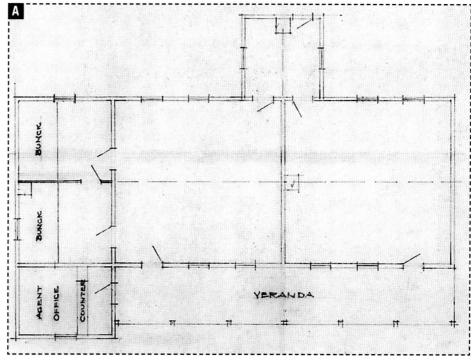

A

BUNCK

BUNCK

AGENT OFFICE COUNTER

VERANDA

of the Calgary immigration hall make it somewhat unique, though a short-lived copy was built in Medicine Hat the following year.

In 1890 a new model was introduced for two much-smaller immigration halls erected in Regina and Whitewood (Figure 3.12). Only one storey, these small, side-gable buildings with clapboard siding were supplemented by a kitchen bump-out and a shed-roofed ell that incorporated baggage storage and two small chambers for use as an office or caretaker's residence. From the veranda extending across the front facade, separate entrances at either end access the two rooms of the hall, a partition dividing the space equally. Two doors from the kitchen access these sex-separated rooms. Given the function of these buildings as mass housing, rather a lot is expected from this compact unit. In fact, as discussed below, there were ongoing issues with the primitive conditions and overcrowding in Regina, as well as in Prince Albert and Strathcona, where copies of this design would be built in 1892. Nonetheless, this 1890 model became the preferable design over the course of several years, because it was much cheaper to build and maintain than the 1883 design — one storey, with no stairs, it also had a smaller footprint, fewer windows and stoves, and no built-ins. The new frame structures sat on wooden piles and could be constructed quickly and cheaply. The Dominion government seems to have concluded that the earlier immigration halls were overbuilt, given the seasonality of immigration and the rapid turnover of guests, most of whom required only a few nights' stay. As the minister remarked in the House of Commons in 1891: "After it was found that these expensive immigrant sheds were not used as we expected, the policy was changed, and last year two sheds were built" for significantly less money.[37] Appropriations clearly reflect the policy change: the Brandon and Qu'Appelle immigration halls had cost $11,000 each; Calgary about $5,000; with Regina and the other small halls of the 1890s coming in at $800 to $1,000 each.[38]

The earlier form seen at Brandon and Qu'Appelle did not disappear entirely, however. It was latent in the design of the 1890 immigration hall for Winnipeg (Figure 3.13), which needed to be a more substantial structure than the ones being erected in smaller and less-developed Prairie towns. A broad, two-and-a-half-storey, gable-roofed structure, the 1890 Winnipeg hall was divided into eight bays, each with a trim dormer capping a vertical line of double-hung windows. At each end of the facade, a kind of bow window served as a bookend, replacing the sex-separated entrances seen in the 1883 designs. Here, a raised entrance was placed in the central bay, marked by a covered vestibule, over which hung a sign denoting the building's purpose. Plans for this building have not survived, but these modifications of the 1883 design indicate two functional shifts. First, the central entrance indicates the increased value placed on surveillance and monitoring of the comings and goings of immigrants; that is, it suggests a central point or office to which immigrants could report, and where they could be served and tracked. This facilitation of control and protection was of great consequence in Winnipeg, the western headquarters of the immigration branch: many

3.13 (*opposite, top*) Winnipeg immigration hall of 1890, in a photo taken that decade. The building is reminiscent of the earlier halls in Qu'Appelle and Brandon, but with an occupiable attic. Some of the windows are shown with awnings or curtains, though it is unclear how these related to different functions.

3.14 (*opposite, bottom*) Postcard of the Lloydminster immigration hall, modelled on the Dauphin hall, built five years earlier. In this case a small dormer marks the central entrance to the building. Its staid, quasi-Georgian style contrasts with the false-fronted commercial buildings along the street, and it is the sole property in this image that is fenced, suggesting a concern for the security of the structure and of the immigrants.

Broadway, Lloydminster, looking South. The first building on the left is the Immigration Hall.

thousands of immigrants would visit this building each year. Second, the disappearance of the separate entrances, which in the earlier designs had accessed sex-separated mess halls and dormitories, hints that traditional sexual mores were becoming less crucial than the ability of officials to effect centralized management of the immigrant population.

Nevertheless, sex-separated spaces – but not entrances – endured in several immigration halls of a new design, which were erected around the turn of the century. Harking back to the Calgary hall, the overall form – of a gabled, five-bay structure – would become axiomatic for the next several years. The main change from the Calgary building is that these later iterations of a five-bay design situated the entrance in the central bay and finished the structure in horizontal clapboard siding. The form is already familiar, seen in the early-twentieth-century photograph of Saskatoon (see Figure 3.5). The original iteration of this new, symmetrical, five-bay design seems to have been the hall built in Dauphin in 1898, as it is regularly mentioned as a model in immigration-branch correspondence: subsequent halls in Yorkton, 1899, and Rosthern, 1900, were copies of the building at Dauphin. Lethbridge received the same form in 1902, and the same design, with a small central dormer, was erected in Lloydminster the following year (Figure 3.14). The 1899 Strathcona immigration hall was built along the same lines as well, conforming to the geometry of the five-bay facade; but given the settlement's importance as an immigrant distribution point, a long two-storey annex attached to the rear of that building held a larger communal kitchen with an extra dormitory above. Unfortunately, no plan drawings for this version of the immigration hall design seem to have survived. The Saskatoon building is described in departmental annual reports as having only two rooms on each floor, one for each sex; a central stair hall separated them in a traditional hall-and-parlour-type

plan, with chimneys serving heating stoves built against each end wall.[39] Basically, the plan is a stacked, somewhat broader, two-storey version of the design for Regina and other small halls. Compared to those minimalist structures of the early 1890s, the new two-storey halls represented a marked improvement, as reflected in the $3,000-to-$4,000 price tags for their construction.

Contemporaneous with these turn-of-the-century buildings in Saskatoon and elsewhere, Dominion government architects began to experiment with spatial planning, layering in more complex circulation, differentiating between functions, and creating a larger variety of rooms designated for specific purposes, particularly to separate families from single male migrants. In fact, by 1904, commissioner Smith judged the Dauphin building – and its many copies – "to a large extent, useless," because it was not commodious for families.[40] A somewhat-more-complex plan from 1902, for an immigration hall in Red Deer, shows the central entrance leading into a stair hall, off which opens a small office for the agent, men's and women's common rooms, and the kitchen at the end (Figure 3.15). Two chimneys serve stoves on either side of the central stair hall. Baggage and wood sheds attach behind the kitchen, while the latrines remain in a separate outbuilding. The plan shows upstairs two family rooms, in addition to men's and women's dormitories, and wash rooms with sinks. Red Deer never received the building shown here, and it is unclear whether any Prairie immigration halls were constructed to this exact plan. The simpler versions built at the time, such as the one in Saskatoon, lacked the smaller rooms that cluster around the central stair, and the chimneys were located on the end walls.

Over the front elevation of the proposed Red Deer hall, a government architect has sketched two dormers, perhaps foreshadowing the more substantial design that would soon appear in Brandon and Edmonton, another variation of the five-bay

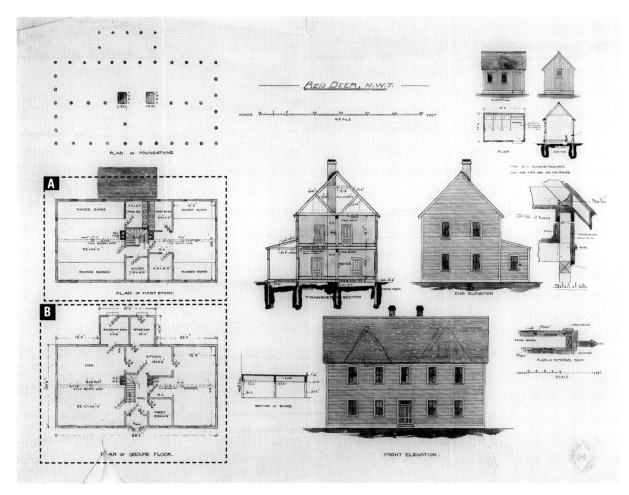

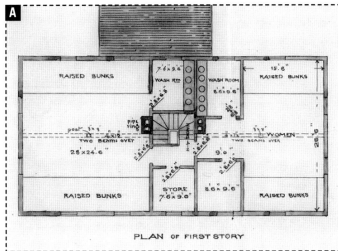

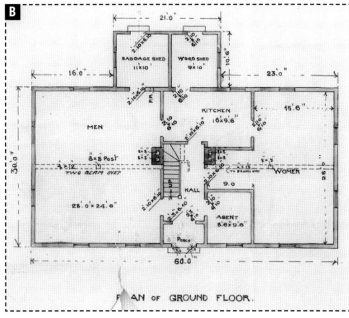

3.15 Full drawing sheet for the Red Deer immigration hall, showing the plan, section, elevations, and details for the five-bay design used in the early twentieth century. Here the built-in bunks lack the headrest detail found in the earlier halls.

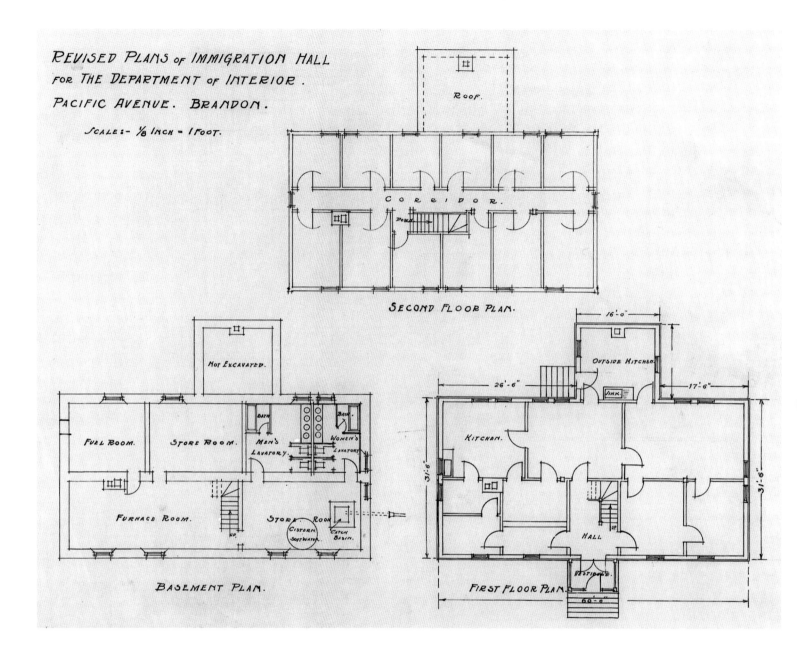

REVISED PLANS OF IMMIGRATION HALL
FOR THE DEPARTMENT OF INTERIOR.
PACIFIC AVENUE. BRANDON.

SCALE:- 1/8 INCH = 1 FOOT.

ROOF.

CORRIDOR.

WOMEN.

SECOND FLOOR PLAN.

NOT EXCAVATED.

BATH
FUEL ROOM. STORE ROOM. MEN'S LAVATORY. WOMEN'S LAVATORY.

FURNACE ROOM. STORE ROOM. CISTERN SOFTWATER. CATCH BASIN.

BASEMENT PLAN.

16'-0"
OUTSIDE KITCHEN.
26'-6" SINK 17'-6"
KITCHEN.

31'-6" HALL. 31'-6"

VESTIBULE.
FIRST FLOOR PLAN.
60'-0"

3.16 Plans of the 1904 Brandon immigration hall. The same design was used in Edmonton and Medicine Hat.

design that began to be used in 1904. These new immigration halls incorporated even-more-striated plans. The new hall in Brandon exemplifies this modernization of the plan, section, and elevation (Figures 3.16 and 3.17). On the ground floor, the central entrance hall provides easy connections via numerous doors to the common rooms, the office, the kitchen bump-out, and the staircase. For the first time, the entire left side of the ground floor is devoted to a caretaker's suite with its own separate kitchen. Upstairs, a double-loaded corridor leads to a dozen sleeping rooms, more or less equal in size, to allow for both singles and families. Gone are the large dormitories for men and women. In a semi-finished basement, we find baggage storage, wash rooms with bath-tubs, and a central heating system — the latter a significant step up from the potbelly stoves seen in immigration halls only a year or two previously.

Beyond just having more complicated plans, the new halls like Brandon's boasted some minor decorative elements and were constructed more substantially. Exactly the same design was used two years later in Edmonton (Figure 3.18). On the facade of these buildings, the central bay was emphasized with a projecting formal portico, fronted by a stair. The roof of the portico is balustraded; behind this, a double window gives it the semblance of a regal balcony. Extending vertically above the balcony, and cutting through

3.17 Section and elevations of the 1904 Brandon immigration hall.

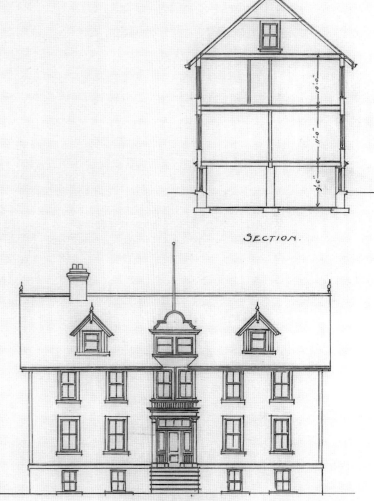

Immigration Hall, Edmonton, Alberta

3.18 Edmonton immigration hall of 1906, in a period postcard. Supplementary tents can be seen in the background. Edmonton is still largely wilderness at this moment, and the Dominion government immigration hall is enough of a landmark that it rates a postcard.

the cornice line, is a large dormer capped by a neoclassical, rounded pediment. Two smaller dormers, like those sketched on the Red Deer drawings, are placed symmetrically on either side of the central one, aligned in between the bays of the facade. A single, sculptural, brick chimney appears on the far right (on the left in Brandon). In each gable end, simple decorative brackets give the tiniest hint of a tympanum. This version of the immigration-hall type sits higher above grade on a concrete-block foundation, which allowed for a more impressive street presence and the development of the basement. These more-substantial

structures of the new century cost more than twice as much as the simpler five-bay halls of the same time period, coming in at about $9,000.

This more expensive design seems to have been reserved for more-prominent regional hubs; only three were built, the third being in Medicine Hat. In smaller towns, the less-substantial version of the immigration-hall type continued to be constructed up until about 1908. By that year, another new design would be developed for Prairie immigration halls (to be discussed in chapter 4). Meanwhile, Regina's new immigration hall of 1904 seems to have been a unique hybrid of the two approaches being pursued by the Dominion government at the time (Figure 3.19). It was slightly larger than the inexpensive five-bay structures, and it shared the more-complex interior layout seen at Brandon and Edmonton. This is evident from the window arrangements: paired windows above the central entrance mimic the balcony windows in the decorated version; and on the end walls, the narrower pairing of windows on the second storey denote the ends of a double-loaded corridor, as seen in the Brandon plans. Yet, the Regina hall lacks the raised concrete basement and the amenities this offered, such as central heating, and it is stripped of the grand portico and other decorative elements. Immigration officials were fully aware of these fine distinctions among the various iterations of the building type. In fact, when the Chief Architect's Branch proposed to re-use exactly the same design it had built in Regina, commissioner Smith was provoked to "strongly recommend that something a little better and larger than this be erected in Edmonton, where the Minister of the Department himself resides." He successfully argued "that the building in Brandon be duplicated" in Edmonton.[41] Oliver had replaced Sifton as minister only a few months earlier, and the civil servants in his portfolio were eager to please their new boss.

Over the two decades after 1883 — and, indeed, during the next two decades as well — the various designs of Prairie immigration halls shared many aspects. Each had a communal kitchen and common rooms on the ground floor. Dormitories and, later, family rooms were arrayed on the ground and upper floors. When possible, given the

3.19 Immigration hall in Regina, erected in 1904. The building is five bays wide, with a central entrance. Outbuildings are visible behind the hall, and the property is fenced.

available floor space, rooms were reserved for an office and a caretaker's apartment. Latrines and fuel storage were in attached or detached sheds. These commonalities added up to a new building type, which is to say a form designed to satisfy a particular social need and retaining its fundamental elements, even as it was refined and modified over time. However, it cannot be argued, as some have done, that, by early in the century, "there was a standard three story wood-frame design for immigration halls and most new halls were built to that standard design."[42] There were half a dozen or more designs deployed for Prairie immigration halls prior to 1905, and no one design possessed a longevity greater than a few years. Rather, it is the differences among the various designs, and in the execution of individual iterations, that reveal changing priorities and attitudes among immigration officials and their architects. For example, as suggested by the shift to centrally placed entrances, the strict sex separation seen at the earlier buildings slowly gave way to different expectations of protection and control. And although the five-bay design continued to include separate dining halls and dormitories for men and women as late as 1903, this changed with the updated, more substantially built, halls of the next few years. The plans of the new Brandon hall show no such sex separation, though we know that single male and female travellers would still be housed separately from families. Around the turn of the century, the obsession with gender was slowly was giving way to official concerns over ethnic segregation. During the Sifton years, when the gates were opened to immigrants from more places and cultures, immigration halls became characterized by attempts to demarcate architecturally the difference between British and "foreign." This ethnic segregation will be discussed further below.[43]

Throughout the history of this building type there always would be specific spatial sortings defined on the architectural drawings. In practice,

however, rooms were occupied by whoever was present at a particular moment. As needs arose, a group migration of one ethnicity might arrive and occupy an entire hall; seasonally, single men waiting for placements as farm or construction labourers might occupy the rooms; or, in slow times, a family or two might spread out into several rooms for a longer-term stay. Moreover, everyone mixed in the communal ground-floor spaces of the immigration halls. Government officials increasingly seem to have recognized the futility of enforcing segregation in these small, no-frills buildings. Thus, there was a broad gulf between the intentions indicated on architectural drawings, and their implementation in the field.

Compounding the lack of space in immigration halls, the facilities themselves failed to provide the desired segregation due to their minimal construction and lack of finishing. In 1896, more than a decade after the completion of the Calgary hall, the agent there begged the deputy minister in Ottawa to see his "way clear to furnish eight cheap doors" for the stalls in the latrine. You "can readily understand," he wrote, "how very disgusting it is not to have a door to each W.C. compartment, the entrance to the male & female W.C.s are so very close to each other, that men will often unintentionally enter the females W.C. which is anything but decent, when the compartments have no doors."[44] The early Prairie immigration halls of the Dominion government in fact were built quickly and cheaply. Structures would be bid on and built the same spring that settlers were to begin arriving; minimal site preparation, green wood, and a lack of furnishings, finishing, and amenities were typical.

Indeed, getting the halls built by the Department of Public Works was one thing; getting them furnished was yet another, as we have witnessed with the west-coast quarantine stations. This problem was exacerbated by a general neglect of western-Canadian infrastructure by civil servants in Ottawa. Officials stationed in remote towns, and even the Winnipeg commissioner, found it could be extremely difficult to get basic work done or supplies purchased. For instance, it was necessary in 1902 for the commissioner to write Public Works complaining how that department had, in Calgary, "a year or so ago erected an addition for an office but have not yet provided our Agent and Caretaker with a desk and office chair."[45] Half a year after the new Strathcona hall was completed, a local official reported that it had "not as yet been made ready for the accommodation of settlers … furnished with a cooking range, adequate utensils and furniture, fuel &c.; and, if its management is to reflect credit on the Department, it is absolutely essential that a smart janitor shall be employed."[46] While the necessity of these turnkey measures seems obvious, Ottawa lagged behind in accomplishing these basic tasks. Things were made more complicated by the bureaucratic structure. Upon the completion of the new Regina hall in 1904, correspondence among multiple departments and locations was needed to determine exactly what furnishings would be provided by Public Works. Cooking and heating stoves, various tables, window blinds, and an office chair were in its purview; but the immigration branch had to find its own suppliers for dining chairs, benches, bedsteads, mattresses, bedding, mirrors, and cooking utensils, and to pay for these out of its own operating budget.[47]

The Dominion government's neglect of its own infrastructure could reach levels of absurdity. A new, one-storey immigration hall was built in Prince Albert in 1892. In 1895, a travelling inspector pointed out that there was "very little in the way of furniture" at the hall, only "a few benches, a small table … and some pails and kettles." There was no outbuilding in which to store baggage, fuel, or storm windows, and because of this the latter were "certain to be broken." Moreover, access to the hall was over "a large ditch." Nothing had

changed by 1900 when a Dominion Lands official reported on the Prince Albert building, which by that time was "settling into the ground" on its wooden sills. Astonishingly, he reiterates that the hall "can only be directly reached by … crossing a gully of stagnant water, now 18 inches deep and 8 feet wide. Two round trees have been thrown across this gully and the only way of reaching the shed is by walking or crawling over these trees, a difficult task even in daylight and almost impossible after dark, which is the time at which the train arrives." By 1902, still no outbuilding had been provided, and the firewood had "invariably been stolen."[48] Back in Regina, a decade earlier, the local immigration agent similarly had requested an outbuilding to prevent the theft of fuel, as well as "to save the main building from being used to saw and split wood in during wet weather."[49] Later, in Craik, the regional Saskatchewan inspector requested for the third time that locks be put on the doors of the outhouses to ensure that the toilets be "kept clean and sanitary for the absolute benefit of emigrants, and not be generally used by section men, and other people as has been the case."[50] Ottawa departments were slow to act on these requests, and continually lost money on capital investments due to the lack of security and maintenance at Prairie immigration halls. In practice, of course, it was the immigrants themselves, and also the immigration agents, who suffered hardships and indignities from the lack of furniture and landscaping.

Most of the immigration halls remained without public utilities until well into the twentieth century. For much of its life, for instance, the Calgary building lacked water, sewage, and electrical connections, despite their local availability and repeated attempts to convince Ottawa of their necessity. In 1892, a land agent reported that the building "is not as comfortable or as convenient as it should be, as Public Works Department sent their local architect to look over the premises some two months ago. I asked for the electric light and for the water to be put into the building … but up to this time nothing has been done." Local newspapers and prominent citizens weighed in, trying to embarrass the Dominion government into acting.[51] It was to little avail: the Department judged the cost of connecting to the sewer and water works to be prohibitive, while electric light was seen as an unnecessary luxury. Ultimately, due to the unsanitary condition related to its lack of utilities, the building came close to being condemned by the City of Calgary in 1910. The municipality relented when the Dominion government promised to replace it with a brand-new structure; the Department of Public Works slowly got around to doing that some three years later.

Sometimes, local immigration officials took maintenance matters into their own hands, such as when the Calgary agent had the interior of the hall kalsomined and painted in 1896. He wrote a somewhat apologetic but glowing description of the cleaned-up building to his superiors in Ottawa, as if he was concerned they might not approve the expense. Local visitors, he assured the deputy minister, "all speak highly" of the renovations, while "the immigrants express their delight at having such a building to come to, & they do not forget to speak of the Government's kindness for providing such good accommodation." The interior walls had been rendered in a "stone color" with two shades of grey trim and "black-painted finger plates on each side of each door & each room numbered in paint."[52] Eleven years old at the time of this interior facelift, the Calgary immigration hall would be required to serve twenty more with few other upgrades.

Unfortunately, the Calgary agent does not describe an exterior paint scheme. The evidence suggests that, at some point in the late-nineteenth century, the Dominion government settled on white walls and roofs (when the latter were of wooden shingles), all accented with green trim. It

was a variation on the appearance of Hudson's Bay Company trading posts, which formerly had been the most significant Prairie landmarks, painted all white and usually with black or red trim. Moreover, it possibly drew on the American tradition of painting hotels white to signify places for travellers to find a bed and other amenities. By featuring this standardized colour palette, these public buildings distinguished themselves as places for immigrants "to come to." The standard colours made the immigration halls easy to recognize at each stop along their journey. The white buildings would have been highly visible against the yellows, browns, and greens of the Prairie, or even under the starshine of the blackest nights, when immigrants stepped down from the train. Needful immigrants would be grateful to find the safety of the halls so readily.

In general, though, the Dominion government seemed not overly concerned with the aesthetics of its Prairie immigration halls. At most, it could be said that the semi-standard designs deployed up to 1905 all assumed an understated Georgian style of architecture, with their broad and symmetrical front facades of repeating bays, symmetrically-placed entrances, and horizontal cornices and roof planes to cap the composition. The earlier halls appeared in what we might call a simple Georgian vernacular popular with Canadian builders. The more substantial later design, which received the classical flourish on the central dormer, can be formally associated with a learned Georgian-revival architecture. As a classical style that could be achieved with minimal decoration, the Georgian was an appropriate – if somewhat outdated – choice. Its lineage connected the immigration halls to an earlier period of British imperial expansion and colonial development in the Canadas. The choice of style reflected the expectation that public buildings would represent order and deliver a modicum of national and imperial culture to western Canada. Even more broadly, Canadian architecture of immigration drew on well-established traditions in the design of public institutions. Architectural historian Annmarie Adams writes that "[s]chool and hospital architects used classical details and symmetrical planning to bestow their institutions with a dignified community presence."[53] The designers of the Prairie immigration halls shared similar means and ends, and worked with familiar architectural idioms and planning techniques, even as they developed a uniquely Canadian institutional typology.

INSTITUTIONAL PRECEDENTS FOR PRAIRIE IMMIGRATION HALLS

In developing a new building typology that was meant to house immigrants overnight or longer, government officials drew on a wide range of institutional precedents. Nineteenth-century reform institutions, such as schools, hospitals, or prisons, were designed so that their inmates were categorized, organized, and edified by the architecture itself: different grades or genders, different risks of contagion or class, different races or required levels of security, could all be sorted out spatially and expressed in classical idioms of order and decoration. Exploiting adjacencies, sight lines, controlled circulation, and spatial hierarchies, these buildings permitted nurses, teachers, guards, or other caretakers to survey and control their charges in an effective manner.[54] As we saw in chapter 2, hospital wards were arranged with surveillance and efficiency in mind. The most apposite Canadian reform institutions, which appeared as a reverse corollary to immigration buildings, were the residential and industrial schools meant to effect the assimilation of aboriginal peoples. The "Indian Residential Schools," like many schools at the time, were designed according to a binary or mirrored plan, with separate entrances, staircases, corridors, and classrooms to ensure the separation of boys and girls, brothers and sisters. Moreover, they were isolated from aboriginal communities to enforce the separation of the children from their families and traditions, and to ensure the pupils' total immersion in the western culture promulgated by these institutions.[55]

The design ideals of reform institutions are reflected in Canada's immigration halls in the way they centralized access and sorted populations. From check-in at the agent's desk, just inside the main entrance, newcomers were distributed to dormitories or chambers based on gender, family status, or ethnicity. Matrons and caretakers were entrusted with sorting, monitoring, and modelling proper behaviour for the immigrants under their charge. Inside Prairie immigration halls, inmates would be isolated from outside populations, and would leave rejuvenated and well-informed, prepared to return to — or newly enter — society. But the immigration halls were not reform institutions in any strict sense of the term. The government never aspired to make them into total institutions, in which immigrants would be improved, cured, or even assimilated. Newcomers — that is, settlers — were perceived and treated differently than aboriginal peoples.

At best, immigrants might be exposed in the halls to advice and expectations regarding the modes and manners — the practices — needed for everyday survival in Canada. Their use of the halls was optional, and immigrants could come and go as they pleased. Prairie immigration halls thus manifested a soft mode of reform, an assimilation-in-passing more akin to that made architectural in Progressive-era institutions like settlement homes, vocational schools, or YMCAs.[56] Social control was a central concern of these late-nineteenth-century institutions, but necessarily was indirect and reliant upon the choices and self-regulation of the clients. Individuals had to be encouraged to enter these spaces to take advantage of the reformatory services offered — skills training, but also education in cultural mores. Architectural design and the daily activities led by representatives of these urban institutions combined to project an image of modern society. A similar kind of mild reform of immigrant subjectivities began when they crossed the threshold of the Prairie immigration hall, were assigned to rooms, and apprised of the house rules. As Chilton has highlighted, migration "involved a series of situations in which an individual's sense of identity might be challenged and reformed, situations in which appropriate 'Canadian' norms of behaviour were conveyed and reinforced."[57]

During their stays in Dominion government immigration halls, immigrants' behaviours were governed by posted regulations: "Clothing must not be washed in the bedrooms, nor hung in the windows to dry. All slops or wash water must be emptied into the sink and not thrown from the windows. Occupants must eat their meals in the DINING ROOM and not in the SLEEPING QUARTERS. DRUNKENNESS will not be tolerated on or about the premises."[58] The site and the appearance of the buildings would be preserved by controlling inmates' behaviours, belongings, and detritus. Spaces would be defined by function, which was perhaps seen by officials as a necessary corrective to peasant habits formed through the inhabitation of vernacular one- or two-room abodes. The building would not be defaced by laundry lines, widely believed to be an eyesore and a marker of class; trash would not be pitched from windows as in filthy nineteenth-century cities and towns. (Even so, as late as 1907, Winnipeg's City Health Officer lodged an official complaint regarding inmates throwing refuse from the windows of the immigration hall there.[59]) Another poster, approved by Ottawa to be printed in English, French, and German, outlined the "rules for the government of the building" in Strathcona. Water, fuel, and light would be provided "free of charge," although "occupants are expected to render assistance in keeping the building and premises orderly

and clean." The local officials reserved the right to "order the removal of any person declining to render such assistance or who may be otherwise guilty of objectionable conduct."[60] The latter remained undefined, but no doubt included inebriation. By these instructions, the hall was asserted as a space secure from potential misuse, unruliness, or immorality.

The regulations and operations of Prairie immigration halls shared affinities with other kinds of institutions that provided temporary accommodations for indigents and travellers. These included hotels, police stations, municipal lodging houses, workhouses and poorhouses, and the bunkhouses of resource-extraction and construction camps. Nineteenth-century North America was characterized by large numbers of mobile persons, especially men, some of them recent arrivals from the Old Country, some of them not. Cities and towns experimented with different solutions to control and shelter these transient populations, which spiked during recessions and when seasonal work was unavailable. Of primary importance, writes hotel historian Andrew Sandoval-Strausz, "was a desire on the part of communities to avoid having to support outsiders." As the number of outsiders increased with immigration, labour mobility, and improvements to transportation networks, "hotels replaced a household model of hospitality [inns or taverns] with an institutional model" characterized by managerial efficiency. The hotel typology's combination of open public spaces for dining and socializing, with the cellular plans of bedroom wings, certainly inspired Prairie immigration halls. Other aspects of hotel culture also seem to have influenced Dominion government practices at the halls. For instance, immigration agents escorting newcomers on the train, or meeting them on the station platform, replaced the "runners" hired by hotels to direct travellers to their businesses, and immigration-hall ledgers mirrored the guest registers used in hotels, asking arrivals to answer most of the same questions: name, number in party, and place of origin.[61]

However, not all travellers were able or willing to pay for room and board at a hotel. From the 1850s to the 1890s, the most common form of temporary free lodging was found at the police station. As revealed by urban historian Eric Monkkonen, "police departments regularly provided a social service that from our perspective seems bizarrely out of character – they provided bed and, sometimes, board for homeless poor people, tramps." These men "found accommodations ranging in quality from floors in hallways to clean bunkrooms."[62] They entered late in the evening and left early in the morning, so police stations offered only the most minimal amount of institutional care.

Toward the end of the century, social reformers became critical of the no-strings-attached nature of "police lodging." Soon replacing it was the municipal lodging house, which, historian Todd Depastino explains, "entailed a rehabilitative component," in which good hygiene and a strong work ethic would be modelled for inmates. The municipally operated free hostel

> would open its doors in the early evening; inmates would register, strip, shower, have their clothes fumigated, and be led to rows of cots; in the early morning, inmates would arise, dress, work in the wood yard, stone pile, or on road repair before being served a breakfast of bread and coffee and released to the streets. To prevent freeloading, the lodging house would allow inmates to return for one or two additional nights only.[63]

Sleeping arrangements were dormitory style, with narrow beds or stacked bunks. It is worth noting that these institutions put into effect a disinfection and fumigation regime analogous to that seen in Canadian quarantine stations, but here designed to be performed within a single urban edifice. Rootless tramps, like immigrants, were stigmatized as infectious and unclean. The police station and the municipal lodging house were temporary solutions to shelter large numbers of travellers – the basic requirement of Prairie immigration halls. The rehabilitative aspect of the municipal lodging house was necessarily partial, like the assimilative potential of the immigration halls. As precedents, however, these urban examples were limited. The populations of police and municipal lodgings were limited to white men of working age – that is, those with unrestricted mobility – while Prairie immigration halls had to serve multi-ethnic migrants, women, and whole families, in addition to single male transients.

Workhouses (also known as almshouses or poorhouses in different contexts) were more-inclusive institutions. Operating throughout the period of this study, these were last resorts for the indigent to ensure their basic survival when jobless, indebted, or incapacitated due to age or infirmity. Like the Prairie immigration halls, they were meant to be "a temporary refuge," and "inmates could enter or leave almshouses" with ease, since this "was not a penal institution." However, social-welfare historian Michael Katz notes that poorhouses "required inmates to work off the cost of their care." The inmates often did "a great deal of the routine work," such as cooking, cleaning, gardening, and nursing others.[64] The buildings typically incorporated extensive work yards and gardens to allow for this payment in kind. At the Prairie halls, immigrants were usually expected to take care of themselves on a day-to-day basis, but their stays were not monetized in exchange for a certain amount of labour. Poorhouses were stigmatized as places for the lowest of the low; in Toronto in the 1870s, residents who had immigrated a year or more previously applied to the immigration agent at the depot for relief, so that they could avoid "the only other institution available to them: the workhouse."[65] The Dominion government strove to evade the negative reputation of the poorhouse in the development of its immigration architecture, which represented merely a brief leg up for newcomers, where recidivists would not be tolerated. The Prairie immigration halls were meant as a first resort, rather than a last.

The shortcomings of North American workhouses were identified by numerous critics after about 1850. It was argued that the underfunding and mismanagement of these institutions, and a loss of control over the institutional space by untrained and outnumbered staff, were to blame for the chaos found within them. In particular, these institutions were castigated for failing to classify, sort, and segregate different ages, genders, races, and classes of indigent – even though the buildings themselves were typically designed to effect strict, often diagrammatically symmetrical, separations in plan, and to represent absolute order in their classical facades. Reformers especially targeted the blurring of gender and ethnic boundaries, such as the indiscriminate mixing of women and men, which inevitably led to morally alarming consequences; they feared for the destitute white widows and children forced to share space with racial others. In the view of these critics, the spaces of institutions ought to reflect the social divisions and identity formations found outside their walls.[66]

These critiques of the workhouse help to explain the overriding concerns for gender and ethnic separation – to be overseen by attentive agents and caretakers – that characterize the design of Prairie immigration halls. In fact, we find a similar sense of moral alarm about mixing in various reports from the chaperones of group migrations. One such representative of London's East End Immigration Society had his views of reception infrastructure published in the Canadian press. When the migrants in his charge "land in the country they are herded together in a way that you would not herd the vilest that walk the street ... there are sheds indeed, but all the married people have to sleep without the least pretence of partition. Is this decent?" Though they "may be poor," he avers, and have little choice but to "remain in these sheds," they nonetheless "have the instincts of modesty and honor." The deputy minister is quoted in the article, denying all, and stating that there "is a distinct separation of sexes in every immigration building." Moreover, he adds for good measure, "Canada has done more for immigrants on arrival than any Government on the continent."[67] Nevertheless, further reports were submitted to Ottawa by Father Morin, a Catholic priest who led several Québécois parties that were relocating to Alberta in the late 1890s. "The Immigration Hall in [Strathcona] is absolutely unfitted to receive and lodge the families," he writes. There were only two rooms in the one-storey structure built in 1892, and these were open to each other, so that they could be "heated by a single stove placed in the centre of the place." As a result, "English, Galicians, French, Russians, Belgians, Doukhobors, all are obliged to live together and cook in common." Morin singled out in particular "a Russian family" residing in the hall, who were

unworthy to appear in the midst of well brought up people; the woman especially knows nothing at all of the laws of decency; my settlers are not bigots but I assure you that I was ashamed to leave young people, young women, even mothers of families in presence of such nudity... of such a spectacle. To be precise that woman (without evil intention I am sure) went to the door, raised her clothing and cleaned herself of vermin in the presence of everybody. It seems to me that such a thing should not happen.[68]

Immigration officials also expressed analogous critiques of the inadequate sorting mechanisms of the early immigration halls. For instance, in his assessments of the same Strathcona hall in 1894 and 1895, the travelling inspector noted that it lacked many basic necessities, including architectural separation: "men, women and children are mixed up without any chance of privacy," and therefore "the better class of immigrants do not use the building." In his recommendations, the inspector proposed doubling the size of the hall, and delineated an architectural program that would "provide separate rooms for 1. Families and females – 2. men without families – 3. foreigners – and 4. Dining or living room."[69] In this recommendation we witness the beginning of a subtle shift, from a dualistic segregation of men and women, to sorting by both gender roles and ethnicity. "Foreigners" are considered apart from women, families, and even single men, the implication being that only well-bred British immigrants rated or required separation by gender and age.

This kind of ethnic distinction was seen elsewhere at the time. A distinctively North American, perhaps even Canadian, form of mass housing for men was the bunkhouse common in work camps. While a new arrival would not yet have been familiar with these quasi-institutions, it is reasonable to assume that many of the immigration agents, land guides, and caretakers had first- or second-hand experience of camps. Bunkhouses were simple, square or rectangular, one-storey dormitories, often windowless, crowded with two-tier bunks and sodden work clothes drying around a central stove. While the camps were architecturally minimalistic, it is their spatialized social structure that is of interest in comparison to Prairie immigration halls. According to a famous study of "bunkhouse men" conducted during the first decade of the twentieth century, "always in evidence" was the division of the camps into "two distinct groups of workers … the 'whites' and the 'foreigners.'" The latter was "a generic term" applied to all non-English-speakers who toiled in hard labour roles. By extension, the former thus referred to the "race" of English-speaking skilled labourers.[70]

Historians have demonstrated that a binary such as this was not so black and white. It was complicated by ethnic and linguistic diversity and differential access to whiteness, as well as by the class consciousness of skilled versus unskilled, and wage versus contract, labour. For example, in her study of gender and ethnicity on the frontier, Sheila McManus demonstrated that, initially, "race was the overriding factor" dividing settlers from the First Nations inhabitants of the Prairies. But as soon as the population of European arrivals grew, the category of "whiteness" would be "subdivided and ranked," just "as the Canadian government had done in its views of immigrants."[71] Indeed, an ethnolinguistic differentiation between so-called British and foreign immigrants was always manifest in how the Dominion government articulated its vision of desirable and undesirable settlers. As Chilton argued decisively, in Canadian immigration discourse, "ethnicity was classed."[72]

Even when it actively began to encourage continental and eastern-European immigration in the late 1890s, the government maintained a binary distinction among classes of immigrant which extended to the design and usage of its immigration halls. Internal government correspondence of the period is shot through with the contrast between the British and the foreign. Commissioner J. Obed Smith nicely summed up the overall tone, addressing the deputy minister in 1902 on the status of halls in Winnipeg and the west: "I take it for granted that your desire is that the British immigration shall have first preference, if there be an opportunity of giving a preference in the way of accommodation etc." In another letter between the two men, regarding the condition of the original immigration hall in Regina, Smith expressed the prejudice architecturally: "The old shack which is there now should be set on fire immediately, and a new building erected at least the same size as the one which was erected at Saskatoon or Dauphin but with a somewhat different internal arrangement to accommodate the different classes of people. There should be separate entrances so that the foreigners may be kept apart."[73] Within a year, the new building was erected in Regina (see Figure 3.19). Ironically, though, the Regina hall was a five-bay design with a sole central entrance and staircase; its shared common areas demonstrate that precise and symmetrical architectural segregation was unrealistic in small immigration halls, even when explicitly demanded by the commissioner.

As the inclusion of smaller family rooms became more common in Prairie immigration halls after the turn of the century, sex separation of the dormitories was less prominent in the discourse. In practice, of course, such separation had always been fraught. Winnipeg commissioner William T. McCreary, Smith's predecessor in the role, wrote of the "model" Dauphin design when it was under construction in the spring of 1898: "I think the building is very well laid out at present, although the divisions for men and women will not be strictly adhered to" due to the demographic fluctuations among inhabitants. Because single female travellers represented a small portion of the overall need for accommodations, they could be grouped in one of the smaller family rooms. Large numbers of single male travellers remained a central concern, though, as did the prejudices of certain immigrants who deigned to share spaces with cultural others. McCreary claimed to "have known English-speaking people ... to go without food, preferring that to cooking with a gang of Galicians around the stove."[74] Eventually, architectural drawings from the Department of Public Works would idealize a different binary: British men separate from foreign men in two dormitories within the same building (see Figures 4.21 and 4.22). But in small immigration halls with a limited number

of rooms, strict ethnic segregation was no more practicable than gender separation.

One solution, which began to appear in the final years of the 1890s, when central European immigration ramped up, was to house British immigrants in different buildings entirely. The situation of Edmonton's various halls serves to illustrate this approach. The first two immigration halls here were erected in Strathcona, the village south of the river, where the railroad connected to Calgary and the CPR main line. The second hall went up in 1899, when the first was egregiously overcrowded; being newer and more commodious, it would be reserved at first for English-speaking settlers. But even these new accommodations were insufficient to cope with the rush of homesteaders seeking free land in the region. To relieve overcrowding at the two Strathcona buildings, and to coincide with the completion of a new bridge, the "town" began "discussing the project of putting a building on the north side of the river at the disposal of ... the better classes of settlers." With two sites in Strathcona and Edmonton, ethnic distinctions could be distributed topographically, seeing different "classes" of settler—which in immigration-branch correspondence always referred to ethnicity rather than economic class—separated by the river valley. The Dominion government concurred, at first renting a building north of the river, then building its first Edmonton hall a few years later (see Figure 3.18). These would both be made available to the "better class" of immigrant. Characteristically, landscaping around the rented hostel was lacking, as indicated in a report from the Winnipeg commissioner: "a rough sidewalk [should] be put in down from the track to the building. At the present time there is no means of getting there except ploughing through the mud, which may not be taken very much to heart by the foreign speaking element, but the English-speaking people who occupy this new building exclusively should not be compelled to put up with that kind of thing."[75]

The language distinction, here reinforced by a dehumanizing contrast between "element" and "people," reveals a clear ethnic hierarchy made manifest in the architecture of immigration.

Thus, efforts toward the containment of difference are most apparent in the ethnic separation afforded by operating multiple buildings in the same town. As will be seen in the next chapter, a similar spatial segregation was achieved in Winnipeg. While officials in larger towns were able to contemplate the separation of ethnic classes in different buildings, social divisions were less clear in the small, unitary structures typical of most Prairie locations. Architectural plans and correspondence indicate that the government was concerned to maintain segregation. But these design ideals could not prevent social mixing in embryonic frontier spaces, especially in halls built with only a single entrance, kitchen, and sitting room. The comings and goings of immigrants were fluid and related to diverse parameters like train schedules and weather patterns. At any particular moment, immigration halls may have been inhabited by British or "foreign" men, women, or children. All were inmates of the same institution.

The architecture of institutions produces an inside and an outside, so that inmates can be differentiated and removed from other populations. Even before it could sort and distribute men and women, whites and others, to their proper sleeping and eating areas, the Dominion government needed to establish who was allowed access to Prairie immigration halls. Who, exactly, was an immigrant? As with all early social-welfare programs, distinctions had to be made between deserving and undeserving recipients of government aid. The rules posted in three languages began by circumscribing who could receive the supports of the institution. "Notice. This hall is intended for the accommodation of immigrants lately arrived in the Country, and for none others."[76] However, "lately" is left undefined; and eastern Canadians

relocating to the Prairies received the same privileges as anyone from eastern Europe. Nonetheless, officials in Ottawa regularly remonstrated with local agents and caretakers to ensure that they satisfactorily restricted free accommodation in the halls to genuine immigrants. The Calgary agent received an unequivocal explanation from the secretary of the department in 1892:

> I understand ... that the immigration shed has been used in the past by people who are not strictly speaking immigrants. The intention of the Government in furnishing an immigration shed is that the building shall be used merely by people who have just arrived in the country, and are without the means of paying for shelter in a hotel while they are looking up homesteads for themselves, or employment, as the case may be. If the shed is being used by any other class, then it is being put to use which was never intended. I shall be glad to have a report from you on the subject as soon as possible.[77]

There would be no flexibility in the expenditure of government resources; no one but admissible inmates would benefit from the protection and shelter of the state institution.

Despite the surety of this missive, the realities on the ground were inconstant. The immigration hall in Calgary appeared on Ottawa's radar again four years later. During the recession of the early 1890s, when there were fewer immigrants arriving in the city, the minister had made a temporary deal with the mayor to allow charity cases to stay at the hall, "on requisition from the Chairman of the Police and Relief Committee." It seems that the hall served as overflow for police-station lodging. The caretaker of the hall, though, took this as sanction to shelter any needful person. The Winnipeg commissioner was quick to dispel the notion that it might be permissible to admit anyone "other than bona fide immigrants." The Calgary caretaker's "practice of taking upon himself to admit strangers is highly objectionable, and I am to say that at the time the immigration work was brought under the control of this Department [of the Interior], it was found that a similar state of things existed in the Winnipeg Building, and we had some difficulty in putting a stop to it." Undoubtedly, this slippage in gatekeeping existed at many of the halls. Though he took action to correct the caretaker's ways, the Calgary agent's response to the commissioner is instructive, for it pushes the boundaries delimiting the function of the immigration halls. In addition to sheltering "bona fide immigrants," he writes, past practice had been to allow admission to men "going to and returning from work … in the lumber woods to the West." With the CPR providing "a nominal rate" to these workers, the immigration sheds were "used for lodging both ways, by those parties, and to that extent the interests of Immigration were promoted, as much as they are by their ordinary use." The agent proposed the continuation of this practice. Furthermore, he proposed, surely "no fault can be found" with sheltering those females "who have come down from the North, looking for positions as Domestic servants." Once these categories of guests were accounted for in the accommodations register of the Calgary hall, "there will be found several who might possibly be best termed as 'indigents,' a percentage might probably be termed the 'tramp' pure and simple."[78] These men, henceforth, would be turned away. Perhaps surprisingly, given the officially stated intent of the immigration halls, head-office approval was given to shelter the domestic servants and the labourers in transit; although not strictly speaking new arrivals, they nevertheless were deemed worthy of government aid and – especially in the case of single female jobseekers – its paternal protection.

Notwithstanding these internal debates over the designation "immigrant," many settlers continued to believe that they could return to the immigration halls whenever they happened to be in town. The Red Deer agent complained in 1894 that, because his "office duties" were located elsewhere and there was no caretaker installed at the hall, "persons not immigrants were in the habit of going into the building and sleeping there without his leave." Upon investigation, a North-West Mounted Police (NWMP) sergeant reported that these "were parties who had previously slept there as Immigrants, but had taken land in vicinity, and on coming into Town, to save expense had gone to the Immigration Building."[79] Likewise, the Edmonton agent in 1899 informed his superiors that "when Galicians come in from Edna they still expect to find shelter in the immigration Shed, and often force themselves in at nights." The following year he reported that "about 300 men" working in construction camps "have been coming back at intervals, and invariably would stop in the building two or three weeks … They had no money, therefore could not go to a boarding house and from their appearance I question whether a lodging house would take them in." On another occasion, two "Galician" women with their ten children had been lodging at the immigration hall the entire winter when it was discovered that their husbands had abandoned them there and returned to the Old Country.[80] Similar rule-bending practices were engaged in by other local representatives of the immigration branch. How the government chose to respond – with flexibility, or with outright bans on those no longer considered immigrants – depended greatly, at different times and places, on the personalities and politics of local and national civil servants, the expectations of the immigrants themselves, the economic situation, and just how busy it was at the immigration hall in question.

Just as early social-welfare programs in North America struggled to distinguish between the deserving and undeserving poor, Dominion government immigration officials strove to ensure that the protections and free accommodations of the halls were restricted to "bona fide immigrants." However, despite ever-present critiques of government spending – especially spending on any kind of social-welfare program – there were incentives for the authorities to act with kindness and flexibility toward new arrivals and former immigrants. Offering accommodations to poor farmers and labourers deflected requests for relief at local charities and churches, and discouraged folks from camping in the streets and empty lots of a town. As well, government agents and caretakers could set the tone for newcomers and others, modelling good citizenship. Providing government-welfare supports enacted a gift-giving relationship in which the giver could expect something in return. A sense of gratitude or indebtedness to the government might motivate an immigrant to become a good citizen or, more immediately at least, encourage them to stay in Canada and contribute to the country's population and economic growth, rather than returning home or remigrating to the United States.

The amount of indebtedness or gratitude felt by new Canadians is impossible to track. However, a collection of testimonials penned in 1905 by guests at the Edmonton immigration hall is suggestive of the ways that migrants may have responded to government institutional supports. The testimonials were gathered by the Edmonton agent as assurance to his superiors that the hall was well managed. As he explained:

> complaints have been made by some of the English families that came in last spring and took advantage of staying in the Hall 3 to 4 months, and then went on the homestead and stayed there till fall, then came back and wanted the same privilege which I could not allow, for if I had granted this privilege I would have been obliged to take in all that would apply … A number of single men from

England have also kicked because we would not give them their meals, free, whilst staying in the Hall, and they have also asked to have their boots blackened. The more you do for this kind of settler, the more they want. We have had settlers from Scotland, Ireland, Germany, France, Denmark and Switzerland, as well as from all parts of the United States and Canada, and all express themselves delighted at the good accommodation provided free.

The complaining class of immigrants with no sense of gratitude – in this case, English greenhorns with a sense of white privilege – were a continual source of frustration for Dominion government immigration agents.

In contrast, two more-experienced English itinerants, both of whom had spent time trying to settle in Australia, compared the infrastructure found there to the hall in Edmonton: "having seen a few immigration buildings I can truthfully say that this is as clean as any I've seen anywhere," wrote one who had spent fifteen years Down Under. His friend agreed, stating that the Edmonton hall "compares and exceeds any I have been in"; that the "chief official here is a courteous gentleman not sparing himself if he can by any means help the new arrival"; and the matron "a kind hearted motherly woman." Another guest went further, calling her "a good christian woman, doing her best to make all newcomers feel at home." A Missouri couple were surprised that the free accommodations at the hall "were better a great deal than what we expected," their preconceptions perhaps coloured by the reputation of other North American institutions for the destitute or transient. Instead, they found the immigration hall "pretty well filled with a respectable class of people, who appear to be contented and happy over the courteous treatment accorded them." A man from Lancashire, who had arrived in Edmonton ten months earlier, reflected on the intrinsic purpose of the government's immigration infrastructure: the "few days I spent there gave me a chance to husband my resources." The parents of a family of seven from St Louis wrote to "cheerfully recommend" that all migrants "take advantage of the many privileges this temporary free home offers," including its comfortable and clean beds, its kitchen and utensils, and its "reading room." Since the government agent was "a veritable encyclopedia of valuable knowledge … [we] believe many a family of small means has steered clear of shipwreck … For all practical purposes the emigration hall is a training school to the new arrival." Finally, some Iowans declared that they "would advise intending settlers" to rest at the hall, which was neat and clean and "good enough for any respectable temperance people." They concluded with an expression of gratitude: "we highly appreciate the privileges and accommodations the Government offers to people coming into Canada."[81] New arrivals who made use of the immigration halls recognized the educational and recuperative benefits represented by these uniquely Canadian institutions, and were sure to credit the Dominion government for providing them.

Canadian immigration buildings therefore lie somewhere between the hard reform institutions and the soft, behaviour-modelling spaces of the nineteenth century. At Prairie immigration halls there were aspirations toward strict control over gender and ethnic mixing among a trapped audience. But the guests at these institutions were not incarcerated. Certainly, many newcomers had little choice but to take advantage of free accommodation, and were subject to hierarchical sorting and institutional regulations, such as set times each evening when the stoves were extinguished and visitors were required to leave. Outside of these official impositions, however, migrants were free to come and go during their stay, and their stays were of short duration. Inmates could cook their own

food, mostly maintain their family groupings, let children romp in the hallways, go out job hunting, and move on when they were ready. The contingencies and practices with which migrants actually occupied these institutions are explored more fully in the next section.

SPACES FOR IMMIGRANTS

A Ukrainian memoirist who migrated to Canada in 1900 provides an apt metaphor to describe his observations of the immigration hall he stayed in: "There I found a great commotion, like that of bees in a beehive. The men were unpacking their boxes of clothing while the women, having sorted out the linen for their brood, went into their rooms to change. They washed the dirty linen in the hall or outside in tubs or pails. Others groomed their children."[82] Normally quotidian activities were condensed into the first moments on solid ground after a long journey. Another man, writing about his family's 1902 passage from eastern Europe to northern Manitoba, compiled a specific and detailed depiction of the 1890 immigration hall in Winnipeg, our only real information regarding the interior of this particular structure:

After four days the train arrived in Winnipeg. A man who spoke Ukrainian, met them on the train. He told them that he was going to lead them to the immigration building, where they could rest up before going farther.

It was a large wooden building consisting of assorted sizes of compartments to fit various sizes of families. These compartments had triple decked wooden bunks without any bedding. There were stoves for cooking meals and facilities for washing. Occasionally people came to the building selling vegetables like cabbage and potatoes. Most people were happy to have some cooked food, a change from the dry brown bread.

To the weary travelers it seemed like a good place for a quiet rest. But not so. As soon as it got dark, a bloodthirsty attack was on in full force. Bedbugs and lice! In the morning, the women were busy shaking out the bedding, changing and washing clothing to clean out the infestation … There was another immigration building in Dauphin. This one was not infested.[83]

This account introduces several motifs common to migrants' recollections of their stays in Prairie immigration halls. These include the opportunity to unpack and freshen up; the rudimentary nature of hard beds and communal cooking; the halls as spaces of female domestic labour; the presence of outside visitors, often selling something; of inside visitors out for blood; and the variability of conditions from one hall to the next. Of course, immigrant perceptions of the halls were contingent on many factors, from the physical conditions previously experienced on ships and trains, to family health and resources, individual expectations and capacities, and the maintenance and operation of the buildings themselves.

The basic experience could be similar even in the most rudimentary form of official accommodation. One woman recalled the spatial practices needed to survive: "after we arrived in Wetaskiwin we stayed in the immigration tent. There were several families already in the tent so there was no privacy. Each family squatted in a corner, made beds all over the floor. There was some sort of stove to cook on. It must have been an awful worry for the mothers with two or three dozen children stampeding around."[84] Sometimes the built infrastructure of the halls was little different from the canvas accommodation. When a group of 340 destitute Jewish refugees arrived in Winnipeg from Russia in summer 1882, they were sheltered long-term at the original immigration shed, by then superseded, but still standing empty and neglected down at the Forks. Since all the furniture had been moved to the new hall by the CPR station, it was like camping out in the building. The Winnipeg Jewish community of eight families cooked the first meal for the group and organized local charity support; the town council provided outdoor relief; others helped by hiring the newcomers for odd jobs. Some of the refugees went to work on the rails, others became peddlers or opened small shops. About two dozen families endured overwintering in the unheated, uninsulated, and dilapidated sheds.[85]

In contrast, the stays of most migrants were brief, matter-of-fact, expedient, and not necessarily an emergency. Stopping at the spanking-new Brandon immigration hall in 1883, a young English labourer wrote home to his parents: "Here it does not cost me anything for lodging, and I can board myself for about $2 a week, whereas the cheapest boarding house in town is $5 a week." For him, as for many single male travellers in search of their fortune, the halls were not so different from the police stations and municipal lodging houses favoured by transients at the time. After the immigration hall in Brandon, this lad ended up in the homosocial bunkhouses of an Alberta railway-construction camp (where a few months later he succumbed to typhoid and perished).[86] Another pair of English adventurers got to Medicine Hat in 1888 and, according to an interview conducted with one of them, "we went to the immigration hall … [and] stayed there until we got employment."[87] For these mobile working men, the halls were practical, but seemed nothing out of the ordinary, given their likely familiarity with the compatible forms of mass accommodation available to their class.

During the day, typically, the prairie immigration halls were perceived as feminine, or family, spaces of domesticity that offered social supports such as shared child care and conversation. Participants and observers often describe women cooking or washing clothes while children played in kitchens and other rooms of the immigration halls (Figure 3.20). Husbands were expected to be out hunting for jobs, land, goods, or contacts from the Old Country. Because of this, though, a woman's experience of the halls could also be one of isolation in a foreign land. One woman recalled her voyage to Canada as part of a group of seven Ukrainian families who arrived in Strathcona the autumn of 1899. After two nights at the immigration hall, five of the families left to join friends.

3.20 Interior view of communal kitchen and dining area, Edmonton immigration hall. This photo was taken in the area marked "outside kitchen" on Figure 3.16. The archival citation identifies the woman serving soup as the building's matron. While women and children predominate in this photograph, two men also join in the meal.

The two remaining husbands went out, and for "a whole week they tramped around, hungry and on foot looking in forest, sand, and swamp for home-steads, but they couldn't find any good land." Then, the other family discovered friends nearby and left to join them; her husband continued searching for days to find friends or transportation to the Ukrainian settlements down river. "I was left alone with my little children in the Immigration Hall," she writes. "As long as others were there I wasn't so lonely but when my friend left and my husband was out all day in town … [I would] feel so alone that my heart felt like it would break from grief. I'd cry. The children cried. I thought I'd go insane from despair." Following two weeks in the hall, her husband built a raft, on which they floated several days down the North Saskatchewan River, with all their children and trunks, through a blizzard, until

they were marooned on a sandbar. Ultimately, the frozen wayfarers were rescued by an aboriginal family and helped along to their destination near Victoria Settlement.[88]

Others experienced less-traumatic arrivals. An English family arrived in Calgary in 1903 and stayed at the twenty-year-old immigration hall. The daughter's memoir — she was ten at the time of migration — describes the lodgings there:

> It was a pretty rough affair, but money was limited; mother had our fortune … tucked in a small pouch pinned into the top of her corset. As the hall was free, here we took up our abode. There was a large room downstairs furnished with a rough table and chairs and a stove where food could be prepared; the upper floor was divided into cubicles with straw mattresses on the wooden bedsteads. After the cramped quarters on the train, this was almost luxurious! The [immigration] agent and his wife … invited us all for supper that first night; the others in the hall were foreigners and not very compatible. [The agent's wife] informed mother of some other quite different type of foreigners that inhabited that place and mother took prompt action! She purchased, upon advice, quantities of sabadilla powder and other horrible smelling stuff, and so saturated all our clothes and possessions with it that we dripped and smelled of it for weeks. It was unpleasant but preferable to American bed-bugs, as they were called at the time … After a few days we moved into some rooms in a block on Stephen Avenue, which was only a little better.

As English-speakers, this family received special treatment from the immigration official, the Dominion government's architectural segregation reinforced by social connections, even among strangers. The agent immediately finds paying work for the men of the family, while the "foreigners" are not mentioned again — except in the waggish analogy to pests.[89]

The vermin infesting the immigration halls made no such discriminations by ethnicity or class. Attacks of bedbugs, lice, and other pests were often mentioned by migrants. The young man we met earlier, who slept on the floor of the Davidson immigration hall, claims he did so because the beds and mattresses — and the other lodgers — were lousy. Another man, who migrated as an adult in an extended family group, remembered the Dominion government immigration hall in a way that officials did not intend: "My experience in this first Canadian hostel I shall not forget for the rest of my life. In one night I was bitten so badly by fleas and bedbugs that … [my] mother wept when she saw me."[90] A history of Ukrainian immigration to Canada notes that, during the sojourns of their families at the halls, one "of the women's duties was to pick lice from the hair and clothes of their children." The continual turnover in the bunks, with people travelling a month or more in teeming spaces, produced excellent habitat for vermin. McCreary wrote to the deputy minister: "You can imagine the condition of the Sheds when I tell you that I have discovered gray-backs crawling up my neck-tie" following visits to the dormitories.[91] Internal correspondence frequently discussed techniques for disinfection and defumigation borrowed from those established at the quarantine stations, and then proven in the Winnipeg hall. For example, detailed instructions for washing walls with mercury solution, and safely burning sulphur in pans (without setting fire to the hall), were sent to the Strathcona agent in 1894. He was chastised by his superiors because a travelling inspector had found the bunks "so infested with vermin as to be untenable. The Commissioner directs me to say that whilst he recognizes that it is practically impossible to keep a building of this description free from these pests, nevertheless, by proper care and cleanliness … the vermin brought in by every succeeding batch of immigrants can be reduced to very few in number."[92] Agents and caretakers would need to practice eternal vigilance against these invaders.

Commissioner McCreary, having his office in the Winnipeg hall, and spending his days among the immigrants, readily acknowledged that a certain amount of annoyance was inevitable, whether due to pests, social conflict, or cultural differences. He did not hold it against his charges. Quite to the contrary, after being elected as a member of parliament in 1900, McCreary found himself in the House of Commons staunchly defending the character of eastern-European arrivals, when confronted with bigoted attacks on the government's policy to encourage non-British immigration — even as he tacitly accepted the distinction between foreigners and English-speakers. His lengthy speech is worth a thorough exposition, not least for its portrayal of spatial practices at the immigration hall, and how McCreary deploys them to make a political statement:

With regard to getting immigration from Great Britain … reports of the last ten years have pointed out the difficulty … [As to] the question of foreign immigrants, especially the Galicians and the Doukhobors … I submit, after an experience of four years in dealing with that class of settlers, that they are going to make good settlers … As regards the cleanliness of the Doukhobors and Galicians … the moment a train load of these immigrants arrives at Winnipeg, and before they are there an hour, the water is boiling, and those people are washing night and day until they are just as clean as any other settlers. When I remonstrated with them about their condition, they said to me, with tears

in their eyes, how could we help it, our linen was clean when we left, but the vessel was in such a condition that we could not keep ourselves clean, packed as we were in a small hold … The first party of Doukhobors with which I came in contact numbered 2,100. They arrived in January 1899 and had been painted to me in such colours that I was afraid we were going, particularly at that season, to have terrible difficulty with them. I put 600 in the immigration hall in Winnipeg, 300 in a building 300 or 400 yards off, and a little over 1,000 in the immigration hall at East Selkirk. I … allowed the Doukhobors to look after the buildings, see that the fires were kept up — it was intensely cold — and they kept the buildings and did their business in such a way that few business men could have kept them better … I spent the winter of 1899 with them … around me in the hall where my office was. I was passing out and in among them all the time. I had the best citizens of Winnipeg come to see them. On Sundays, these immigrants generally occupied the evening in singing their psalms, and I had the choirs of the various churches come in. There were people about them there all the time.[93]

As on the docks and train platforms, the immigrants could be a kind of spectacle for local curiosity seekers. At the same time, McCreary was demonstrating to these observers in the immigration halls that the controversial, non-British newcomers were independent, hard-working, and god-fearing future Canadians. The agent at the Regina hall concurred, stating in his annual report of 1900 that "Doukhobors and Galicians took shelter at the building at all times of the year and of the day, coming and going all the time … I secured work for them … and all, without a single exception, have given good satisfaction to their employers … It is surprising how quickly most of them pick up the English language … I am sure they will make in a short time good citizens." Interactions at the immigration halls supported the acclimatization of the newcomers to different jobs and a different language, while the agents and other interested parties could observe their practices and progress.[94]

The East Selkirk hall that McCreary refers to was not a purpose-built structure, but rather an old railroad roundhouse rented by the Dominion government and refurbished with floors, partitions, and cooking appliances. It was about forty kilometres from central Winnipeg and the main immigration hall. This overflow space, opened for that first party of Doukhobors, was used until 1906 to accommodate the large group migrations that were growing in regularity. The roundhouse accommodated greater numbers than were possible in any immigration hall built up to that point. Sergey Tolstoy, the chaperone of the Doukhobor party we met in quarantine on Lawlor's Island (see chapter 2), provides a sense of the spatial organization and practices in this former industrial building:

When everybody had got off the train and gathered in the large dining-room of the immigration hall, McCreary gave a welcoming speech to the Doukhobors. The *starichki* responded with expressions of gratitude, and, to McCreary's great surprise, more than a hundred of them carried out the traditional bow to the ground. The building in which the Doukhobors are now housed is a large round brick building, with the roof and ceiling resting on rails. In the centre is a vast, high-ceilinged hall; around the sides are sleeping areas, where triple-decker bunks have been constructed. The kitchen and bakery are next door. It is rather crowded, but it is warm and comfortable.[95]

According to Vera Lysenko's *Men in Sheepskin Coats*, Ukrainian immigrants who bunked in the East Selkirk roundhouse would write home to say "I live on the third floor and we crawl in and out on a ladder because in Canada they do not build stairs." She also relates how one of the first parties of Doukhobors to stay there built clay ovens "after the style of the old country" in order to bake their bread while overwintering. In later years, Ukrainian immigrants were happy to put these ovens to use as well, cutting "long poles of poplar wood for the rakes."[96] Given a converted industrial building for their accommodation, these groups shaped it as best they could into a space of domesticity.

Despite his defence of the government's strategy to encourage eastern-European immigration, McCreary's experiences with large groups in the Winnipeg hall were not always positive. For example, according to Lehr, when the "mass immigration of Ukrainians began in earnest in 1897," immigration-hall staff "soon found themselves overwhelmed." Confrontations arose as officials attempted to distribute these immigrants to desirable land. When some of the Ukrainian arrivals discovered they were being sent to establish new colonies distant from preceding Ukrainian settlers, they resisted the move by occupying the Winnipeg immigration hall. Things came to a head when another train carrying more than five hundred Ukrainian immigrants was due to arrive at the depot; these newcomers also expected shelter at the hall. After refusing various alternative settlement sites offered by the commissioner, the first group was "forcibly removed from the Immigration Hall and placed on a train for Yorkton." As McCreary concluded, "a certain amount of force has got to be used with this … ignorant, obstinate, unmanageable class." Due to conflicts such as this, government agents began to determine immigrants' destinations as soon as they debarked into eastern port buildings, or at least on the train before its arrival in Winnipeg. In addition, to avoid the lure of land speculators and misinformed locals, trains sometimes would run straight through Winnipeg without stopping, only depositing their passengers at immigration halls down the line.[97]

Large groups like the Doukhobors, or the mass migrations of Ukrainians, were able to remain somewhat aloof from other migrants and locals, protected by chaperones, government agents, and assigned interpreters. They travelled and occupied immigration halls as culturally and religiously homogeneous groups, with the goal of block settlement en masse. The experience was different for smaller groups, families, and individuals who, as strangers in a strange land, by necessity had to seek out residents who shared their place of origin, religion, or language. One Icelandic man claimed that the only "information or advice" at the Winnipeg hall when his family arrived in 1893 was "that from friendly Icelanders who had been here quite some time."[98] Even with the development of a network of immigration architecture, many newcomers still fell through the cracks of the paternal bureaucracy and were forced to rely on the advice of other locals. The quality of that assistance varied greatly. For example, numerous sources suggest that Ukrainian immigrants were susceptible to countrymen who convinced them to detrain at Winnipeg, even though government officials had land or jobs reserved for them farther along the line. Perhaps this was a symptom of a long-held distrust of state functionaries. Later, those immigrants regretted their decisions to detrain when they witnessed in person the poor quality or quantity of lands and jobs still available around Winnipeg. "Yes, people should have listened to his advice," remarked one man, remembering the attempts of the interpreter at the immigration hall to dissuade his extended family from taking up poor land just because it was close to other Ukrainians.[99] When hundreds were in the

halls, not everyone would have a chance to confer with the agent, interpreter, or commissioner – and not everyone would take the advice conferred by these figures. It was also impossible to control the comings and goings of locals, with good intentions or not, without transforming the halls into more-secure, carceral institutions. The latter course would have represented an expense, and an imposition on the immigrants, that the government was loathe to undertake.

Despite the tendency of migrants to seek out compatriots, and even with ethnic segregation an architectural goal of the Dominion government, individual practices in immigration halls were shaped and flavoured by social mixing. Sometimes exposure to cultural differences, forced upon migrants in need of free lodging, was rebuffed as "incompatible," to borrow the word of the English girl who stayed at the Calgary hall. Others embraced the chaos of a crowded immigration hall with a kind of bemused awareness that all were in the same boat, or at least the same dormitory (Figure 3.21). As one Ukrainian migrant recalled, of his stay in Winnipeg:

People fill up the place like a swarm of flies. Darkness and commotion engulf all. A very dim light from a small lamp barely illuminates one corner. Everyone chatters at the same time, and their voices blend into one loud confusion. Here, one can find Frenchmen, Swedes, Germans, Russian Jews, Scotsmen, Ruthenians, Poles, and others. Some are undressing and getting ready for bed. One is whistling; one is gabbing away and laughing lustily. In a corner, a religious Frenchman is crossing himself, and right in the middle of the floor is our *muzhyk*, making himself at home as he repeatedly prostrates himself, forehead to floor, till the room resounds with thuds. Not understanding the meaning of this ritual, the spectators watch his gymnastics, shake with laughter, and assume that perhaps this is the proper thing to do before retiring for the night.[100]

Aside from, perhaps, modes of transportation, the immigration halls were the first Canadian spaces of multicultural encounter for many migrants.

The observation holds true for Canadian-born residents as well, for whom the immigration halls could be spaces of wonder, and even, perhaps, personal transformation. For McCreary, a British-Canadian born and raised in Ontario, the experience of working in the Winnipeg hall, in the midst of hundreds of diverse souls, evidently changed his thinking on the character and abilities of different "classes" of immigrant. A Winnipeg girl, whose Icelandic father was often called in to interpret for his compatriots, visited the immigration hall around the turn of the century and remembered it in her autobiography as a site of radical difference. The "grimy, forbidding place, with dirty windows and battered doors" happened to be crowded with Doukhobors when she arrived:

3.21 Men's dormitory in one of the immigration halls in Winnipeg, likely the 1890 hall seen in Figure 3.13. The walls of the narrow attic room are finished with flocked wallpaper. A single bulb provides electric light, in addition to the small dormer windows that would be to the rear of the photographer.

a hundred human forms stretched out upon the dirty floor ... all wrapped in grayish, woolly, skin garments ... they seemed a race of hairy monsters, stewing in their own reek, like the animals in the circus. I could not skip through them fast enough. That is how I came to trip, sprawling on a huge fellow who lay spilled out in peace ... [I dropped my] gift of flowers, and if I didn't scream, it was because the fright was shocked out of me when the huge bolster jacked-up like a spring and the big bearded face ... crinkled with smiles. What was more, the surprising creature retrieved the bouquet of flowers ... [and] a woman beside him snatched them from his hand, and buried her hot grimy face in the sweet petals.[101]

In this passage, she first dehumanizes the exotic immigrants, but by the end she seems to rehumanize the smiling, helpful man and the woman appreciative of beauty. Was this a moment of insight for the young girl? In his book *Creating Societies*, Hoerder comments that Winnipeg before the turn of the century was a "thriving interracial community." Even if a migrant paused there for only a short time, the immigration halls were a focal point for this kind of interaction.[102] After being newcomers, migrants became locals; for many, the immigration halls continued to play a role in their everyday life, and in building a sense of community.

SPACES FOR COMMUNITIES

In the early years of small Prairie towns, the Dominion government immigration hall was often the first, and sometimes the only, substantial structure other than a train depot. As a result, these government buildings came to serve a number of purposes related to early settlement. Primarily, of course, they served as temporary lodgings for arriving immigrants with few resources to recover from transatlantic and transcontinental journeys.

Immigrants and support staff were the primary users of space in most immigration buildings. However, the Prairie halls were significant institutions in their communities as well – as landmarks, and as places to people-watch, to find labourers and sell food or equipment, to access government functions, and to attend meetings or entertainments. Local residents, many of whom would have stayed there themselves, knew it as the place to send bewildered newcomers. And in the newspapers, immigration halls were of considerable interest to readers in the community.

Sometimes the immigration halls received negative attention, such as when the newspapers reported on overcrowding, dilapidated conditions, or other problems. As with the very earliest immigration buildings of the 1830s, when the convalescent sheds were chased out of town, leading to the establishment of the first quarantine islands, the siting of Prairie immigration halls could be controversial. Before construction started on the hall there in 1885, an editorial in the Calgary *Herald* politely suggested that it "may be as well to inquire if the shed is placed in altogether a desirable situation from a sanitary point of view." Sure, it would be close to the platform where immigrants debarked, but it would be "a long way from water, and a very short way from the heart of the town." In a place with two fast-flowing rivers, where "water is the most abundant gift we have," and if "cleanliness is at all a desirable thing about an immigrant shed," the editorial advocated that it be built on one of those rivers. Moreover, if "immigrant fever" broke out, "as it is most likely to do, the shed is in a place where the prevailing wind will be most likely to carry infection into town." Stigmatizing immigrants as unclean, and drawing on the well-worn miasmic theory of disease, the editorial – unsuccessfully, as it turned out – called on the town council to intervene.

The local press regularly reported on the arrivals and departures of new settlers at the halls, as news items akin to the society pages. For instance, the Calgary paper in 1888 took note that the "last of the immigrants that [the agent] had in stock, have gone north to locate. The immigrant building is now 'empty, swept and garnished,' and ready for another consignment."[103] Reportage on the presence of new batches of immigrants at the halls could bring employers and suppliers of fresh food. It also brought in people off their homesteads to search for friends and family, farm help that spoke their language, and news of the Old Country. Farmers also could make a few dollars with their wagon and team, transporting newcomers onto the land. The immigration hall in Strathcona in the years around the turn of the century served as a kind of regional community centre for Ukrainian-speaking settlers. It was fondly known as "the Emigrant," and many tearful reunions took place there.[104]

Sometimes immigrant tears were shed for other reasons as well: their anxious arrival in some small, remote town where they stood out as different and did not know the language. For example, the Strathcona immigration agent complained to Ottawa in 1895 that immigrants were being mocked by locals on the train platform, while a policeman was present. The NWMP inspector fully admitted that the incident had occurred, though the policeman stationed there had left before it happened. Significantly, the inspector dismissed it as a frivolous grievance: "this is a very ridiculous matter to make a complaint out of, the whole thing arising out of some laughing remarks made about peculiarities of dress of some of the Immigrants, and which they could not possibly understand, or be annoyed at, being unable to speak English."[105] It seems unlikely that the new arrivals were ignorant of this rude welcome. Historian of Ukrainian immigration to Alberta, James MacGregor, calls out the ruling-class attitude represented by the inspector, while noting that locals saw the arrival of immigrants both as opportunity and spectacle.

On every hand horse traders sought out the unwary, and other vendors, horse-trading types too, offered second-hand machinery and vehicles. For many had come to sell to these foreigners – some who were honest and many who needed watching. Others who had nothing to sell came to watch. For here, centred around the South Edmonton station grounds and the immigration hall, was a rare spectacle indeed. Many of the onlookers brought their children so that they might not miss this … colourful pageant few of the spectators would ever forget … [the locals] by their looks, actions, laughter and gesticulations expressed not only idle curiosity and surprise but varying degrees of scorn and disapproval. Though there could be no verbal communication … the unfeeling eyes of the crowd did nothing to comfort the new colonists … showing as clearly as words or blows that they were not welcome.[106]

Being able to escape these intimidating stares by withdrawing to the immigration hall could give newcomers a sense of protection and legitimacy within the local community that would not have been possible if they were left to their own devices in scattered hotels and encampments.

Sometimes the protection was needed. So-called "Galicians," Doukhobors, and other non-British newcomers of course faced prejudice and a negative attitude toward their immigration. As historians have recorded, they were pilloried with "xenophobic fervour" in the House of Commons, the press, and on the street.[107] In a rare incident – occurring at a moment characterized by great numbers of eastern-European arrivals, and growing agitation against Dominion government policies that encouraged them – the Strathcona immigration hall actually became the target of an attack, likely motivated by anti-immigrant sentiment. "[O]ne night in 1899, 'drunken toughs' tried to invade the immigration hall, pounding on doors and breaking windows." When neighbours came to the rescue, the attackers fled.[108] Fortunately, on the Prairies, this kind of violence never escalated to the level of the race riots seen on the west coast.

Conversely, the earliest Prairie immigration halls played some small role in the racial violence of the North-West Rebellion of 1885. The large immigration halls of Qu'Appelle and Brandon (see Figures 3.7 and 3.8) were marshalling stations for troops from the east. When the "special train" arrived in the latter town, the "men were immediately marched to the immigration sheds" to set up camp. Meanwhile, farther west in Medicine Hat, there was "intense excitement" because the "Indians are reported on the warpath." Local residents had "applied to the Government for arms, ammunition, and reinforcements," and were bracing for attack by occupying the most substantial public building: "The immigrant sheds will be barricaded and prepared for the reception of women and children."[109] In bellicose moments, the halls could convert from the protection and control of immigrants, to the protection of white settlers and control over a space of engagement.

Sometimes added legitimacy was achieved for the institution when immigration halls were supplemented with other government uses in the same structure. This only made sense, since they were the sole public building in many towns, and typically used on a seasonal basis. For example, the 1883 hall at Qu'Appelle, which the department soon realized was larger than needed, was partly converted into an NWMP post and a courtroom. First the troops, and then police, had begun to overwinter in the building in 1885; no immigration agent was stationed there by the end of the decade. A plan from the early 1890s shows the allocation of space after the alterations (Figure 3.22). The portion of the ground floor reserved for use by immigrants as a common room and mess hall is about one-third of the total area; the kitchen bump-out attaches here. The central third comprises the courtroom, while the final third includes an office and a bedroom, plus saddle storage, for the NWMP officer stationed there. Upstairs, the immigrant quarters retain about two-thirds of the area for dormitories, while the rest is devoted to a jury room and a meeting space for lawyers.[110]

The Calgary hall of the same era, half the size of Qu'Appelle's, also received a temporary courtroom conversion. By 1889, the Calgary press was decrying the lack of adequate and gender-appropriate space for the accommodation of incoming immigrants: "the best half of the immigrant shed is now occupied by the department of justice and the other part of it is not all it should be … there is no possible means of privacy for females." According to the editorial, there would be no problem at all in renting another space to house the courtroom, which should vacate the premises "at once." The local newspaper closely tracked the renovations that were undertaken that summer, and, upon their completion, provided a particularly detailed description of the hall, now in "first class order." The immigration agent took over the room previously used as the judge's chamber, newly kalsomined and looking "very well." The rest of the ground floor comprised a lobby and baggage room; a wash room "for the use of females"; a dining hall with tables and benches; a large kitchen with sink, shelving, work table, utensils, and "a $65 cooking stove." The upper floor had the men's wash room, and "sleeping rooms sufficient to accommodate probably 30 persons at a time," though the article does not indicate if these were dormitories or family rooms — at this date, they were likely the former. The wash water was pumped from the well to a tank on the roof, which gravity-fed the sinks. Two stoves provided heat, in addition to that in the kitchen. The clipping concludes by naming the various contractors for the project and the

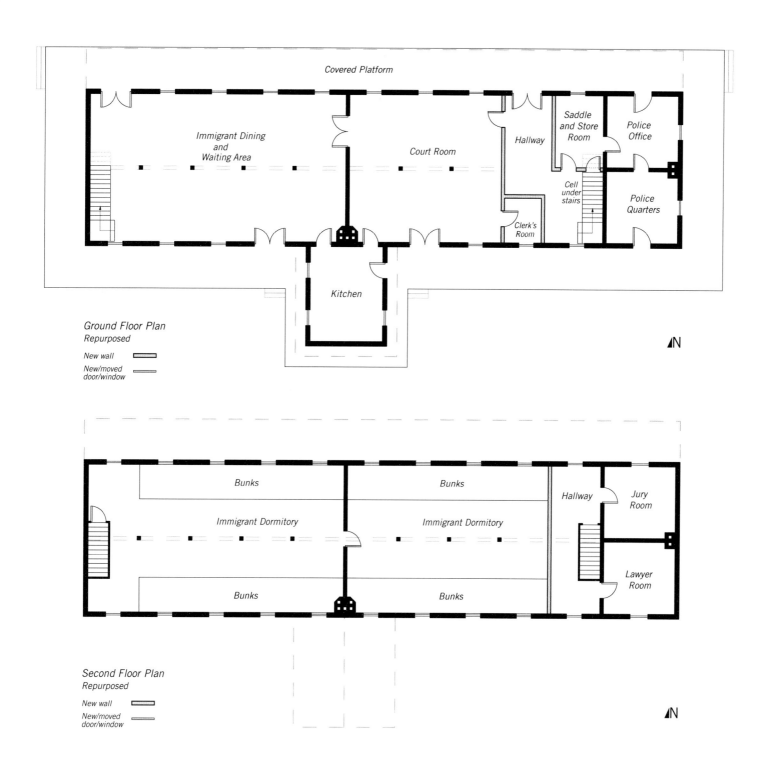

Covered Platform

Immigrant Dining
and
Waiting Area

Court Room

Hallway

Saddle
and Store
Room

Police
Office

Cell
under
stairs

Police
Quarters

Clerk's
Room

Kitchen

Ground Floor Plan
Repurposed

New wall
New/moved
door/window

N

Bunks

Bunks

Hallway

Jury
Room

Immigrant Dormitory

Immigrant Dormitory

Lawyer
Room

Bunks

Bunks

Second Floor Plan
Repurposed

New wall
New/moved
door/window

N

3.22 Redrawn plan of Qu'Appelle immigration hall,
showing the layout of rooms and functions by the 1890s, or
about a decade after the building's construction.

local Public Works architect who had "succeeded in keeping within the estimate."[111] The presence and status of an immigration hall was considered an important marker of a town's development, and these institutions regularly received attention in the press.

The Prairie immigration halls also appeared in local newspaper advertisements as the sites of various public events. Hoerder describes how new settlements on the Canadian Prairies developed a communal life, organizing mixed socials, dances, youth clubs, ethnic associations, and so on. "Many communities set up drama clubs and staged theatrical productions ... Theatre as an oral art had a long European village tradition."[112] But where would these meetings and events be held? Given the lack of urban infrastructure in early Prairie towns, the large dining rooms and dormitories of the immigration halls lent themselves well to these local entertainments. A Medicine Hat history records how the "halfway home to immigrants ... also served as a dance hall on Saturday nights and as church and meeting house on Sundays. It was a scene of weddings as well."[113] An especially good record of non-governmental uses of the Qu'Appelle immigration hall has come down to us in archives and newspapers. In 1891 alone, when the NWMP essentially was in charge of its management, local applications were approved to use the building for town-council meetings, exhibits, lectures, church meetings and services, plays, and Christmas pageants, by groups as diverse as the Agricultural Society, the Qu'Appelle Station Operatic Society, the Royal Templars of Temperance, and "the ladies of the town."[114] We get a fuller sense of these public roles of the immigration hall from a dissertation by Ian McWilliams, who describes how the large ground floor room would often be used for dancing or other entertainments, with refreshments set out upstairs in the dormitory space – no doubt taking advantage of the built-in bunks as makeshift, sloping tables.

McWilliams also sketches out the contours of a debate that erupted in 1890 between Presbyterians and members of the Church of England, during a lecture series on the history of religion taking place at the hall. Ultimately, the reverend and the bishop agreed to disagree during a public meeting on the "neutral ground" of the immigration hall, "an important place for the exchange of ideas" in pioneer Qu'Appelle.[115]

Architectural historians have shown that a popular piece of infrastructure to be built by nascent North American settlements was the town-hall opera house, which provided space for both council meetings and performances.[116] As McWilliams suggests, the Qu'Appelle immigration hall effectively came to serve in this role. In addition to the lively performance schedule outlined above, the municipal council took a lease on the immigration building to serve as its town hall. When they occupied it in 1893, the council fixed up the hall and removed the built-in bunks upstairs, since "they rendered the room useless for any purpose" other than sleeping.[117] That said, there seems to have been an understanding that migrants in need of shelter could still come to the building as needed – although by this time not many were arriving in this settled region. The council met in the courtroom, although the latter intermittently continued in use for its judicial function. The Department of Justice seems to have retained a sense of ownership over its portion of the structure, and, in fact, twice sent a sheriff in 1904 to evict the town council from the building. This occurred in the midst of several years' correspondence between Ottawa, Regina (where the regional judge and Public Works architect were based), and Qu'Appelle, trying to sort out rights and responsibilities for the 1883 hall. Notwithstanding all these shifts in tenants and functions, the structure continued to be known locally as the "immigration building" until it was finally sold in 1906. At this point, McWilliams reports that it was relocated and converted into several units of terrace housing.[118] As we will explore further in the next chapter, Prairie immigration halls ended up satisfying all kinds of different local needs after their usefulness for immigrant reception was past.

CONCLUSION

In the late-nineteenth and early-twentieth centuries, the core process of the Canadian state was the National Policy, with two tenets being railroad construction and the promotion of immigration. Federal government immigration halls were part of National Policy infrastructure. The halls were portrayed as a financially practical means by which immigrants to the Prairies would be received, and their transition to Canadian life eased. They also helped establish a federal presence on the Prairies, beyond the few police posts scattered near the border with the United States. Historian A.A. den Otter has argued that, although the railways were the product of Canadian state-making, the experiences of immigrants on the CPR did not constitute an effective process for their assimilation into a national identity. He asserts that their "only experience with Canada was the blur of lakes, trees, and occasional cities outside the westward-speeding train window."[119] The architectural history of the Prairie immigration halls indicates that this was not the case. At the very least, to many immigrants "Canada" meant a series of spaces designed to guide, protect, and direct their movements and actions. In dozens of Prairie towns, immigrants' last point of contact with the Dominion government was not on a colonist car, but in immigration halls, where they could stay for days or weeks, receiving free shelter with few strings attached. The railways may have marked a federal presence, though it is difficult to know whether new immigrants would perceive the close ties between the CPR and the Dominion government. Government immigration agents might meet colonist trains right on the CPR platform, but train platforms were de facto public space in that era. Meanwhile, Dominion immigration halls stood adjacent to Prairie railroad stations, often on CPR land. But immigrants paid fares to travel on CPR colonist cars, clearly a commercial interaction. They experienced free stays in immigration halls while en route to claim free Crown lands. The state was present at each step of the journey. The immigration halls were spaces where policy, experience, and practice intersected in a way that did not occur on CPR colonist cars, or in settlers' everyday lives on homesteads or in urban areas. The buildings were an extension of the Dominion government – indeed they were often the only physical manifestation of federal authority in new Prairie towns.

In Canada, there was no singular location where the greatest portion of immigrants were received. On the east coast, the importance of Quebec City was diluted by the winter ports of Halifax and Saint John. Hoerder writes that, although "none of the seaboard towns developed an entry-gate myth, Winnipeg's immigration sheds were remembered by many. The modest accommodation matched their future modest lives of hard work."[120] A more apt metaphor may be provided by a different kind of gate: the locks that allow vessels to ascend a river that otherwise would be unnavigable. At each lock, the vessel shelters in a safe place while the waters below it are replenished, lifting it to the level of its surroundings. When the vessel has risen, the gates of the lock open to let it rejoin the stream. Passing through the locks is a methodical, step-by-step process, which is how the Dominion government envisioned the arrival and distribution of immigrants. At each stop in the network of immigration architecture, the migrant would pause to be replenished with sleep, nourishment, and advice, so that they could continue inland and begin homesteading or working with the same level of potential success as their neighbours.

Undeniably, as Hoerder notes, Dominion government "institutions, such as the immigration hall and land office, remained brief stopovers."[121] These were not reform institutions, where the transformation of subjects was enforced over the long term. Schools, hospitals, workhouses, and the like aimed to produce skilled, healthy, and disciplined citizens. In contrast, it was hoped that Dominion government recruitment strategies, and the difficulties inherent in long-distance migration, would weed out the undisciplined and unhealthy immigrant. Still, new arrivals were likely to be poor, and remained at a great disadvantage compared to those who already knew the language, the lay of the land, the value of their labour, and the norms of North American society. Indigent settlers therefore would be supported at the inauguration of their endeavours — and sometimes thereafter as well. In the process, perhaps immigrants would learn something of Canadian life, and the expectations for good settlers.

Here in the context of immigration architecture, we see Canadian social-welfare policy in its infancy; but it is important not to overstate the case. Historian of state welfare programs Alvin Finkel declares that, in Canada, there was "fairly limited involvement of the state in people's lives in the late nineteenth century."[122] Beyond the relief offered in immigration buildings, and early public-health measures that partly grew out of the Dominion government quarantine system, few programs provided ongoing support for settlers or industrial workers prior to the 1920s. And yet, in its desire and its actions to assist immigrants upon arrival, Canada began to define itself as different from other New World nations on the receiving end of nineteenth-century migrations. Migrants understood that Canadian reception practices were different, more welcoming and helpful. Promoters of immigration were quick to assure potential recruits that clean, well-tended government buildings awaited them, and that they would receive reliable guidance within them. Local agents assured Ottawa officials that the reception architecture was needed and appreciated; the newly opened immigration hall in Edmonton, wrote one, was "a great success, the people who occupy it give the Gov. wonderfull praises for the good accommodation provided."[123] The payback for paternalism went beyond just keeping newcomers out of the local poorhouse.

CHAPTER 4

Prairie Immigration Halls in a New Era of Reception

At the time of writing his 1909 book, *Strangers within Our Gates*, J.S. Woodsworth was the superintendent of a Winnipeg settlement house, and minister to new arrivals at the immigration hall in that city. In its pages, he evokes the excitements and uncertainties of the immigrant's journey, and describes, in the racist essentializing language of his era, the different classes and ethnicities on display during the voyage, and upon debarking into a Dominion government pier building. "An immigrant ship in mid-ocean," he writes, "here is more of human interest to the cubic foot than is to be found anywhere else on the face of the globe … What a field for study!" And what a motto for the present volume, a study of migrants' experiences and practices in the spaces of Canadian immigration architecture.

Despite writing in the first person and drawing on his experiences in the ministry, Woodsworth relies on official sources for most of his information about immigrant recruitment and reception practices, excerpting in his book a recent lengthy article by L.M. Fortier, chief clerk of the immigration branch in Ottawa:

The process of uprooting and transplanting is a painful one, but it is undergone by many a family to the great betterment of their prospects in life; and when the momentous decision has at last been bravely reached, the Canadian agent again steps in and renders assistance in the way of advice on transportation matters, "what to take," etc., besides offering various little attentions, which as a rule are gratefully received at such a time … on reaching port in Canada they are always welcomed by Government officials, who direct them and see to their comfort in every possible way …

And so Canada gives no cold and niggardly reception to desirable settlers who seek her shores in response to her invitation. At the same time it is always well to have it understood that we fight shy of criminals and undesirables generally. Canada is not a healthful or inviting country for them to come to, and they are gently but firmly turned back, for their own good and ours.

At [the ports] comfortable and commodious buildings are maintained, in which the immigrants spend the waiting time between landing from the ship and entraining for the railway journey. The women and children have their own quarters and a matron and assistants to attend to them. If there is sickness, medical aid and comforts are at hand …

Arrived at Winnipeg, all go into the Immigration Hall for rest and refreshment, and from there in due time find their own place in the new land.[1]

From previous chapters we are familiar with these sites of immigrant reception. Here, Fortier represents immigration as a systematic, guided, step-by-step process in which migrants move through a series of managed spaces en route to finding their "own place." In addition, he notes that there is now incorporated an aspect of immigrant selection in the process of immigrant reception — he completely elides the often-race-based assumptions and decisions that inflected that selection process. Regardless, the upshot is that new policies and procedures introduced after the turn of the century began to change the spatial practices of quarantine, pier, and Prairie immigration architecture.

This chapter continues the story of Prairie immigration halls, picking up the narrative just before 1905 — where the previous chapter ended — and pursuing it to 1930, when the last of this building type was constructed. First, though, I discuss the changing context of Canadian immigration architecture in the early-twentieth century, which is the era covered in the final two chapters of the book. Compared with earlier decades examined in chapters 1 to 3, the new century was a time of modernization for the immigration branch and its building program. Through new legislation, means of communication, and management practices, the network of immigrant-reception architecture became increasingly systematic. This was a necessary development to allow the Dominion government to control a large increase in the number of arrivals and to protect the immigrants themselves. This modernization of immigration-branch activities is symbolized partly by the erection in Winnipeg of a large and expensive new headquarters building, the principle case studied in this chapter. Then, to further flesh out an understanding of

Prairie immigration halls, the chapter examines the community contexts, local practices, alternative uses, and architectural plans germane to other sites outside Winnipeg. Although the story of this chapter and the next is one of modernization, much remained the same in the quotidian operations and spatial practices at the halls. Finally, the decade of the 1920s receives attention as a moment when several large immigration halls were built of permanent materials, even as the demise of the program seemed increasingly inevitable.

THE MODERNIZATION OF IMMIGRANT RECEPTION IN CANADA

By the turn of the century, concerted efforts by landholding corporations and by the Dominion government in promoting and recruiting abroad had begun to bear fruit in growing immigrant numbers. New technologies emerged that eased Prairie farming, chain migrations were established, and with the "closing" of the American frontier in 1893, more immigrants began to arrive in the "last best West." The Census decade 1901 to 1911 was the first since Confederation to record net growth in Canada's population. Immigration continued to grow almost annually in the pre–First World War period, with 1913 being Canada's peak immigration year. These booming immigration years in the decade prior to the war saw the most construction activity in the immigration buildings program, as settlers poured through the ports and quarantine stations, and fanned out across the Prairie provinces of Manitoba, Saskatchewan, and Alberta in the wake of railroad construction and Dominion land surveying. In parallel with this great influx, Dominion government officials also began to develop the ways and means to reject or deport undesirable new and recent arrivals, which resulted in new architectural spaces. Arrivals slowed during the First World War, though established American farmers continued to take advantage of free land on the Canadian Prairies. In the postwar years, the economy was less anchored in agriculture, and more immigrants went to cities where hotels, rooming houses, relatives, and friends could accommodate newcomers.[2] Still, the late 1920s saw a brief resurgence in the construction of immigration infrastructure, particularly in the major transportation hubs, reflecting a sudden increase of new arrivals related to US immigration restrictions and Canadian assisted-migration schemes.

The increase in immigration to Canada after the 1890s is often linked to Clifford Sifton's spell as minister of the interior. Sifton significantly densified the previously diffuse network of Canadian immigration buildings, and populated them with his "well-organized chain of officialdom." Numerous contingencies had to be managed by these officials: transportation schedules between and across continents; weather patterns and the seasonal navigability of rivers and roads; the progress of the Dominion Land Survey, of railroad construction, and of enterprises that offered employment. As historian John Lehr writes, the "logistics of mass settlement" were complex, and "the government could not afford, either financially or politically, to have angry and often destitute settlers crowding the immigration halls in the major distribution centres."[3] Everything depended upon the continuous flow of immigrants across the network of reception architecture. For example, when several bridges south of Dauphin were "washed away" in the spring of 1902, the Winnipeg commissioner reported that "we have at least four hundred people on our hands for that point and points beyond whom we cannot distribute." Bridge and track were swept away again two years later, north of Regina, "causing the congestion of immigrants at this point." Although the immigration branch spent a lot of money to house and feed them, the agent reported, "the expense of doing so was advisable as very few, if any, of the newcomers became

discontented and refused to go on to their original destination." Communications along the network could help distribute impatient immigrants in available nodes. It could also save them from leaving comfortable accommodations in hubs like Edmonton when the more remote immigration halls were already full – or when the latter were under quarantine, as several northern Alberta halls would be during the influenza epidemic of 1918–20.[4] Improved information and communication also allowed officials to gauge when to shut down idle immigration buildings "as the tide of immigration passed beyond them."[5]

It was Sifton's successor, Frank Oliver, who codified many of the de facto practices from previous administrations, and it was during his tenure as minister that Canada's immigration boomed. Whereas in previous decades there had been few restrictions regarding who could enter the country, with the massive growth in the number of new arrivals came concerns over monitoring and assessing the qualities and characters of immigrants. Oliver's Immigration Acts of 1906 and 1910 introduced selectivity and various kinds of restrictions into the process of immigrant reception. This led to building renovations at the ports, and to entirely new facilities, such as the immigrant hospitals built during the first decade of the century, and the detention centres of the 1910s: these will be discussed in chapter 5. That being said, the fundamental motivations behind immigration architecture remained consistent. The presence of supportive institutions to welcome immigrants, where the paternal protection of the state was made available to them, would distinguish Canada as a destination. And even as nineteenth-century towns grew into twentieth-century cities, with ample hotels and boarding houses, YMCAs, and established ethnic communities, there remained a pragmatic need to shelter immigrant families without means, single male transients, and female domestic workers – anyone distributed from hubs like Winnipeg and Edmonton – along with those arriving at the end of steel on the open Prairie.

The great growth of immigrant numbers required the more thoroughly organized system of reception described by Fortier. The immigration branch had always thought of its architecture as a network; transportation routes stitched together the nodes in this network (Figure 4.1). Though subject to the decision-makers in Ottawa, agents stationed at these nodes had exercised a significant amount of independence and personal judgment in carrying out their duties. The information they passed on to the immigrants was gathered and distributed face-to-face or by letter post.[6] In many ways, these practices remained the same in the new century. What seems to have changed is the subtlety and efficiency of the network and the modernization of its bureaucracy. "Polite and attentive officials" meet and guide the immigrants at the old pier building, a Quebec City newspaper reported with a tone of great surprise in 1910, "there is no confusion, no disorder, no agitation,

4.1 Map showing the location of government immigration halls, tents, and rented accommodations across the Prairie provinces, drawn over the Dominion Land Survey grid.

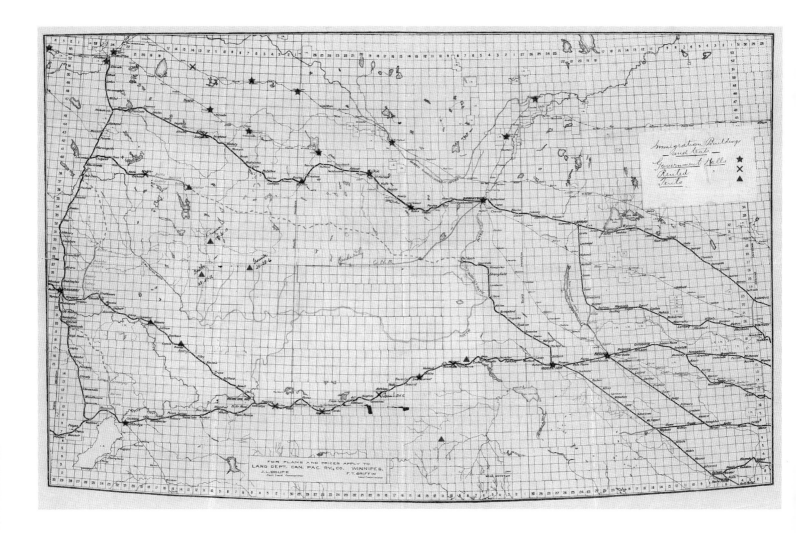

but a quiet, systematic method throughout."[7] The Dominion government's network was so successful that a series of articles in the *New York Times* argued for the Canadian method of reception, compared to that of the United States: "The keynote of the Canadian immigration system, as has been shown, is to make Canada attractive to the immigrant." The result had been the development of "what is probably the most carefully considered, elaborately planned, and scientifically executed immigration system ever adopted by any new country."[8] This was high praise coming from the city that boasted the Ellis Island immigration station.

The systematization of Canadian government immigrant reception shared many aspects with other modernizations undertaken by public and private institutions in the late-nineteenth and early-twentieth centuries. Under the influence of social reformers, the isolated charity institutions of earlier decades slowly gave way to a distributed network of voluntary and state social-welfare agencies operated by professional public-health and social workers.[9] In Canada, different organizations worked to do good for children, mothers, the elderly, the injured, and the newcomer. Space was made available for these kinds of charitable groups to do their work in Canadian immigration architecture. Church groups and the Red Cross Society moved into the port buildings to greet and aid new arrivals. Like most of the churches in Winnipeg, Woodsworth's All People's Mission maintained a presence among the immigrants: "In the Immigration Hall we have been assigned a desk, and during the immigration season a college student devotes his time to this department ... He meets the Old Country Methodists, helps to direct and advise them, and conducts religious services in ... [an old building nearby] which we regard as our Immigration Chapel."[10] This structured social-welfare support was extended within the rubric of the Dominion government's system.

Meanwhile, corporations and governments partook of a managerial revolution to handle the increased size of workforces, the control of operations over great distances, and the complexities of communication, production, and distribution of services.[11] The immigration branch was no different. Managerial efficiency was already in evidence when Sergey Tolstoy was in Winnipeg and going "to the immigration office every day" to deal with the "affairs" of the Doukhobors. He provides a detailed description of the modern business practices in place at the hall in 1899:

> The office includes a large room, the centre of which is encircled by counters, as in stores. The space between the walls and the counters is taken up with various agricultural implements, samples of seeds, tariffs, land maps, popular brochures on land available and so forth ... Behind the counters are the administrative offices, as well as an enclosed office for the director, equipped with desks, typewriters and telephones for a secretary and clerks ... Because of the democratic openness of interpersonal relations and the absence of formality, the work proceeds quickly and straightforwardly; there is a feeling of activity; time-wasting in official correspondence has been reduced to a minimum ... Here long documents are not returned for retranscribing simply because the department head decides that "bearing in mind" should have been written instead of "taking into account," as once happened to the writer of these lines when he was serving in a similar office in Russia.

The commissioner at the time was William McCreary, who Tolstoy portrays as a "self-made man," very busy, working long hours, "dictating to the typists, talking on the telephone, giving out information to various people," but nevertheless "dressed in a plain jacket."[12] That is, the director worked as hard as anyone else in this "democratic" office, which was the nerve centre for widely distributed operations that could be controlled using the modern communications technologies there enumerated. Efficiency was the watchword. For this reason, the chief architect of the Department of Public Works objected to the excessive white space left in a typed report on the immigration hall in Edson, noting that this "wastes paper and fills up files." The correspondent was duly reprimanded: "In the interests of economy and to make your reports more businesslike, please instruct your typist to leave less margin."[13] When public funds were at stake, paper would be used – and buildings would be designed – in a cost-efficient manner.

More immigrant arrivals and more immigration buildings meant more government employees and bigger budgets. That meant greater scrutiny in the House of Commons – a powerful impetus to develop managerial systems to keep budgets and employees under control. Any aspect of immigration-branch operations might be subject to formal or informal auditing. For example, in 1901, ardent questioning by the Opposition revolved around whether immigration agents at the pier buildings should be issued one or two uniforms per year, or "[s]imply one suit and an extra pair of pants."[14] On another occasion, the minister of public works was interrogated about the cost of a boiler installed at the quarantine station on Grosse-Île. The Opposition member insisted that the department had been "imposed upon," being overcharged by 125 per cent on this "article carried by all first-class plumbers in stock." "There are boilers and boilers," was the minister's glib response. "I have seen a lot of boilers in my time, and have not seen two that were quite alike." Nonetheless, he assured the House that he was happy to have the "accounts brought up" and "investigated" in a business-like manner.[15]

More broadly, the idea of conducting the work of government as if it were a corporate undertaking was never far from the mind of immigration officials or politicians; the language of business permeated their correspondence, debates, and statements. Speaking to the press in 1907, Winnipeg commissioner J. Obed Smith described the commercial justification for the work of the immigration branch: "I believe that it is as much good business to look after the immigrant's welfare when he comes, as it is to secure him for the country. He becomes an advertising agent for us if he prospers." The good words of well-served customers would bring more settlers. Prefiguring the *New York Times* articles, the Winnipeg reporter rightly concluded: "No other government in the world has so systematized its work nor embarked upon it on so large a scale." Meanwhile, on the managerial side of things, she reports recent changes that allowed the business of the Winnipeg headquarters to be "carried on expeditiously." Smith had been given the authority to cut cheques and make payments instead of sending them to his superiors in Ottawa: "The immigration department is the only government office in the west to which this privilege has been accorded."[16] It was, at this time, the Dominion government's most important enterprise on the Prairies.

In this context of House oversight and bureaucratic managerialism, every decision had to be justified, and this meant a tremendous increase in the paperwork required of civil servants. When the deputy minister responsible for immigration appeared before a House committee in 1901 he actually used the growth of paperwork in the Ottawa head office as a metric to demonstrate the success of the branch: "The attachments made to our files were 16,683 in 1900, as compared with 13,798 in 1899, and 13,390 in 1898."[17] As we move into the twentieth century and the modern era of medical

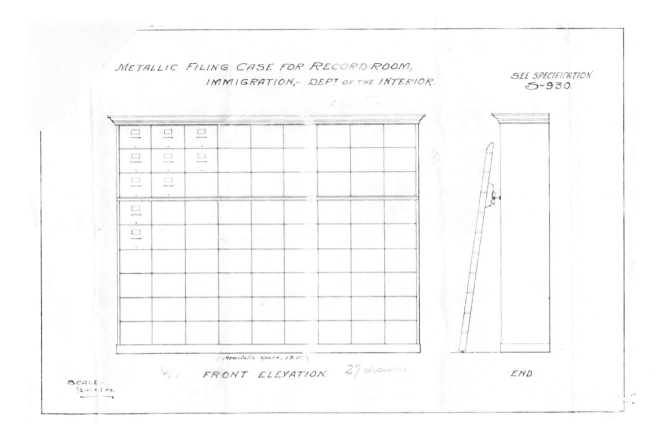

4.2 Built-in filing cabinet for the Record Room of the immigration branch in Ottawa.

and civil inspection, or immigration restrictions, and of deportation, each individual immigrant had to be distinguished and documented in forms and ledgers. However, as the global-migration historian Adam McKeown writes: "Identification of the corporeal human was of little social significance if it could not be embedded in an institutional memory as retrievable data." Government authorities everywhere pursued "the development of complex relational filing systems."[18] Surviving in the archives of the Department of Public Works is the design drawing for an early-twentieth-century metal filing cabinet for the "Record Room" of the immigration branch in Ottawa (Figure 4.2). Thirteen feet wide, with a whopping eighty-one drawers, this case required a rolling library ladder to access its upper levels, which were tucked below a neoclassical cornice. Even the design of the

office fixtures would be managed. The formality of the specification for this filing cabinet provides a symbol of the second era of Canadian immigration architecture, beginning about 1905. The more prominent immigration buildings in transportation hubs from Halifax to Victoria no longer would be wooden sheds. Built with modern conveniences, permanent materials, and formal styles, these came to resemble the other public buildings going up across the growing and modernizing Dominion.[19] The brick-and-stone facades of this new architecture emphasized the stability and confidence of the government, extending expressions of federal power into communities across Canada.

On the Prairies, the first foray into a brick-and-stone architecture of immigration was the construction of a new Winnipeg headquarters between 1904 and 1906. The old 1890 hall endured as the main building there during the early years of the new century, and it was entirely inadequate to handle immigrant numbers to the west, which would double during the first decade of the 1900s. In defence of his government's meagre budget for public buildings in the Province of Manitoba, one member claimed in the House of Commons that the old Winnipeg immigration hall was just fine as it was. Former Winnipeg commissioner turned member of parliament (MP) William McCreary was quick to provide a rebuttal, which aligned the quality of the accommodations with the class of the immigrants to be housed there:

> I beg the hon. gentleman's pardon, the buildings are not in good condition. I know the Dominion government immigration hall at Winnipeg pretty well, and ... [it] should be reserved entirely for foreign immigrants, and for British immigrants there should be a new building distinct and apart from it. The best class of immigrants do not care to go into the Dominion immigration hall ... Every year, about March or April, there are some contagious diseases, and the building is in such a condition that it is almost impossible to keep it as it should be kept. What I did two years ago, was to rent a building ... and put the British immigrants there, reserving them a place for themselves.[20]

The inadequacy of the hall led to the continual need for rented structures at Winnipeg, the large East Selkirk roundhouse being the most prominent example.

Another MP corroborated the criticisms during a later debate: "The present building, as any one knows who has visited Winnipeg and seen it, is unfit for the purpose to which it is assigned. The compartments in which the immigrants have to sleep are placed around the sides of the wall, and are much like stables ... There is no ventilation and very little light ... [and the hall] is situated on a low flat spot, which is very muddy."[21] As the immigrants themselves recalled, the hall was hardly comfortable by twentieth-century standards. In the words of a non-British immigrant arriving in Winnipeg about this time: "I borded the Emigrants Hall and laid me down on a big table for the night, there was only setting accommodation in the Hall, so this did not solve the problem of sore bones acquired in the train."[22] His experience sleeping on the table may have been due to overcrowding, or could reflect his interpretation of the rudimentary built-in bunks that were common in the earlier immigration halls.

So, just as the previous chapter began with the attention of the minister responsible being drawn to the hardships experienced by immigrants in 1881 Winnipeg, twenty years later we witness more of the same. Instead of a brief lag between the completion of the railroad station and that of the new immigration hall, now there had been several years of neglect and expedient measures characterizing the state of immigrant accommodations in that city. Things came to a head in the spring of 1903, in reaction to the rush of a new immigration season. A lengthy debate erupted in the House regarding the status and sufficiency of "Accommodation for Immigrants." Opposition members from Manitoba attacked the government on the issue. Nathaniel Boyd read into the record an article from the *Winnipeg Telegram* that avowed: "So great was the number of arrivals on Thursday night that it was impossible for them to secure accommodation in the immigration hall or at the hotels. The Canadian Pacific Railway officials threw open their waiting rooms and hundreds slept on the floors." Using that as his opening salvo, Boyd asserted "that the members of the government who are responsible for this, when they lie upon their downy beds sleeping the sleep of the just and the righteous – whatever opinion we may have of them on this side of the House – I think you will agree with me that they must feel some remorse when they think of these poor people whom they are inducing to come into the country … that they should have made some provision for them instead of allowing them to lie on the floor." Given the aggressive immigration strategy of the Dominion since the appointment of Sifton six years before, it "cannot be said that this rush has come upon the government unexpectedly." Piling on, another member from a rural Manitoba riding reckoned if "the government are so anxious to take to themselves the credit of these people coming into Canada, they must also bear whatever blame attaches to them if these people are not properly looked after … Something should have been done to erect public buildings, especially immigration halls, where these people would have had proper accommodation." But how could anything be done, he asked, when the government had appropriated a measly five thousand dollars for the construction of public buildings in the entire Province of Manitoba, including "the important city of Winnipeg, the gateway of the west, the headquarters and distributing point of all these immigrants?" According to this member, three times that much was spent on a single post office for a small town outside Montreal.

McCreary next stood to "endorse the remarks" of the Opposition members. "I regret very much to have to criticise the action of the government which I am supposed to support; at the same time in this matter I believe they have been neglectful of their duty." As he had been predicting for several years, immigration to the west had boomed and the inadequate accommodations in Winnipeg had become a crisis. McCreary confirmed that, a few

days earlier in Winnipeg, he had seen great "numbers of immigrants around the streets, who could not get work on account of the cold weather, as work had not begun, and who could not get west, and who had no place to sleep. They went to the police station … and the Canadian Pacific Railway did what they never had to do before, they opened up their station and allowed them to sleep not only in the ladies' and gentlemens' waiting rooms, but in the corridors, between the offices upstairs." McCreary then went on to remind the House of the importance of first impressions. If immigrants, and especially the most desirable "English colonists," were to write home upon their arrival in Winnipeg, he opined, "I do not think they would write very cheerful or encouraging letters or letters which would induce more immigrants to come out." In these partisan, and friendly, critiques of government inaction, we see concern over the welfare of the immigrants themselves, and over the reputation of Canada as an immigrant-receiving nation, as well as continued frustration with the representational and financial bias toward central Canada.

In the absence of the minister of the interior from the House that day, it fell upon the postmaster general, Sir William Mulock, to respond to the critiques. "I entirely sympathize," he claimed, while confirming "that immigrants shall be furnished with every possible reasonable accommodation for their comfort, so that they may, with the least inconvenience, be able to start well in their new venture in life. It is of the utmost importance that these immigrants should receive a good impression of the country, and that they should find that the country, and the government representing the people, are not indifferent to their needs, but are ready to welcome them with open arms." After thus summing up the competitive and paternal rationales for Canada's immigrant-reception network, the postmaster general then offered some dismissive absolutions for the government's lack of preparation for the immigrants it knew were coming. For instance, he remarked "that others besides the government have failed in foresight"; the business facilities, hotels, boarding houses, and railroad connections in Winnipeg all were inadequate for the "immense immigration" of that season. Moreover, despite some inconvenience, these new arrivals still were much better taken care of than in previous years: "Whilst I would not compare the hardships of the past with those of today, or suggest that these immigrants are having a softer time than our forefathers did, it is always well to bear in mind that there is always more or less discomfort connected with the movement of people from one country to another." That said, of course the Dominion government wanted to portray itself as ameliorating that discomfort — in comparison with other countries — by providing a network of immigration infrastructure.

The last words in the debate were taken by Opposition leader Robert Borden, who quickly put paid to Sir William's flimsy excuses.

> While it may be true, as my hon. friend says, that the conditions faced by these people may not be so severe as the conditions which were faced by the pioneers of this country a hundred years ago, that does not as an argument amount to very much at all. What we have to do is compare the conditions which the immigrants of today have to face not with the conditions of one hundred years ago, but with the conditions in the United States, our great competitor. [23]

This was a pointed statement; it exposed the government as planning for past wars, rather than recognizing and anticipating the modern circumstances of migration, and the expectations of migrants. Ad hoc and rustic accommodations of the nineteenth century needed to be replaced with well-built, well-organized, and sanitary

institutions. Finally, since he missed the House debate, government MP Frank Oliver — who within two years would become minister responsible for immigration — added his piece in a respectful letter to Sir William. Summarizing the situation in Alberta, Oliver took "the liberty of saying that there is no duty before the Government at the moment, so important or so urgent as providing reasonable shelter for the thousands of desirable settlers now rushing into the Territories."[24]

Newspapers in Ottawa, Winnipeg, and Edmonton seemed to agree, and reported or editorialized on the subject of the debate. Even the *Detroit Evening News* recapped the House "discussion" of immigrant reception. This paper believed it to be "of interest all over the state," since "[t]housands from Michigan are in the ranks of these settlers" relocating to the last best west. In the article, Boyd is cited extensively, though the Detroit paper exaggerates his words. The treatment given settlers was "shameful," the paper concludes, and "everything was topsy-turvy." The implication was that Midwesterners should reconsider succumbing to the lure of free land grants north of the border, since the reception system was in crisis. This bad press in the United States so angered someone in the Ottawa office of the immigration branch that they scrawled in large cursive script across the news clipping: "Boyd is an ass."[25]

Still, two days after the debate, the deputy minister wrote to commissioner Smith that "there is some anxiety with regard to the accommodation for immigrants. Sir William Mulock is particularly desirous that there should be no complaints." By this point, the two immigration officials had already exchanged several emergency telegrams. After checking in with the agents at the other Prairie immigration halls, to ensure that there were "no complaints or hardships experienced anywhere," Smith telegrammed to report that "there is no apparent reason for the anxiety shown in house of Commons. We will cope with

Difficulties as they arise and there is no reason to fear immigration will be retarded." Smith also clarified that he received "nearly all the country papers in the North West Territories, and have spent some time in trying to find mention in the local columns regarding lack of accommodation for immigrants at any of these points." Finding no such mention, he "was considerably surprised" by the House debate, and "fear[ed] the result will be an enormously increased expenditure for that branch of our business … [and] difficulty in future in persuading those at the various points to depend upon their own resources rather than those of the Government." That is, local communities were also expected to provide hotels and boarding houses, and those who could afford it were expected to make use of them – and not to stay at government immigration halls. Indeed, a puzzled recruiting agent wrote from Minnesota that, if it was Ottawa's intention to house every new arrival, "it would be necessary to have large buildings at the distributing points … and after the rush is over the sheltering places would be practically useless for another year. When the great rush in the Western States took place some few years ago, there was not such attempt made on the part of the authorities to look after the housing of people as there is made by the Canadian Government today."[26] This agent seems to have missed the memo that justified immigrant reception: the whole point of the Canadian network was to offer supports that were unavailable south of the border. And yes, many of the Prairie immigration halls sat idle in the off-season.

Despite Smith's reassurances, the Ottawa office felt obliged to react to the negative attention. In ordering the commissioner to rent as much extra space as he could in Winnipeg, and to dispatch tents to Saskatoon and other "points where the people may leave the cars," the deputy minister concluded: "Whether we need to use all this accommodation or not it is considered far better

to be prepared." Smith soon telegrammed with an inventory of all immigrant shelter available in the west, spread across almost fifty different sites. He followed it with a more detailed letter to Sir William, describing how his action "therefore assures accommodation at every point where it is possible for settlers" to detrain, including 16,500 new bed spaces due to rentals and tents, to supplement the 9,500 spaces that the branch already had prior to the House of Commons debate. A couple of days after the fuss started, Smith had rented a skating rink in Winnipeg which would receive a wood floor and partitions and be equipped with surplus stoves from other halls. Smith confirmed that "we are having the old Immigration Building cleaned out of foreigners and placing them in the Rink," while the former "we are painting and cleaning up so as to utilize the two buildings here for English speaking people."[27] Officials were concerned about any immigrant who received a bad first impression, but they clearly were more concerned about the preferred classes having a negative experience. Ironically, the immigration hall that now would be reserved for the "best class" of newcomers – with a fresh coat of paint slapped on – was the same old building that McCreary had described in the House as objectionable to English-speakers. As for accommodating foreigners, Smith resolved that renting the rink was preferable to borrowing the Dominion government Drill Hall – a course advocated by Ottawa officials – because the latter was too far from the train station, and too much exposed to public scrutiny, which "would create criticism of a severe kind against the Department, particularly in view of the fact that the Drill Hall is situated in one of the best residential portions of the city." As with the very early quarantine hospitals, the "best" neighbourhoods were likely to object to the presence of indigent outsiders, especially those that did not speak English.

The local solution proved temporary, however, as the owner of the skating rink decided to demolish it three months later. After putting a significant amount of money into renovations, the immigration branch would have to vacate. Since there was "apparently no other place to be got in the city," Smith decided to bring back to the 1890 hall any foreigners he could not accommodate at East Selkirk. To this end, he partitioned off some of the larger rooms in that building, which could "be utilized from the rear of the premises where we have outside staircases." English-speaking immigrants would not be required to use the same entrances as foreigners. Because this meant "practically a division of the Immigration Hall in two parts," it necessitated the retention of the "Galician caretaker" from the rink "to keep control over these people." Ten days later, Smith reminded Ottawa of a months-old requisition, mired at the Department of Public Works, "to erect the fences so as to divide the yard" around the old immigration hall, since "you can imagine how disagreeable it is for the Britishers to mix up with the various

classes of foreigners."[28] Whether in entirely different towns like East Selkirk, in different structures with decisively different levels of comfort and quality, or in the open dirt compound around a couple of immigration buildings, officials would make efforts to keep Anglophones from others, as the press of immigration increased.

The second of the two buildings mentioned by Smith as available for English speakers was a new immigrant hospital, just then being completed next to the old immigration hall in Winnipeg (Figure 4.3). Immigration-branch hospitals will be discussed more fully in the next chapter, but this one in Winnipeg often served as overflow shelter during busy times at the hall. Its correspondence with the Prairie immigration halls did not end there, either: it also was a two-and-a-half-storey, wood-frame, pseudo-Georgian structure with clapboard siding. This materiality contrasted with the later immigrant hospitals, which would be made of brick and stone. In fact, the design of the Winnipeg hospital may have been the inspiration for the more substantial halls that appeared in Brandon, Edmonton, and elsewhere over the next few years (see Figures 3.16 to 3.18). Sitting on a raised stone basement, the hospital's two-bay wings symmetrically flank a prominent centre section, which projects forward on the facade, and on the roofline results in a kind of bas-relief hip or pavilion superimposed on the gable roof. This centre section, though wider than those on the subsequent immigration halls, is characterized by a tall, elaborate balcony on top of a raised entry porch. The stacked columns and pediments on this grand projection are the principal elements of neoclassical decoration on the building. When it was ready for use in the summer of 1903, its basement was immediately given over to emergency overflow shelter, with forty mattresses on the floor — reassurance for Sir William and other anxious Ottawa decision-makers. It would continue to be used as extra accommodation during the next

4.3 Immigrant hospital, Winnipeg, in a photograph taken when it was near completion in the spring of 1903. To the left can be seen the back side of the 1890 immigration hall, with its large shed-roof kitchen bump-out.

three summers, while a new immigration hall was under construction.

Although for several years McCreary, Smith, and others had been lobbying the government to build a new immigration hall in Winnipeg – in addition to the hospital – action seems to have been prompted finally by the 1903 debate in the House. By fall, the House of Commons had approved funds for a new building. There was little questioning of the appropriation, and the brief discussion revolved around whether "to retain the old buildings," in order to "make a separation between the immigrants, some of them being of an inferior class."[29] Although the minister of public works, who presented the estimate in his budget, believed that only the new hospital was to be preserved, in fact both buildings continued in use after the completion of the new immigration hall – for some twenty years thereafter. Meanwhile, the deputy minister was advising Sifton to demand "a more prepossessing building" that would "impress new arrivals, especially from the Old Country, as having good comfortable accommodation provided for them." Immigrants would be awed and sorted, as they were being supported. Also prompting the construction of the new Winnipeg hall was the concurrent development of a new Canadian Pacific Railway (CPR) station and hotel complex, which would encompass the lots on which the old immigration hall and new immigrant hospital stood. A land swap was arranged with the CPR, so that the new immigration hall could be located adjacent to the new station, allowing immigrants to be met on the train and on the platform and directed to a special access. The existing buildings were moved almost two hundred metres to the new site, no small feat given their size; they were placed on new concrete foundations and partly reclad in brick to match the new hall. The old hall and the hospital became known as Buildings No. 2 and No. 3, respectively, when the construction of No. 1 was finished in the summer of 1906.[30] Once all

these structures were available, immigrants would be assigned to one of the buildings according to their ethnic status. As we will see, British immigrants received the most-modern quarters in No. 1. Non-English-speaking newcomers went in No. 2, the less-commodious, wood-frame structure of 1890. Immigrants were further subdivided into all-male dormitories, dormitories for single female travellers, and family rooms.

ARCHITECTURE AND SPATIAL PRACTICES AT THE NEW WINNIPEG HALL

What became known as Building No. 1 was the main headquarters of the immigration branch outside Ottawa (Figure 4.4). It certainly was more impressive and monumental than other Prairie immigration halls, or any other Canadian immigration architecture up to this point. As Janet Wright describes it, the new Winnipeg immigration hall "was an imposing four-story building, constructed of steel and reinforced concrete, sheathed with brick. Although located alongside a railway track, it had the appearance of an important public building, with its classical elevation." The architecture was in an Edwardian Baroque style popular for government and commercial structures across the Anglo-American imperial world during that decade.[31] The principle elevation faced the CPR tracks, like a billboard welcoming the immigrants. It was fifteen bays wide, composed of a high, rusticated, limestone base with round-arched windows; three stories in buff brick, accentuated by grey masonry keystones and stringcourses; and a strongly articulated cornice line with dentils. Doric pilasters ran up between the base and the cornice, framing each pair of end bays, as well as the three central bays, where the pilasters formed a muted temple front. The pilasters visually supported triangular tympanums over the bookends, and a rounded Baroque pediment over the centre bays. Where the pilasters

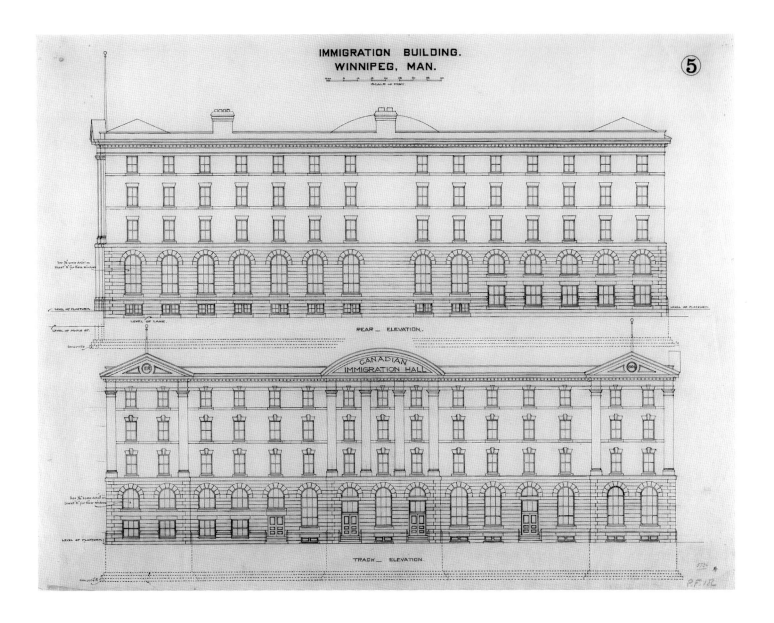

REAR ___ ELEVATION.

CANADIAN
IMMIGRATION HALL

TRACK ___ ELEVATION.

P.F. 112

4.4 Elevations for the 1906 immigration hall in Winnipeg.

sat atop the transition from stone to brick, the rustication bulged outward, suggesting a series of buttresses supporting the added symbolic weight of the classical-temple elements. The central buttresses also served to frame the main entrances in imitation of a triumphal arch or Romanesque church facade. The narrower end elevation, which faced the new CPR station complex, also featured a triangular pediment surmounting its central bays. Indeed, the brick-and-stone finishing of the hall complemented the materials used for the railway's buildings. The other end of the immigration hall, and its rear elevation, were plainer. The classical tripartite division was maintained on these elevations, with the base, middle floors, and cornice line, but without the ornamental details of the more public facades.

The contrast between the rusticated base and the brick of the upper stories emphasized the separation between the ground-floor office spaces of the building and the more prosaic dormitories, family rooms, and communal kitchens found above. The ceiling height and arched windows of the ground floor provided a rather grand reception area and office, where immigrants applied for government advice on land and employment at a long counter (Figure 4.5). During the first decade of the century, sixteen immigration officers were employed there, safely ensconced behind the counter that controlled immigrants' access. An ample waiting area provided the space for large numbers of arrivals and visitors. Nothing could be further from the situation described by the *Winnipeg Telegram* three years earlier (and read in the House by Boyd) when "the immigration offices were far too small to accommodate the inquirers

4.5 The reception area and office space where the immigration officials pictured here would meet with and advise new arrivals. Copious electric task-lighting was necessary, since trains arrived at all hours. The space is garlanded with wheat sheaves and other bounty from the Prairies, and framed images of agricultural activities. Though it is formal, airy, and bright, the pipes and radiators are exposed, a reminder that this is a structure built with public monies.

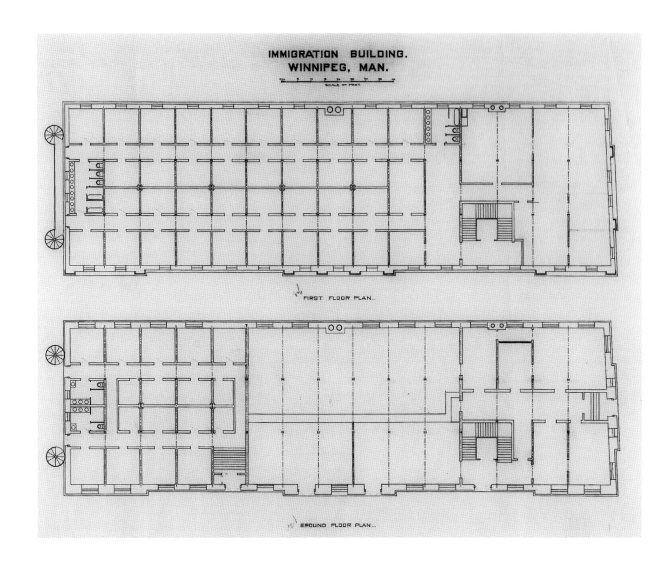

IMMIGRATION BUILDING.
WINNIPEG, MAN.

SCALE OF FEET

FIRST FLOOR PLAN.

GROUND FLOOR PLAN..

4.6 (*above and opposite*) All floor plans and roof plan from 1904 for the new immigration hall in Winnipeg. The upper floors were identical, though they were later altered. The wagon wheels on the left indicate the fire escapes.

at the counters. Some of the officers were outside, and others surrounded at their desks giving information to the anxious inquirers." As can be seen on the plans for the building, this reception area took up just over one-third of the ground floor, or six bays (Figure 4.6). At the far-right end of the space, the counter took a bend to allow immigrants access to a hallway, where they would find the main staircase and even an elevator to the residential floors; here there is another outside door, directly accessing the elevator lobby. Beyond that, there were some private, high-ceilinged, corner offices for the Winnipeg immigration and land commissioners, and these had their own entrance under the lateral temple front. At the other end of the ground floor was a mezzanine level, with its own outside access; it included sleeping rooms and toilets, but lacked areas for cooking, eating, and bathing. Some of the smaller rooms here were likely reserved for immigration agents who

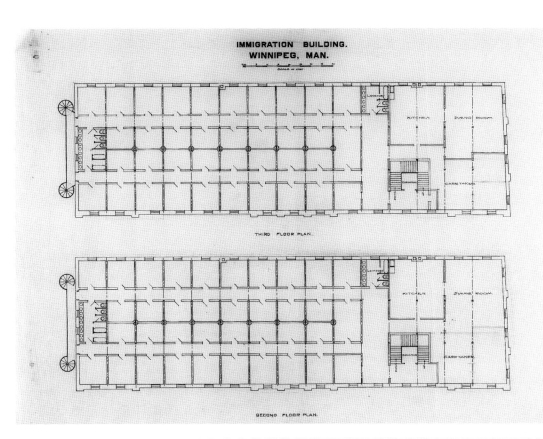

IMMIGRATION BUILDING.
WINNIPEG, MAN.
SCALE OF FEET.

THIRD FLOOR PLAN.

SECOND FLOOR PLAN.

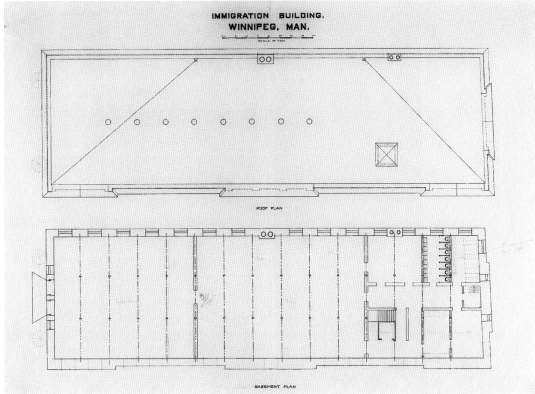

IMMIGRATION BUILDING.
WINNIPEG, MAN.
SCALE OF FEET.

ROOF PLAN

BASEMENT PLAN

travelled back and forth on the trains, land guides, and others who might have to keep odd hours.

The mezzanine level was inserted above the large basement baggage room, which could be accessed by ramp from the train platform. At the other end of the basement, near the elevator and stair, were to be found bath tubs and toilets, including a small staff washroom, a laundry room with ten tubs and running water, and next to this a drying room. In the centre of the basement was a boiler room for heat and hot water, including space for fuel storage, and an incinerator. The upper three floors were devoted to accommodations, with

4.7 A painting by Harold Copping of a bedroom in the 1906 immigration hall at Winnipeg.

one end of each reserved for a spacious kitchen, dining room, and caretaker's bedroom. The immigrant sleeping rooms on these floors were arranged along two parallel, double-loaded corridors, which meant that only about half of them had exterior windows; this would cause problems later. The windowless rooms were also smaller than the others. Two bathrooms served either end of the floor, the one adjacent to the kitchen likely being for women, and the other, larger one, for men; both had toilets, lavabos, and bathtubs. As we have seen before, Canadian officials were particularly concerned to provide ample bathing and laundry facilities for the class of settlers expected to be in need of free accommodations. Moreover, the cleanliness of the immigration halls themselves would be a model for future citizens.

The English travel writer Arthur Copping provides an evocative and especially detailed description of the living spaces in the Winnipeg hall, where he stayed while researching his 1911 book, *The Golden Land: The True Story and Experiences of British Settlers in Canada*. He begins in the baggage room, where immigrants could leave their belongings at "no charge for safeguarding … and for afterwards forewarding." From there, Copping and his brother Harold, a professional artist who contributed illustrations to the book (Figure 4.7),

> were taken up in a lift to the second story, and ushered to our room, which proved large, light, lofty, and scrupulously clean.
> It was furnished with a writing-table, two chairs, and a broom, in addition to a certain strange iron mechanism clinging against the walls. The attendant showed us how, on the release of a clutch, each apparatus unfolded as a pair of bunks; whereupon we appreciated the forethought which had so equipped an apartment that, when serving as a parlour by day, it was redeemed from the aspect it wore as a bedroom by night. Blankets were neatly

folded on the flock mattress that reposed upon springs.

Exploring the corridor, we found our way to lavatories and bathrooms that shone with cleanliness. Open doorways gave us glimpses of domestic serenity — women busy with their needles, men writing letters or reading, the little ones at play on the floor.

The author continues for several more paragraphs recounting his own uncouth experiences of "masculine ineptitude" as he attempted to navigate the entirely female spaces of the kitchen and laundry room. Overall, Copping writes, the "Immigration Hall in Winnipeg astonished and delighted us. I have never seen a more striking illustration of paternal government at work." Still, the government would only go so far, because it "was concerned to foster self-reliance, and to discourage a slothful spirit, in its guests. The presence of that broom in our room was a hint that we were expected to keep the floor tidy."[32] Immigrants in the halls were learning how to comport themselves in Canadian spaces.

Despite the grand, classical exterior, and the generally more modern and organized interior of durable materials, migrant experiences recorded at the new Winnipeg building were similar to those at earlier halls. One man arriving from Leicester in 1907 was enthusiastic in his memory of Winnipeg No. 1: "We reported to the Emigration Hall on the station which even in those days was very large and roomy, all particulars were taken of every emigrant stopping there … There was a canteen and accommodation … which I made use of the first night." He had travelled across the Atlantic in steerage class, but in British steerage, separated from "foreigners"; appropriately, he was accommodated in the new hall, while those other steerage passengers were sheltered in the old building next door. This newcomer could afford to move into a hotel on his second night in Winnipeg, but he would return to the hall later when looking for employment advice.[33]

Perhaps the most complete portrayal of immigrant spatial practices in Winnipeg Nos. 1 and 2 is a long 1907 article in the magazine section of the Manitoba *Free Press*. This article, by journalist Florence Hamilton Randall, very much reflects the ethnic split effected at the Winnipeg compound, both in what she describes and how she describes it. In fact, Randall's depiction indicates a tripartite organization of space: the "British, English-speaking foreigners, and Galicians have each separate quarters." These were, respectively, the upper floors of the new immigration hall, the mezzanine floor, and the entirely separate 1890 structure. The distribution of the "semi-foreign quarters" to the mezzanine reserved the "brighter rooms" with windows for families, "while single men take willingly enough the rooms on the dark side of the corridor."[34] This sorting by sex likely prevailed on the upper floors as well. The placement of these immigrants on the mezzanine, or "half-floor" as she calls it, and Randall's evocation of them as half-British — a characterization she no doubt absorbed from the immigration officials she interviewed — are wonderfully poetic indications of the hierarchy of access to citizenship at the time.

In a section subtitled "Woman's Work in the Kitchen," the article goes on to contrast domestic scenes in the British and foreign quarters. Upstairs on the British floors of the main building,

some of the newly arrived were cooking their dinner … In the room adjoining, the dining room, several pretty, flaxen-haired little English girls, with soft voices and nice manners, were playing "Old Maid" to while away the tedium of the rainy day. Here the children are allowed to romp and enjoy themselves, playing tag, "horse," or any childish game … Sometimes, too, an invitation comes to an evening "children's party" at All People's Mission, when cake is consumed in large quantities.

Meanwhile, across the yard in the 1890 hall, it was

> down in the basement kitchen of this building that the most picturesque sights may be seen, from the point of view of the artist. He might find the atmosphere a bit stuffy at times but he would get wonderful studies of the foreign element in their population of the west ... I watched with delight the children playing about on the bare floor, the elderly woman bending over a soup pot bubbling on the huge range, the young girls with their bright handkerchiefs and aprons, holding the omni-present baby.

The "foreign element" is portrayed as totally other: colourful, unusual, overly reproductive, content to sit and play on the bare floor of the kitchen. In contrast, the British are blonde and attractive, polite, sitting primly at the dining table to play cards, only interrupted by the occasional frolic.

For this reporter, the principle marker of difference between established local citizens and arriving British was the amusing misuse of Canadian cooking stoves by the newcomers – using oversized logs or lighting the fire in the oven instead of the compartment underneath. Comparatively, she notes that the foreigners were deemed so different as to be supplied with their own "post office where the non-English speaking receive their letters ... The postmaster and his assistant occasionally find it pretty hard to decipher these names, 'but it's all in getting used to them,' I was told."[35] Meanwhile, there was no need for Canadians to "get used to" the Britishers; already the latter were being invited to community cake events.

During her visit to the compound, Randall spent time interviewing Commissioner Smith, who discussed with her the "many ramifications" of immigration-branch work centred in its Winnipeg headquarters. "Unless they go up in a balloon our immigrants cannot escape us," he is quoted as stating:

> That is why the government practically gives us carte blanche, and that is why it is possible to do all we do. Last winter, you may have heard, we sent out our patrols into certain districts to see that the homesteaders did not starve because of the exceptional conditions ... they sent whole families in to us, to tide them over the bad days ... This spring we had to advance an enormous amount of seed grain to those farmers who were forced to use what they had during the winter.

In these cases, the immigration halls in Winnipeg and elsewhere became emergency shelters. The branch administered both indoor and outdoor relief. To support this work, a "record is kept of all who pass through the office," although Randall makes much of Smith's ability to remember faces and stories from the thousands of immigrants under his charge. The personal touch tempers the bureaucratic surveillance and record-keeping represented by the formidable new Winnipeg immigration hall. Benevolently, the government's record-keeping allowed for the reunion of families and the discovery of malingering fathers, elopers, and other reprobates. The modern hall witnessed marriages, births, and deaths as well.[36]

A fuller understanding of the office work at No. 1 can be gleaned from the *New York Times* articles mentioned above, which were concerned particularly about the care taken in the selection and maintenance of healthy, productive immigrants:

> Winnipeg is the distributing centre for Western settlers. They pour out through the great

station into the adjoining huge Immigration Hall, where they undergo inspection once more. Before they left the ship they had been inspected closely by immigration agents, and again in Montreal they had undergone careful scrutiny, so this is the third time. If they are intending homesteaders, seeking Government farms, the plans and details are all there in the Government land office, with courteous officials to help them understand. If they are workers seeking employment, there has been gathered for their information the latest reports on the demand for labor.[37]

The "wise men" managing the Dominion government immigration system are portrayed as heroic figures. When the *Times* reporter visited, Smith had been promoted to serve as assistant superintendent of emigration in London, England; his replacement was the "suave" J. Bruce Walker:

In a large sunny room on the ground floor of the Immigration Hall in Winnipeg ... a sturdy, pleasant-faced man of fifty sits at a big flat-topped desk.

The sunlight streams in through the tall, wide windows upon his white hair and the huge bowl of fresh sweetpeas at his elbow, bringing out the orderliness of the letter files and law books surrounding him, the keen blue eyes, strong features, and shrewd smile that flashes over them as the man talks. Room and occupant seem to match each other in a way that rooms have of reflecting the personality of forceful tenants. Action and optimism pervade both.

The man at the desk never seems to stay there for prolonged periods... standing up to emphasize some statement with outstretched forefinger, or bending forward to drive home some argument with clenched fist on open palm. It is characteristic of him that he prefers to stand to use the telephone ...

[T]here is a steady stream of baggage-laden immigrants in and out of the building past the window of the sunny room in which the sturdy man is at work. There seems to be no detail in the personalities in that stream that escapes his attention, no variation in its volume or characteristics that he does not note. For that is his business.

From this office emanated the modern network of immigration-reception architecture in Canada, over which Walker, as the article explains, held full command. The reporter proceeds to laud the efficient organization of the system, extending from the demands of local employers or areas in need of eager settlers, through local immigration agents at the Prairie halls, the Winnipeg headquarters, the Ottawa offices, to superintendents in London and the United States monitoring the supply and quality of immigrants. The superior Canadian system sifted out "undesirable" immigrants, and funnelled in the most desirable, northern-European – and midwestern American – agriculturalists and labourers targeted for specific national needs. The *Times* reporter expresses some chagrin that Canada "gets the cream of immigration," while the United States gets the "skim milk." Walker's response is emphatic. "Why shouldn't we get the best immigrants?" he asks. "What care do you take of them? You receive them, but then you leave them to sink or swim." There follows several paragraphs describing the social-welfare programs that ensure the health and productivity of settlers in the first year or two after their arrival in Canada.[38] The implication was clear: the efforts of government officials were good for the immigrants, but were also perceived as vital for the country. By looking out for the welfare of newcomers all across its network of immigration architecture, the Dominion government could attract more settlers to populate the west, keep them, and ensure their gratitude to the state.

OTHER IMMIGRATION HALLS AND THEIR PLACE IN THEIR COMMUNITIES

During the decade prior to the First World War, immigration halls continued to be sites of interest to local communities across the Canadian Prairies. Local newspapers, lobbyists, and governments all paid attention to the provisions for immigrant reception in their towns, crying fair or foul. To satisfy what it determined were genuine local needs, the Dominion government in this period developed a standard design for a cheap and easy-to-build, wood-frame immigration hall that would be used in more than a dozen new communities. At the same time, though, just as many immigration halls were shut down as were built new. When all the land or jobs in a small community were taken, the necessity for accommodations disappeared. At that moment, or before, locals often stepped in to borrow or buy the surplus hall and convert it for other community uses.

When a hall was in operation, a regular news item in local papers was the "Immigration Returns." As noted in the previous chapter, newspapers printed the weekly or monthly numbers of arrivals and departures at the local immigration hall, often listing as well the ethnic origins and ultimate destinations of the newcomers. For example, in reporting the returns for the second week of July 1909, the *Edmonton Bulletin* noted that among "the arrivals the majority were of English birth, with several more Germans and Americans … The homesteaders arriving at the present time will make the very best class of settlers." On another occasion, the same paper strove to explain longer-term stays at the immigration halls: "The officers have not encouraged early entry into the country as it is hard to obtain suitable

accommodation and too cold to go out in search of land." However, the agent was encouraging those "who have sufficient means to take up lots in the city and build temporary shacks where their families could be housed till the men secure land in the country districts. " This would make room for new "inmates," such as the dozen "good looking men" just arrived from England. In rare instances, the reports were less upbeat, such as at moments of severe overcrowding or when the immigration hall was in quarantine due to an outbreak of some contagious disease.[39] In these cases, the news items were like public-service announcements, warning away potential employers, vegetable sellers, and others.

Sometimes there were things for town residents to see at the immigration halls. Readers of one local newspaper were recommended to appreciate the "fine assortment of floral plants given to the immigration department … tastefully arranged in two beds, one on either side of the entrance to the hall … a fine touch of color to the otherwise sombre surroundings" in the vicinity of the rail yards. The halls also hosted exhibits of Prairie produce to edify immigrants and render locals proud (Figure 4.8). In 1910, for instance, it was reported that there was "on view at the Immigration Hall specimens of oats, wheat, buckwheat and poppies grown at Athabasca Landing and contributed by residents of that district to tempt the incoming settler."[40] It was another way of providing information about good homesteading land. Meanwhile, the immigrants themselves read the papers for local information and for news of home. For one Winnipeg newsboy, intimate knowledge of the ethnicities present in the immigration halls was a matter of good business. Bribing the guard or caretaker with a free newspaper, he could sell copies to inmates by matching headlines to their countries of origin. At the same time, he kept an eye out for Jewish arrivals who might need translations or other aid from his father, a local merchant.[41]

One measure of something's prominence and familiarity within a community is that jokes are made about it. The local newspaper reported how a "young German immigrant" caused some amusement in Edmonton when he attempted to enter the immigration hall by the fire escape. When a station guard spotted him "half way up to the roof," climbing the iron ladder and "lugging a heavy valise after him," the guard's "words rang out in stentorian tones across the 100 yard interval" between depot and hall: "Hi, there! Where are you going?" The reporter is led to ponder the nature of spatial practices in unfamiliar terrain: "Whether he was accustomed to exterior stairs or expected new things in a new country, he at any rate decided that this was the way into the big wooden building where he could find a temporary home." Another

4.8 Immigration hall exhibit of sheaves of wheat and other Prairie produce, in Edmonton or Strathcona, in 1902. The image reveals the agent's office space with small desk, letter press, British and United States flags, and photographs of western Canada, as well as the king and the prime minister.

local rag published this jokey item: "A Welsh immigrant who visited the immigration hall was arrested on a charge of insanity the other day. He was gesticulating wildly, and no one seemed to be able to understand him … It developed that he had been only trying to make himself understood in his native tongue."[42] Though British subjects, the Welsh seem to have been considered, at least in the context of this wisecrack, among the semi-foreign. That this item appeared in a newspaper printed in

4.9 Unofficial immigration shed erected from scrap materials in Moose Jaw, 1902.

This tent was of a size sufficient to cover their most ardent dreams regarding the number of immigrants coming in, but they are now satisfied that the Department had a better idea of what accommodation was really necessary at that point than they had themselves … there never was, and is not now, nor likely to be in the future, the necessity for any such accommodation … and I am quite satisfied if the tent had been fully occupied very much discomfort would have ensued, as nothing but a shingle roof will keep out the heavy rains we have been having.[43]

All was not lost, however. Smith had the lumber salvaged and recommended that Ottawa approve a small amount of money to help slap together a small, one-storey immigrant shed just to keep the town happy – though no government agent would be stationed there. This shed remained in use for almost a decade (Figure 4.9). A proper Dominion government immigration hall for Moose Jaw was finally announced in 1909, to be built according to the standard plans of that period. The local press concluded that the "decision to erect this hall is … another indication that the wheels of progress are moving rapidly in this city this year." However, two summers later the Board of Trade was again ruing the "wholly inadequate" situation for immigrant reception in Moose Jaw, claiming that the new immigration hall was too small. Their grumbles were raised in the House of Commons, and summarily dismissed.[44]

In Edmonton, the immigration branch had been renting an old hotel as an immigration hall for half a dozen years when local citizens had had enough. At the start of 1905, complaints originating with immigrants staying at the rented hall made their way back to the Emigrant's Information Office, a British government clearing house, and Ottawa was notified by the Canadian commissioner of immigration stationed in London. Prominent

a town where there was no immigration hall at all attests to these being such well-known institutions that they played a role in popular culture.

Towns that lacked an immigration hall would lobby to get one built. The implication often seemed to be that to have a Dominion government building meant that the town was better developed than the next one along the rails. The boosters in these towns felt the lack of an immigration hall as a snub. If the government was not forthcoming with a building, towns sometimes took matters into their own hands. The Moose Jaw Board of Trade, "owing to this place's importance," had been lobbying the Dominion government unsuccessfully for more than a year when, in spring 1902, the town erected a 3,300-square-foot tent with wood flooring, partitions, and bunks for the accommodation of immigrants. Commissioner Smith was unimpressed when he visited on an inspection tour a couple of months later. He "ordered" the removal of the temporary structure and described the scene for the deputy minister:

Edmontonians seem to have caught a whiff of the complaints, with both the Board of Trade and the Liberal Association writing strong resolutions to the Dominion government demanding a new immigration hall. MP Frank Oliver wrote his support directly to the minister. Two months later, Oliver was the minister responsible for immigration. By that summer, the site was determined for a new hall, though construction did not begin for another year, due to delays at the Department of Public Works.[45]

Successful lobbying efforts sometimes could backfire, however. In Edmonton, the design for the new immigration hall was determined – nay, copied from Brandon – without any spatial-planning research to understand the local needs (see Figure 3.18). Before construction commenced, the Edmonton agent was warning his superiors that the borrowed plan to be used there was too small for this busy transportation hub. However, his superiors decided it was too late to effect changes in the plan, because Public Works was too slow in accomplishing any request. Change orders might mean another year's delay. Instead, immediately upon the completion of the building in the winter of 1906–07, a "temporary addition"

was placed at the rear, probably without any input from the Chief Architect's Branch. This one-storey, shed-roofed addition comprised a long common room flanked by narrow sleeping compartments entirely filled with built-in, sloping, shared bunks. A second, identical addition would extend the complex further by 1909 (Figure 4.10). In the words of one official, these additions were "wooden erections scarcely inferior to an ordinary homesteaders [sic] stable."[46] But as the Edmonton *Journal* reported, the gross underestimation of the space needed for immigrant lodgings was not the sole "bungle" in the design and construction of the 1906 immigration hall. When the contract for the main building was let, it did not include provision for the heating, plumbing, or electrical systems. Construction being finished, the ceiling had to be "ripped up" so these could be installed. In the meantime, the first addition was completed without any toilets or wash rooms, forcing those staying there to tramp over to the main building – once those services had been installed there. It was

4.10 Edmonton immigration hall of 1906 on the right, with the two additions and a wash house with toilets (the "lean-to"), as of the early 1920s.

"a rather deplorable state of affairs," and the "city sanitary inspector" gave the Dominion government twenty-four hours to provide proper privies, or he would shut down the whole complex. Local citizens had held high expectations, concluded the *Journal*, but "instead of taking proper pride in the new building, it is regarded out of place in a city with the prospects of Edmonton."[47] As it was, the new immigration complex was an embarrassment to boosters, rather than an asset to be boasted of.

A few years later, similar ignominy was associated with the old 1885 immigration hall in Calgary. The need for a new hall there was identified at least as early as 1906, though the new building would not open for many years. At the start of 1909, the city clerk corresponded directly with the minister, advising him of a council motion to appeal for a new immigration hall. "I do not think it requires any argument on my part," he wrote, "to show that the building is entirely out-of-date, so far as size and convenience are concerned, and not modern in any particular." A year later, having received no response, the City moved to condemn the structure. By mid-1910, Commissioner Walker was in town to announce that a new hall was to be built, "modern and up-to-date," and on a "concrete foundation, with red brick and white facings." This was a lot of architectural detail, considering that the Chief Architect's Branch had not yet embarked upon the design of the new building. Walker sent his specifications to Ottawa a week later, and it was clear that this structure would be more impressive than the basic wood-frame immigration halls being erected elsewhere. In fact, it would be in the spirit of the recent Winnipeg No. 1, if not on quite the same scale.[48]

By the fall, though, little had changed, and stakeholders began to express their frustration. The local agent wrote bitterly to the commissioner, asking for "any information" he had regarding the pending project. If it was not to be built immediately,

then something will have to be done with the one we have, as it is settling so that the plaster is cracking and falling off the lath. I have been obliged to saw off one corner of the doors in order to shut them, and I am expecting every day that the health inspector will come and nail up the doors of the water closets.

There is not a day passes over my head that I am not asked if the Government is not going to build a new immigration hall at Calgary this year or not, for they say the one we have is a disgrace, and it is the truth too.

To compound the problem, Calgary experienced a typhoid epidemic that fall, and several hundred residents were hospitalized with the infection. As a result, the sanitary inspector informed the immigration branch that the City was "enforcing sewer and water connections in every building where a sewer is on the street." The Dominion government had resisted the expense of connecting to public services in Calgary for almost twenty years, and the present building had only outdoor privies. Now the government had to pay for a connection to a building about to be demolished. Later that fall, Walker was writing angry letters to Ottawa:

I regret to learn that notwithstanding the elapse of months since the information required by the Public Works Department was placed at their disposal, nothing seems to have been done towards making a beginning with the new building ... there is a great deal of public indignation expressed both in the City Council, and through the public press of Calgary ... [and] a great deal of blame is also unjustly placed upon the Immigration Branch.[49]

Throughout this period, newcomers were taking up lodgings in the creaky old hall with its jury-rigged plumbing and drafty doors; unfortunately, their impressions were not recorded. The story resumes two years later, with the immigration branch still occupying the 1885 hall. In the interval, the Liberal government – which had overseen so much immigration construction activity during its fifteen-year reign – had been defeated. No doubt, many federal construction projects were delayed due to the turmoil of parliamentary transition. The building was eventually prodded along to completion by newly elected local MP, R.B. Bennett, through his interventions with the ministers of the interior and of public works.

In Calgary's second immigration hall, which was finally completed in 1913, four large dormitories in the attic point to the ideal of sorting by ethnicity (Figures 4.11 and 4.12). In the middle floor, a dozen bedrooms are provided for family groups and women. On the ground floor, a central entrance, vestibule, and hall are flanked by the agent's office and the caretaker's suite to the left. Immigrants' communal rooms are behind and to the right of the stair hall, with the large kitchen and its storerooms taking up much of the rear of the building. The basement is reserved for services: WCs, bathtubs, showers, and laundries for immigrants to scrub off the dirt of travel, plus a large furnace room and fuel storage to provide central heating. On the exterior, the hall is characterized by classicism in red brick with masonry trim, not unlike that used on Winnipeg No. 1 (Figure 4.13). The specific details, which add up to a French Second Empire style of architecture, are strangely *retardataire*, however. The elevations, though less ornamental, strongly resemble those of the Customs House in Victoria, designed by the Chief Architect's Branch over thirty years earlier. There, as architectural historian Harold Kalman has noted, the mansard roof, pedimented dormers, and tall chimneys were "sufficient to convey the federal image."[50] Here in Calgary, people could also identify the immigration hall as a public

building, even if it greatly departed from the style and colour scheme of the wood-frame halls in other Prairie towns.

After taking so many years to get built, the new Calgary hall hosted relatively few immigrants. With the outbreak of the war about a year after the building's completion, immigrant numbers dwindled for most of a decade. In the interim, the building was used to house troops during deployment and discharge. In 1917, when the hall was occupied by thirty returning veterans, the boiler in the basement exploded, "wrecking the rear of the building and doing considerable damage" to the kitchen. The officer in charge related that the "crash of the explosion, with the shaking of the building was strongly reminiscent of the trenches."[51] When the Dominion government undertook repairs in 1920, it converted much of the building for use by the Seed Branch of the Department of Agriculture. The immigration and land agents retained offices on the ground floor, but no immigrant lodgings were preserved.

Having an Alberta MP as minister ultimately helped to get the Edmonton hall built and the one in Calgary under way; the intervention of the local representative, a member of the new government elected in 1911, was required to get Calgary's finished. Perhaps the most extreme case of immigration halls being built as a political favour were three that appeared in Quebec early in the twentieth century. The Dominion government did not see the Province of Quebec as a primary destination for immigrants. However, Quebec politicians wanted to repatriate francophones who had moved to New England factory towns. Various organizations offered ready-made farms and other incentives to remigration. It would look good – in Quebec, at least – for the Dominion government to appear supportive of this movement, and the prominent francophone journalist and MP Henri Bourassa extracted promises from Sifton to erect immigration halls for the purpose of repatriation.

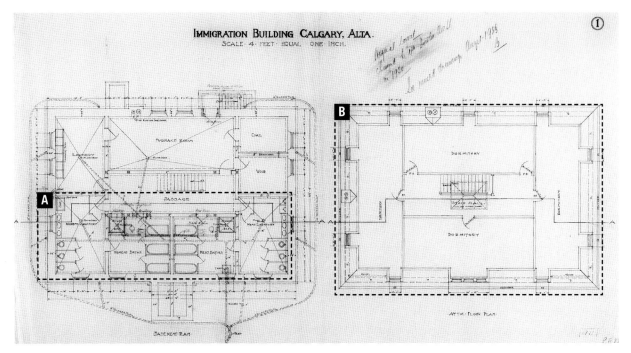

IMMIGRATION BUILDING CALGARY, ALTA.
SCALE · 4 · FEET · EQUAL · ONE · INCH.

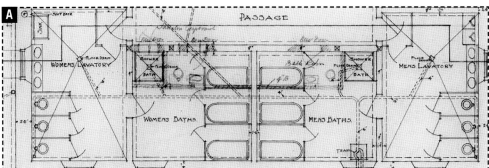

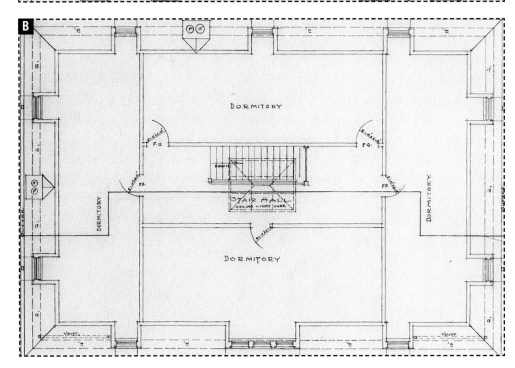

4.11 Basement and attic plans, Calgary immigration hall. The plans are dated 1911, the structure was built in 1913, and the handwritten note indicates that there were alterations made to the building in 1920 by local Public Works architect Leo Dowler (a Conservative Party appointee back in 1912), and again in 1933.

4.12 (*opposite and overleaf*) Ground- and first-floor plans, Calgary immigration hall.

IMMIGRATION BUILDING CALGARY, ALTA.
SCALE · 4 FEET · EQUAL · ONE INCH

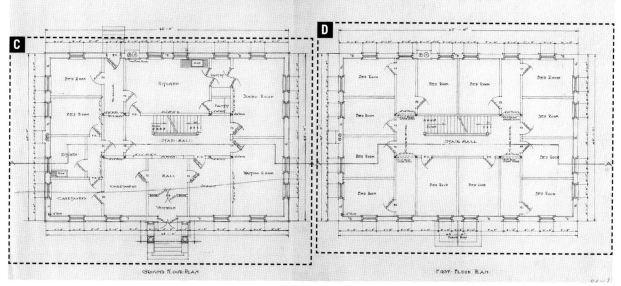

GROUND FLOOR PLAN

FIRST FLOOR PLAN

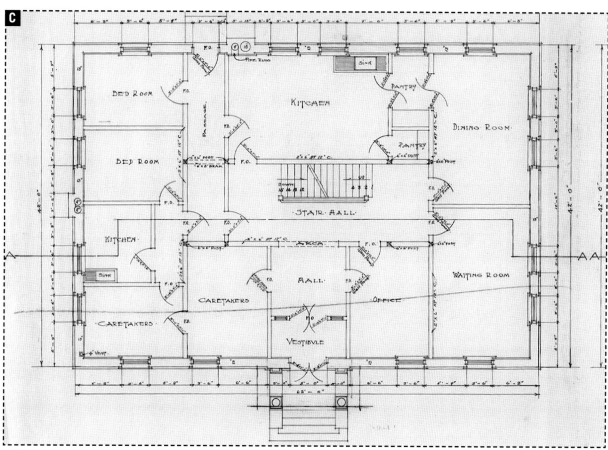

D

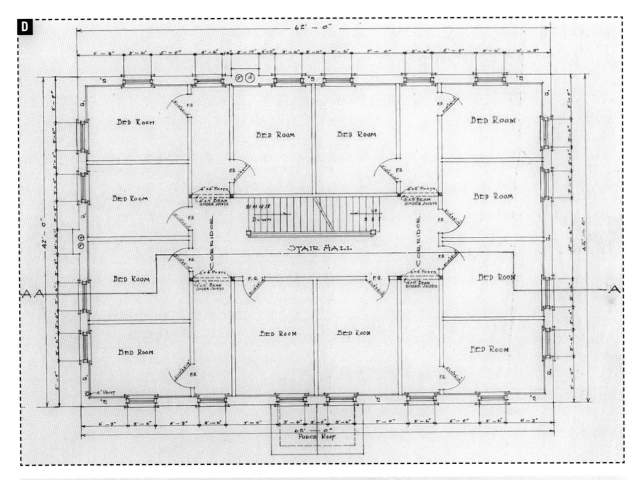

BED ROOM

BED ROOM BED ROOM

BED ROOM

BED ROOM

BED ROOM

STAIR HALL

BED ROOM

BED ROOM

BED ROOM

BED ROOM

BED ROOM

BED ROOM

PORCH ROOF

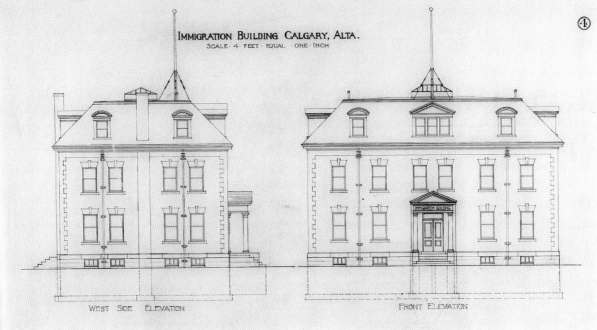

IMMIGRATION BUILDING CALGARY, ALTA.
SCALE · 4 · FEET · EQUAL · ONE · INCH.

④

WEST SIDE ELEVATION

FRONT ELEVATION

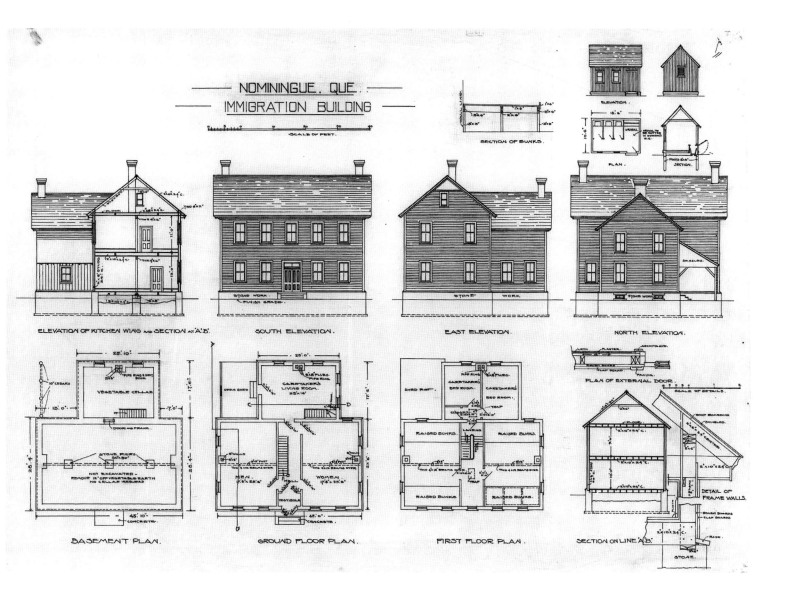

NOMININGUE, QUE.
IMMIGRATION BUILDING

SCALE OF FEET.

SECTION OF BUNKS.

ELEVATION.

PLAN.

ELEVATION OF KITCHEN WING AND SECTION AT 'A.B'.

SOUTH ELEVATION.

EAST ELEVATION.

NORTH ELEVATION.

PLAN OF EXTERNAL DOOR.

BASEMENT PLAN.

GROUND FLOOR PLAN.

FIRST FLOOR PLAN.

SECTION ON LINE 'A.B'.

DETAIL OF FRAME WALLS.

In 1904, the deputy minister wrote the chief architect asking for a favour: "If you have a set of plans and specifications which you could let me have I would be much obliged." He had in mind, for cost and design, "something the same as the one in Dauphin" built half a dozen years earlier.[52] A copy of the five-bay, two-and-a-half-storey Dauphin immigration hall soon appeared at Nomininge, in Bourassa's riding (Figure 4.14). At about the same time, a somewhat larger hall was built farther east in Roberval, according to the modernized,

4.13 (opposite, bottom) Elevations, Calgary immigration hall. The design's Second Empire style features a mansard roof, quoins, and strongly articulated window frames in varying forms (flat with keystone, segmental, and classical pediment).

4.14 (above) Immigration hall in Nomininge, Quebec, built in 1907. The main volume is a copy of earlier halls in Dauphin and other Prairie locations, but here we find a unique, two-storey bump-out housing the kitchen and bedrooms of the caretaker. The building never housed immigrants.

4.15 Immigration hall in Edson, Alberta, built in 1911 according to the new standard design. Three-quarters of the site is fenced with a high board fence for security and privacy, but the building is fronted with a charming and domestic white picket fence.

five-bay plan by then in use on the Prairies (see Figure 3.15). It appears that the immigration branch did not formally request Public Works to oversee construction of the three halls in Quebec, nor is there evidence of an appropriation of funds for them. However, the caretakers at these halls did draw federal salaries on the approval of the prime minister himself.[53]

A couple of years after the Nominingue hall was built, internal correspondence marvelled that there was no record of any immigrants or re-turning Québécois ever having stayed there, though some of the latter had used the building as an information and left-luggage bureau. Meanwhile, provincial government employees had offices in the building without the knowledge of the federal Department of Public Works. The caretaker at

Nominingue, who was the provincial colonization agent and a Liberal Party organizer, made the hall a personal residence for his family of five. In 1909, he had the audacity to request some repairs and renovations: painting, adjustment of doors and windows to correct issues arising from the wet lumber used in construction, a concrete floor for the root cellar, a porch roof, and a new entrance better situated to improve the livability of the house.[54] It seems that none of this maintenance was ever performed. The caretaker was sacked and evicted after the 1911 change in the federal par-liament. The paper trail disappears until 1920, at which point Ottawa officials admitted that their most recent information about the Nominingue hall was the 1909 request for repairs. In the early 1920s, Public Works stepped in to dispose of the structure and land.[55]

The halls in Quebec likely represent the last de-ployment of those particular five-bay designs from the turn of the century. Around 1908, the immigra-tion branch began to use a new standardized hall design (Figure 4.15) in smaller communities such as Vermilion, Swift Current, and Wilkie, followed by Yonker, Wainwright, Philips (1910), Unity, Edson, Entwhistle (1911), Castor (1912), Gravelbourg and Athabasca Landing (1913), Grande Prairie (1914), and both Spirit River and Peace River (1917). This simplified design would be easier to build, maintain, and monitor. Used for about a decade, it would become the longest-serving standard plan for Prairie immigration halls. Even so, despite this standardization, the newly appointed travelling immigration inspector expressed bewilderment at the variety of different hall designs he was encountering across the Prairies in 1912, writing that "there seems to be a lack of principle or systematic uniformity as regards the laying out of the various Halls."[56] As we have seen, there had been at least half a dozen different designs used in the previous thirty years, and there were examples of most of these still in use. Prompted by this inspector, the new standard plan

for smaller halls, by then in use for some years, was refined and codified to an extent not seen with earlier designs (Figure 4.16).

Compared to the most recent, five-bay versions of the building type, the new standard design was only one and a half storeys; it was of a similar depth, but about twenty feet longer than the older halls. The greater length allowed for all the principle functions of the immigration hall to be accommodated on the ground floor. The entrance porch opens to a lobby monitored by the agent's office, and easily accessible to a washing room with several sinks. The caretaker's suite occupies two

4.16 (*below and overleaf*) Blueprint of the standard design used for small-town immigration halls from about 1908 to 1917. Note that these buildings did not boast central heating, electrical wiring, or modern plumbing; the plan, section, and elevation of the outhouse – or outdoor privies – are at the bottom right.

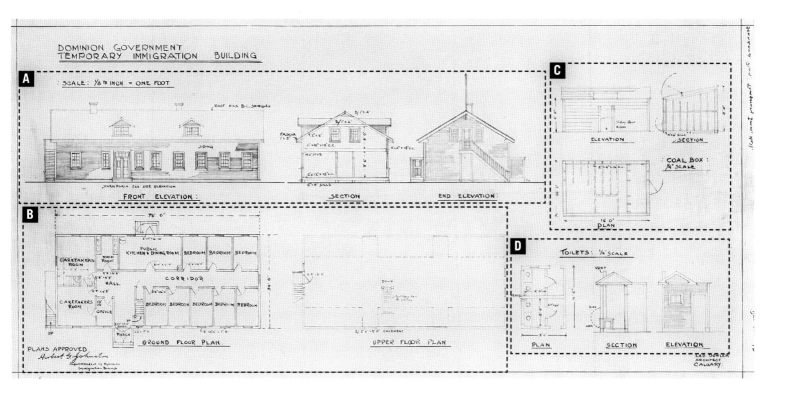

A

: SCALE : ⅛ TH INCH = ONE FOOT

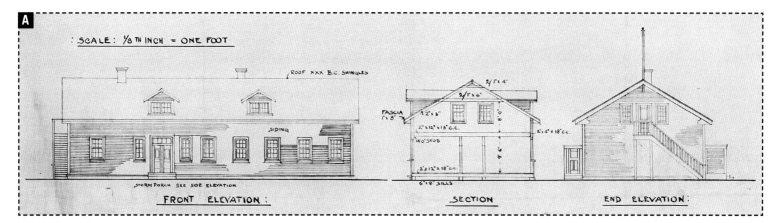

ROOF XXX B.C. SHINGLES

SIDING

STORM PORCH SEE SIDE ELEVATION

FRONT ELEVATION :

FASCIA 1"x 8"

2/1"x 4"
2/1"x 6"
1/2"x 6"
2"x12"x18" c.c.
4"x 4"x 18" c.c.
14'0" STUD
2"x12"x18" c.c.
6"x 8" SILLS

SECTION

END ELEVATION :

B

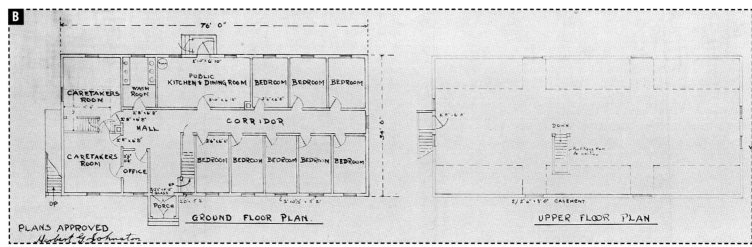

76' 0"

CARETAKERS ROOM
WASH ROOM
PUBLIC KITCHEN & DINING ROOM
BEDROOM
BEDROOM
BEDROOM
2'8"x 6'8"
HALL
CORRIDOR
34' 0"
CARETAKERS ROOM
OFFICE
2'8"x 6'8"
BEDROOM
BEDROOM
BEDROOM
BEDROOM
BEDROOM
UP
GLASS
PORCH
UP

GROUND FLOOR PLAN.

2'8"x 6'8"
DOWN
Partitions run to ceiling
2/2'6"x 3'0" CASEMENT

UPPER FLOOR PLAN

PLANS APPROVED
Hubert G Johnston

C

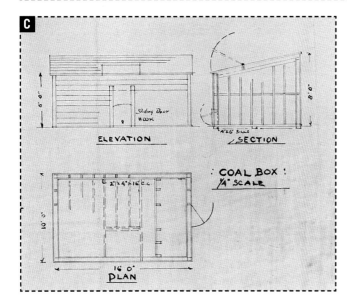

Sliding Door HOOK

ELEVATION

SECTION
8'0"
4"x 6" SILLS

COAL BOX :
¼" SCALE

2"x 4"x 16" c.c.

16' 0"

PLAN

D

TOILETS : ¼" SCALE

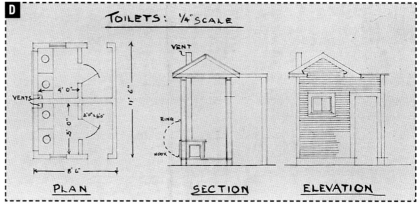

VENTS
4' 0"
5' 0"
2'0"x 6'0"
8' 6"
11' 6"

PLAN

VENT
RING
HOOK

SECTION

ELEVATION

generous rooms on the far-left side of the plan. From the lobby, a long, double-loaded corridor passes the immigrants' kitchen and dining room, and eight bedrooms all of approximately the same size. One long, narrow attic room, with four dormers punctuating the sloping ceilings, served as overflow sleeping space for single male transients. These attic rooms could be left unfinished and inaccessible if officials did not anticipate that much traffic at the location. In fact, in the earliest iterations of this design, the attic was accessible only by ladder. In later examples, such as that seen in the blueprint, a staircase has been inserted adjacent to the main entrance, and an external fire escape was added in the gable end. There are no modern conveniences included in this bare-bones design: there is no plumbing, with sinks draining directly to the outside; toilets are in outhouses; heating is limited to kitchen stoves; and there is no electrical wiring. This rusticity endured as a key aspect of the immigration-hall experience. The Winnipeg commissioner confirmed in 1930 that, due to the cost, "we have so far not authorized the installation of electric light in our second class immigration halls."[57] These amenities were reserved for the larger immigration halls, such as the new ones built in Calgary (1913) and Prince Albert (1927).

The exterior of these standard halls presented a trim and modern appearance, with horizontal siding painted bright white, with green trim (Figure 4.17). In the picture, a flagpole extends up from the peak of one gable. Unlike the Georgian symmetry of previous wood-frame immigration halls, the entrance here is off-centre in the third of eight bays. The appearance is modernistic, with the elevation reflecting the functions within: beginning from left, wider window spacing marks

4.17 Immigration hall, Grande Prairie, Alberta, erected around 1914, photographed in the mid-1920s.

the caretaker's suite; a smaller window indicates the tiny footprint of the office; on the other side of the entrance porch, another small window lights the staircase to the attic; finally, to the right of this extend the bedroom windows in a somewhat more regular rhythm. There is no ornamentation. Although the architecture of these standard halls differentiated them from single-family houses, their low-slung, linear form was less of a landmark than the tall, gangly immigration halls of earlier years. By this point in the history of the immigrant-reception system, perhaps the Dominion government felt comfortable that new arrivals were cognizant of the halls, and easily able to find them. Alongside the standardization of the architecture, the same travelling inspector urged the standardization of furniture and supplies in immigration halls. Ottawa agreed by 1914: "The Minister has decided that we should have a uniform practice in the West with regard to supplying sheets, pillows, pillow slips, blankets, etc. ... to all Immigration Halls, including, of course, the Halls at Winnipeg ... It is also desired that when a new stock of blankets is purchased the same shall have woven into them the words 'Dom. Imm. Hall'... When ordering a new supply of dishes the same words should be stamped on the cups, plates and saucers."[58] The immigration branch was discovering the power of branding its material culture. As we will see, though, this level of standardization was short-lived: the few immigration halls to be built after the war were larger structures, situated in the main distribution points, and these would be one-off designs like the 1913 Calgary building.

Despite this new design, other aspects of the experiences and practices of guests and staff at the immigration halls remained consistent throughout this period. Stays continued to be governed by posted regulations, though the list became longer and more detailed, probably based on past experience. For instance, new regulations specified that cleaning and cooking tools were not to be removed from the premises, that "Electric Lights or Oil Lamps" were not to be tampered with, and that no one was allowed in the baggage room or shed "unless accompanied by an officer." Even so, the immigration branch would "assume no responsibility for loss or injury to baggage" at the halls, nor would it be stored indefinitely. The maximum length of stay was stated to be seven days, while "[l]oungers or idlers would be ejected from the building, and tramps would be handed over to the police."[59] Regardless of the regulations, however, the length of stay remained flexible. In the annual report of the Winnipeg commissioner for 1912, Walker states that "new-comers are cared for" at forty "PRAIRIE IMMIGRATION HALLS," where they are "received and provided with accommodation, light and fuel. While there is officially a fixed period of residence in an immigration hall, at the same time practical caretakers of these buildings see to it that if the new-comer is making an honest effort to settle, no stated limit of residence is imposed upon him."[60] In these contexts, regulations were symbolic but not pragmatic.

The quality of design and maintenance continued to vary across the network of immigration halls, depending on the age of the structure, the demand and turnover in the lodgings, the commitment of the staff, and the responsiveness of their superiors. For instance, on a Saskatchewan tour in 1905, an inspector found the halls at Regina and Craik both in "very good condition," but the one at Rosthern was "filthy," it having "been the rendevous [sic] for everything strolling on the prairie." He recommended "the appointment of a competent care taker at this point."[61] Indeed, agents or caretakers were regularly dismissed for neglecting to keep their halls tidy and sanitary – or for failing to keep good paperwork on the immigrants passing through. As well, disorganization at the Chief Architect's Branch continued to cause problems for immigration officials. Getting simple work orders accomplished seemed

FOR THE TEMPORARY ACCOMMODATION OF SETTLERS

184

well-nigh impossible at times. A year after the opening of Winnipeg No. 1, Commissioner Smith sent an emergency telegram to Ottawa: "Mosquitoes growing rapidly. Public works have estimate for mosquito screens nearly two months nothing doing."[62] This was a regular refrain in the decade prior to the First World War, as government architects struggled to keep up with the rapid expansion of Canada's population, urban development, and architectural requirements.

By the turn of the century, almost all immigration halls had a caretaker or matron living on site year-round. The caretakers would have an apartment carved out of the overall square footage of the building. We can read the plan of a typical three- or four-room house, with its own kitchen and sitting room, within the footprint of the larger immigration buildings (e.g., Figures 3.16, 4.10, 4.14, 4.21, and 4.23). In other frontier institutions at the time, such as bank branches, domestic space complemented public rooms in an intimate manner. A period photograph of the Medicine Hat immigration hall similarly reveals it as a domestic space: potted flowers are visible behind lace curtains in the windows of the caretaker's apartment. The immigration branch saw the caretakers as protecting its investment during the off-season, when the buildings were largely empty, and providing essential cleaning and maintenance during the spring and summer immigration season, in addition to hosting and record-keeping duties. Often, couples would divide the duties, with the husband as agent and handyman, while the wife cleaned and prepared the rooms and dormitories. In the early 1920s, Victoria Cross medallist John C. Kerr and his wife were caretakers of the Spirit River immigration hall when the Dominion government closed it for three years due to the low number of new arrivals; the Kerrs were allowed live in the building "to keep a careful eye on the property." By 1941, Mr Kerr had remobilized as a military policeman; Mrs Kerr was managing the hall on her own when she chose to join her husband stationed on the west coast. Vacating the hall, she allowed a wounded Second World War veteran and his wife to move in temporarily. Not having any instructions to the contrary from Ottawa, which was a long way from Spirit River in a time of war, Mrs Kerr did not want to leave the building empty, because there were "too many windows ... to tempt small boys."[63] Even in retirement, she continued to care for the facility.

Some caretakers, though, were tempted to become complacent and abusive of their position after several years characterized by low immigrant numbers and/or the neglect of the physical plant by Ottawa authorities. During the 1920s in Winnipeg, the caretaker of hall No. 1, a widower who had an apartment in that building, married the matron of No. 2, who had an apartment there. The newlyweds lived in No. 2, while the caretaker's adult daughter and son occupied the No. 1 apartment, even though neither were employed by the Dominion government, and the latter had a good job at Ashdown Hardware. Despite a local MP lodging a complaint about this situation, Winnipeg commissioner, Thomas Gelley (who replaced Walker at the time of the war) did not seem overly concerned.[64] It is similarly unclear whether any action was taken on another occasion when a concerned citizen wrote from Edmonton to inform the minister that, when he was "on the Depots" he had "overheard immigrants complaining of the treatment they received" from the matron at the immigration hall there. Upon taking "up conversation with them," the immigrants told him "that they were snubbed and ordered around like a bunch of dogs ... separated from there [sic] families [despite] empty rooms in the building." The correspondent states that the parents of the matron had been living "for a long time" in one of the upstairs rooms meant for immigrants. He felt that "surely the Government does not have to give charity to these people, when the Matron's

Father who I know personally can play the Wheat Markets every day." This concerned citizen believed that "everything should be done to make the newcomers feel at home" in Canada and at the immigration halls.[65]

As we see here again, the surrounding community served as "caretakers" for immigrants staying in the government halls. A Polish woman who migrated to Canada in 1923 recalled her foray onto the streets of Edmonton:

When I was in Immigration House I was very hungry and I went outside … and I think it where I can go buy some bread? And I stop there and stop and two fellow come in passing one morning first thing, was morning. "Is the lady from the old country?" I say yes. "Does the lady need anything?" I want buy something bread, but I don't know where. Oh, go to my, did you see that little house over there? There is my sister, you go there and knock on the door, she is alone there and she open you door and ask her she go with you to store and that was Ukrainian people. And I do that and sure, that lady right away offer me she go with me … And [also] she take me and I buy very nice woolen dress because it was fall.[66]

Another Polish immigrant remembered his arrival in Prince Albert in the middle of the night, when he was led, with several others, off the train, "to a barrack for immigrants. Inside there were some wooden camp beds and an iron stove with a few people standing around it. The agent … spoke Polish very well … He told us that we could use the stove and sleep without being disturbed." After a short stint as farm labourers, he and his friend walked all day through melting snow and "returned to the same barrack that we had left the Saturday before – muddy, tired, and hungry as well." That night he found food at the Chinese restaurant, and the "Chinaman" took pity on him and provided

several days' work washing dishes.[67] If only temporarily, immigration-hall residents were treated as neighbours – and this seems to have held true in larger cities like Edmonton as much as in small frontier towns.

An excellent description of the architecture and usage of the immigration hall in one small town, Athabasca, gives us a sense of experiences there in the early 1920s for immigrants, staff, and neighbourhood children. The meticulous writer of this memoir grew up on her grandparents' farm outside of Athabasca; her uncle was caretaker at the hall, and it became her "home for many happy summers and for a period of three years" while attending high school in town. In her words, the caretaker job was a plum position; her uncle had

found he was not adapted to farming …
As soon as he had "proved up" on his homestead, he moved his family to town … At the time of acquiring the caretaking of the Hall, he was working in a sawmill, so was not at all sorry for the opportunity of something less strenuous.

The job at the Hall was seasonal from April to November. It paid a modest salary, but had the advantage of rent-free living in the building the year round, with heat and light provided. He supplemented this income by doing janitor work [for various local businesses] … and they managed very comfortably and stayed there until the Hall had fulfilled its purpose, a period of about 20 years.

The immigration hall in Athabasca was of the standard type built during this period (see Figures 4.16 and 4.17). The caretaker's suite was to the left of the entrance porch; to the right, as she describes:

Extending the length of the building from the lobby was a long hallway with a window at the bottom. There were five bedrooms on one side and six on the other and they were, indeed, cheerless cell [*sic*]. They had bare, boarded walls, one uncurtained window, equipped with a green blind, and oiled floors, and were furnished with a double bed-stead, a straw-filled mattress and dark grey blankets …

At the lobby end of the Hall was a large kitchen with a cook stove, a rough worktable, woodbox, another large table for eating on, and numerous chairs. In one corner, on a stand, was a large uncovered water cistern … this was the only water provided … but not too tempting to look at, having washed the shingled roof, nor was it too palatable to drink. There were many complaints about it, but there was nothing my uncle could do but advise the people to boil it.

On the kitchen and bedroom wall was tacked a printed list of regulations, regarding length of stay, use of property, and general behavior. Since a very large percentage of im-migrants spoke a foreign language, this was quite useless and unheeded. Adjacent to the kitchen was a large storeroom where cooking utensils, cutlery, tin and enamel dishes, and the ever-necessary coal oil lamps were kept for the use of the "guests."

The outside … [had] a double outhouse, each unit being equipped with two holes. The front unit was for the caretaker. They were partitioned only part way up and if one cared to stand on the seat, he could look over the petition [*sic*] and view the occupant on the other side.

A solid, unpainted board fence enclosed three sides of the property and the front sported a white picket fence. A neat little board sidewalk led up to the entrance … The buildings were painted white with green trim and looked quite impressive from the outside.

She writes that many immigrants stayed there over the years, coming as families, extended families, and singles: "Once there was an influx of fifty, and that was the only time that the huge, barn-like up-stairs room was used. Some of the men were sent up there to sleep on cots." Actually, she mentions one other time the upstairs room was in service; her uncle moved all the family's "furniture and be-longings, except the stove," up there during spring flood, when the waters of the Athabasca River almost reached the front step (Figure 4.18).

Due to its size, paint scheme, and location, the immigration hall was easily visible from the train station, and immigrants could walk over with their baggage. Upon arrival, the weary travellers

crowded into the tiny office where Uncle Frank made note of their names, where they came from and a few other pertinent facts in a ledger … If the language barrier seemed difficult, he had them write the answers to the questions and then copied them as best he could. Then, he took them to the store-room for the utensils they needed, showed them the working of the kitchen equipment and allotted them their rooms …

Among the many who came, I remember one young woman in particular … She arrived quite alone, red-eyed and weeping … and then went to her room and closed the door. The sound of heart-broken sobbing could be heard all the way down the hall. We saw little of her for the next two or three days, but if by chance one of us passed her in the hallway and spoke to her, she became very distraught and broke into fresh weeping. She had not gone out to buy any supplies, nor had she used the stove.

Aunt Annie, who was generous and kind-hearted, became very concerned and at lunchtime fixed a very tempting tray of sandwiches, fruit and cake and a pot of tea.

4

4.18 Immigration hall in Athabasca, as seen from across the river, with scows heading downstream to Fort McMurray.

The girl opened the door at my aunt's knock, and seeing the food, began to cry and wail piteously ... so my aunt set the tray down on a chair and withdrew. Later, we picked it up outside her closed door. Nothing had been eaten. Fortunately, someone came for her that afternoon and she departed, still weeping ...

One spring, a group of young English boys arrived. They ranged in age from sixteen to eighteen years and were sent out to work as farm laborers for very low wages. They were heartbreakingly forlorn ... While waiting for their prospective employers, they lounged on a grassy spot outside the kitchen door and talked of home, comparing their known and loved environment with this strange and alien one and their desperate homesickness was quite apparent.[68]

As we have seen in the last two chapters, well into the 1920s Prairie immigration halls remained rudimentary accommodations, one step up from roughing it in the bush. In addition to hosting the mundane tasks of everyday life, they were sites of interaction and engagement with a broader world, witnessing great emotion and anticipation, both positive and negative.

By their function, Prairie immigration halls had a limited lifespan. As our Athabasca memoirist wrote, by the early 1930s "[f]ew immigrants were now making use of the Hall and Uncle Frank knew it would be only a matter of time before the Government ceased to finance the project and they would have to find a new home."[69] Her uncle and aunt needed a retirement plan. But what of the building itself? Sometimes these were demolished, but often they found new uses in the community. Local interest in the halls extended beyond their useful life to the immigration branch, and they were often adapted to new uses. Other Dominion government agencies, and then local organizations, seen to be acting in the public good, were given first priority in disposal of the buildings. For example, in Yorkton the 1899 immigration hall became a Dominion armoury in 1911. In Vermilion, the hall served the immigration branch from about 1908 to 1918, then as a post office in the 1920s, and as an armoury during the Second World War. The immigration hall at Rosthern was donated as early as 1906 to the Alexandra Hospital, which moved it to another site. The Grande Prairie immigration hall was turned over to the Royal Canadian Legion in 1938 for the nominal rent of $1 a month; the Legion then purchased the building in 1947. Sometimes, alternate uses were temporary, such as when 1931 Census commissioners took advantage of free accommodations in rural Alberta immigration halls. In Spirit River later that decade, the University of Alberta borrowed the immigration hall to offer a few courses; in 1942, the Department of Public Works leased it to the local school board as a residence for boarding students from the surrounding countryside. The newly formed School District bought it four years later, even though the thirty-year-old building was in poor condition by then. Records of the adaptive reuse of the halls typically are accompanied by tales of dilapidation caused by lack of maintenance, heavy use, and the corners that were cut during construction.

Prior to leasing the immigration hall to the Spirit River school board, Public Works had deflected several overtures from potential private tenants, including a provincial member of the legislative assembly, whose children needed to live in town for school. Private solicitations for the purchase, rental, or even charity inhabitation of Prairie immigration halls were common in small towns with limited building stock. Depending on its condition, a hall might be sold off for scrap or for reuse. It might be moved, or sometimes the building and land were sold as a package. In Dauphin, the immigration building was sold to a local entrepreneur in 1911 for a 30-per-cent down payment, with the Department of Public Works carrying the debt. He converted it to a store, but initially had trouble finding a tenant. After a few years in arrears, he managed to close his debt.[70] Sometimes the former immigration hall remained in a town for decades after its last use as such. Back at Yorkton, the caretaker of the hall wrote to Public Works during the Second World War, asking permission to forward tenders for the sale or demolition of the "old wooden structure which has been a landmark for over 40 years."[71] As noted with the Qu'Appelle immigration hall, another option for purchasers was to cut up the structures into smaller residences

4.19 Peace River immigration hall, or at least a third of it. Built in 1917, divided in 1937.

189

to be moved to new sites. A developer did this at Peace River in 1937, where one-third of the 1917 immigration hall survives today as a single-family home (Figure 4.19).[72] This modest Peace River house is the only portion of a small-town, wood-frame Prairie immigration hall known to be extant. A few of the more substantial concrete-and-brick structures of the 1920s also endure.

CHANGING CONTEXTS FOR IMMIGRATION HALLS IN THE 1920S

Immigration from Europe slowed during the First World War. However, established farmers from the US Midwest continued to take advantage of free land in the Canadian Prairies. They passed through immigration halls in hubs like Prince Albert and Edmonton on their way to newly opened land farther north. New immigration halls had to be built during the war in small communities of the Peace River district, along the line of the newly completed Edmonton, Dunvegan, and British Columbia Railway. These halls were of the standard design initiated in 1908 and perfected before the war. For the most part, though, this was a time of attrition in the building stock of the immigration branch. At least sixteen Prairie halls had closed by 1920, and many had been converted temporarily for other uses. Even the Winnipeg headquarters of the immigration branch was not immune to the encroachment of competing space requirements, and officials worried about the future of their work. "I don't think that we should encourage the idea," wrote Commissioner Walker in 1917, "that all our organization, including the equipment of our halls, should be destroyed, because that primarily during the war immigration is momentarily at a standstill. I am looking for better and brighter days ahead when these halls, and the Winnipeg Immigration Hall among them, will be very badly needed."[73] Despite the branch's rearguard action, it was impossible to protect idle infrastructure

when war mobilization resulted in formidable space demands.

Dominion government pier buildings and many of the Prairie immigration halls became sites for the marshalling and movement of troops. Several immigration halls were converted into armouries, as at Yorkton. In Winnipeg, the Post Office could not get a new building erected due to wartime spending priorities, so it assertively arranged — after much correspondence — to move its CPR-station branch into one-third of the lower two storeys of No. 1. The upper two floors became a veteran's convalescent hospital, which operated until 1922, and the immigration branch would not regain control of its entire headquarters building for another two years after that.[74] Alternative uses also predominated at other halls immediately after the war, reflecting the defining events of that moment: the influenza epidemic and mass un-employment. The Yorkton armoury now became an influenza hospital, as did several halls across northern Alberta. Meanwhile, Winnipeg No. 2 and Edmonton No. 2, the long addition to the rear of the hall there, both served several years as shelters for jobless men.

Not until after 1923 did immigration begin to pick up enough to justify the re-opening of Prairie immigration halls. At this time the Dominion government began to relax restrictions enacted during the war that prevented many potential European immigrants from leaving their home-lands: for example, a ban on the entry of those considered enemy aliens, and the requirement that immigrants entering the country had a sub-stantial amount of cash to support themselves. The focus remained on attracting more British settlers. An information booklet published at the time by the CPR was unequivocal: "The fun-damental of Canadian progress is immigration. Canada needs immigrants; in particular she needs British immigrants."[75] The booklet was flush with the exciting new Empire Settlement Agreement, which, according to immigration historians Kelley and Trebilcock, "provided transportation assistance to four classes of immigrants: agriculturalists and their families, farm labourers, domestics, and juvenile immigrants." Subsidized travel for these Britishers "was complemented by various other inducements, the features of which depended on the targeted group." By 1925, the need for industrial labour in a rapidly expanding economy also brought single men from all parts of continental Europe. Their numbers grew rapidly after the ratification of the Railways Agreement, which more or less gave carte blanche to the CPR and Canadian National Railways to recruit, transport, and distribute immigrants across the country. Annual arrivals grew by 60 per cent during the decade after 1920, though the numbers never reached half of the peak 1913 level.[76] After the slow years of the early 1920s, the number of immigrants staying annually in Prairie immigration halls fluctuated between fifteen to twenty-five thousand in Winnipeg, five thousand to seven thousand in Edmonton, fewer than one thousand in Prince Albert, and no more than a couple of hundred in the smaller halls that survived.

Most of the 1920s immigration-assistance schemes involved significantly discounted or free ocean crossings and rail journeys to predetermined destinations in Canada where employers had indicated a need for labourers. Migrants were keen to take advantage of this subsidized transportation, whether as bona fide settlers, as sojourners, or as tourists; they were not necessarily so eager to go where the Dominion government, railway companies, or industrial concerns wanted them to go. As they passed through the larger cities and train depots, many attempted to slip away and go off independently. Some were successful in doing this, but many met with armed guards on the train platforms and elsewhere, ensuring that they would end up at their allotted destinations.[77] Boarding them at the extant immigration halls on

the Prairies was one way to keep an eye on these assisted immigrants.

In the case of single female immigrants, the Dominion government strove to have them escorted from port of departure all the way to their local employment situation. Established in 1920, the Women's Division of the immigration service provided matrons, conductresses, information, and assurance that government immigration buildings were of a layout, cleanliness, and condition suitable to receive young single women and respectable families. The supervisor of the Women's Division regularly reported on the presence of separate WCs, female dormitories, and family bedrooms. For example, on her 1927 inspection tour of the Prairies, she applauded the attention paid the immigrants by the caretaker and matron at the Winnipeg compound, the latter having made mattress covers and pillow slips herself. Things were not so rosy at the old Edmonton hall, where the "mattresses and pillows had no covering whatever," and the building was "in an exceedingly dirty condition." Perhaps worse, the women's supervisor decried the fact that there was too much intermingling of the many male inhabitants with the British women and children in the common rooms and at the overtaxed WCs. "Decent, clean families object to being housed in such quarters," she argued, "and the publicity we get from this source will not be very favorable."[78] Once again, officials worried over the mixing of different classes and genders in immigration-hall spaces – soon a new hall for Edmonton would be planned and built. Officials wanted to ensure that single female domestic labourers actually took up the jobs waiting for them, and for which governments had paid their transportation, but they were also concerned that the personal safety and mores of these women would be preserved. After a visit to Winnipeg No. 1 in 1923, the Ottawa secretary of the branch worried "that both men and women seemed to be accommodated" on the same floors.

"The object of this letter," he continued, "is to call attention to complaints we have had from other points, particularly from ocean ports … We have had some regrettable incidents occur owing to the failure of officers to enforce the segregation of the sexes."[79] Although separation by sex had been eclipsed in official correspondence starting in the late 1890s, when the administration of ethnic divisions became paramount, here the protection of single women re-emerges in the spatial practices at Prairie immigration halls.

Many of the promotions and agreements to bring immigrants to Canada were failures in some way: not enticing enough British settlers or domestics, or marooning farm and industrial labourers far from their homes when work dried up. One scheme was harvest excursions, which transported unemployed British labourers in 1923 and 1928 to perform seasonal work on Canadian farms. On several occasions, disgruntled "harvesters" occupied the Winnipeg immigration compound, creating havoc there in an attempt to draw attention to what they perceived as their neglect by the Dominion government. This resulted in a controversial episode, in which the harvesters were escorted from the immigration halls under guard to a holding pen in the train station, from which they were transported to the immigration-pier building at Quebec City for passage to Britain. When kept in the immigration halls, malcontents would strike out at the built fabric, leaving their angry marks. Commissioner Gelley related how the minister had passed through Winnipeg and "inspected Immigration Hall No. 1 a few hours after a number of British harvesters, who were being returned to the Old Country, had left the building and he was shown the damage done in the rooms by the breaking of doors, glass, hardware, etc. He also took notice of the filth they left after they had gone, not only on the floors, but the defacing of the walls and the writing on same." In addition, Gelley continued in another letter, he had been "obliged

to secure the services of the Mounted Police," because the harvesters would "steal" and "use abusive and filthy language, and it was only the 'Red Coats' who made any impression on them."[80] As we witnessed in previous chapters, the protection proffered in immigration buildings could swing quickly to control by government authorities – and those subject to this power associated it with the architecture itself.

In response to these new immigration schemes, and a quick upsurge in the number of new arrivals, discussions resumed about new construction. In Winnipeg, it was apparent that both No. 1 and No. 2 halls, after years of alternative uses, would need to be updated. As early as 1913, when No. 1 hall was just over seven years old, the City of Winnipeg had banned the use of all the upper-floor bedrooms on the inner side of the double-loaded corridors, because they had no access to fresh air or natural light. Upon re-inspection ten years later, City officials were surprised to find British harvesters housed in those same inner bedrooms. They concluded in disgust that No. 1 had been "designed with a gross disregard of the necessity for adequate lighting and ventilation … If these rooms were in a building owned by any person but the Dominion Government they would be closed up as insanitary."[81] In addition, Winnipeg staff had come quickly to the realization that the location of the immigration compound, right next to the tracks, was "the cause of much dirt and smoke settling in the building," which affected the quality of the workspace and the cleanliness of the immigrants' quarters. Just before the war, the immigration branch had envisioned an entirely new, and even more monumental, headquarters building, to be erected a couple of blocks away. Plans were drawn up, but this project was put on the back burner because of the war, and the branch did not manage to revive it afterwards; its fate was similar to that of the large new hospital begun on Grosse-Île in 1913, but never completed. Ultimately, the western headquarters of the branch remained in No. 1, and the bedroom problem was solved by moving the kitchens and dining rooms to the inner sections of the second and third floors, and converting the previous common rooms into dormitories.[82]

Dormitories had begun to make sense again in the immigration halls, even at the expense of losing some of the family rooms. The immigration-promotion schemes of the 1920s, especially the Railways Agreement, brought many unattached workers each summer, whether farm hands, industrial labourers, or domestics. Prairie immigration halls still in service by that time were often severely overcrowded. Slowly, in the late 1920s, the immigration branch moved to improve accommodations at a few key points outside Winnipeg. Three substantial, two-storey, brick-and-stone-clad immigration halls were built on the eve of the Great Depression in Prince Albert, Edmonton, and North Battleford. All three appeared in a kind of moderate classicism used by the Chief Architect's Branch for post offices and multi-use public buildings across Canada at that time. Hallmarks of the style were symmetrical facades focused on a grand entrance stair or porch, with the entrance framed in ornamental columns, and the windows sometimes framed with subtle classical details.[83] Though the words "Immigration Hall" were carved in stone over the main entrance of each building, these were generally less ornamented than the other types of public building (Figure 4.20). Reinforced concrete frames and foundations, indoor plumbing, central heating, and electric lighting were standard conveniences in these modern buildings, even if they took on historical styles. These three structures represent the continued significance of these cities as transportation hubs for the access of immigrants to land and jobs after six decades of populating western Canada. But they also mark a transition in the immigration-hall building type. Conforming to the functional requirements of the type, these

three are, however, one-off designs generated by the Chief Architect's Branch. These were not standardized, expedient structures erected moments before the first immigrants arrived in the spring travel season. No doubt due to the substantial construction of these three buildings, two of them remain in use today, as non-governmental shelters for populations at risk.

The story of why and how these late 1920s Prairie immigration halls were built is instructive. In Edmonton, the 1906 hall was still in service and "altogether inadequate" to the work of tracking and sheltering immigrants in transit, especially "due to the movement of continental farm labour under the Railways Agreement." The railway companies had been forced to provide "boxcars for boarding houses," right in the shunting yards. The shed addition, where central Europeans had been warehoused without light or heat, was condemned and demolished in 1927; the main hall, in use for British immigrants, was also considered to be in violation of local building codes. In his justification of an appropriation for a new building, the deputy minister summed up these reasons, concluding that: "New arrivals cannot be dumped down in these main points and left to their own resources while awaiting overnight train connections or pending placement, as to do so would render them easy prey for unscrupulous individuals who are awaiting on the ground looking to exploit them in any possible manner."[84] Interestingly, alongside the long-term neglect of the physical plant, the letter cites the immigrants' need for the Dominion government's paternal protection from predatory sharps; in this, 1930 was little different from 1830. Surely a new immigration hall, modern in every way, and more akin to other public buildings, would place the reception and distribution of immigrants in Edmonton on a more professional level.

In the meantime, over in Prince Albert, local citizens and the press had been lobbying for a new

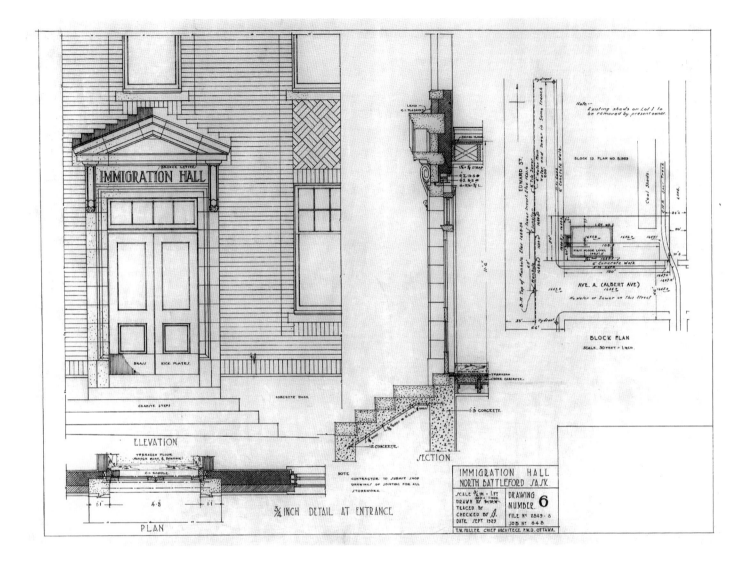

ELEVATION

IMMIGRATION HALL

BRASS KICK PLATES.

CONCRETE BASE

GRANITE STEPS

PLAN

4·8

¾ INCH DETAIL AT ENTRANCE

SECTION

NOTE
CONTRACTOR TO SUBMIT SHOP
DRAWINGS OF JOINTING FOR ALL
STONEWORK

BLOCK PLAN
SCALE 50 FEET = 1 INCH.

EDWARD ST.

AVE. A. (ALBERT AVE)

IMMIGRATION HALL
NORTH BATTLEFORD SASK

SCALE ¾ IN = 1 FT
DRAWN BY
TRACED BY
CHECKED BY
DATE SEPT 1929

DRAWING
NUMBER 6

FILE Nº 2619-6
JOB Nº 848

T.W. FULLER CHIEF ARCHITECT. P.W.D. OTTAWA.

4.20 Detail of the classical-temple-style front entrance to the 1929 immigration hall in North Battleford. This building had a unique plan, with a small caretaker's suite, kitchen, and a long dormitory on the ground floor, with the upper devoted to eight family rooms. There were modern bathrooms on both floors.

immigration hall ever since the Empire Settlement Agreement had been inaugurated in 1923. The City Health Officer itemized the sanitary deficiencies of the hall then in use: it was a complicated and "slow process" to heat wash water on the stove top; "all the waste water and swill is thrown on the ground outside the building, together with any garbage"; the dippers had been stolen from the barrels of drinking water, so "wash bowls" were being used in their place; and the kitchen tables were made of wooden boards, "the crevices being filled with an accumulation of filth. There can be no pretense of cleanliness as regards these." The outside privies were "nothing less than an open cesspool, and in such a poor state of repair that the filth is exposed to the public." No action was taken by the Dominion government for another three years, while the locals continued their campaign for a new structure. By this time, though, immigration officials had begun to think that accommodations indeed were needed in a few key places, such as Prince Albert. The Ottawa commissioner briefed the deputy minister:

As you know the Department during the past year has had several requests from different points in Western Canada for the opening of Immigration halls, but the policy is pretty well established of not opening up new halls for the reason that as the country has become developed there is no need for such accommodation for incoming settlers, distribution being easily and comfortably made from Winnipeg and other central points… In so far as the situation at Prince Albert is concerned, this city is the distributing point for the North country where there is unquestionably a good field for the placement of farm labourers and settlers. Daily trains are not always available and parties … have often to remain for two or three days in that city.

The network of Prairie immigration halls was undergoing a process of centralization that entailed replacing blanket coverage of the frontier with a few regional distribution points.

Furthermore, there was powerful motivation to modernize the few necessary immigration halls to conform with contemporary expectations of immigrants, staff, and local officials. Wooden sheds were no longer appropriate in the context of built-up cities that had a range of public buildings erected by different levels of government. To compete for presence within the built fabric of growing Prairie cities, federal architecture would need to become increasingly monumental. Nor did inexpensive wooden construction project the image of a modern, independent nation with a professional civil service. In 1926, the "present building"

in use as the immigration hall in Prince Albert had been constructed only fifteen years earlier, according to the standard plan described above and used in locations from Edson to Athabasca and Spirit River. But now, according to the commissioners in Winnipeg and Ottawa, this "second class frame building … is a one story shed and cannot be called an Immigration Hall in the proper sense of the word."[85] They do not provide a "proper" definition of the building type. What they had in mind seems to have differed from earlier Prairie immigration halls mostly in materiality and modern conveniences: reinforced concrete and steel, stone-and-brick facades, indoor plumbing, and electric light.

Functional programming of the building type remained the same. However, at this time the Dominion government did experiment with the layout of the basic features. Records of the early 1927 design process for the Prince Albert hall reveal several iterations and critiques. First, Public Works proffered blueprints of the prewar standard design. Clearly, this would not do, since the building to be replaced had been built to that very same design. Then, the Chief Architect's Branch supplied "sketch plans" for a much longer building with a full second storey (Figure 4.21). In this design, a symmetrically placed central entrance leads to a hall crossed by a double-loaded corridor, off which are arrayed immigrant bedrooms, kitchen, and caretaker's residence. The layout of this floor is quite similar to the standard plan of the 1910s. Upstairs, though, radiating from a central hall, are four dormitories, two of which are labelled distinctly for British and Foreign single men. A two-storey bump-out on axis with the central entrance bestows ample toilet and bath facilities on both floors – the sole washroom on the upper floor being provided for men only. About half of the extra length on this plan is taken up by discrete entrances and stair halls placed at each end of the building, unique to this iteration, and a complete throwback to the original Prairie designs

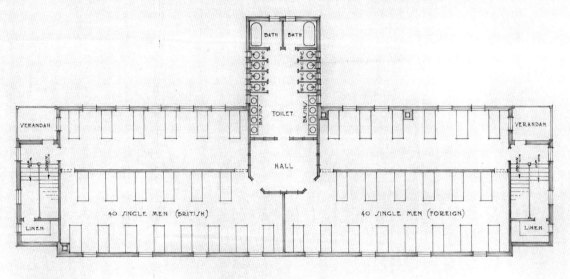

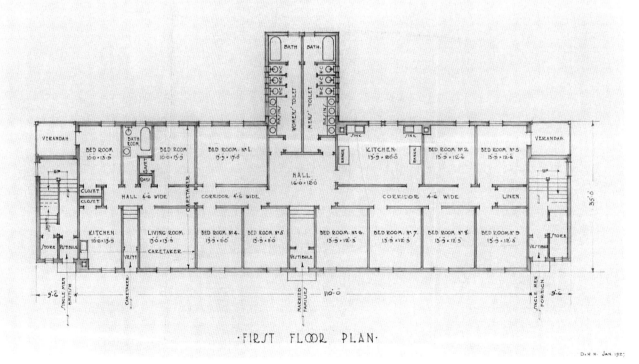

4.21 Initial draft of plans for the Prince Albert
immigration hall, 1927.

4.22 Plans of the 1928 Prince Albert immigration hall, based on the Winnipeg commissioner's Sketch No. 2. The original sketch had included the unusual chamfered corner. which creates a kind of feature window in the corner of the caretaker's living room. Note the duplicated staircases in the central hall and the position of the washrooms.

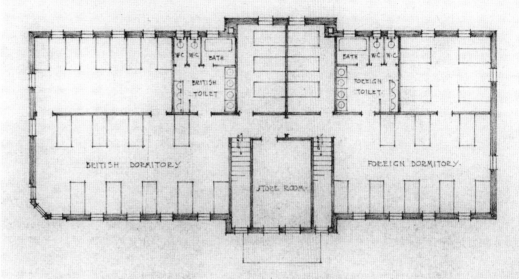

PRINCE ALBERT SAS.
REVISED SKETCH PLANS FOR PROPOSED IMMIGRATION HALL
CHIEF ARCHITECTS OFFICE DEPT OF PUBLIC WORKS OTTAWA.
SCALE 8 FEET EQUALS 1 INCH.

BRITISH TOILET

FOREIGN TOILET

BRITISH DORMITORY

STORE ROOM.

FOREIGN DORMITORY.

SECOND FLOOR PLAN

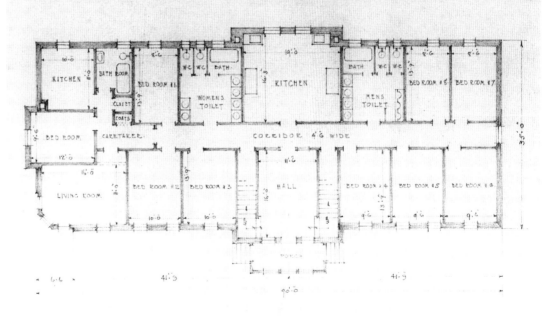

KITCHEN

BATH ROOM

BED ROOM #1

WOMENS TOILET

KITCHEN

MENS TOILET

BED ROOM #8

BED ROOM #7

CLOSET

COATS

BED ROOM

CARETAKER.

CORRIDOR 4'6 WIDE

LIVING ROOM.

BED ROOM #2

BED ROOM #3

HALL

BED ROOM #4

BED ROOM #5

BED ROOM #6

PORCH

FIRST FLOOR PLAN

of 1883. These two end halls would have ensured the segregated circulation of British and foreign men, while minimizing the necessity for their presence in the corridors outside the family rooms on the ground floor. Of course, strict separation dissolves in the shared central halls, washrooms, and kitchen. On reviewing the plans, the Ottawa commissioner was quick to point out that the separate entrances were extraordinary: "I am afraid that a building of this kind will cost more money than the situation warrants … we could cut off the two ends and have just one entrance … [the one] now marked 'Married Families.'" He also preferred to economize further by removing the bump-out, so that the central halls "on both floors could be eliminated and less toilet facilities furnished."[86]

Two alternate sketch plans appeared about a month later, reflecting Ottawa's critique. These were amateurish plans, probably drawn by Gelley in Winnipeg. In Sketch No. 1 the ground floor is again laid out similarly to the 1908 standard plan, but with men's and women's washrooms shoe-horned in off the entrance hall – the 1908 design never included indoor plumbing. A single staircase in the hall leads upstairs, where there are four, awkwardly arranged, dormitories of different sizes, plus one big bathroom. In Sketch No. 2, a larger entrance hall sustains two staircases accessing separate British and foreign dormitories, each with its own washroom; the two ethnic classes would have "no communication between them," in the words of Gelley, who clearly favoured this plan. He was particularly enamoured with the increased surveillance afforded by Sketch No. 2. Equipped with a desk and benches, the large entrance hall would serve as the office and checkpoint for all immigrants. Meanwhile, the placement of men's and women's toilets on opposite sides of the communal kitchen would create a kind of safe space "for single girls and women … at the caretaker's end of the building." The plan thus would "give the Caretaker better control" over comings and

goings, and interminglings, at the immigration hall.[87] Six weeks later, the Chief Architect's Branch was formalizing measured drawings for Gelley's preferred Sketch No. 2, which ultimately was built (Figure 4.22). Effectively, the design settled on was a hybrid of immigration-hall layouts that had been in use before 1908. It combined the symmetry and efficiency of a central entrance and double-loaded corridor on the ground floor, with the reintroduction after many years of the meticulous division of space by both ethnicity and gender.

The movement of so many singles under the auspices of the various Agreements and promotions caused concerns among officials that were made manifest in the design of the Prince Albert immigration hall. These concerns were less explicit, but still legible, in the plans for the new Edmonton hall, built two years later (Figures 4.23 and 4.24). That is, the rooms on the Edmonton plans were not labelled "British" and "Foreign," but the building's layout indicates that segregation was in the minds of the designers. On the top floor of this three-storey structure, two pairs of dormitories are arranged symmetrically on either side of a central stair hall; each pair is isolated from the other, behind a door and down a short corridor, where each pair also has its own men's washroom with urinals. This upper floor thus was reserved for single male travellers, who could remain segregated by ethnicity. The middle floor featured eighteen smaller rooms, also symmetrically placed behind closed doors on either side of the stair hall, each group with its own washroom facilities. On this floor, both men's and women's facilities are duplicated inefficiently on the two sides of the hall, indicating the significance of ethnic segregation even in the spaces for single females and families. The bottom floor is a kind of half-basement; from the main entrance to the immigration hall, one had to descend half a flight of stairs to access it. On one end of this floor was a three-room caretaker's suite, as well as the large communal kitchen and

4.23 Edmonton immigration hall, as completed in 1930.

dining room flanking the corridor. At the other end of the half-basement was the coal storage and boiler room, immigrants' laundry, and a suite of offices, the largest of which monitored the stair hall through an internal window or counter. Despite the suitable location of these offices for the purpose of surveillance, immigration officials immediately objected to the insalubrious location, "surrounded by" the utility rooms; moreover, wrote Gelley, the exposed piping on the ceiling of the half-basement "detracts considerably from the appearance of the office, which is going to be used by the general public." The piping was similarly exposed in the grand, high-ceilinged offices of Winnipeg No. 1, but nobody complained about that when the building went up in 1906. It seems the civil service had acquired a better opinion of itself since then. Soon after the completion of the new Edmonton building, the offices were moved into a few of the family rooms on the middle floor, where there was "better lighting."[88]

Notwithstanding the construction of three expensive immigration halls in the final years of the 1920s, the writing on the wall foreshadowed

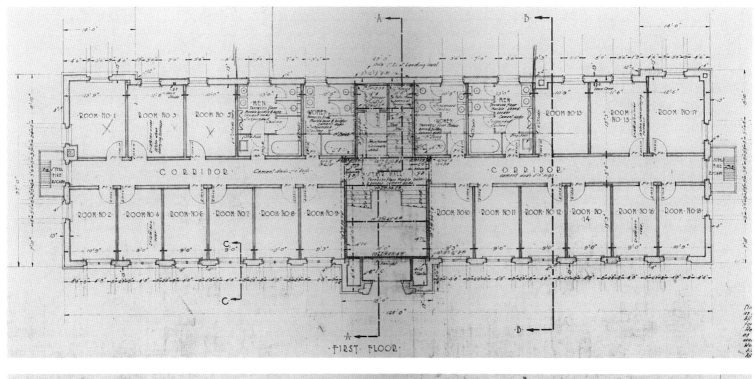

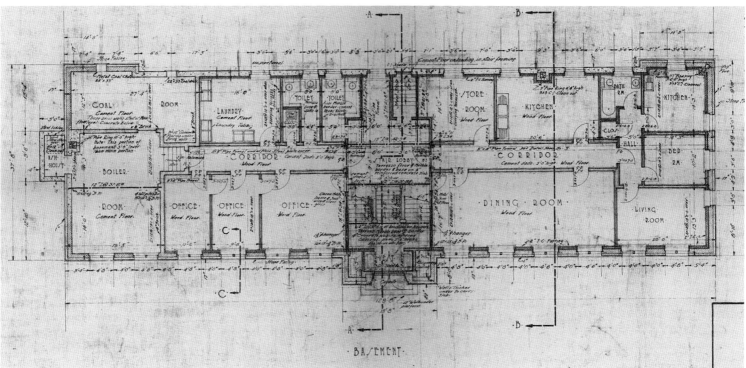

4.24 (*above and opposite*) The three floor plans of the 1930
immigration hall in Edmonton.

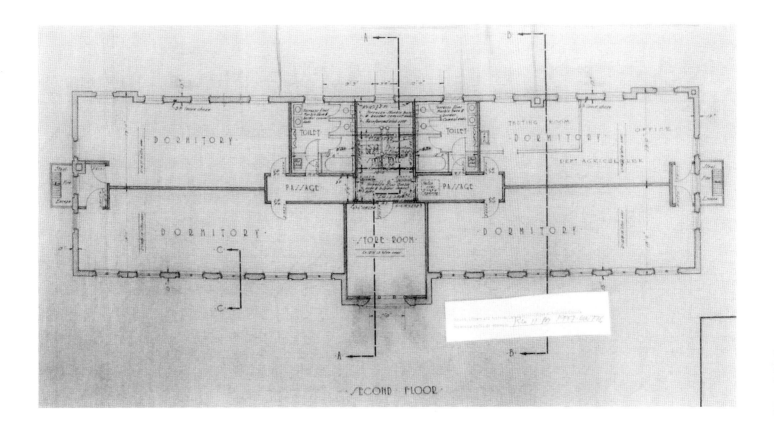

the termination of the building program. When the appropriation of $45,000 for the Prince Albert hall came to a vote in the House of Commons in spring 1928, it did not pass without commentary by Opposition members. "What is the need for this building?" asked one, perhaps out of genuine curiosity. "It is the Prime Minister's riding; why should there not be a building there?" answered another. "They deserve something," added one more. To defuse the situation, the minister of public works cited the town's population growth, and blandly proceeded to read into the record the justification for the new hall that had been penned two years earlier by the immigration branch. The appropriation passed, along with the next one on the list, a $50,000 addition to the public building in the same town. "Prince Albert is well looked after," was the parting comment of one Opposition member.[89]

Accusations of pork-barrelling aside, the Opposition's first question seemed to be growing more pertinent: were Prairie immigration halls still necessary? Commissioner Gelley, for his part, raised doubts regarding "whether it would be advisable for the Department to build" the new Edmonton hall, just before its construction began at the end of 1929. He was concerned that the new Natural Resources Acts, which transferred control over Crown lands and their resources to the Prairie provinces, would "affect the immigration policy" of the Dominion government. In this case, responsibility for the reception and care of new arrivals would likely devolve to the provinces and railways.[90] He did not cite the Great Depression as a context for reduced immigrant numbers — Black Tuesday having occurred only two months earlier. Even so, within a year the City of Edmonton secured use of the dilapidated 1906 immigration hall as an unemployment shelter, since the new one was not complete. By 1932, the brand-new immigration hall in Prince Albert was also being used as a shelter for the jobless. Meanwhile, the smaller, or second-class, immigration halls on the frontiers seemed less and less necessary. Transportation connections were better than in previous decades, and Prairie towns had hotels and rooming houses, not to mention distant relatives, church members, or ethnic associations to host immigrants in transit. During a tour of the Peace River district in 1929, the Ottawa commissioner "found that a very considerable proportion of the persons using the Immigration Halls are not of the immigrant class." Depending on the site, the ledger books showed that 25 to 30 per cent of recent guests had been Canadian-born, and another 20 to 30 per cent had been in Canada more than two years. "As the homestead lands become filled up around these centres, there is a lessening use of the Halls for real immigration purposes." He concluded that "it is only a matter of a short time before" the facilities will be closed.[91] Perhaps the final ignominy came during a 1929 House of Commons debate over the branch's budget "for the equipment and maintenance of immigration halls at various points in the west." A Toronto MP stood to ask the simple, but damning, question: "What is an immigration hall?"[92] Clearly, the Prairie network which once boasted over fifty sites was in rapid decline.

CONCLUSIONS

It was in the best interests of the Dominion government to attract immigrants to populate western Canada. Throughout the period of immigration history covered by this book, 1870 to 1930, it did this through offering the enticement of free land, transportation assistance, and the provision of certain protections along the migration route, specifically in its network of buildings and services made available to immigrants. The Dominion government thus took a paternalistic attitude that the immigrants must be guided and protected along the way from port to Prairie. In particular, it was frequently stated as far back as the early-nineteenth century that newcomers were easy marks for hustlers and exorbitant rates at way stations, hostels, and restaurants. Under the guidance of the immigration branch, what reporter Florence Hamilton Randall called "that most paternal of organizations," new arrivals would get good advice and conserve their limited funds for homesteading.[93] Immigrants could be steered to particular locations or jobs, depending on the opening of land by surveyors and transportation networks, the season, and other local factors not known at their ports of entry. Simultaneously, bureaucrats could collect population data from immigration-hall caretakers and agents. In this way, the network of immigration buildings across the country helped the government track the success of individual immigrants and the programs that supported them.

For their part, it was a boon to migrants to take advantage of government incentives and infrastructure during dramatic life changes like moving between continents. Most had severely limited funds for their journeys, and required some "seed money" to establish themselves on the land. Hotels and restaurants were expensive for large families, while many single men migrated with the shirt on their back in the hope of finding day labour and free room and board as a farm hand. Accommodations, meals, baths, and laundries at an immigration hall would smooth their arrival, allowing them to research land or present themselves to employers. Sometimes, when necessitated by harsh winters, outdoor relief in the form of emergency food or seed was extended by the Dominion government to newcomers in their first year or two of homesteading; sometimes recent arrivals were able to return to the immigration halls in between jobs or when visiting town for various reasons.

These supports were considered an extension of immigrant-reception work; in contrast, there were few social-welfare programs for those no longer considered immigrants. However, the receipt of government services always operated in a kind of reciprocal economy. For immigrants to Canada, reciprocity initially meant merely staying in the country and contributing to its demographic and economic development. Mutual benefits established a relationship between government and population that would only extend as immigrants became settlers and then citizens, and as the nation moved toward becoming a modern welfare state offering a range of services and protections beyond the immigration portfolio.

The demise of the Prairie immigration halls, followed by the rest of the Canadian immigration infrastructure, coincided with the growth of welfare-state supports more familiar to us today. As the city and town infrastructure of the country developed, there seemed to be less need to protect new arrivals and more duty to facilitate them in their life course. J.S. Woodsworth, the keen observer of the immigration question, argued this point in his address to parliament in 1926: "We must not consider our work done even though we bring these immigrants carefully to this country, see them through our immigration halls and personally conduct them out to the local communities.

We must go further than that and see that they have full educational opportunities," so that they can become more than just "hewers of wood and drawers of water." The Dominion government should sponsor "a more definite organization of community life," such as providing medical services in rural areas, rather than "dumping the immigrants in and then leaving the local governments … to do the work necessary to building a community."[94]

Woodsworth was a bit of an idealist. But during the 1910s and 1920s the provinces had begun to implement workmen's compensation and mothers' allowances; in 1927, old age pensions became the first shared federal-provincial welfare program.[95] These social programs targeted needful and deserving recipients already established in the country. As state spending on these kinds of programs grew, so did the powers – and the desire – of the Dominion government to designate recent arrivals as ineligible for them. An application to any government body for welfare support was a leading justification to deport a recent arrival; infirmity, criminal behaviour, or radical political beliefs were others. As we will examine in the following chapter, the rise of selectivity, inspection, and investigation of immigrants at the border and after their arrival, resulted in significant architectural changes and entirely new building types.

CHAPTER 5

Canadian Immigration Architectures of Inspection, Detention, and Deportation

Until it was demolished in 2015, a four-storey building with the word "Immigration" carved into a stone lintel over its main entrance stood behind Canadian Pacific Railway (CPR) Windsor Station in Montreal (Figure 5.1). Like the later immigration halls in hubs like Edmonton and Prince Albert, this structure was of modern construction, and it was clad in a classical vocabulary, here achieved in buff brick and grey masonry trim. Again, like the Prairie immigration halls, this Dominion government building in Montreal offered free accommodations and guidance to new arrivals awaiting transfers or hoping to settle in the region. However, around at the back of the building, away from the street and the railway depot, were some architectural elements not found on the Prairies: barred windows, and verandas enclosed by iron-mesh cages (see Figure 5.34). In fact, the original name of the Montreal building indicates a new typology that was developed during the decade leading up to the First World War: the "immigrant detention hospital." So called on the architectural plans and in government correspondence regarding this and several other buildings, the nomenclature indicates that other functions supplemented simple shelter. The new building type acknowledged the government's continued interest in disease control and public health that we witnessed at its

quarantine stations, but also expanded and formalized a new function that was becoming increasingly significant at the time: detention.

Policy changes put into effect during the first decade of the twentieth century introduced new aspects to immigrant reception. In previous years, once a European immigrant was clear of the quarantine stations, their interaction with Dominion government officials was largely in the context of advice and welfare support along the way. With few exceptions, Canada had wanted and welcomed everyone who was willing to come. Now, very many were coming, and the country wanted to be more selective. New policy and procedures focused on border crossing and on assessing the immigrant's potential for economic productivity and good citizenship. Medical inspection of immigrants was introduced at Dominion government pier buildings at the end of 1902. By 1910, several other criteria had been added that could ban an arrival from entering the country. These included conditions that were more cultural and economic than medical, and which would be identified in the increasingly strict civil inspections that immediately followed the medical exams. In addition, the power to reject immigrants at the border was extended spatially and temporally, such that they could be deported, from wherever they had settled,

even several years after their date of arrival, due to conditions arising that were not apparent at the port of entry. Ultimately, the circumstances that could lead to removal from Canada ranged from contagious diseases, mental-health issues, and unemployment, to poverty and radical political beliefs. The result of all this was the development of new processes and incumbent spaces for

5.1 Former immigrant detention hospital, Montreal. Built in 1914, demolished in 2015.

immigrant inspection, detention, cure, investigation, and deportation.

The immigrant detention facility in Montreal was built and modified over the years to accommodate these changes in policy, proceedings, and political context. In fact, it became the immigration-branch headquarters for east-coast detention and deportation. The building type evolved from architectural precedents with which the branch began to experiment immediately upon the introduction of medical inspection. Superficial line inspection, as practised by immigration doctors in the pier buildings, was rarely sufficient to determine a new arrival's inadmissibility. Immigrants would often be detained for further tests or observation before a decision could be made; some newcomers could be cured easily with Canadian medical care, if it was believed they would make good workers and citizens once returned to health. To accommodate all these detainees, hospitals were built in the eastern ports. Both immigrant and public health would be protected. Soon enough, though, the control, rather than the cure, of newcomers became the more conspicuous motivation behind this architecture. This tendency was epitomized on the west coast of Canada, where detention buildings were erected in Victoria and Vancouver, amid a regional context of racist anti-Asian sentiment. Although they ostensibly shared the functions of the east-coast hospitals, the British Columbia buildings comprised extralegal space, where immigrants were held longer, while officials tried to prove their inadmissibility. Thus, not all the detention hospitals were meant to serve the same clientele. Eastern Canadian sites largely handled medical and political cases, whereas the buildings in Victoria and Vancouver were devoted to the racialized deterrence of Asian immigrants. Detention hospitals were also used — sometimes along with other immigration buildings as well — to hold persons subject to deportation: those awaiting hearings and those awaiting transoceanic transportation to their ports of origin. By the start of the First World War, when Montreal received its detention hospital, a new immigration architecture had been established.

This chapter examines the architectures of inspection, detention, and deportation from 1903 to 1935. At the beginning of this period, we observe the first forays into the medical inspection of immigrants. The end is punctuated by a Depression-era boom in deportation proceedings, as the Dominion government attempted to cull welfare recipients and suppress political radicalism. Beyond dormitories, communal kitchens, and commissaries, these new institutions featured examination rooms, wards, surgeries, and cells. Although many immigration historians have written about the restrictive and selective policies of this era, there are few first-person sources that record experiences and practices in these new kinds of carceral space. To supplement those that do exist, we will view the detention of immigrants through the eyes and opinions of their supporters in the community, and of officials reporting on the conditions of incarceration and on the daring escapes achieved by desperate inmates. In the end, an Epilogue traces the subsequent narrative of Canadian immigration architecture as the buildings go silent — or are put to alternative uses — during the later 1930s and 1940s, briefly come to life to receive displaced persons and refugees during the 1950s and 1960s, and are shuttered finally after that.

INSPECTION PROCEDURES AT DOMINION GOVERNMENT PIER BUILDINGS

When the minister responsible for immigration, Clifford Sifton, was interrogated on the floor of the House of Commons in 1899, the "subject of the medical examination of the immigrants" was a pointed line of questioning. An Opposition member noted that a US immigration agent had observed in the pier building at Quebec, "not without surprise how seldom the Canadian immigration officials will turn back undesirable immigrants." In response to this accusation of "laxity," the minister expressed his hope that "the hon. gentleman is aware that we have no provision in the law at present to enable me to exclude certain people from the country. They have a right to come and they do come." And when they come, he added somewhat disingenuously, they "are subjected to a careful and thorough medical examination" by the quarantine service at Grosse-Île and other stations.[1] Within ten years, the situation would be wholly different. Critiques of immigration procedures in the House and the press became more and more common as the Dominion government controversially encouraged continental European immigrants and continued to allow arrivals from Asia. Amendments to the timeworn 1869 Immigration Act introduced the medical inspection of new arrivals at the port of entry. Before that 1902 amendment, the screening of immigrants indeed had been limited to the quarantine doctor's visit to the ship, where he searched only for evidence of epidemic diseases like cholera and smallpox. Now, a more broadly defined set of conditions would be watched for by doctors who were to be stationed in the ports. Immigrants could be prevented from landing at all if seen to be suffering from any disease or ailment. Thus, writes sociologist Alan Sears, portside "inspection was introduced on top of existing quarantine procedures to assess the suitability of individual immigrants according to broad public health standards."[2]

Late in 1902, therefore, doctors were appointed to examine all arriving immigrants in steerage and second class. The following summer, the deputy minister was brought before the House of Commons to elucidate how these practices played out at the pier buildings. As he explained: "From complaints made in the newspapers and elsewhere, the government was of opinion that more strict measures should be adopted ... to provide for

better inspection, outside altogether of the quarantine inspection." As a result, the immigration branch had "adopted precisely the same system" as that used in the United States. The deputy minister then proceeded to read into the record the "Departmental Instructions to Inspecting Physicians." Along with the duty to examine all arrivals immediately upon debarkation, "and before they are identified by the agent," doctors were given the power to deport those "suffering from loathsome, dangerous, or contagious diseases." However, in the case "of the milder class" of illness, "if the party afflicted ... or his friends are in a position to pay the expenses in connection with it, [the doctor may] permit him to enter a hospital at the seaport, and to be kept there until fully recovered before being allowed to proceed."[3] Those landed in this latter context were, according to historian Barbara Roberts, "the curable sick who were otherwise fit" and could be converted into productive farm or industrial labourers.[4] The Dominion government still preferred to welcome all comers, even if it had to bring them up to health before being released into Canadian society. One decade into this new program of medical intervention, an outside observer concluded that "much good has been effected" by avoiding the infection of Canadians and by retaining the useful but "suffering immigrant" – because every rejection "constituted an economic loss of man-power to the Dominion."[5]

The introduction of medical inspection had abrupt architectural and procedural consequences in Dominion government pier buildings. The first doctor appointed by the immigration branch, writes Roberts, found that both the "physical layout" of the spaces and the methods of documenting immigrants "made adequate inspection impossible." Initially, new policies and practices would have to be accommodated in old buildings. Early in 1903, the port doctor was provided with some converted rooms on the second floor of the

Quebec pier building (see Figure 1.8). There was a staircase from the ground floor; immigrants may have come up to the medical-inspection chambers from there, or perhaps there was an outside fire escape. Later, an overhead bridge would be constructed to take immigrants directly from ship to medical inspection. The correspondence is unclear, but the adjacent men's dormitory seems to have doubled, during inspection, as the waiting room. A significant amount of space was needed for immigrants to queue up and walk slowly past their examiners – because "line inspection," as it was known and used at New York's Ellis Island, was the only practical organization for examining hundreds of people per hour. In a few seconds, a doctor would watch an immigrant walk several paces, looking for debilities in gait and posture, then, as the immigrant passed by, quickly examine their skin, scalp, and eyelids. Pulling those with obvious illnesses aside for further examination or hospitalization would allow officials a better opportunity to judge if they were desirable immigrants.[6]

A description comes down to us in the memoir of an immigrant from London who passed through medical and civil inspection in 1905, when the procedure was still relatively new:

Although we arrived at Quebec on the Thursday night, the 3rd class passengers were not allowed on shore till next morning. After breakfast about five o'clock we went on land and were marshaled along to a point where those going to the States were separated. Those for Canada were herded into an immigration hall where after waiting for an hour or two, we marched one by one past two doctors … Thence we passed to two immigration officers who were fortified with information which we had had to fill out on shipboard, information as to nationality, country of birth, profession, age. One of them asked me if I

was going to teach. When I answered, "Not much," he smiled … Next part of the proceedings was the claiming of baggage.[7]

The initial medical inspection, as the narrative suggests, had to occur in daylight hours, so that doctors could detect debilities. The delays caused by this requirement were a continual source of complaints from the transportation companies, whose ships, arriving in the evening, were forced to stand off until a doctor was available in the morning.[8] With no illnesses detected, this English immigrant passed through without being detained for further medical consultation or hospitalization; statistically, most did. Moreover, at this time, the subsequent interrogation by civil immigration agents remained a relatively minor part of the process, especially for an educated Englishman who professed his intention to homestead.

Half a dozen years later, another English arrival required a couple of hours to be processed through the same building, along with hundreds of steerage-class immigrants. As he writes, "with the occasional opening of a gate, batches of our party were received within a railed enclosure … instructed to remove our hats and proceed down an indicated corridor." They were "scrutinised and interrogated by four officials," and although the questions asked were routine, the inspecting doctor "was anxious about our eyes."[9] Indeed, visible infections like trachoma, which causes a kind of rash under the eyelids, could be discovered easily in the brief line inspection possible when hundreds of immigrants debarked. As the doctors became more experienced with the process, they claimed to be able to recognize the subtle outward signs of a wide range of physical and mental disabilities.[10] Visible symptoms were markers – for doctors and bureaucrats – of potentially deeper flaws of character and heredity.

Historians in both the United States and Canada have emphasized that the motivations behind these inspection procedures were social and cultural as much as medical. For instance, to the inspectors, trachoma might indicate crowded living conditions, uncleanliness, or a lack of moral fibre associated with urban dwellers – as opposed to vigorous agriculturalists. It was an era when poverty and petty criminality were seen to be genetic failings, rather than symptoms of social inequalities. Moreover, with the support of eugenics theorists, the immigration branch assumed that certain races were prone to disease and degeneracy. Inferior classes and races, if allowed to enter Canada in great numbers, would dilute and eventually degrade the robust genetic stock that had established the young nation. Inspection at the port of entry would allow for a more specific classification of immigrants than the simple split between British and "foreign." Indeed, as Roberts argues, the immigration doctors tended to believe that "[r]acial criteria were even more important than medical ones" when it came to decisions about populating the country.[11]

In these opinions, the doctors had wide support among politicians, the press, and the general public. As Geoffrey Bilson concludes, those most "concerned by immigration" from non-British sources "were likely to emphasize … disease as confirmation of their suspicions that these immigrants were not 'suitable' for Canada." But even the British could be suspect, depending on their background. "If Canada is to be turned into a devil's island for the convicts of England," trumpeted a Quebec member in the House of Commons in 1907, "it will not be to the interest of the French Canadians, [and] it is certainly even more to the discredit and disadvantage of the Englishmen's sympathizers and co-imperialists."[12] However, there also were powerful forces arrayed to ensure a continual influx of inexpensive, unskilled labour. Employers across Canada, from the railroads and resource fields, to farms and industrial concerns, wanted access to an unrestricted flow of new arrivals. This is the context in which we must understand the immigration branch's willingness to hospitalize and treat – rather than reject outright – those arrivals who were quickly curable. Indeed, the strictness with which immigrants were examined and rejected fluctuated in response to the need for labour.[13] For instance, a Norwegian migrant remembered his 1923 debarkation at Quebec City, just as the economy and immigration numbers ramped up: "many rumours circulated about regulations for going ashore," such as the need to possess a minimum amount of landing money, and these "rough labourers" feared the power of the doctors and border agents to send them back home. As it turned out, though, "the examination and questions were very superficial."[14] Despite the extensive apparatus of inspection developed by the Dominion government after 1902, portside decisions on admissibility were subject to ministerial decrees driven by racial and class prejudices, and the unending need for workers.

Medical inspection therefore was a crucial first step toward immigration restriction on the east coast. But, as Roberts showed, its importance was soon eclipsed by other reasons for exclusion. In the beginning, doctors were relied on to provide the principal rationale for rejecting an immigrant: the latter's health and, by extension, their potential economic productivity. Within a few years, the doctors were downgraded to an advisory role, with immigration-branch border agents making final decisions on admissibility during their civil inspection.[15] The Immigration Act of 1906, the first new Act in three decades, codified medical inspection, but also added, as reasons for rejection, an immigrant's personal history of pauperism, criminal behaviour, or disability. Four years later, the 1910 Immigration Act further formalized procedures and stiffened entry regulations. These Acts established "the principle that the absolute right of the state to admit and exclude new members was an essential feature of state sover-eignty."[16] The branch was empowered to exclude entire classes or races of immigrant. Border agents were given greater responsibility for a wider range of restrictions; accordingly, the tone of these agents' interactions with immigrants also seemed to change. A recent English arrival described to a newspaper his 1910 experience of a Dominion government pier building:

> It is impossible to time the arrival of a liner at her destination like a railroad train and for this reason, no doubt, can be attributed the long wait of three hours on a bitterly cold frosty morning, for the arrival of the immi-gration authorities on our disembarkation at Quebec. Put a bit of gold lace on an ignor-amus, place him in the position of a Govern-ment official, and a "Bowery tough" is a lamb by comparison. I don't care what nationality a man is, if he is worthy of the name of a man, he merits treatment different to that received by many whilst passing through the Immigration sheds. Think of it: three and a half hours herded together in a stuffy room, the atmosphere of which you could cut with a knife, and not allowed to move. I sat next to a quaintly dressed woman and her family from one of the tribes of Northern Russia, where they never wash for fear of getting pulmonary trouble. When I stretched my legs and endeavored to get near the key hole for a breath of pure air, I was asked if I did not feel well by a supercilious individual. I was told to take my seat, and gently, but firmly, pushed into it … Certain officials of the immigration sheds should be made to understand they are dealing with human beings.[17]

This gentleman had the privilege and the public voice to criticize officials and the other immigrants around him – including the Irish, the London

Cockneys, and the "foreign element" with whom he had shared the ship. Unfortunately, we do not have the perceptions of his neighbours in the waiting room.

THE DEVELOPMENT OF IMMIGRANT DETENTION HOSPITALS

By law, rejects and deports had to be conveyed to their ports of origin by the transportation com-panies. However, ships did not necessarily turn around right away and begin their return jour-ney. This was the case with steamers stopping in Quebec City to debark steerage and second-class passengers considered immigrants. The ships continued on to Montreal with first-class pas-sengers and tourists, and it would be several days before these vessels got back to Quebec City to re-embark those barred entry at that port. Simi-larly, deportees who had been in the country for a while had to be collected wherever they were and sent to one of the ports to await available space on a returning vessel. Finally, if the government was going to offer medical support to unwell arrivals who might be admitted to Canada, there needed to be spaces for consultation, intervention, and care. Local hospitals in the port cities could not accommodate the numbers of detained transients under custody of the Dominion government. In the meantime, all these different detainees had to be housed in a facility from which they could not simply walk away. During the first six weeks after the 1902 inauguration of medical inspection, when the transportation companies "undertook to provide a place for the treatment of certain pa-tients" in sheds on the wharf, no less than forty-seven of these detainees escaped.

The lack of detention facilities was identified immediately, though in early discussions immigra-tion officials seemed a little sheepish about their carceral nature. The deputy minister apologetically described the need for a "detention house" to the agent in Quebec City: "You understand, of course, that it will practically be a jail but in no case would immigrants be detained longer than a few days." Later, the agent referred to the proposed structure as a "prison." As was explained to the minister, it would be best if the government was to build and operate detention facilities itself, so it would have "absolute control of the building and the treatment of these immigrants, and there would be no danger whatever of escapes or of any conflict of authority" with the transportation companies.[18] At the same moment, a committee of prominent public-health physicians was asked to report on the theory and practice of portside medical inspection, following half a year of its operation. They "began by recommending that proper buildings be created to detain immigrants at the ports," recounts Roberts. By the start of 1904, the immigration branch had engaged one of the committee members, Dr Peter Bryce of Toronto, as its chief medical officer.[19] In addition to overseeing the doctors performing inspection work in the pier buildings, Bryce would shepherd the construction of "immigrant detention hospitals" in Quebec City, Halifax, and Victoria, over the next few years. Bryce and the other immigration-branch doctors saw the "splendid detention hospitals" as giving "immigrants every assurance of safety and comfort," where they would be grateful and content to receive "the best expert medical treatment."[20]

At first, though, temporary measures would be taken by the rental of detention space. The most useful and available structures in the east-coast ports were old hotels or "tenements" close to the waterfront. However, in both Quebec City and Saint John, the neighbours – even the Harbour Commissioners in the former city – protested vigorously against the quartering of sick immigrants in these "extemporized" facilities. Immediately upon his appointment, Bryce was sent out to secure suitable hospital sites. Within a month, he had the government purchase a large building

(formerly a farmhouse and inn) on the outskirts of Quebec City; the site became known as Savard Park, after the seigneur, who continued to hold much of the surrounding land. The distance of the site from the immigration pier building remained an issue throughout its years of service, as the branch had to arrange for the separate transportation of both sick and well detainees some five kilometres through the streets of the city. The superintendent of the hospital also worried that anglophone detainees might be concerned about their sequestration in rural francophone territory; he believed they would be reassured by the presence of the Union Jack:

I understand that out West every public building … have one hung up in permanence at the top of an appropriate flag pole. I should think that no place more than the immigration hospitals should have its complete outfit where it is important that the foreigner's eye should be struck with the national emblem. I might say further that in Quebec it is not less important in view of the Britishers themselves, where those detained have the impression sometimes that they are kidnapped by a foreign population.[21]

In response, the flag would mark Savard Park as a Dominion and imperial institution.

Some expense was incurred in converting the existing structure for hospital use, but a year later it was consumed in an inferno caused by a turpentine explosion. All the functions were transferred temporarily to a hastily partitioned wooden barn on-site, while plans for a new hospital building were prepared. It would be two years before the completion of the new building, and another year after that before separate isolation cottages for measles, scarlet fever, diphtheria, and observation were added to the complex. When completed, the main hospital building at Savard Park

5.2 Immigrant detention hospital at Savard Park, in Quebec City. The immigration branch hired a professional photographer to capture the building just as it was being completed in July 1907, so they could use this image in promotional materials. The verandas on the long side of the building are being screened in; those on the narrow end lack screens, because these fronted on the staff quarters. The brick-filled bay of the veranda in the foreground served as a stenographer's office, added to the plans as an afterthought. Two bays to its left, the large bow window draws daylight into the operating theatre.

(Figure 5.2) was a nondescript structure, devoid of decoration. Its appearance, on the principal south and east facades, was characterized by "conveniently arranged" verandas on both floors, so that "patients suffering from the effects of foul air on ship board would convalesce more rapidly through spending hours in the day time in the open air."[22] The verandas on the long side of the building were accessed from the wards via a central hall, so these outdoor areas were enclosed by floor-to-ceiling iron screens to prevent the escape of patients.

The immigrant detention hospital in Halifax was also built on a suburban site, just north of the city boundary at the time. It was under construction simultaneously with Savard Park, according to more or less the same design (Figures 5.3 and 5.4). Both buildings were rectangular, two-storey blocks, with utilities in the basement, which included central heating, hot water, plus large kitchens and laundries to serve both staff and inmates. There was some kind of disinfecting apparatus in the basements to deep-clean immigrants' clothing and bedding. The main entrances to these hospital buildings were on the narrow end, in contrast to the Prairie immigration halls. Radiating off a main lobby were a public waiting room, staff dining, and a doctor's office with surgical suite. From the lobby, a corridor connected the entrance hall to a secondary hall, around which were arranged three wards of different sizes; in the midst of all these wards was placed a guardroom with attached

5.3 Elevations of the immigrant detention hospital in Halifax. Screened verandas cover two sides of the building, and the building is finished with a subtle classicism indicated by the Renaissance-style masonry lintels over the windows and doors.

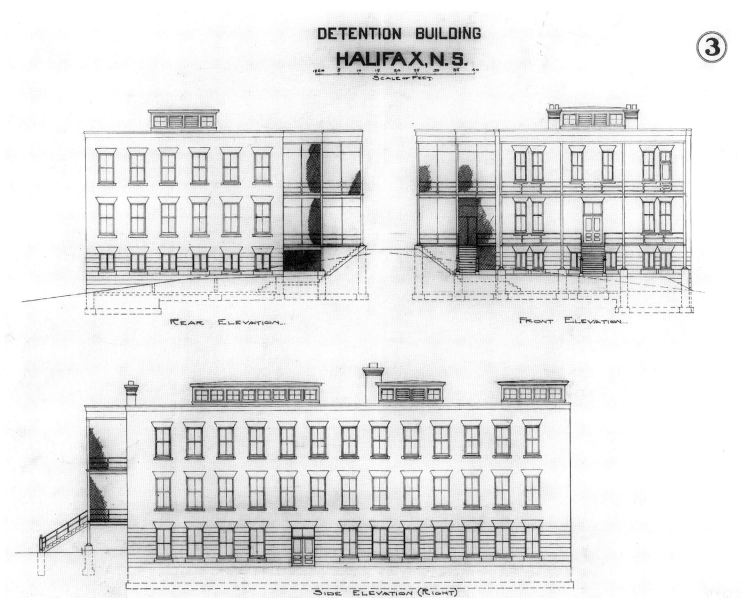

DETENTION BUILDING
HALIFAX, N.S.
SCALE OF FEET.

③

REAR ELEVATION...

FRONT ELEVATION...

SIDE ELEVATION (RIGHT)

160

DETENTION BUILDING
HALIFAX, N.S.

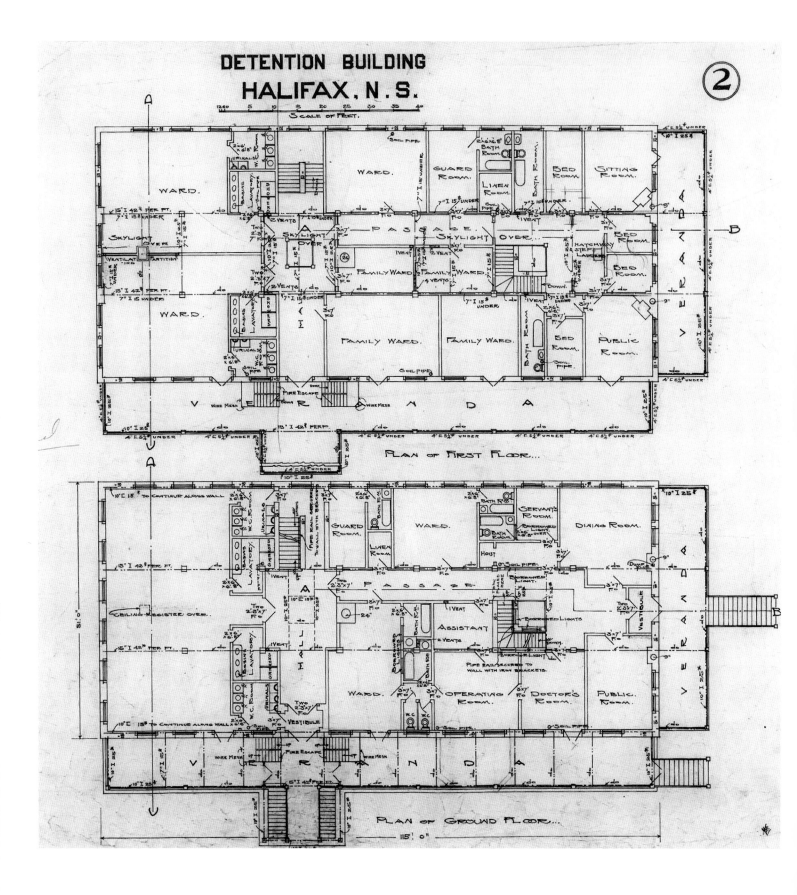

PLAN OF FIRST FLOOR....

PLAN OF GROUND FLOOR....

bathroom. Clearly, the guard was meant to live in his room for long shifts. On the upper floor there was a second guardroom and several wards of various sizes, some marked "family" (Figure 5.5). At the front of the buildings were bed, bath, and sitting rooms for the nurses. In both buildings, the floors were divided by sex, with women and children located on the upper floor with the nurses' residence. The Quebec plans indicate that men's and women's wards were further segregated by British and "foreign" populations.

The immigrant detention hospitals thus were arranged in the ward system that continued to be common in smaller, publicly funded, hospitals. They incorporated ventilating skylights (which continually leaked and drained warmth from the wards), verandas, and large double-hung windows to ensure airflow – all hospital design tropes left over from the era when miasma was blamed for infection. The Quebec and Halifax hospitals were inexpensive wood-frame structures with lathe-and-plaster walls. While interior finishings in the doctor's offices and surgical suites were smooth and hard (Figure 5.6), indicating the significance of non-porous surfaces to combat germ infections, outside these rooms only a nod was given to new hygienic materials in the specifications for ceilings and floors. The bare concrete floors proved problematic, with perpetual dust irritating the eyes of the trachoma patients; numerous fixes were tried, but the immigration branch was loathe to spend the money necessary for the most modern, seamless flooring materials.[23]

Despite being designed as medical spaces under the supervision of doctors, the buildings were not simply hospitals – they were *detention hospitals*. Reflecting the contrasting imperatives of medical and civil border-control officials, the immigration branch effectively invented another new building type. Different forms of detention were combined in architectural space: the hospitalized, who likely

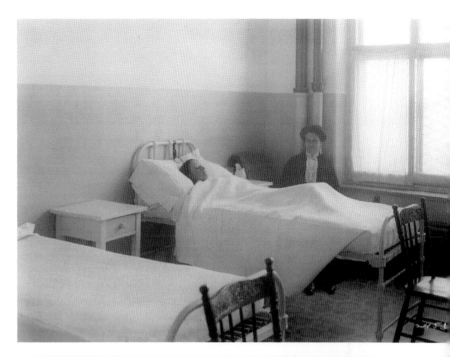

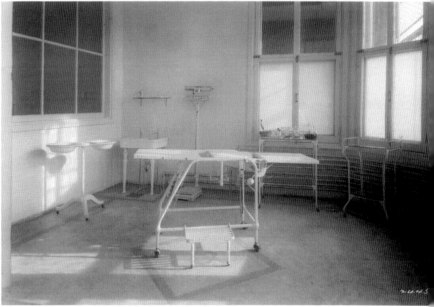

5.4 (*opposite*) Ground- and upper-floor plans of the immigrant detention hospital in Halifax.

5.5 Women's ward in the Savard Park immigrant detention hospital at Quebec City, c. 1911.

5.6 Operating room with bow window in the Savard Park immigrant detention hospital at Quebec City, c. 1911.

would be admitted to the country, mingled in the corridors and bathrooms of these detention hospitals with both sick and healthy immigrants awaiting deportation for social, political, or economic reasons. While some of the wards had their own toilet, bath, and shower facilities, in other cases the patients would have had to pass down the corridor and use those in neighbouring wards. This was not the best setup to prevent cross-contamination; more significantly, it mixed spatially immigrants on their way into the country with deportees on their way out. The crossbred building type resulted in confusion and security problems right from the start.

To migrants, the immigrant detention hospitals represented the terrifying incarceration of themselves or their family members in an unfamiliar or dreaded type of institution. The healthy loitered outside for news of their relatives who were undergoing treatment, waiting for opportunities to visit or pass them home remedies. The doctor in charge at Halifax strongly represented the need for perimeter security there: "I wish to call attention to the surroundings of our Hospital," he wrote to Ottawa: "For want of a fence friends of Immigrants come to the windows and screens and hand them all sorts of things up to whiskey."[24] Beyond the fears and concerns of family members outside, it doubtlessly remained unclear to patients why they were incarcerated and whether they would be allowed to proceed to their destinations. Upon discharge, would they be deported along with others kept in the detention hospital at the same time? Not surprisingly, many migrants and deportees, both sick and healthy, decided to break out. Reports of escapes enter immigration-branch correspondence as soon as detention spaces were rented in 1903, and they continue unabated after the new buildings were put into operation. For instance, Bryce communicated to Ottawa a few months after the opening of the Halifax detention hospital that certain design details were incomplete: "while the original plan of the building is carried out with regard to the iron grating upon the verandah yet these gratings have never been closed as in the hospital at Quebec, with the result that … 3 patients escaped from the window." He requested the completion of the enclosure "so that after supper patients may go on the balconies and yet be prevented from escaping."[25] A balance had to be struck between the medical benefits of fresh air and the inmates' inclinations to flee.

Civil detentions rose rapidly in this period with updates to the Immigration Act. Immigration-branch doctors were swamped with civil detention cases by 1910, and remained perplexed as to why they were responsible for these non-medical inmates. The doctor at Halifax was particularly vocal about the issue. He declaimed the class of "penitentiary immigrants awaiting deportation … [who] are brought in handcuffed." There was no safe place to put them in the hospital, and he asked for a locked room to be constructed in the basement. Three years later, Bryce continued underscoring to Ottawa the need for renovations, including this basement cell and a series of iron partitions to separate the wards between medical and civil detainees. In the meantime, escapes continued apace until the reduction of immigration caused by the First World War.[26]

Beyond the protection and control of the staff and inmates, there was the risk of spreading infection. Of "what use is all our precautions," demanded the Halifax doctor, when, by mixing the well with the sick, officials were "conveying infection and scattering it broadcast over the land?" Why were officials at the pier building, where there was space for sixty to sleep, transporting to the hospital "healthy immigrants to live in the same rooms with cases of Trachoma?" Answering his own question, he proffered an argument that probably horrified immigration-branch bureaucrats: "They are sent out here to prevent escaping from there," but in his opinion it was "far better to have several well persons escape than to have one infected." To no avail, the doctor tried to sway Ottawa with the threat of a scandal: "There will certainly be trouble if a hostile press gets hold of this."[27] It is clear that the public-health imperative of the doctors conflicted with the broader mandate of the immigration branch to create a new kind of cordon sanitaire – no longer against the threat of disease, but against criminals, paupers, and the chronically ill, whose problems were seen as genetic defects that would dilute the Canadian population. Ironically, in so doing, officials recreated the earliest conditions on Grosse-Île, where quarantine doctors had struggled to segregate the sick from the well, and many of the latter were infected.

RECEPTION, INSPECTION, AND DETENTION AT THE PIER BUILDINGS

While the introduction of medical inspection altered the way immigrants were processed through space, other aspects of reception continued as before. However, the east-coast buildings were simply inadequate for the immigrant numbers of the new century. A 1907 newspaper article described the arrival of a shipload of more than 1,500 immigrants at the "sadly lacking" Dominion government facility on the pier at Quebec City:

The examinations being completed, the immigrants first sought the railway office to secure their tickets. Then they were free to pass the time as they willed. Compelled to stay within the barriers, which guarded them from the tracks on one side and the river on the other, there was not a great deal to do …

The supply of benches was soon used up and there was only one alternative for the late-comers, the floor. The floor space inside and outside was filled in the course of time and the long stretches were filled to capacity …

The big grocery shop did a rushing business and … the main form of entertainment for the immigrants was to eat and for hours … [all] were munching on some form of food …

It was a perfect Babel of languages that fell upon the ear in the immigrant quarters in Quebec … and it was only when the phantom of false dawn was near that wagging tongues were stilled in slumber.

It is seldom that the quarters have to shelter immigrants by night, and it is well … The place is limited, the accommodation is insufficient, and so cramped is the space that while the arrival of the [rail] cars was being awaited, these people were strewn all over the floors, men, women and children huddled like animals.

The experience in the Quebec pier for these potential "citizens of Canada" was, the newspaper concluded, "not an auspicious one." It laid the blame squarely on the politicians: "Twenty years ago the sheds of Quebec may have been models in their way, but today they serve only as monuments of what was good … The conditions as they exist are not the fault of the officials; these men did their best under trying circumstances. The fault lies higher up and if some Cabinet Minister had been compelled to pick his way through the heaps of sleeping humanity … new arrangements would probably be in order."[28] Though the 1887 pier building had incorporated dormitories for the use of immigrants, these had been given over to inspection lines and detention rooms by the time of this article.

The immigration branch was well aware of the structure's inadequacies. The Canadian Pacific Railway (CPR) had argued the need for a new immigration building as early as the summer of 1903, reflecting the new medical procedures and the growth in the number of arrivals. At any one time, three ships might be at the pier, with thousands of steerage passengers in need of processing. The Chief Architect's Branch was preparing plans by 1906, when the Quebec agent was asked to enumerate the spaces needed. Along with the typical functions of feeding and informing the immigrants, the agent stressed that "ample space … must be given for the medical inspection and detention rooms." Then, nothing happened. By 1909, the immigration branch was seeking the intervention of Prime Minister Wilfrid Laurier, in whose riding the piers of the Louise Embankment were situated. He promised to give the matter his "immediate attention." However, Laurier would still be trying to get construction started on the new pier building during the election campaign of 1911. The Ottawa superintendent complained to Minister Frank Oliver that there were "strong influences at work" delaying the progress of the new building. Forceful memos flew between ministries and civil servants, outlining the desperate need for the project. The old pier building was "just sufficient" for the immigrant traffic when built in 1887, wrote the superintendent, and now the number of annual arrivals was five to eight times greater.[29]

Tenders were finally requested on the eve of the election in September 1911. Construction commenced that fall despite – or perhaps due to – the deposition of the Laurier government. It was a substantial building project that would take several years to complete. By the end of 1912, the local agents and doctors were able to occupy offices in the new pier building, but the immigrant reception spaces would not be ready for another year. Since the old structure was demolished by that point, the branch was forced to rent and renovate a Harbour Commissioners warehouse in which to inspect and process new arrivals.

The long period of construction allowed ample time for the various social-service organizations and transportation companies to appeal for office or counter space within the new structure, or

to bicker about their placement. The CPR complained that the lunch-counter customers would interfere with the queues at its ticket wickets. The churches were provided with one large office to share, but soon enough the Roman Catholics and Anglicans had lobbied to have their own spaces partitioned off, and other churches then made similar requests. The superintendent in Ottawa thought that additional space for any clergy was unjustified, since newly "arrived immigrants are naturally more interested in their temporal than in their spiritual welfare." By early 1914, just before the building finally opened to immigrants, he was exasperated by the barrage of letters from charitable organizations: "I may say that if one half the requests … were granted there would be no space left for the immigrants."[30]

The most substantial request for space, though, came from within; the Quebec agent had the sudden inspiration to add an entire floor to the new pier building to accommodate civil detention cases. The House of Commons had in fact appropriated funds for an entirely separate, portside detention facility to keep civil suspects and deports out of the hospital at Savard Park, where they crowded the wards and continued to escape on a regular basis. Placing this detention function on top of the new structure would save precious space on the crowded pier and economize on catering, since the detainees could be fed from the immigrants' restaurant kitchen. Conveniently, four more detainees escaped just as the arguments in favour of the extra floor for the pier building were being made in Ottawa.[31] The immigration branch and the Public Works Department moved surprisingly quickly to instigate this extra storey, although

5.7 (*opposite, top*) Elevation of the 1914 immigration building at Quebec City.

5.8 (*opposite, bottom*) Immigration building at Quebec City in a rendering from 1923, originally published in the Canadian Pacific Railway Bulletin.

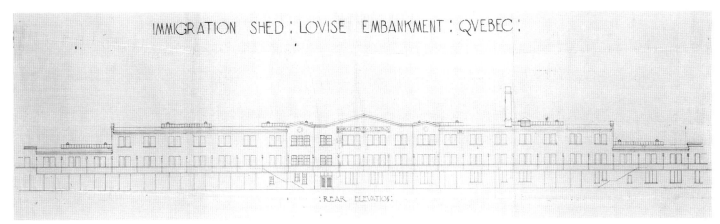

IMMIGRATION SHED : LOUISE EMBANKMENT : QUEBEC :

: REAR ELEVATION :

CANADIAN PACIFIC PIER

COVERED PASSAGE TO IMMIGRANT RECEPTION HALL

IMMIGRANT RECEPTION HALL

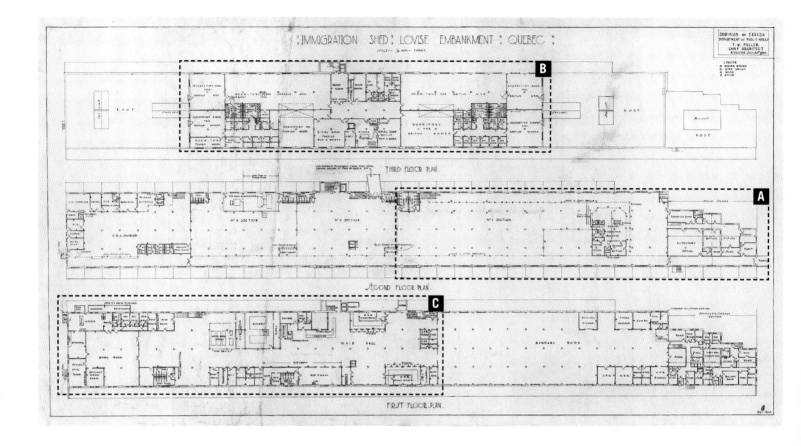

:IMMIGRATION : SHED : LOUISE : EMBANKMENT : QUEBEC :

THIRD FLOOR PLAN.

SECOND FLOOR PLAN.

FIRST FLOOR PLAN.

5.9 (*above and opposite*) Plans of the 1914 immigration building at Quebec City. North is to the left. The stepped form of the south end of the building reflected the curve of the railroad tracks as they passed by to access sheds further along the pier.

it was still under construction when the lower two floors were fully in service in the spring of 1914.

The new immigration building in Quebec City was a modern steel-and-concrete structure that presented a largely industrial appearance (Figure 5.7 and 5.8). Long elevations faced the waterfront and the lower town across the railroad tracks. A repetitive rhythm of paired, double-hung windows was broken up by groupings of three arranged below three false gables. The central gable rose the highest, establishing the symmetry of the composition, and fronting the partial third storey,

with its detention spaces. A plain cornice and some brickwork details in the gables were the only hint of ornament.

The new pier building covered the site of the previous structure and more, incorporating some 125,000 square feet of additional interior space. Most of this extra floor space was devoted to inspection and detention (Figure 5.9). Immigrants would arrive by gangway and elevated passage to the middle floor of the building. From the entry on the southeast corner, a corridor extended almost the entire length of the floor, as far as the US pre-clearance area; on the left of the corridor were windows facing the city, on the right was chain-link fencing demarcating huge waiting rooms accessed by gates. On the opposite side of the waiting areas were chain-link baggage cages, where immigrants could store their hand luggage

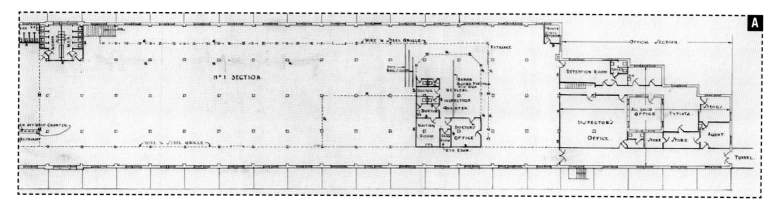

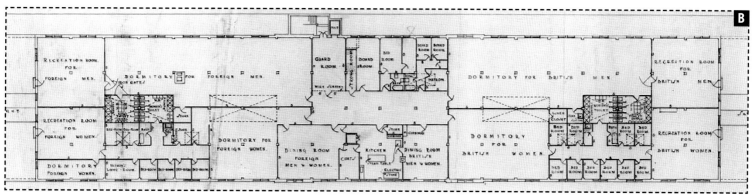

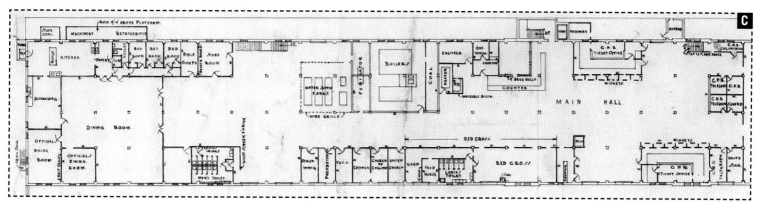

(or carry-ons) temporarily while proceeding through medical and civil inspection. These large waiting areas allowed more than two thousand passengers to be assembled and organized at once.

At the south end of the largest waiting room, parallel rows of pipe railings channelled the flow of immigrants back and forth in a labyrinthine procession in front of the doctors. Adjacent to this was a suite of doctors' offices and examining rooms, including a dark room for eye exams. Immigrants could be checked further here if they had been identified as symptomatic during the line inspection and extracted from the flow. Around the far side of the medical suite, another grouping of parallel pipe railings sorted the immigrants who had been passed medically into queues to await civil inspection interviews, which were held at a series of desks. An area to the side here contained agents' offices, file and supply storage, holding cells, and guardrooms.

Those arrivals to be detained overnight, or longer, were transferred to the top floor, via the staircase in the bump-out halfway along the west side of the structure. This partial top storey was subdivided several ways: for male and female, British and foreign, medical and civil, detention cases; these identity categories required no less than four dormitories and four hospital wards, the latter supplementing the facility that continued to operate at Savard Park. Placing the partial storey in the longitudinal centre of the plan provided outdoor roof decks at each end of the building, so inmates had access to fresh air and recreation space, with a view of the city. These two terraces were each divided into fenced male and female areas; likely, British and "foreign" medical and civil inmates were permitted to exercise on different schedules. A residential guard's room rounded out the plan of the top storey.

For those who were passed by the civil inspectors and welcomed into the country, another corridor passed alongside the baggage cages on the west side of the middle floor. Immigrants could retrieve their hand luggage from openings on the corridor side of the cages before descending the stairs leading to the ground floor. This lower floor was given over to amenities for the immigrants, beginning at one end with a spacious dining room served by a professional kitchen (this included bedrooms for the chef and two assistants), and an elongated waiting area punctuated by counters, wickets, and offices, where they could access snacks and supplies, tickets, information, advice, postal service, and moral support from caterers, railway and steamship officers, and representatives of various social-service agencies, churches, and provinces. About one-third of the ground floor was taken up by the baggage room, arranged for the efficient transfer of immigrants' trunks and crates from ships' holds to railroad carriages. Provisions

for staff were not neglected, including a private officers' dining room within the restaurant. At the opposite end of the ground floor, in the narrow, stepped extension of the plan, was a suite of living spaces – several bedrooms, a kitchen, and a "billiard room" – arranged around a light well. These were the quarters for the matron and assistant matron, as well as guards and sometimes doctors, when necessary.

It is important to note that, in contrast to other pier buildings, there were no overnight accommodations for immigrants in transit at the new Quebec City facility, so this was no different from the situation identified in the 1907 newspaper report. The imperative was that passengers would be debarked, efficiently processed along the building's human assembly line, then fed, informed, and entrained before the day was through. If officials suspected there was insufficient time to complete the process, then immigrants would stay aboard ship until morning. Instead of free accommodations, the lion's share of floor space in the new Quebec pier building was devoted to various kinds of inspection and detention. These spaces also received the most attention from the clients and designers and were prioritized for space planning, because this architecture of process and incarceration made manifest the new tone of the latest Immigration Acts of 1906 and 1910. The layout of the ground floor, with many stakeholders negotiating their territory even after the building opened, seems to have been something of an afterthought.

About one year after the new Quebec facility was finished, a new pier building also opened in Halifax as part of a modernization of the harbour. This building on Pier 2 included the same functions as the one in Quebec, but was configured differently and had less interior square footage. Likely the Intercolonial Railway had something to do with this building's design, which resembled a terminal station, with that company's tracks

5.10 Halifax Pier 2 immigration building, erected in 1915.

running straight into the heart of the structure. On the street side, a symmetrical masonry facade with some neoclassical details, such as the grand arch over the track entrance, conceals a simple industrial shed (Figure 5.10). This is the only Dominion government pier building that assumes this track layout and architectural style. Immigrants were received and processed on the upper floor, where they also could buy rail tickets. Services and waiting rooms flanked the tracks on the ground floor.

A series of interior photographs taken just as the facility was completed provide an opportunity to appreciate the level of finishings and arrangement of spaces in the pier buildings of this period. In the "assembly room," church-like rows of pews separated by aisles face the front of the

room (Figure 5.11). Lit by a clerestory and a long glass partition, the space is otherwise plain, with its post-and-beam structure exposed. The picket fence in the background would have marked the area set aside for the temporary storage of hand luggage during the medical and civil examinations. After this, immigrants proceeded to the inspection lines, which were divided by pipe railings and contained in a long, narrow, monochromatic corridor (Figure 5.12); they would advance to the tables in the left foreground, where hand baggage would be inspected. From there, immigrants who passed muster would gather in the booking hall (Figure 5.13). Although suffused with ethereal light

from the cathedral window – formed by the top of the grand arch on the building's facade – the booking and waiting room was exceedingly industrial in character. The ticket wickets were less prominent than the forest of pipework and electrical conduits, the deep concrete beams, and the freestanding radiators.

This Pier 2 building would be replaced again by the end of the 1920s with the opening of a new facility at Pier 21, which became an immigration station somewhat inadvertently. In fact, local immigration agents had no desire to leave Pier 2, and passively resisted being put in Pier 21. But transatlantic arrivals henceforth would debark at this new wharf, part of a massive project known as Ocean Terminals, a deep-sea port constructed on fill, which was begun during the First World War, and included a new Union Station and railway hotel. Tracks were laid so that the colonist trains could pick up new arrivals directly from the immigration facility (Figure 5.14). The Pier 21 building was designed by railway engineers to be a cargo shed, and construction was under way in

1928 when immigration officials were forced to plan their spaces within it. The branch was offered a large, unfinished, open space on the second floor of the building. Using partitions under the open, steel-truss roof structure of the shed, officials carved up the space into offices, waiting rooms, an infirmary, and a detention centre. It was not enough space to accommodate the full immigration process, however, so they insisted on the construction of an annex across the tracks. Built at the same time, the annex housed customs and baggage

5.11 (*opposite, top*) Pre-inspection waiting area, or "assembly room," at Pier 2, Halifax, in 1915.

5.12 (*opposite, bottom*) Corridor with hand-luggage inspection lines, Pier 2.

5.13 (*below, left*) Booking hall on the upper floor, Pier 2.

5.14 (*below, right*) Aerial view of the Halifax waterfront. In the middle ground, the immigration shed at Pier 21 sits just to the right of the ocean liner. It is a long, low structure, the facade broken up by a red-brick entrance pavilion with moderate neoclassical detailing. In the foreground sits the Nova Scotian Hotel.

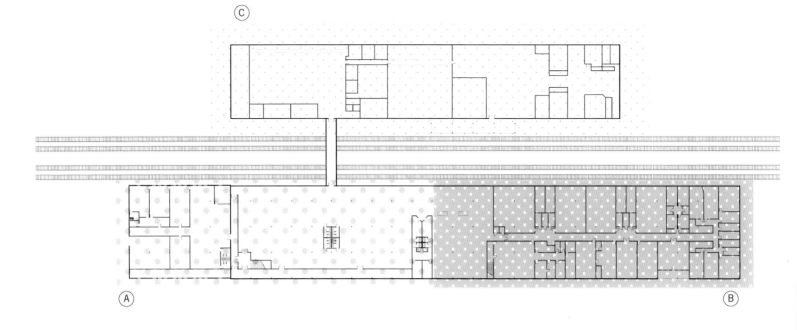

5.15 (*above and opposite*) Redrawn plans of Pier 21,
main immigration shed, detention areas, and annex.

LEGEND FOR OPPOSITE PAGE

1	US Clerks	16	General Office	31	Social services
2	US Inspector	17	Agent	32	Waiting room
3	US Agent	18	Stores	33	CPR Ticket office
4	US Border	19	Boardroom	34	CNR Colonisation
5	US Inspection	20	Detention Sailors	35	Money changer
6	US Assembly	21	Kitchen	36	CNR Ticket office
7	US Doctor	22	Detention British Men	37	Kitchen
8	Baggage racks	23	Detention Foreign Men	38	Red Cross
9	Assembly	24	Detention Foreign Women	39	Nursery
10	2nd Medical Inspection	25	Detention British Women	40	Ramp
11	Medical Inspection Line	26	Cubicles	41	Baggage room
12	Doctor	27	Recreation Room	42	Baggage room continued beneath
13	Breezeway	28	Balcony	43	Waiting room
14	Desks	29	Ward Foreign Men	44	Train platform
15	Civil Inspection Line	30	Ward Foreign Women		

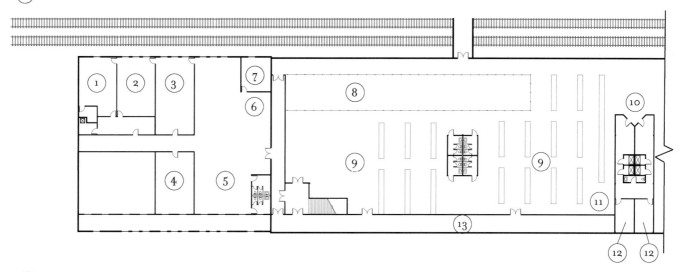

A   PIER 21

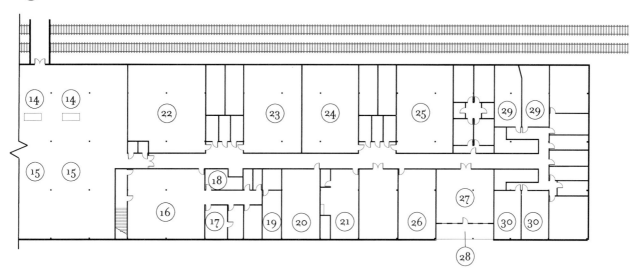

B   PIER 21

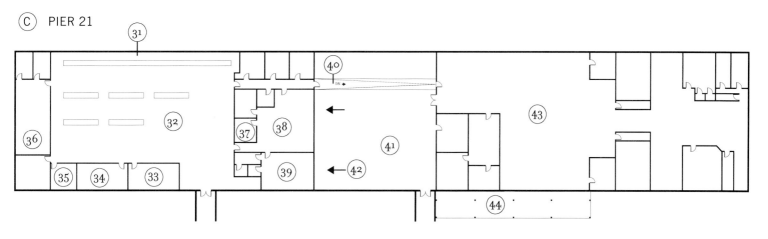

C   PIER 21

FOR THE TEMPORARY ACCOMMODATION OF SETTLERS

5.16 View from a passenger liner with eager immigrants at the rail, Pier 21, Halifax. Immigration agents and doctors ascend the gangway from the second-floor assembly rooms where immigrants would debark. Family members and other interested parties wait on the pier and in the building.

handling, railway ticketing, provisioning, and the social-service agencies, including a nursery operated by the Red Cross (Figure 5.15).[32]

In this new Halifax terminal, ships pulled up and docked next to the anonymous industrial facades of multiple cargo sheds, a continuous wall more than one thousand feet in length, and

not a particularly attractive view from the ship's rail (Figure 5.16). Cargo could be stevedored from ships' holds into the warehouses, while immigrants debarked directly to second-floor assembly rooms, where benches to seat almost a thousand immigrants were arrayed facing the desks of officials. Closed doors led to mysterious rooms, into which select immigrants were taken for further examination. The high ceiling of the warehouse space, receding above the partition walls, suggested untold areas where immigrants might be detoured by bureaucracy. A giant Union Jack hung from the ceiling, exerting authority over the reception process. At the same time, the exposed steel-truss ceiling, aloft over the tops of partition walls, must have seemed impermanent and non-monumental. After medical and civil inspections were complete, newcomers passed to a corridor that connected them with the baggage cages, and then to an enclosed bridge connecting the annex. On the bridge they passed through their first Customs inspection, that of their hand luggage. From here, they passed into the annex, where they might retrieve from the nursery their children who – quite often, if they were identified as tired, hungry, or in need of a bath – had preceded them into the country unexamined. A long ramp in the annex then led down to track level, where there was a waiting room for the trains, and the baggage room. While they were being processed upstairs, the immigrants' baggage had been transferred from the hold of the ship through the ground floor of Pier 21 and into the baggage room. Here, the immigrants claimed their trunks and other large items, but not before they had been inspected by Customs officials.

Saint John likewise received a new immigration pier building after the war, on time for the winter season of 1920–21. About half the size of the one in Quebec City, it was arranged similarly to Pier 21, with the ship's berth on one long side and the railroad tracks on the other. Although the immigration branch annual report merely refers to it as a heated "baggage shed," it also provided "eminently satisfactory" space in which "both medical and civil examiners have every opportunity to perform their work."[33] The old Dominion government pier building (see Figure 1.18), connected to the new structure by an elevated passage, was converted into long-required detention quarters, as well as short-term accommodation. The CPR controlled most of the immigrant traffic through Saint John. In its colonization-department periodical, the company lauded the modern conveniences and finishes found in the new pier building: electric light, steam heating, and emergency exits; plus

"excellent" interiors, "the floors in polished hardwood, the walls and ceilings in pedlar metal sheeting, harmoniously painted in two shades of gray." For the CPR, though, the "superiority of the new accommodation lies mainly in the provision for continuous handling of passengers" and baggage through all the steps of the arrival process, without any "confusion and delay incident to" the experience. For the transportation company, efficient movement of people and cargo was the watchword. But it did not forget to address a public often skeptical or fearful of immigrant otherness. In the new Dominion government "shed," it assured readers, the "social side has consideration in the fact that British-born, both men and women, have special dormitories, and like arrangements and comforts are provided for foreign-born." Moreover, the periodical averred: "Sanitation is the governing factor throughout the entire plant. The fumigation system is of a modern type ... All clothes of the inconnue are subjected to the close scrutiny of immigration officials, and a thorough cleansing is carried out in all cases by the modern process."[34] Despite the modernity of the architecture and the procedures at these new pier structures, at least some of the nineteenth-century discourse about immigrants and contamination – and the architectural features that responded to these prejudices – still seemed salient.

In fact, some older agents had difficulty coming to terms with the subtleties and implications of the new architecture and policies. Soon after the new Saint John complex was completed, a controversy erupted over the interpretation of the rules by the agent there, who continued to allow representatives of non-governmental organizations access to new arrivals aboard ship. As the commissioner in Ottawa clarified for the new deputy minister: "This somewhat irregular practice would appear to have arisen at St. John by reason of an error of judgment by our Agent who is ... a product of the time when there was practically no immigration inspection and consequently has a somewhat hazy idea of the proper administration of the Immigration Act." Almost twenty years after the introduction of medical and civil examinations in the pier buildings, the commissioner still had to reiterate "that no outsider should be permitted to come in contact with passengers prior to inspection." In particular, immigration-branch officials worried that clergy or others allowed access to immigrants on ships or in waiting rooms would coach, provide "material advice," or pass envelopes of cash "from relatives" to aid new arrivals posing as agriculturalists in possession of the required landing money.[35]

Immigration-branch correspondence suggests that Ottawa had been willing to look the other way when its antiquated agents allowed Christian clergy to meet and minister to immigrants ahead of medical and civil inspections. Rabbis were a different story. Reflecting the well-documented anti-Semitism of Canadian immigration officials, the Ottawa commissioner wanted to draw the line at rabbis. To him, the neatest solution was to debar everyone from communicating with immigrants prior to inspection. This decision created a furor among clergy who had been accustomed to the liberty of immigrant-reception spaces. Roman Catholic priests even used boardrooms in the pier buildings to hear confession. In face of protests from well-connected churchmen, the commissioner was overruled: clergy would continue to have access to new arrivals in advance of immigration doctors and border agents. "If chaplains are permitted generally to board vessels ... and to come in contact with passengers ... then I do not see how we can very well refuse the representatives of Jewish and other organizations," the commissioner concluded bitterly.[36]

Regardless, this upper-level decision did not prevent other techniques of discrimination against Jews trying to leave war-torn Europe and post-revolutionary Russia. The immigration branch mobilized all aspects of the Act to prevent their entry, from bogus medical reasons to claims of insufficient landing money, to the continuous-journey clause (discussed below). Sometimes three to five hundred Jewish refugees would be detained from a single ship and held in the pier buildings of Quebec, Saint John, or Vancouver while their cases were judged and immigrant-aid societies appealed to the courts, and to public opinion, to stay deportation proceedings. In Saint John, the assistant to the antiquated agent worked hard to prevent family members residing in Canada from visiting loved ones prior to their deportation. The lawyer for the refugees called for this assistant agent's dismissal and prompted a special investigation. The agent kept his job. Of almost two thousand detained Jewish arrivals in 1920–21, about 13 per cent escaped from Dominion government pier buildings, detention hospitals, and returning ships, from which they jumped in the night and swam for shore.[37] The experiences of these Jewish refugees are reminders that Canadian immigrant-reception architecture also effected control – and even enabled persecution.

The reception of these immigrants deemed undesirable contrasts sharply with other experiences. An English teenager arrived at Saint John with his family in 1919 among the few civilians travelling with returning troops, and during an influenza epidemic; they entered the old pier building to a welcome of cakes and sandwiches. This was an especially felicitous case. Most arrivals entailed mixed feelings of excitement and anxiety. The memoir of a Dutch woman who debarked as a child in 1925 Saint John is indicative:

> The smell of rotten fish filled the air. The weather was dull and dreary ... the old unpainted buildings lining the pier looked shabby and drab. But ... there was a festive mood aboard ... Suddenly everyone spoke the same language: "Canada! Canada! Canada!" Gingerly, we walked down the long

wooden ramp and, one by one, we placed our feet firmly on the solid footing of our new world. In a matter of minutes, the dock became a confusing mass of humanity … Babies were crying; children were clinging to their parents; others sat forlornly on the mounds of baggage … Red Cross angels of mercy were aware of the significance of the day. They spoke with smiles and handshakes while serving free cookies and hot cocoa to everyone.

In the era of medical and civil inspection, many immigrants remembered the examinations, even if they recalled little else from their time in the pier buildings. A British "Home Child" who arrived in Saint John wrote: "As soon as we disembarked, we were met by Sisters … Canadian doctors gave us another quick medical, and then we were loaded on a train." For this boy, the most traumatic aspect of his 1920 arrival was the sudden separation from friends made on the crossing.[38]

As always, immigrants found ways to navigate the spaces and to survive the procedures instituted by officials in the pier buildings. A Dutch home-steader described the arrival of his ship in Halifax during a spring snowstorm in 1927: "The formal-ities got under way quickly. First we passed by an eye doctor, who rapidly examined us and held back an occasional one in order to take a more care-ful look at his eyes. After that we were dealt with by another official who checked our papers and asked how much money we had. He was delighted with my answer. A Limburger had two dollars left in his pocket and he declared three hundred! All you need is a little nerve!"[39] Meanwhile, a young Hungarian girl arrived in the same pier building that year, accompanying her father and sister. Her story is worth quoting extensively as it is a unique and sensory first-person account of being pulled from the inspection lines for a visit to the doctor's examination room:

The gangplank was extended, and the pas-sengers began to file off into the customs and immigration section to verify passports and visas, completing government's [sic] business …

My father turns to me and says, "Come on now! You're being tardy. Hurry up! We have to go through the customs together, not separ-ately. They have rules to obey here."

He was nervous.

In the customs office, problems were cropping up. The name on my official papers was different than my family name, a mixup to be sure, but after much investigation, and questioning, the customs agent agreed that I was indeed, "a daughter to this father," and someone "over there" said the agent, mean-ing Hungary, "must be dull at his job." My father was preparing to respond to this minor insult, I could see it in his eyes, but then giving second thought, troubles enough, he kept silent.

Now the custom [sic] agent turns to my sister Klara and another problem comes up. Remember that sore on her upper arm that my sister Klara always had? Well, listen to this: that sore on her arm was another inci-dent almost cancelling our entry into Canada, the customs man spotting the sore, redness on her upper arm, asking about it, saying … "Who is this one? Is she your daughter too?"

My father nodded his head, wondering again what's up. "Yes, she is my daughter Klara and she is a very good child."

"Where did she get this serious infection?"

"Well, it is not serious, she has always had it, my father said …

"I'm afraid we will need to have a doctor judge it," said the official, "It might be a com-municable disease like syphilis or something. We don't want diseases coming into Canada from other countries."

My father's face was reddening. To suggest the presence of a dreaded social disease in his daughter was powerful …

"What are you talking about? What are you saying? What's the matter with you? She is a child with a sore, nothing more. You talking of syphilis? The people of Besce are not of that kind …"

Here we are in the customs and immigration offices, wire mesh on the windows, the smell of Lysol everywhere, and it is beginning to look as though we were going to be shipped back to Hungary, resulting from my father smart-talking this immigration official …

We were taken away to an anteroom, and made to wait, each of us becoming more anxious, sitting all in a row on a bench …

The day became very long. We had to wait until … the immigration physician would make his rounds, passing judgment on this one or that, and sometimes closing the gate forever on those whose illnesses are forbidden. Hours of waiting. My father insisting that we remain seated. No wandering. No walking around. He would not even allow me, knees crossed, to rock my leg back and forth, relieving some of the stored up energy. I was ready to burst. My skinny bum, no flesh on it, was not a good cushion, and I needed to slowly place my weight on one cheek for ten minutes or so, switching to the other when the discomfort presented, my sister Klara, her fat bum providing plenty of comfort, sitting pretty …

Eventually the doctor came in …

"Hmmmm. Is this family #BT893? I have a yellow sheet here requesting a physical examination of Klara #BT893. What city are you from in Hungary? Budapest I hope. As a foreign student, I was fortunate enough to attend university there … I was attracted to its cultural life …"

"No," said my father. "We are from Besce, a town in the southern part, near Yugoslavia. With Budapest I am very familiar though, many of my friends being there in the arts …

"Yes," said the doctor, "I noticed in living there, that the arts are simply taken for granted, everyone interested, an everyday thing."

Now, my father cleared his throat, his eyes to the ceiling, he began to quote from memory the epic poem *Az elveszett alkotmány*, which is a solid mixture of love and patriotism, and about a half hour long. This was recited in Hungarian, and the good doctor, with only limited knowledge of the language, obediently waiting for the lengthy poem to end. When it did, he gave congratulations to my father … "You are a remarkable man and a talented presenter. I thank you for the recitation, and I regret there is no way for me to repay you."

My father became daring. He said, "Well, you could repay by helping me through the immigration process here," and then he finished the request in High Hungarian, the dialect of the Budapestian, the doctor thoroughly impressed … So, to express his thanks in an almost embarrassed way, the doctor gave Klara's arm a cursory examination, wrote a few comments on the yellow paper, passed it on to my father, and wished us god speed to our destination in Ontario.

While we were walking to claim our luggage … I said to my father that the doctor was highly impressed with the recitation of *Az elveszett alkotmány*.

"He's a dope," said my father. "The poem speaks about foolish governmental bureaucrats toying with people's lives, and making a mess of it. In other words, the poem made sport of him, and he didn't even recognize the condemnation … When it comes to the arts, he is just a duffer."[40]

It seems that medical inspection, though based in science, was equally a negotiation of both architectural and national space, and was characterized by prejudice, error, empathy, literary criticism, and chutzpah.

The highest officials recognized the significant limitations of industrialized immigrant inspection in effect at the pier buildings. By the 1920s, responsibility for medical inspection had been transferred from the immigration branch to the newly formed Department of Health. The minister summed up the issues undermining the mandate of the port physicians to protect the public from incoming immigrants with diseases or congenital conditions: the "opportunity for picking out these individuals is a limited one. The train is going to leave in an hour, and another one is going to leave in two hours, and the railroad company is in a hurry, and everybody is in a hurry. We have arranged that our medical officers will stand at the head of the lines. We make the individuals walk a 'maze' and during that time our medical officers pick them out … and if their defect is not very obvious, they very frequently get through."[41] This truncated medical inspection occurred only at Canada's east-coast ports. At the other end of the country, doctors and immigration agents had more time to observe newcomers who were typically detained by default. Under the Chinese Immigration Act – and racist interpretations of the general Immigration Acts of 1906 and 1910 – reception and inspection took on different procedures, meanings, and spaces.

ASIAN IMMIGRATION AND THE VICTORIA DETENTION HOSPITAL

When the deputy minister for immigration was in the House of Commons in 1903 explaining the newly instituted medical-inspection regime, a member wondered whether these procedures were confined to the east-coast ports. "What about the back door of Canada, how do you manage your immigrants who come in through British Columbia?" The deputy minister responded that he had "not heard that very many immigrants come to us through that route." "There are lots of Celestials," the member assured him, using a racist term for Chinese people common at the time.[42] The deputy minister's ignorance, feigned or not, may surprise us, given what we have seen of the William Head quarantine station in chapter 2. By the time of this exchange in the House, some thirty thousand Asian migrants had entered Canada through its west-coast ports. Most of these were governed by the aptly named Chinese Immigration Act of 1885. And yet, these west-coast arrivals of Asian origin were not considered by government officials to be *immigrants*.

Before the 1890s, Chinese mostly came to Canada as prospectors or contract labourers, and they were not expected to stay. They were not seen as settlers or future citizens. But many did stay, and those who became successful wanted to bring over relatives and Chinese labour to support their business operations. The white settler colonies establishing themselves in British Columbia resisted any increases in Asian populations – much as white settlers did all over the Pacific Rim. The Dominion government, which was at least partly sympathetic to the racist calls for a "white Canada," first responded with a head tax, imposed on all Chinese arrivals of the labouring class. At times, the head tax was successful in reducing the number of Chinese coming to Canada; often, though, the demand for labour was enough for employers to pay or loan the necessary funds. As well, many Chinese entered the country, legitimately or not, as members of the exempt classes of merchant, student, diplomat, or child of resident. The Chinese Immigration Act and its associated head tax were managed by the federal Department of Trade and Commerce; since they were conceived of as sojourning labourers, the arrival of these

Chinese men was understood as a purely economic transaction.[43] Meanwhile, quarantine inspection, limited to epidemic diseases like cholera, continued to be managed by the Department of Agriculture, from which the immigration branch had been removed a decade earlier. Therefore, socially as well as bureaucratically, the Chinese were not immigrants, a status so eloquently indicated by the ignorance of the immigration branch deputy minister: his department had nothing to do with them.

Asian immigration to Canada's west coast thus existed in a kind of bureaucratic grey area that increasingly became a point of contention and confusion in light of formalized medical and civil inspection procedures in other North American ports. What practices were in place at Canada's "back door"? In fact, there were few practices instituted there, other than collection of the entry fee. Certainly, from its beginning in the 1890s, the process at William Head had been more invasive for Chinese immigrants, who, by default, were detained, disinfected, and defumigated regardless of the presence of any quarantinable disease. But if they or their friends could afford to pay the head tax, these new arrivals basically were admissible. They could avoid the head tax by posing as a returning resident or a member of an exempt class, though this would mean a delay at the port of entry while these claims were investigated. Meanwhile, due to a US pre-clearance agreement, Chinese immigrants awaiting funds or identity checks to enter that country – and those rejected by it – had to be kept in Canadian ports. With no institutions established in west-coast cities, detainees were put up in "Japanese boarding houses" and Chinese "Joss houses," from which they would often disappear.[44]

Following the east-coast model, a medical inspection separate from quarantine was instituted in Victoria and Vancouver during the fall of 1904. There now would be three layers of federal bureaucracy governing incoming Asians, and the lack of any kind of facilities was immediately felt. In the port of Victoria, arrivals were received *en plein air* at the end of the wharf, where only a dilapidated shack offered shelter or security. Neither in Victoria nor in Vancouver was there a place for document processing or, more importantly, a doctor's examining room or ward for the treatment of trachoma and other ailments. The CPR, which transported most Asian immigrants on its steamship line, agreed to provide space in a large, wooden, gable-roofed warehouse on the wharf in Vancouver (Figure 5.17). The company installed wards/dormitories, washrooms, and a dining area on the upper floor, with a specialized Chinese kitchen below. A Japanese caretaker managed the facility, and a large Chinatown business, Wing Sang Company, undertook the catering contract. The CPR provided security during the day, and a "white guard" was hired by the immigration branch to handle the night shift. Even so, escapes occurred regularly from this makeshift detention facility.[45] Officials in the United States, where Asian immigration was restricted more severely, complained that lax Canadian inspection and detention practices allowed Chinese labourers and other undesirables to slip away in the ports and cross the border along remote forested routes in the interior of British Columbia, or among the islands and bays of the coast.[46] Indeed, the CPR shed became notorious as the site of corrupt immigrant-reception practices, which paved the way for illegal entry of Chinese.

The multiple departments, transportation companies, middlemen, languages, and interpreters involved in the reception of Chinese and other Asian immigrants provided situations ripe for exploitation. As Asian-studies scholars have demonstrated, starting with the Chinese head tax of the 1880s, it became incumbent upon officials to identify individual immigrants through interviews and document checks, in order to determine their status as members of exempt classes or whether they had already paid the entry fee. The

middlemen who previously organized the migration of work gangs for specific contracts, were now replaced by brokers of individual passages, who arranged for real or false papers and familial connections. Historian Adam McKeown writes that, due to the "Chinese exclusion laws" of white settler colonies, the "activities of most brokers were pushed into shady areas beneath public awareness and at the marginal interstices of law … [which] held a wealth of opportunities for the broker, from coaching migrants on how to deal with immigrant officials to directly smuggling them across borders."[47] That many Asian immigrants chose to land in Canadian ports prior to crossing illegally into the United States only upped the stakes.

In a fascinating monograph, historian Lisa Rose Mar has described the career of Vancouver's most powerful immigration broker, Yip On, who in 1904 was appointed the official Dominion government

5.17 CPR detention shed on the pier in Vancouver. Note the tall fence around the exercise yard to the left, and the shed-roof addition housing the toilets, which drained to the water.

interpreter stationed at the newly established, CPR warehouse facility. In effect, since white officials in the building did not speak Cantonese, the appointment installed the politically active and transnational Yip, "an implacable foe of anti-Chinese immigration laws, as the nation's de facto chief enforcer of the Chinese head tax." Yip took advantage of his access to the immigration facility, to immigrants, to white officials, and to political patrons both local and national, to operate a global business in illegal entries. His network included a brother in Hong Kong who prepared and sent migrants, and his uncle's Vancouver concern, the Wing Sang Company, which, as the caterers at the immigration building, facilitated communications, the passing of money to pay bribes and head taxes, and likely escapes as well.

Mar recounts the memoir of a Chinese migrant who arrived in Vancouver at the age of nine and was detained in the CPR warehouse:

> The guards locked Wong in a cell with iron bars until his father ... could travel to Vancouver to claim him. Wong had never been outside China and was terrified. The British guards teased him mercilessly, calling him a "pig" and other names he did not understand. They also cut off his queue ... As each day passed in jail, Wong and the other Chinese passengers grew more anxious, fearing that they would be sent back to China. To free his son, Wong's father first had to bribe the Chinese interpreter, Yip On [who] interviewed the father and son separately in the presence of [an] official ... who did not understand Chinese. Yip declared that the father's answers matched those of his son and the father was a legitimate merchant whose family was exempt from paying the head tax.[48]

By 1910, Yip faced a challenger for his post as interpreter, a young lawyer from within Vancouver's Chinatown, who exposed Yip's activities to the press and police. The result was a Royal Commission investigation that tabled in 1911 "a voluminous report consisting of nearly ten thousand pages," in which "it was asserted that while the administration of Chinese immigration at Victoria had been as effective as possible, there had existed at Vancouver ample opportunity for the illegal entry of Chinese."[49] In the aftermath of the inquiry, several white officials stationed at the CPR warehouse were removed from their posts, and the Dominion government transferred responsibility for the Chinese Immigration Act to the immigration branch. Another result was the introduction

of photographic identification for Chinese immigrants and residents registering to travel abroad. Although Yip On had been forced to flee the country because of the investigation, within a few years other family members occupied the interpreter post and operated the illegal operation. Wing Sang Company, which by the mid-1910s established itself as "Canada's premier brokerage firm," continued to hold the catering contract at the immigration facility throughout this period, even after the Dominion government erected its own building in Vancouver.[50]

In the first years after the introduction of medical inspection in the west-coast ports, two new sources of Asian immigration also became suddenly significant. Japanese arrivals to Canada (and the mainland United States) spiked first, with South Asians from India also arriving in greater numbers starting in 1907. The annual numbers from each country, in the low thousands, were small by east-coast standards, but they alarmed white settlers in British Columbia to whom this seemed an invasion. The federal courts and government had to annul more than twenty discriminatory statutes directed at the suppression of Asian immigration and community participation that were brought forward by provincial voters and politicians. To British Columbians, Ottawa seemed a long way away, while Asia was just across the water.[51] Anti-Asian sentiment erupted in the ugly Vancouver riot of 1907, which ripped through Chinatown before being brought to a stop in Japantown.

It was within this heated context that the immigration branch moved to provide purpose-built facilities on the west coast for the proper inspection and detention of immigrants from any point of origin. Because Vancouver at least had the CPR warehouse, Victoria would be the first west-coast port to receive an immigrant detention hospital similar to those then being built in Quebec and Halifax. Dr Bryce visited Victoria as early as 1905 to initiate such a project, but an appropriation from parliament had not been forthcoming at that time. The attitude of the Dominion government changed as Japanese and Indian arrivals peaked, and construction would begin in 1908. In the meantime, passengers detained in Victoria were being transferred awkwardly to the Vancouver CPR building, or sometimes even to a US facility in Port Townsend. Those undergoing medical inspection or treatment in Victoria had to line up "on the sidewalk of the street" outside the immigration doctor's private practice. This situation was, he reported, "objectionable to the public."[52] The new building in Victoria would solve these practical problems, while at the same time communicating to locals that the federal government was listening to their demands for a solution to what was perceived locally as the "Asian problem."

From the start, though, the Victoria project was characterized by confusion and controversy in the immigration branch, the press, and the House of Commons. It was unclear what the building was supposed to be. Early in the design process, the immigration doctor stationed in Victoria was reprimanded by Bryce for referring to the building as a "detention shed" in a local newspaper report: "I hereby give you warning that from this time forth if you do not use the more dignified terms 'Immigration Hospital' or 'Immigration Building' in connection with the proposed elegant structure … you will get into trouble." Bryce claimed to be joking, but reiterated the caution three times in a one-page letter, emphasizing the need to "lend all the dignity we can to the new building."[53] Ottawa saw the proposed structure as akin to its new hospitals in Quebec City and Halifax; however, speaking to local audiences largely opposed to immigration from Asia, the Victoria doctor portrayed it as purely a detention facility. Meanwhile, the Winnipeg commissioner, J. Obed Smith, visited Victoria at this time and stated to the press that the new building would have "full accommodation

for immigrants such as the Dominion government provides elsewhere."[54] He thought the Victoria structure would provide shelter for new arrivals, like the Prairie immigration halls under his charge. In early designs and then as built, the Victoria immigration building in fact would differ from both models; it would be neither hall nor hospital.

Bryce and the Victoria doctor were heavily involved in the initial designs for the building. At the end of 1906, the latter forwarded to Ottawa a programmatic description, sketch plans, and a cost estimate "made by a competent person." The correspondence back and forth reveals the intentions of the doctors in providing hospital space comparable to that in the east-coast ports, mingling with the concerns of the immigration branch as it first began to deal with Asian arrivals. Racially segregated wards with barred windows would be provided, while special sanitary provisions were discussed and analyzed. The original proposal included a separate, octagonal wash pavilion, with basins and floors sloping to a central drain, emphasizing white perceptions that "orientals" represented a "very dirty class," who "prefer bathing themselves standing up, and not by using the bath tubs." In addition, the doctors proposed special, culturally sensitive, water closets "owing to the habits of the Hindoos," who do "not use toilet paper, but wash themselves with water" running over a trough. The doctors also "desired, if possible, to have most of the windows of this building glazed with wired glass, which would not only render the window safe, but partly opaque, and prevent any exhibition by the various immigrants, which might offend the public taste in this public thoroughfare." As post-colonial scholars have argued, white settler colonialism was desperately concerned to manage the abject bodies and orifices of racial others.[55]

An elevation was prepared representing the vision of the doctors, and it was published in the

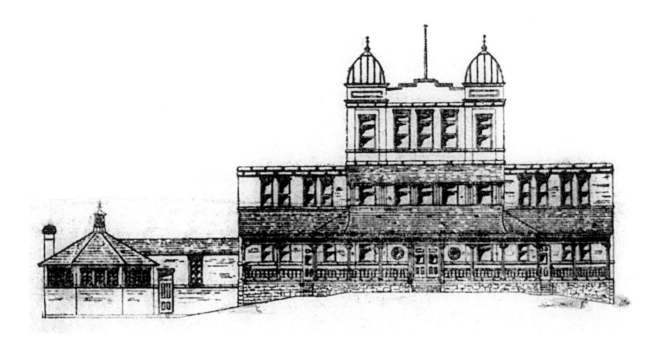

5.18 Elevation depicting the doctors' vision for the new immigrant detention hospital in Victoria.

newspaper alongside the J. Obed Smith interview (Figure 5.18). The bottom two floors indeed have the appearance of a Prairie immigration hall, with a symmetrical facade of repeating bays, a central entrance, and a veranda. Surmounting this, and represented in less detail, is a strange accretion, a partial floor punctuated by two tall, domed towers, like something seen on a contemporary exhibition building at an agricultural fair. It is unclear what the function of these turrets would have been. To the left, connected by a covered passage, is the octagonal wash pavilion, emphasizing the significance of the sanitation function. There are no identifiable stylistic elements. It was an amateur effort by civil servants with only partial authority.

Once the Chief Architect's Branch got hold of the project, the architectural plans and form changed entirely from the earlier concepts. Gone was the bizarre elevation with its turrets, along with the separate pavilion. Instead, we have a more

staid, self-contained block, in the understated classicism of the Dominion government, built in load-bearing brick and masonry (Figure 5.19). The main stylistic details include segmental arch windows and different kinds of classical pediments over the entries; a hint of the turrets remains in the corner chimneys. On the upper floor several bay windows enliven the principal façades, perhaps inspired by the requirement for more daylight in the surgery. In contrast, the rear elevations inside the L-shaped plan, are plain and mostly hidden behind screened balconies that allowed outdoor exercise for detainees. Windows of the dormitories were barred, though none were barred in the wards and offices which faced the public street.

The ground floor of the Victoria building (Figure 5.20) offered a large waiting area, medical-inspection rooms, guard's rooms, kitchen and dining – spaces typical of pier buildings on the east coast, though more modest and missing the social services and commissary functions. Also included in Victoria were a couple of rooms for the US officers conducting their own pre-clearance inspections, and for Canadian Department of Trade and Commerce officials, who in 1908 remained responsible for the Chinese Immigration Act. The upper floor was devoted to detention (Figure 5.21). It included separate wards for Chinese, Japanese, "Hindoos," and "patients," suggesting that the first three groups were not patients, but detainees. Also included were an isolation room with its own toilet, and a small ward for detention of the "insane." Along with the surgery are another doctor's office, and generously sized rooms for a guard and a nurse, the latter monitoring the corridor of patient wards. Similar to other Dominion government immigration institutions, certain employees resided on-site. On both floors, corner offices with

fireplaces were given over to guards and doctors and the dining room, except for the back corner ward upstairs, where "Hindoos" were treated to this architectural feature – likely in order to maintain the pattern of chimney bookends on the facade. As the building boasted central heating,

5.19 (*below*) Victoria immigrant detention hospital, as built.

5.20 (*overleaf, left*) Victoria immigrant detention hospital, ground-floor plan with inspection areas and other functions. The veranda is enclosed by wire screens for security. North is to the left.

5.21 (*overleaf, right*) Victoria immigrant detention hospital, upper-floor plan, with racially designated wards and lavatories, and the rooms for the doctor and nurse.

VICTORIA B.C.
DETENTION HOSPITAL
SCALE ¼ INCH = 1 FOOT

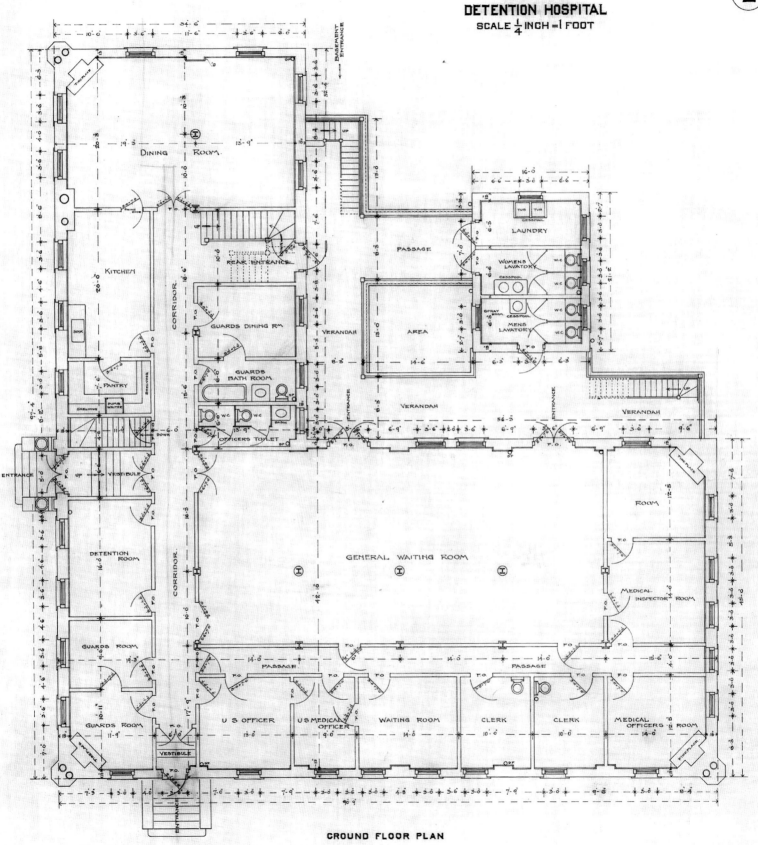

GROUND FLOOR PLAN

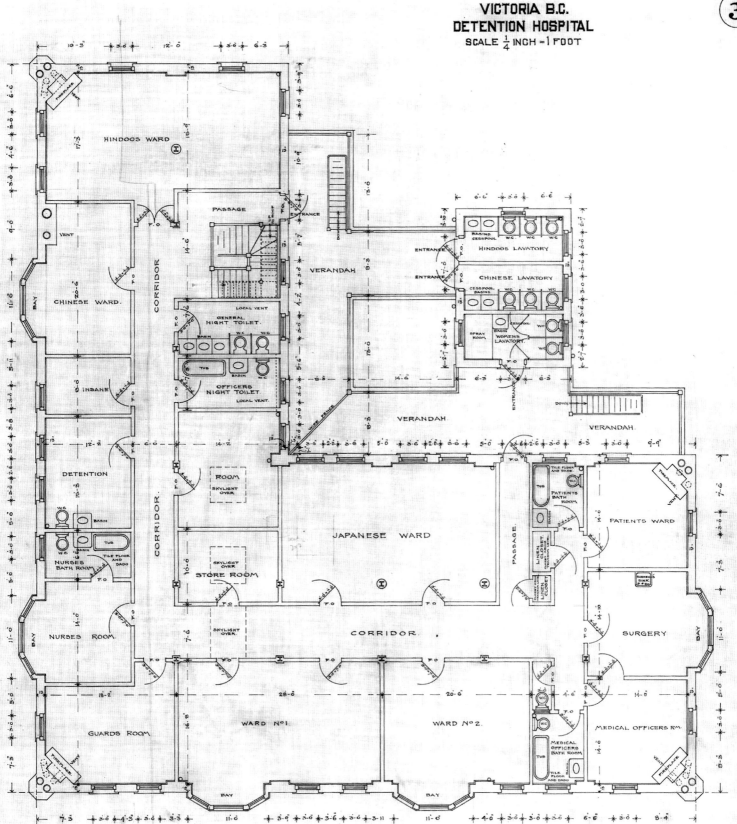

VICTORIA B.C.
DETENTION HOSPITAL
SCALE ¼ INCH = 1 FOOT

③

HINDOOS WARD

CHINESE WARD.

INSANE

DETENTION

CORRIDOR

PASSAGE

ENTRANCE

GENERAL NIGHT TOILET.

LOCAL VENT.

OFFICERS NIGHT TOILET.

LOCAL VENT.

VERANDAH

ENTRANCE

HINDOOS LAVATORY

CHINESE LAVATORY

SPRAY ROOM

WOMENS LAVATORY

VERANDAH.

VERANDAH.

DOWN

ROOM
SKYLIGHT OVER

STORE ROOM
SKYLIGHT OVER

JAPANESE WARD

PASSAGE

PATIENTS BATH ROOM

TILE FLOOR AND DADO.

LINEN CLOSET

PATIENTS WARD

FIREPLACE

NURSES BATH ROOM

TILE FLOOR AND DADO

BASIN

SKYLIGHT OVER.

CORRIDOR.

SURGERY

BAY

NURSES ROOM.

GUARDS ROOM

WARD Nº1

WARD Nº2

MEDICAL OFFICERS BATH ROOM

TILE FLOOR AND DADO

MEDICAL OFFICERS Rᴹ

FIREPLACE

FIREPLACE

BAY

BAY

FIRST FLOOR PLAN.

it seems the fireplaces were purely decorative details, though ironic ones in the latter case. Rather than occupying a separate pavilion, the wash facilities for detainees have been relegated to the basement, in conformity with contemporaneous Prairie immigration halls. A separate Chinese kitchen and dining area was also located in the basement.

After touring the new immigrant detention hospital, a Victoria editorialist – a self-styled critic of everything federal – had to admit backhandedly that it was a well-appointed building: "I have hurled abuse at the Immigration Building, and I still think that from an architectural standpoint it is hideous, but after having been inside I wish to make the 'amende honourable.' The fixings are excellent, and I am seriously thinking of disguising myself as a Yellow or a Hindu-coloured man to have the benefit of living in the palatial residence which has been erected."[56] This writer's white privilege might even have enabled such a gambit. The inmates of the building, on the other hand, struggled to pass as desirable immigrants, and even more so at the moment when the Victoria building was ready for business.

The Dominion government moved to restrict Asian immigration in various ways. The so-called "Gentlemen's Agreement" with Japan limited the number of migrants allowed to leave that country en route to Canada. Then, the "continuous journey" order-in-council was instituted, which required immigrants to arrive on steamships coming directly from their countries of origin. This effectively curtailed immigration from India, since no ships came that distance without stopovers in Hong Kong or Japan. Japanese remigration from Hawaii was also eliminated by this regulation. By the time the new Victoria detention hospital opened in late 1909, Indian and Japanese arrivals had already slowed to a trickle due to these policies. Finally, the new Immigration Act of 1910 introduced what became known internationally

as "the Canadian principle," which empowered the minister and the immigration branch to ban specific races or nationalities from entering Canada for broadly defined economic reasons. For example, Asian migrant groups could be banned outright due to the status of the labour market, or because they were defined as unsuitable workers for the Canadian climate.[57]

During 1908 appropriation debates, the Dominion government was criticized roundly in the House of Commons for wasting money on the Victoria detention facility when all this legislation restricted Asian immigration without any capital cost. An Opposition member stood up to grill the minister of public works: "why do you need this accommodation now? We are told the influx of Japanese has stopped … and the Hindus are not allowed to come further … What immigration is expected that this expenditure should be necessary? … What nationality of immigrants?" Another member added that, "in view of the present agitation against Oriental immigration, there cannot be any possible use of a building to cost $90,000." Moreover, noted another, "even the Japanese," if permitted entry, would "come in by way of Vancouver, and not Victoria." The minister proved rather ignorant of the justification for the new building. His colleague William Templeman, prominent Victoria businessman and minister of inland revenue, jumped to his defence, assuring the House that "many whites" also arrived on the west coast, and that Victoria typically was their first port of call, since the William Head quarantine station was nearby.[58]

In the aftermath of this debate, an editorial in the Vancouver *World* accused the government and Templeman of pork-barrel politics: "Truly it pays to have cabinet representation – especially when cabinet representation is used unscrupulously for the benefit of one's own city." The paper emphasized the importance of Vancouver as the railroad terminus, "where daily trains, not monthly boats, continually land immigrants" from eastern Canada. Vancouver deserved an immigration hall like that found in Winnipeg, the newspaper argued on behalf of local immigrant-aid societies; meanwhile, "the need of such a society has never even been discovered at Victoria." The Victoria *Daily Times*, owned and operated by Templeman since the 1880s, took the high road, restating and augmenting Templeman's apologia in the House, and presenting facts and figures supporting the need for a building. "It is noteworthy that only an occasional vessel coming from a foreign port goes direct to Vancouver," the editorial claimed.[59]

Almost a year later, the Victoria hospital again became the target of Opposition attacks in the House of Commons. A Saint John member pointed out that the immigrant detention hospitals on the east coast were wood-frame structures, "while the Victoria building is evidently of a much superior class." Getting such an expensive project built was a real coup on the part of certain Victoria representatives. Indeed, as an Opposition member from that city sardonically stated, during the previous autumn's election season, Templeman had "published a very fine campaign pamphlet which contained numerous beautifully etched illustrations of the different works he had obtained for the constituency, and amongst these illustrations was one of the immigration building which, during the campaign, was described as the Japanese Hotel." According to several critics in the House, the implication seemed to be that "this building was erected because the government expected a large immigration of Japanese, Chinese and Hindus." Saving face with a roundabout double-negative, the minister of public works did "not think any one would say that in a seaport of the importance of Victoria an immigration building is not desirable." While stressing that he had not been minister at the time, he nonetheless was forced to agree with his critics: it "may be that when the requisition was made … a large number of Asiatic immigrants

were coming in and that the plans were prepared more liberally than they would be to-day."[60] As with the construction programs at the quarantine stations this same decade, the Dominion government again was developing expensive and elaborate architecture to allay fears of immigrant others already addressed by policy and procedures.

The Opposition members were probably accurate in their observations of the Victoria building project. Despite Templeman's protestations, the number of immigrants processed and detained in the hospital was never large. A local news reporter visited and described the typically motley collection of detainees for deportation around the time of the building's opening: they were three stowaways from a Japanese ship, a Belgian, an Italian, and an American for extradition, "three men who were suspected of robbing Redfern's jewelry store," plus "two insane Chinamen [and] two drunks of common garden variety." The CPR warehouse in Vancouver lacked proper wards and cells, so some long-term detainees would now be transferred across the water to the Victoria facility. Not surprisingly, medical detention on arrival targeted Asians almost exclusively. Combing through the building's ledger in 1921, the Victoria agent advised Ottawa that only seven Europeans had been treated in the hospital since its opening over a decade earlier. British immigrants whose destination was Vancouver Island, and who might have welcomed the free accommodations of an immigration hall, shunned the Victoria detention hospital due to its association with Asian arrivals, even though the Ottawa superintendent assured the local newspaper "that there are ample provisions in that building for any 'white people' who may come along, and that care is taken that they shall not commingle with the Orientals."[61] In 1911, an Opposition member from the city queried the minister of the interior about the number and "nationality" of immigrants who had "used the Victoria immigration building since its completion."

The response is telling: "European immigrants from the United States, 197; from Australia, 9; Japanese, 27; Chinese, 147; Chinese detained in building for customs, 57; building also used for registering Chinese outward bound to the number of 1,382."[62] There was no further questioning, since the low numbers of new arrivals spoke for themselves. In the end, it seems that the structure was both overbuilt and inadequate for the varied needs satisfied by other immigration architecture.

As the statistics suggest, the primary use of the building in Victoria was the registration of Chinese who already resided in Canada. After the turn of the century, as successful merchants began travelling to China on holidays and business trips, officials worried how bona fide residents of Canada could be recognized on their return. In an era before passports, the solution was "Certificates Outward," which recorded names and identifying characteristics of these residents. These certificates were completed before departure, and verified upon arrival, in the Dominion government immigration buildings. As a history of the Chinese in Canada described, both registration and return were "humiliating and difficult" experiences:

> returnees were kept behind bars … and immigration clearance might take several days or even weeks, while quarantine was cleared or previous residence (and hence, right to return) was verified. If the returnee were fortunate, a diligent immigration officer would locate a name in an early passenger list that roughly corresponded phonetically to the current rendering of the returnee's name and allow him admission. If not, there were suspicions, humiliations, and delays. The task was not easy for anyone. There were many cases of attempted illegal immigration. Many Chinese were semi-literate in English, had never standardized the romanized equivalents of their Chinese names, and

were easily confused and intimidated by the situation.[63]

A representative of one of the steamship lines described the complicated arrangements in 1912. Most Chinese departed from Vancouver, where their certificates were filed in the government offices at the CPR warehouse. If these Chinese residents returned on lines other than the CPR — which effectively had "a monopoly" on Vancouver arrivals — then they had to be detained in the Victoria hospital until their papers were found and shipped across the Georgia Strait. In cases of first-time arrivals, even "witnesses" to their admissibility had to be transported to Victoria. There was a further complication related to those refused admission in Vancouver: if their ship was travelling on to Seattle prior to returning across the Pacific, then these deportees had to be conveyed separately to Victoria, where they could be held until the ship left US waters. Clearly, in the words of this correspondent, "an Asiatic Passenger Detention Shed to be under Government control and supervision," independent of the CPR, was necessary in Vancouver.[64]

VANCOUVER GETS ITS OWN IMMIGRANT DETENTION BUILDING

As soon as it was clear that Victoria would receive an expensive immigration facility for processing and detaining arrivals, interested parties in Vancouver began to lobby for a comparable institution in their city. City Council, the Board of Trade, the Salvation Army, and the YWCA all made representations to Ottawa. At the peak of South Asian arrivals in 1907, the secretary of the Vancouver Hindusthani Association argued the need for shelter "on behalf of immigrants in general." Almost a thousand Hindus, "recently arrived at this port," with plenty of capital among them, had "suffered terribly for want of proper accommodations

… [and] even the white immigrants are obliged to live in the CPR station." In a curt reply to the City comptroller, the Ottawa superintendent of immigration exposed the local supplicants' ignorance of the broader context:

> so far as the requirements of immigrants arriving by rail are concerned our information is that their numbers and condition are not such as to warrant the establishment of an immigration hall at Vancouver at present. In regard to people arriving by the China and Japan steamers, I beg to say that this Department is not in any way responsible for such arrivals, and does not propose to make any provision for their accommodation beyond the requirements for the detention of such as are undesirable or who require medical treatment."[65]

Asians could not be considered immigrants, and European immigrants destined for west-coast cities were unlikely to be the agriculturalists catered to on the Prairies; therefore, there was no justification for an immigration building in Vancouver.

Immigration officials remained sanguine about their rented rooms in the CPR warehouse only until October 1911, when the branch was given the responsibility of administering the Chinese Immigration Act in the wake of the Royal Commission investigation. During the months that followed, it became evident that a proper Dominion government facility was "essential."[66] The first serious discussions of a new building took place the following summer, but it would be the end of 1913 before tenders were called. In the meantime, the CPR made more space available in its shed; the ground floor would be devoted to Chinese arrivals and departures, with the upstairs rooms reserved for the medical and civil inspection of everyone else.

5.22 Thirty-nine Sikh men were held in the Victoria immigrant detention hospital in 1913. Here the men are shown in the background lining the outdoor staircase behind security screening, while their supporters pose outside the perimeter fence.

The racial separation between the two floors was not just a governmental priority. According to the Vancouver agent, South Asian residents of Canada travelling abroad insisted on being "registered out upstairs." They underwent the same identification process, but separate from other "Orientals" who were not British subjects.[67] The status of non-white immigrants from India was a sticky point for imperial and Canadian authorities, and a basis for continuous challenges to the continuous-journey regulation. Groups of South Asians, detained upon arrival, would retain a Canadian lawyer and attempt to argue in the courts for their admissibility. For example, thirty-nine were imprisoned at the Victoria immigration hospital during the 1913 legal proceedings. A historic photograph shows a number of them lined up behind the wire screens of the enclosed verandas on the rear of the building, while their supporters are arrayed in the foreground (Figure 5.22). Well-dressed in mostly Western-style suits and turbans, these citizens of the British Empire challenged the authority of a colonial outpost like Canada to restrict their mobility and right to work.

There was yet no suitable detention building in Vancouver when the *Komagata Maru* sailed into port after being passed at the William Head quarantine station. In this infamous 1914 event, over three hundred South Asian migrants were refused permission to dock or debark in Vancouver. They were kept on board the ship for two months, short on food, water, and sanitation, while immigration-branch officials sought out all possible ways to reject them. The ship was under guard the entire time, and out in the open for everyone to see, while "the press kept the *Komagata Maru* on the front pages." Throughout the incident, the new Vancouver immigration building was under construction nearby, in view of the ship. The Dominion government may have been able to avoid the whole embarrassing situation if the building had been ready, and the migrants could have been detained away from the watchful eyes of the press and public. For the migrants, detention in Dominion government dormitories on solid ground likely would have been more comfortable and clean, with more assured meals from the kitchen. However, the results of the legal proceedings may have been no more successful. Ultimately, the ship was escorted out of the harbour by a Royal Canadian Navy cruiser, and sent back across the ocean.[68]

As the plans for the new Vancouver facility were drawn, went to tender, and were publicized, there was no pretence of it being a hospital, a Prairie immigration hall, or a pier building like the one then under construction in Quebec City. The chief architect, the Ottawa superintendent of immigration, and the Dominion immigration inspector for British Columbia, all referred to it as "the new Detention Immigration Building in Vancouver," or simply the "detention building."[69] When a rendering of the facility was published in several Vancouver periodicals, the accompanying captions also

emphasized the detention function; none mentioned free lodgings or hospital wards. One caption declared the project a "detention shed and executive building," reflecting both its carceral spaces as well as its role as the Pacific-coast headquarters for the immigration branch.

Another caption applauded the fact that the new immigration building would be "in keeping with the handsome and solid appearance of the other Dominion government institutions in Vancouver." The attractive rendering (Figure 5.23) revealed an Italianate-style building of five, three-bay sections, each with a different hip-roof treatment, some with deep brackets and exposed rafter ends. Ornamentation was limited largely to the ground floor, where classical flat pediments marked the entries, and the windows were capped with round arches filled with a chequerboard pattern and punctuated by tall keystones. A huge Union Jack flew from the central point of the facade. The rendering presented a perfectly charming scene, with trees and a white picket fence in the background; in the foreground, waves lapped at the pier, where men strolled and stood chatting in groups, while a launch steamed past. Deep, inset verandas on the third and fourth floors suggested that this building could be a resort hotel. There was no indication that those verandas would be, in reality, caged exercise yards for detainees.

This artistic rendering is the only drawing of its type that I have discovered in the archives of immigration architecture. Renderings are more typically associated with speculative building projects, or when clients and stakeholders need convincing to hire an architect or approve a project. The Chief Architect's Branch, with its client assured and functional programming being its primary concern, rarely bothered itself with the production of presentation drawings like perspectives or renderings. Therefore, the existence and broad local distribution of this particular representation suggests that it was intended to convey something

5.23 Artistic rendering of the proposed immigrant detention building for Vancouver, 1914.

to Vancouver residents. The importance of public relations may also explain why prominent Vancouver architect E.E. Blackmore was engaged to oversee design and construction in tandem with Public Works architects in Ottawa and Victoria. Blackmore was one of the first private architects engaged on an immigration-branch project since the 1870s, reflecting a more open policy toward out-of-house design instituted by the newly elected Conservative government of 1911.[70] Blackmore's office surely produced the rendering of the building.

The public-relations message seemed to be that, after years of neglect, the Dominion government would now provide a landmark immigration structure on the waterfront, recognizing the importance of Vancouver as the terminal city for

both trains and ships. It was a kind of gift from the new government after fifteen years of Liberal rule. One new MP was H.H. Stevens, a former Vancouver city councillor and well-known anti-Asian crusader, who had been a leading voice in the buildup to the 1907 riots. He appears often in departmental correspondence about the facility. The *Western Call*, a reformist and boosterish newspaper founded by Stevens, included the rendering in a fall 1914 issue. The caption assured readers that the firm contracted to erect the building was founded and operated fully by "Native Sons," referring to a homegrown fraternal association whose

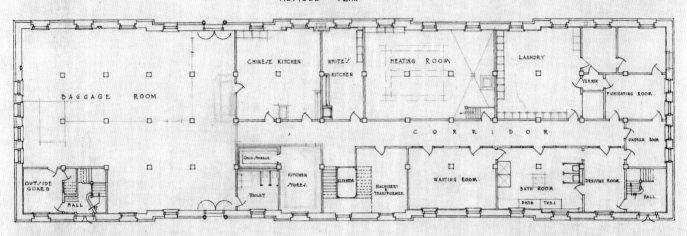

REVISED PLAN.

BASEMENT FLOOR PLAN

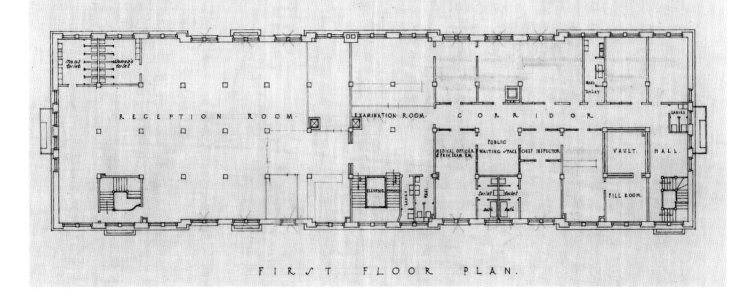

FIRST FLOOR PLAN.

5.24 Basement and first-floor plans of the immigrant detention building in Vancouver.

5.25 (*opposite*) Second- and third-floor plans of the immigrant detention building in Vancouver.

membership was restricted to white men born in British Columbia.[71] The Vancouver detention building was a clear signal that the new government was alive to the circumstances of Asian immigration on Canada's west coast. Bestowing a west-coast headquarters for the immigration branch was no small gesture. In the end, it cost nearly $400,000, outstripping any other project for the branch, even the contemporaneous Quebec City pier building with its extra storey.

What was built on the Vancouver waterfront was a substantial four-storey, steel-and-concrete structure clad in stone and brick in conformity with the rendering. The annual report of the Public Works Department enumerated the myriad functions accommodated in the new building (Figures 5.24 and 5.25). On the first floor were spaces for the business of receiving immigrants at the port: waiting rooms, medical and civil examination

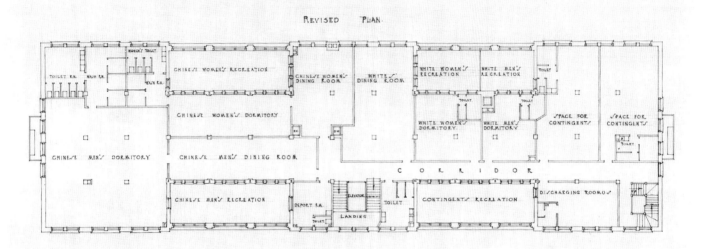

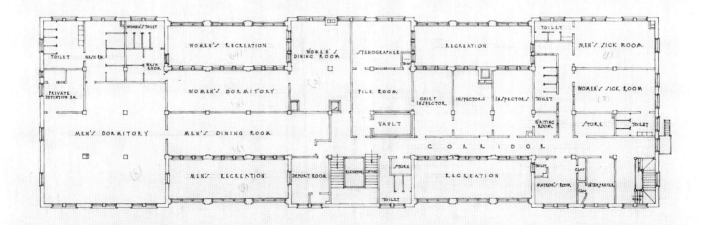

rooms, doctors' and agents' offices, space for several stenographers, plus a vault and file room to store certificates outward and other paperwork. The second floor was residential, divided into separate dormitories, dining halls, and recreation spaces for Chinese and white men and women, and for "contingents" or other races, as needed. The second and third floors also had several "private detention" rooms to isolate special cases and deportees. On the third floor was another set of men's and women's dormitories, dining, and recreation spaces (unassigned), plus two wards for sick detainees. Each dormitory had an enclosed veranda associated with it. Private rooms for a matron or nurse and an interpreter are provided here. One of the rooms would be dedicated to "Hindu registration" outwards. Also here was duplicate clerical space for the US immigration service performing pre-clearance duties, with inspectors' offices, stenographers, vault, and file room. Dedicated staff dining and recreation space on this floor point to the increased size and modernization of the bureaucracy, as did the filing cabinets and secure storage found throughout. Topping out, the partial top floor had three large "unassigned rooms," plus a machinery room for the elevator.[72] The building's ground-level basement contained the large baggage room, entrance halls, and separate kitchens for "whites" and Chinese; immigration officials had learned back at William Head in the 1890s that Chinese cuisine required different equipment, such as huge rice cookers. Also in the basement, the laundry formed part of a cleansing suite that incorporated dressing and undressing rooms and fumigation and disinfection chambers for clothes, belongings, and bodies. Again, the practices established at the west-coast quarantine station convinced officials that all Asian arrivals would be required to undergo a sanitary regime.

The foregoing description is of the facility as built; the function of many of these rooms changed over the years, along with changes in

5.26 Panoramic view of Vancouver harbour centred on the Dominion government immigrant detention building.

policy, practice, needs, and flows of immigrants. For instance, by 1920, the documentation associated with Chinese immigration had "become so voluminous that a separate filing room" had to be added, taking over space previously used for other purposes.[73] And US officials vacated the third floor during the First World War; they returned in 1921 as the US quota laws began to take effect, and pre-clearance again became central to that nation's immigrant-reception procedures.[74]

As indicated by the plans, there were relatively few entrances to the building and, despite the symmetry of the facade, none was centrally placed. On the water side, doors were located at either end, on the right for staff and the left for immigrants. Arrivals entered at the basement level, into a stair hall monitored by a guardroom; this dedicated stair led directly up to the large waiting room. After civil and medical inspection, the central staircase and elevator would take detainees to their accommodations in the upper stories. Double swinging doors also led directly into the baggage room from the wharf; matching doors on axis led out from

the baggage room to the railroad tracks. This latter baggage door is the only entrance to the building facing the city side, but this provision was made merely for moving cargo: there was no imperative here — as at the east-coast ports — to process immigrants through formalities and onto waiting trains beside the building. That is, several doors received and discharged immigrants on the wharf, but no doors were placed to allow direct access to and from the city. Because the building sat on the waterfront at the base of a bluff, it was separated effectively from the everyday life of the city and from the regular passenger traffic served by the grand CPR station which was built at the same time, but atop the bluff.

A panoramic photograph from 1920 reveals the Vancouver immigration building to be sited in an industrial context, surrounded by railroad tracks and surplus materials, warehouses, fuel tanks, boxcars, barges, and log ponds (Figure 5.26). Access to the site is limited to a viaduct from the top of the bluff, or perhaps a long walk along the waterfront. A large open area adjacent to the building suggests the possibility of keeping the

surroundings under surveillance. And yet, the site is not uninhabited. In this panorama, the photographer fortuitously has captured several figures: a workman tends a large brick oven, while another drives a horse-drawn dray out of a Pier A warehouse; there are a couple of "fresh-air inspectors" on the viaduct, and one man strides purposefully along the tracks toward the immigration building. Most curious, however, is the lone man in front of the building, who seems to be communicating with several inmates seen behind the bars in second-storey windows. The man on the ground assumes an awkward posture, as if he is bending to retrieve something tossed down to him. Or perhaps he is in the midst of a strange mating ritual: the rooms where figures can be seen were dedicated on the plans to Chinese women's dining and recreation.

EXPERIENCES AND ESCAPES FROM WEST-COAST IMMIGRATION ARCHITECTURE

Chinese women were often detained in the west-coast immigration facilities to await male suitors or guardians. One bride remembered a five-week stay in the Victoria immigrant detention hospital. In the words of the scholar who compiled her story from family members, she "had paid the higher second-class fare, yet when she arrived in Canada she and other Chinese passengers were segregated by race, not cabin class." Even though she "was freshly showered and in clean clothing ... she was forced to undress in front of a non-Chinese speaking stranger ... and told to wash." After the medical examination and entrance interview, she was held to await the arrival of her fiancé, who was travelling from Brandon. The story concludes that the couple were married in Victoria before returning to the Prairies; the wedding may have occurred in the detention hospital. As described by an Anglican missionary who was allowed to visit Chinese immigrants under detention in both Victoria and Vancouver, brides often "went through the ceremony at the Immigration Offices before being allowed to leave," because they were suspected of being prostitutes or indentured servants.[75]

All Asian arrivals were treated with suspicion, and their experiences were similar to those of prisoners. Our Anglican missionary, who — in parallel with east coast practices — was sometimes allowed to greet new arrivals before they had met with inspectors or interpreters, described the Dominion government facilities:

Arrived at Vancouver, the immigrants were taken to the immigration building, and placed in rooms to await examination. The quarters consist of a dormitory with iron bunks, the number varying according to the size of the party arriving; a dining-room fitted with long tables and benches, where meals in Chinese style were served by Chinese cooks on the premises; and a paved room for exercise with windows down one side, all barred with iron to prevent escape.[76]

Unlike the case on the east coast, though, where few immigrants memorialized their detention, Asian arrivals in British Columbia ports spoke bitterly of theirs: of course, detentions typically were longer in the west. Chinese newcomers remembered the immigration buildings as nothing other than prisons. One 1920 arrival, a thirteen-year-old, recalled that "when I arrived in Canada I was locked in Immigration for 19 days ... in Vancouver, in the old building, behind steel bars, like a jailbird."[77] An eight-year-old who came the following year was detained for three months:

We were like prisoners. There were bars in the windows. There was roll call, bed call, a time to sleep, a time to wake up ... There were guards to keep you in line ... and visitors were regulated.

The food was very bad: generally there was a dish of soup, then they used the same meat from the soup and mixed it with vegetables and served it with rice ... The station was noisy too, with trains going back and forth all day long.[78]

As we have seen, the Chinese caterers were concerned with other aspects of the immigration process beyond just the quality of the food.

Chinese and other detainees were thus subject to the regimentation and repetitiveness of prison life. Not surprisingly, they became bored and resentful, and took out their frustrations on the building itself. Resistance started small. Soon after the opening of the Vancouver building, the local agent complained that the light "switches are all placed inside the detention rooms and can therefore be turned on and off at will by the occupants. We find that the Chinese detained here appear to get considerable amusement out of turning on the lights after they have been turned off by the guards, and also in turning them on and off in the daytime." A few weeks later he informed Ottawa he was having "trouble" with the sinks in the same rooms:

> These basins are the same as will be found in the average hotel, fitted with waste pipe stopper controlled by a rod and porcelain knob on the basin.
>
> We find that the Chinese detained, apparently from want of something better to do, take these appliances to pieces and as a result the basins are practically useless.

He suggested that a "rubber plug and chain" would be more serviceable.[79] There are two conclusions to draw from these stories: first, even though the building had been denominated a detention facility in all of the official correspondence, the architects had not detailed or specified with that in mind; and second, detainees were dismantling this anti-Asian immigration architecture piece by piece.

Perhaps the most significant destruction was done during the postwar explosion of Chinese boy arrivals, some of whom we met earlier. These were the sons or "paper sons" of residents. At times, between fifty and one hundred were detained together in several dormitories of the Vancouver building. As local officials explained, "boylike they are continually sky-larking with the result that boots, boxes, apples, and other miscellaneous objects are thrown against the windows breaking the same … Unfortunately the damage does not stop at broken windows. The electric switches are experimented on with pocket knives, nails, etc., electric globes broken and walls defaced." All this occurred even though "the interpreters are continually warning the boys," and the guards visited the detention rooms "three or four times" every hour. Subsequently, about a year of correspondence between the immigration branch and the Public Works Department debated who would pay for the damages, the latter arguing that this represented something beyond ordinary wear and tear.[80]

More respectable Chinese detainees – that is, second- and first-class passengers – complained about broken glass and plaster and walls defaced by the graffiti of single male immigrants. These complaints seem to have reached the Chinese consul, who brought them forward to the government. Ultimately, the minister of the interior was questioned in the House of Commons about the condition of the detention spaces, but he dismissed the criticisms out of hand: "I have visited the immigration shed at Vancouver, and although it is not by any means a palatial hotel, I think a man could be comfortable there provided he had his own bedding, which nearly all these immigrants carry."[81] Meanwhile, mouldering in the correspondence files were three years of outstanding requests for cleaning and repairs. Maybe the minister had visited only the immigration-branch offices, and was not shown the immigrant dormitories.

The travelling inspector, though, readily admitted that the detention rooms in Victoria and Vancouver were "disgraceful … due to the Chinese immigrants who have been detained there scribbling all over them." The Vancouver agent proposed refinishing the walls with a material that "would make it difficult for persons to mark them up with pencils."[82] It is unclear whether this ever happened, but when the Victoria detention hospital was demolished in 1977, geographer David Lai managed to document some of the poetic words carved and inked onto the walls by Chinese detainees. One poem is a belated warning and romantic paean to freedom:

> Fellow countrymen, read the following notice quickly:
> Having amassed several hundred dollars,

I left my native home for a foreign land.
To my surprise, I was kept inside a prison cell!
Alas, there is nowhere for me to go from here,
I can see neither the world outside nor my
    dear parents.
When I think of this, my tears begin to stream
    down.
To whom can I confide my sorrow,
But to write a few lines in this room.

It is noteworthy that the space itself here becomes the interlocutor. Other poetry and prose record typical experiences in the immigration building. The "black devil … forces the Chinese to sweep and clean the floor" cried one 1911 verse. One detainee described with horror how immigration officials "examined my eyes, forced me to strip to the waist and take off my pants to lay bare my body." Another fragment expresses bitter sentiments, the building's walls echoing with the detainee's lament: "I cannot sleep because my heart is filled with hate. When I think of the foreign barbarians, my anger will rise sky high. They put me in jail … I moan until the early dawn."[83] Many Chinese arrivals spent weeks or months in the Victoria and Vancouver detention buildings. Uncertain about the outcome of their cases, they left their permanent mark on the spaces to remind the world of their existence.

Both legitimate and fraudulent immigrants continued to come from China, even as shipping slowed during the war. Above all, in 1917–18 large contingents of Chinese labourers – "coolies" as government correspondence continued to call them – were billeted at the Vancouver detention building. They were in transit from William Head quarantine station onto eastbound trains, and eventually across the Atlantic Ocean to reconstruction sites in war-torn Europe. The waterfront around the Vancouver detention building was under lockdown for a year in a feeble attempt to ensure the top-secret passage of almost eighty-five

thousand of these labourers. About two-thirds of this number returned by the same route in late 1919 and early 1920 (the remainder went home via the Suez Canal).[84] Into the 1920s, the registration of out- and in-bound Chinese residents of Canada remained the primary business at the Dominion government's west-coast immigration buildings. And, even though the new Chinese Immigration Act of 1923 eliminated the head tax and almost totally restricted new arrivals, the few exempt classes still had to be processed in the buildings.

Other trans-Pacific migrants were also detained in Victoria and Vancouver. Russian Jews began arriving late in 1916, most of them en route to the United States, then a "considerable influx" seeking asylum in Canada arrived from 1919 to 1921. Most Jews were ordered deported, but a well-organized Jewish community filed suits to prevent or delay these actions. In the meantime, the community was allowed to post bonds for the temporary release of individual refugees, for it seemed "inhuman to keep" them locked up in the dirty and damaged immigration building at Vancouver, along with Chinese and other non-white immigrants.[85] The Dominion government's stance toward South Asians softened slightly in 1920. After several years of strict exclusion following the challenges to the continuous-journey regulation, residents now were allowed to bring wives and children to Canada. These family members awaited reunion with patriarchs in the Victoria and Vancouver detention buildings, where South Asians also continued to be registered outwards. Finally, the 1921 implementation of the so-called "percentage Act" south of the border required the detention of *all* US-bound immigrants, so that the monthly and annual quotas for each nationality could be checked. Due to these pre-clearance arrangements, detention rooms were needed in Canadian ports to house immigrants during the process; rooms would even be needed for "white passengers" en route to the United States.[86]

Japanese immigration continued throughout these years, well in excess of the limits placed by the Gentlemen's Agreement. The Japanese interpreter, Fred Yoshy, newly hired by the immigration branch just ahead of its occupation of the new Vancouver building, ensured a robust flow. He ran an illegal immigrant smuggling scheme similar to that of Yip On, using his role as interpreter to sidestep the law for some fifteen years. Investigations in 1931 identified about 2,500 Japanese workers in the country illegally; when rounded up, they were gathered in the Vancouver detention building prior to deportation. Yoshy was tried and convicted. In contrast, the name of the Japanese interpreter in Victoria was never besmirched. Regardless, both interpreters were remembered fondly by Japanese newcomers who were treated to family dinners at their respective homes in the two cities.[87]

Compared to the investigated interpreters, there are few documents that record the experience of other staff members. However, a series of encounters at the Victoria detention hospital prove interesting. In 1921, the Victoria immigration doctor complained angrily to his superiors at the new Department of Health that three of his best examining rooms and wards on the second floor had been converted – without his knowledge – into an apartment for the caretaker and his wife. In a response upheld by the immigration-branch officers in Ottawa, who by this time held a certain contempt for the doctors in the service, the local agent explained that the apartment was a better use of space than hospital rooms. The converted apartment was necessary because the caretaker's wife would not reside in the building otherwise. Previously, the caretaker's suite had been on the ground floor adjacent to the immigrants' dining room and kitchen, but the "living conditions … were simply unbearable owing to the numerous altercations between Chinese detained here where knives and missiles were used. On one occasion, the wife of [the previous] Caretaker … jumped

from her kitchen window and fled from the building." In effect, when it had been "necessary for the caretaker's wife to come more or less in contact" with Chinese, she had had some "rather unpleasant experiences."[88] The odd mixture of uses in the immigration detention building type placed people in all sorts of situations that were foreign, surprising, confrontational, and rife with hierarchies of power. Distinguished doctors were subordinate to civil servants with comparably little training. A white woman, forced to live in the building due to her husband's position, was on the side of hegemonic power, but felt subject to the male gaze and unwanted attention from non-white men. And although the Asian immigrants were prisoners, they were feared within the architectural space just as they were feared in white settler society.[89]

Despite their incarceration, Asian and other detainees acted forcefully within the spaces of Dominion government immigration architecture. The most dramatic evidence of these spatial practices was their daring escapes. Almost immediately upon the completion of the new west-coast detention buildings, inmates began to find ways out. At Victoria in 1912, two Chinese, "wily fellows," as they were called by the Victoria doctor, damaged the bars while escaping from one of the wards. One year later, four Japanese stowaways sawed through the bars and escaped, leaving officials with "a query how they obtained the saw." A year after that, "a number of Hindoos succeeded in forcing a hole" in the wire screen on the veranda and absconding. The litany of escapes continued after the war, with incidents in 1918, 1919, 1920, 1924, and 1925 – at least incidents that were known about. After the 1924 escape of a Japanese man, the west-coast commissioner "noted that the cook who loaned the alien a knife has been replaced."[90] This series of escapes led to modifications in the building: more windows were barred; the staircases down from the detention rooms were en-caged; and locked gates were installed at the ends of corridors that accessed wards and dormitories, since it was easy to breach the wooden doors of these rooms.

Officials had the Victoria escapes in mind as the Vancouver detention building was under construction. The agent there made Blackmore replace the common-and-garden doorknobs specified for the detention rooms, because they were insubstantial and could be unlocked from the inside. Later it was noticed that the hinge pins were also inside the rooms, so the doors could easily be removed by inmates. The two gentlemen also worried that agile immigrants might shimmy down the shafts of the dumbwaiters that delivered meals from the basement kitchens to the various dining rooms on the upper floors. It is unclear whether modifications were made to correct this latter deficiency. Regardless, inmates found many other means. The first recorded escape occurred about one year after the building opened; an eastern-European sailor, detained after deserting his ship, "wrenched free from the door posts" the transom-window hardware, crawled out through this opening, snuck down to the ground floor, and climbed out an unsecured window with "very little trouble." As a result, all the transoms were screwed shut, reducing the quality of ventilation in those spaces. In 1918, following the escape of "several Japanese," it was found that the wire-mesh windows in the doors could "be removed with the aid of an ordinary pocket knife by separating the beading from the door frame, allowing the glass to fall back into the room." A grid of bars over all these windows was the solution. It was to no avail: a group of six Japanese stowaways soon escaped by bending down the tops of the bars which were not fastened to anything and scrambling out over top. Finally, in 1920, two white Americans, possibly on the lam, were abetted in their escape by an accomplice on the wharf, who passed up to their window, on a lowered rope of torn sheets, a tool to cut the bars and two revolvers in case of trouble.[91]

The news of escapes occasionally leaked to the press or was raised in the House of Commons. "Have any precautions been taken to prevent similar escapes in the future?" asked one member in 1923, to which the minister of the interior replied, "Yes."[92] However, despite the immigration branch's continual protestations about security breaches and the urgent need for renovations and repairs, Public Works moved glacially to make any changes. Correspondence could go on for months just to get extra bars or better locks installed. But even these alterations had limited effect, because government architects were unaccustomed to designing carceral spaces. Escapes were difficult to prevent, since government officials were unable to perceive space the same way as desperate inmates. In her essay on the spatial practices of escaped slaves in the antebellum United States, Rebecca Ginsburg demonstrates that "whites often failed to recognize the components of enslaved workers' environments." In order to navigate, hide, and eat, fleeing slaves used their knowledge and experience of a "black landscape" that was separate from, but layered with, hegemonic understandings of space.[93] Inmates of Canadian immigration architecture similarly exploited the ignorance of officials who saw the detention spaces from the opposite side of the doors — and no doubt ethnic interpreters, kitchen staff, and others helped inmates perceive an alternative geography.

While immigration officials were of course concerned about the escapes, they did not wring their hands over them. Perhaps this was because they knew of all the frauds being committed by interpreters and accomplices to aid the entry of newcomers on the west coast. Or perhaps their nonchalance was due to the fact that detainees and deportees were rarely guilty of any serious crime or wrongdoing. A similar attitude about escapes seems to have prevailed at the Montreal detention hospital, as is discussed in the following section.

Ultimately, when we add up the cost of these substantial west-coast structures, their monumental size and style, and their prominent locations on the waterfronts of Victoria and Vancouver, and then compare these observations to their lack of effectiveness in barring – or even briefly detaining – undesirable immigrants, the buildings appear to be symbolic gestures as much as functional institutions. McKeown concludes that, in settler societies, immigration "procedure was a physical and symbolic orchestration of social relationships that situated the participants in relation to each other" according to perceived racial hierarchies. Thus, Canadian legislation controlling the influx of Chinese, Japanese, South Asians, Jews, and others, was represented architecturally by the towering brick walls and barred windows of Victoria and Vancouver detention facilities, which formed ramparts on the western edge of British North America. These walls symbolized segregation on a transoceanic scale.[94]

MONTREAL: DETENTION AND DEPORTATION HEADQUARTERS

The immigration branch did not perceive the necessity of any infrastructure in Montreal for two decades after the closing of the Tanneries building in the late 1880s (see Figure 3.2). In 1893, the Dominion government had banned the landing of steerage passengers in Montreal; these migrants all debarked in Quebec City and for the most part passed through Montreal on the train, perhaps with a brief stop at one of the stations, en route to the Prairie west. To serve those newcomers with local destinations in the Montreal region, the immigration branch seems to have rented some rooms and an office in the years around the turn of the century.[95] As in other cities on both coasts, the situation changed with the inauguration of medical inspection. By the end of 1903, the branch

recognized the need for an immigration doctor in Montreal, largely to monitor the influx of unskilled labourers from across the southern border. For example, rail connections to Montreal from Boston and Portland, Maine, allowed Italians and other suspect Europeans to bypass the Canadian inspection process in place along the St Lawrence River. Some five thousand of these arrivals were inspected by the newly appointed doctor in the first half of 1904. "There were quite a few cases which could have been detained," he explained, "but having no proper place to keep them they were allowed to go on." A further source of anxiety for immigration officials at this time were "persons other than the crew" travelling aboard cargo freighters; because these vessels did not carry listed steerage passengers, they were not required to report at the pier building in Quebec City. During the navigation season of 1903, over eight hundred of these "stowaways" were counted and examined for quarantinable diseases at Grosse-Île, but then they managed to avoid medical and civil inspection when debarking from the freighters in the port of Montreal.[96] A physical presence at the city was necessary to effect proper examinations and detentions for these migrant flows.

As a result of these issues, the immigration branch in 1905 rented an old mansion close to the train stations that could be carved up into offices, wards, and examination and isolation rooms (Figure 5.27). However, with the landlord annually raising the rent, and the Dominion government on the hook for endless repairs and upgrades, the decrepit structure proved a constant headache. By 1910, the floorboards and stair treads were worn through, and the mansion was "very much overrun by rats, which cause the inmates a good deal of alarm," especially a female deportee who found one in her bed. Meanwhile, the doctor there was begging for the installation of electric light in the women's quarters, because of the danger of gas

5.27 Montreal immigrant detention hospital in a rented former mansion, seen in 1910 hung with drapery to commemorate the recent death of King Edward VII.

escaping from leaky old pipes and fixtures. He also worried that "insane" detainees could tamper with the gas. The toilets were in rough shape too; as the doctor declaimed, with so many inmates the facility "cannot do without some modern conveniences." Many immigrants, he added, were sleeping on "the soft side of a plank" due to overcrowding. Finally, it was exceedingly easy to escape from the old house and grounds; he noted the need for a few "strands of barb wire" on top of the fence "in order to lessen the possibility," but it was impossible to overcome the deficiencies of the premises as a carceral space.[97]

A new building had been discussed by officials starting in 1907, when Bryce decried the mixing in Montreal of sick and transient immigrants with criminal or disillusioned deports. About the same time, a newspaper story drew attention to the lack of a Montreal immigration hall in which new arrivals could be properly supervised. A CPR official was quoted at length, listing age-old concerns about the welfare of ignorant immigrants "who wander about the streets" while awaiting their train connections: "Of course, they are free agents. We have no right to detain them. It is such people who fall a prey to the sharks of all kinds who haunt this neighbourhood. The brass watch fakir, the eating houses which charge four prices, the fraudulent employment agencies, and, lastly, the dens in which people are fleeced of their money – all these snares might be avoided if the Federal Government would provide a place in the neighbourhood."[98] As usual, it took more than half a dozen years before the immigration branch managed to provide a proper facility in which to examine, treat, host, and hold for deportation the growing number of immigrants passing through Montreal in both directions. During the decade between the beginning of medical inspection in Montreal and the construction of a new immigrant detention hospital in that city, the building type had evolved to incorporate somewhat different functions in comparison to those at Halifax and Savard Park. The Montreal facility was more akin to the Victoria and Vancouver buildings, mixing immigrant accommodations with hospital functions and long-term detention of deportees.

In particular, the deportation of undesirables became an increasingly important function of the immigration branch with the new Acts of 1906 and 1910, which extended the temporal definition of "newcomer" for two, and then three, years following the date of arrival. In effect, immigrants could be rejected many months after debarking at the port, if they were found to be in contravention of any medical, social, or economic restrictions of the Acts. For example, they were at risk of deportation if they became ill or unemployed and sought out charitable support. Social-welfare institutions, especially those run by municipalities and provinces, had a duty according to the Acts to report these indigents to the immigration authorities. In her admirable book on the subject, Roberts observes that the Dominion "government did not automatically ship out people who had fallen upon hard times. Immigration buildings were sometimes used to shelter immigrants who were temporarily penniless, and Immigration agents tried to help them." We saw evidence of these practices in previous chapters. Nevertheless, Roberts indicates that after 1906 the immigration branch actively began to "seek prospective deports instead

of waiting to have problem immigrants brought to its attention."[99] Thus, the frequency of deportations grew rapidly during the first three decades of the century, and, as we will see, an architecture of deportation grew in parallel with these numbers.

The Montreal office became the headquarters of the repatriation process, because the city was Canada's most important rail hub, and most transatlantic steamers also originated there. As the number of deports rose during the economic recession of 1908–09, the transportation companies that were legally responsible to deliver them back to their places of origin began to demand solid evidence of an immigrant's unemployability, debilitation, or other unsuitability to Canadian residency. Especially during the subsequent decade, "the head office in Ottawa devoted a good deal of attention to instructing the local officers in how to build a tight case for each deportation, a case that could stand up to challenges from the courts, from the transportation companies, from foreign governments, and from interest groups."[100] This all meant more civil servants collecting more information – and documenting it in paperwork stored in the file rooms of major immigration buildings in Vancouver, Winnipeg, and Montreal.

During the investigation of their cases, potential deports were incarcerated in these same buildings. In 1907, not long after the opening of the main immigration hall in Winnipeg (No. 1), new padded cells were installed in the basement to hold deportees before they were sent on to Montreal. The cells were seen by the branch as so vital to its operations that it demanded they be preserved when the post office took over portions of the building during the First World War. The latter department wanted the entirety of the basement and ground floors for its operations; the immigration branch countered with a vertical split of the space, with it keeping the cells and offices in the western half of the structure. The chief superintendent of the Post Office Department wrote a furious letter to his superior, ridiculing the plan proposed by the deputy minister of immigration,

> towards whom I entertain the greatest possible personal respect, but he seriously advances as a reason why this should be done the fact that there are a couple of padded cells in the basement for insane immigrants. It may be, however, that he does not want to give up the luxurious offices on other floors in the west half of the building … it is a puerile argument to advance against the larger proposition of handling the thousands of tons of mail matter that pass through the CPR station at Winnipeg.[101]

This civil servant pointed to the slackening of immigration during the war years as justification for the post office taking over any floor space in the building not already occupied by military barracks. But the postal officials did not understand that deportation proceedings – if not actual repatriations – would continue throughout these years, even if immigrant arrivals had ceased. In the end, the immigration branch was able to protect their cells and their magnificent offices with the high ceilings; the post office received use of only the baggage room and the mezzanine floor above it. Branch officials were prescient: after the General Strike of 1919, three of the "Winnipeg Five" would be held for deportation in the basement cells at the immigration hall.[102]

From Winnipeg, western-Canadian deportees were forwarded to Montreal, where they would join others from Ontario and the eastern provinces to await available ships and trains to Europe and the United States. Sometimes those rounded up for deportation proceedings managed to prove their continued worth to the country and were allowed to return to their Canadian homes. Public-health-policy researcher Fiona Alice Miller found that less than 20 per cent of those investigated by authorities around the time of the 1910 Immigration Act were ever deported. Her analysis of the case files for several dozen Ontario detainees indicates that some avoided deportation, even after they had been removed to the Montreal detention facility to await transportation. For example, in 1913, a Scottish immigrant identified for deportation at the Toronto Hospital for the Insane, once transferred to the Dominion government facility in Montreal, "seems to have impressed the medical staff with his sanity and this prompted a re-investigation of his case." He was allowed to stay in the country.[103]

The new detention building in Montreal, therefore, manifested the systematization of Dominion government deportation policies and practices that was under way in the years leading up to its construction. The immigration branch was up front about this purpose of the building. As in Vancouver, a prominent local firm, Ross & Macdonald, was commissioned in mid-1912 to design and oversee the project. In this firm's discussion of the structure with City permit officials, it became necessary to clarify the exact building typology. The provincial building code required expensive modern mechanical ventilation in hospitals, the architects explained, but it was their understanding that the new Dominion government facility was "not a hospital in the ordinary sense, although it is called a hospital on the drawings." The Ottawa superintendent immediately wrote back to confirm that the project "can in no sense be considered as an hospital," and is rather to be used as an "immigration office" and "for the temporary detention of persons about to be deported." Several years earlier, in fact, when medical inspection proper had been moved to the border stations south of Montreal, it had already been argued that the rented mansion should be recognized "as a detention house pure and simple."[104] Ross & Macdonald proceeded to produce construction drawings without the extra ventilation requirements for hospitals.

However, other stakeholders envisioned the building differently, and managed to get their desires acknowledged in the design. First and foremost, there was the immigration doctor still stationed in Montreal. To him, the facility remained a place to treat sick immigrants, that is, a hospital. As Roberts explains, and as we have seen before, the Montreal doctor's professional practices and priorities were in constant conflict with those of the local immigration agent and the Ottawa bureaucrats, and he "could never quite understand that his patients – deports for the most part – were not entitled to the same level of care" as those detained in the immigration hospitals elsewhere in Canada.[105] Nonetheless, in spite of the building-permit process, the Montreal facility would contain examining rooms, wards, and other hospital functions.

Meanwhile, during the design-and-construction period, a powerful local member of parliament and his philanthropist backers lobbied the branch to include in the project some temporary accommodations for newcomers in transit, especially women and children, along the lines of a Prairie immigration hall. Although the Ottawa superintendent assured him that this sort of accommodation was entirely unnecessary in Montreal, the member won out. When the building was half-complete, the decision was made to add two extra storeys for use as a hostel, with family bedrooms, dormitories for foreign and "English speaking male immigrants," a kitchen, and dining room.[106] In a way, the move was opposite to the one made in Quebec City, where the extra storey was added to the pier building for the purposes of detention, rather than accommodation.

This MP was so pleased with the new institution that he arranged for the immigration branch to host a "housewarming" celebration, an open house with the minister of the interior speaking to a crowd of local stakeholders, including immigration chaplains and female immigrant-reception workers, transportation-company representatives, public-health professionals, police and jailers, judges, newspaper editors, and the consuls from several European nations that sent Canada a lot of immigrants. For this event in April 1914, the Ottawa superintendent commanded the Montreal agent to ensure that all the staff "shall present a good appearance and be in uniform wherever one is worn." They were to be "stationed about the building so as to receive and show the guests some attention." In contrast, he did not think it would "be advisable to have our new building filled with inmates such as deports at the time of the opening."[107] They could be moved over from the old mansion afterwards. Philanthropists could inspect government workers in clean uniforms standing on gleaming maple and terrazzo floors – and be assured of not seeing any depraved or destitute deportees.

Ultimately, the architectural result in Montreal was a hybrid program. The building was a narrow structure with entrances off the street to the general offices, and off one long side to the detention, hospital, and accommodation spaces; a short corridor connected the two entrances. Reading the original plan from street front to back, the ground-floor (Figure 5.28) included the agent's corner office, a large reception and clerks' room, and an office for the Controller of Chinese Immigration. (Chinese often attempted to enter or exit Canada in the east, to avoid the established inspections and brokerage relationships in British Columbia.) Across the hall, two offices were given over to the repatriation agents who handled deportation cases. Next was the doctor's office and surgery, though the surgery was later moved up one floor to access better light. To the rear of the ground floor, and separated by the central corridor, were

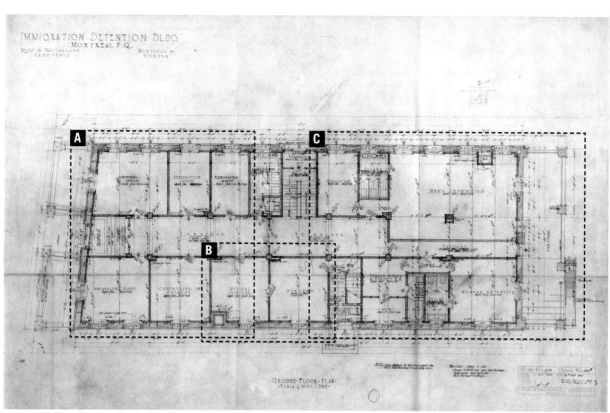

IMMIGRATION DETENTION BLDG
MONTREAL P.Q.
ROSS & MACFARLANE   MONTREAL &
ARCHITECTS   WINNIPEG

·GROUND·FLOOR·PLAN·

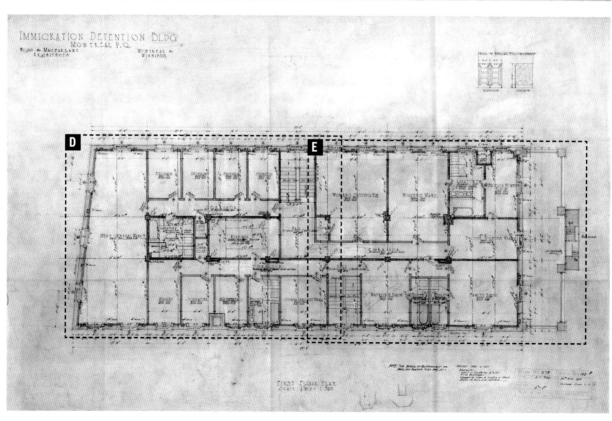

IMMIGRATION DETENTION BLDG
MONTREAL P.Q.
ROSS & MACFARLANE   MONTREAL &
ARCHITECTS   WINNIPEG

FIRST FLOOR PLAN

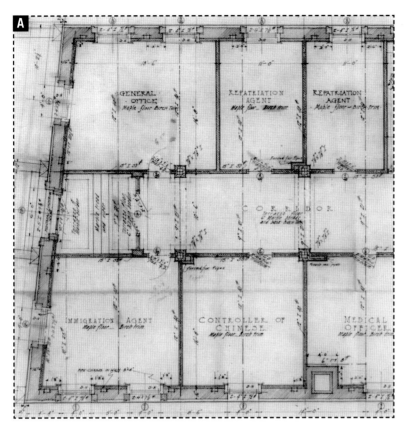

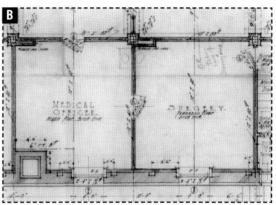

5.28 (*opposite, top, and this page*) Ground-floor plan of the immigrant detention building in Montreal, Ross & Macfarlane Architects, 1912–14.

5.29 (*opposite, bottom, and overleaf*) First-floor plan of the immigrant detention building in Montreal, Ross & MacFarlane Architects.

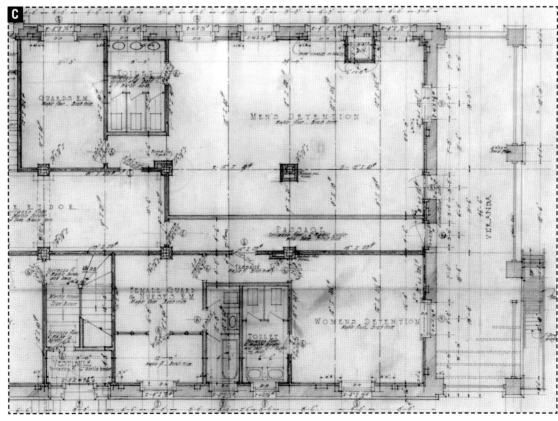

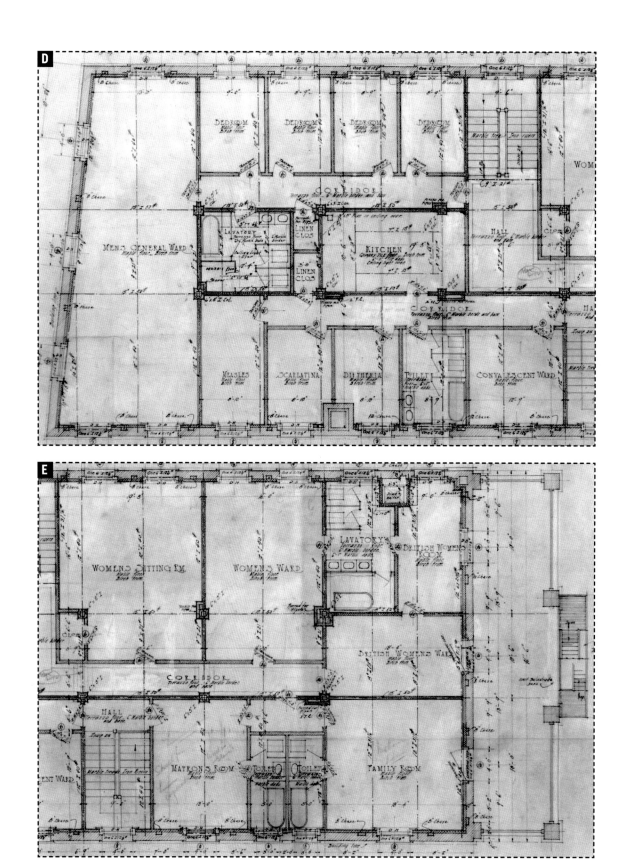

men's and women's detention rooms, each with its own dedicated guard's room (or "female guard and nurse's" room) monitoring the entrance. Both detention rooms open onto the veranda with its security screens, where inmates could take fresh air.

The next floor up was devoted on the original plans to hospital uses, including a separate kitchen, several wards, and isolation rooms for infectious diseases (Figure 5.29). The rear of the plan comprised a large suite of wards for female patients, divided between British and non-British, with access to sitting rooms and the veranda. A live-in matron's bedroom and bath was originally in this area. The segregation of different classes of inmate — male and female, British and foreign, infectious or not, deports and mere detainees — made for a carefully delineated organization of rooms on the first two floors — so much so that

it may have hampered the efficiency of the staff. Everything in the building was walls and doors, with each section of the redundant and dog-legged corridors cut off from other parts of the building.

Land was not purchased until after the original design of the building was complete. Because the new site featured a neighbouring building that was built to the property line, there was only a small gap allowed between structures. The proximity of the neighbouring carriage works necessitated the elimination of a separate entrance and second staircase that would have served the hospital and dormitories separately from the spaces for deportees. Thus, deportees would often mix with

5.30 (*below and overleaf*) Basement plan of the immigrant detention building in Montreal, Ross & MacFarlane Architects, 1912–14.

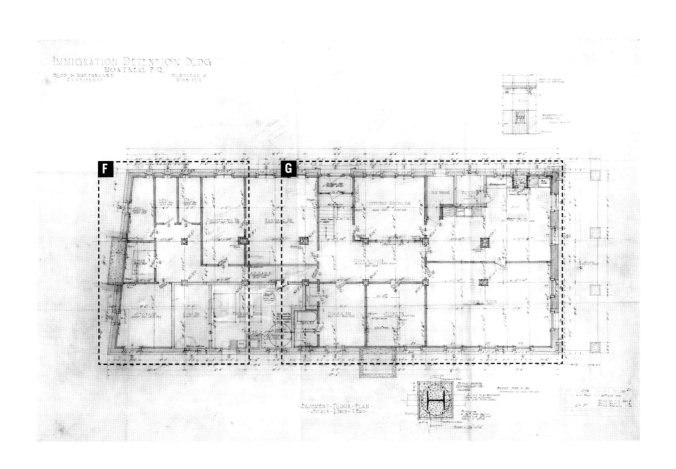

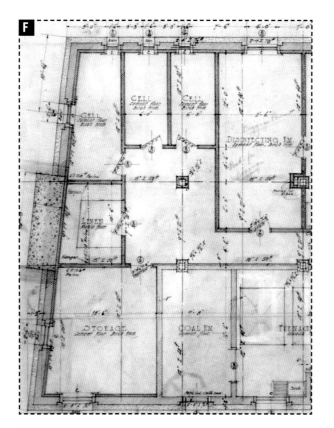

patients, and all shared the main staircase with newcomers seeking free accommodation. Because of the neighbouring structure, the rooms on that side of the building were always dark; local officials repeatedly requested that Public Works paint the neighbouring brick wall bright white, to reflect light into the immigration offices, wards, and dormitories. This does not seem to have occurred. Meanwhile, the omission of frosted glass on that elevation allowed workers in the adjacent factory to peer directly through the windows into the toilet and bath rooms of the women's wards and detention area.[108] Ultimately, the slender gap between buildings also allowed for furtive escapes out the windows on this side of the edifice.

In the basement of the building, support spaces included mechanical, coal, and storage rooms, a large baggage room, laundry and disinfecting chamber, a commercial kitchen, two dining rooms

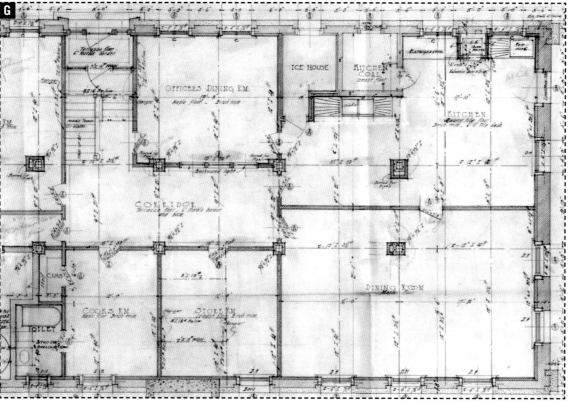

(one for staff), and a small apartment for the cook (Figure 5.30). At one end of the basement, secluded around the corner of an L-shaped corridor, down past the furnace room, were three cells for criminal or insane detainees. Visible on the plan and elevation, the cells had narrow, barred windows. The radiators were recessed in the walls and protected by wire screens. Close to the completion of the building, one of the cells was padded to prevent self-harm during detentions. The architects

of this building were a little more clever than those of the Vancouver detention facility: drawings specify "all cell doors hung on corridor side" so that the hinge pins were not accessible to inmates (Figure 5.31).

The Montreal detention building was originally planned as a two-storey structure, with large skylights illuminating the second-storey hospital spaces. A third and fourth floor were added to serve as accommodation for immigrants

5.31 Details for the cells in the basement of the immigrant detention building in Montreal, showing padding and security screening of windows, doors, and other elements.

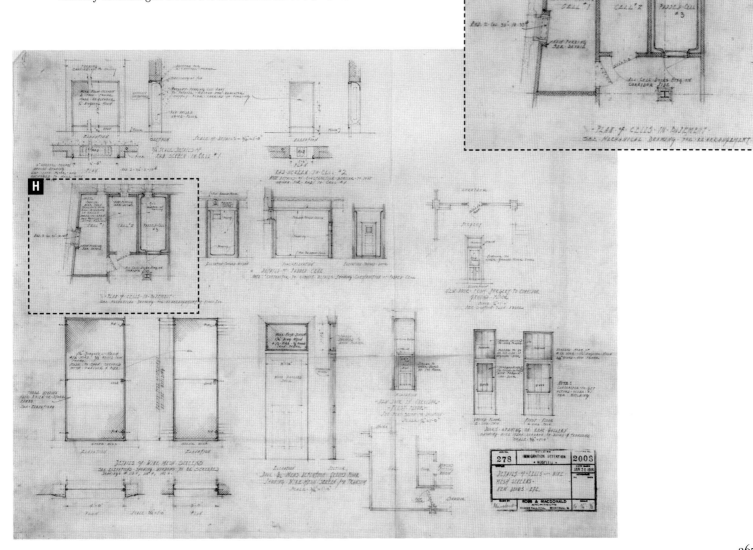

in transit, and these were laid out similarly to a Prairie immigration hall, albeit a rather large one (Figure 5.32). Thirty-eight bedrooms on the two floors wrapped around two light courts, making continuous figure-eight corridors, meeting at the stair hall. A dining room and immigrants' kitchen/serving room on the third floor also had access to the veranda, which did not have security screens on this level. All this would change. Within a few months of the building's opening, only twenty new arrivals had made use of the free accommodations, and these rooms began to be annexed for carceral functions as the number of inmates continuously grew. The third-floor veranda would soon receive its iron grillwork to allow an exercise space for

detainees. Later, in 1927, the area of free accommodations shrank again when the men's detention dormitory was relocated to front rooms of the top floor; the immigration branch hoped it would be harder to escape from that height.

Once the upper-floor bedrooms began to be converted for detention purposes, food was delivered from the basement kitchen to the serving room by a dumbwaiter presciently provided in the original design. Immigrants in transit were expected to provision and cook for themselves, but detainees could not be trusted with knives and fire. Therefore, the immigration branch fed them — at great expense. Statistics recording meals provided to deportees at the Winnipeg immigration hall were published in the *Sessional Papers* for a few years in the 1920s; with a few hundred persons detained for two to three weeks each in Winnipeg, the number of meals quickly reached the tens of thousands per year.[109] The numbers of detainees

5.32 (*below and opposite*) Top-floor plan of the immigrant detention building in Montreal, showing the layout for temporary accommodations of non-detained immigrants passing through or looking for work in Montreal.

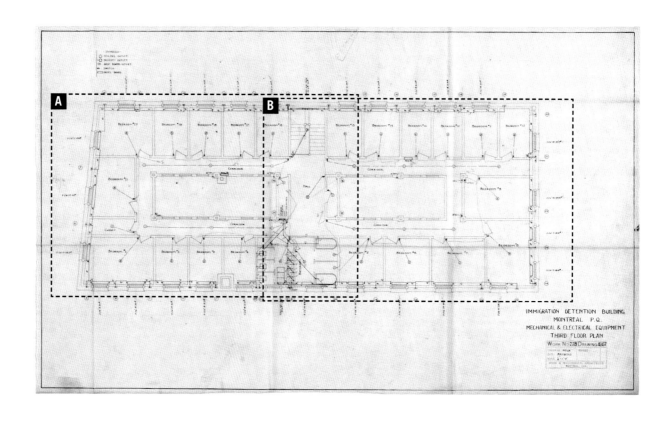

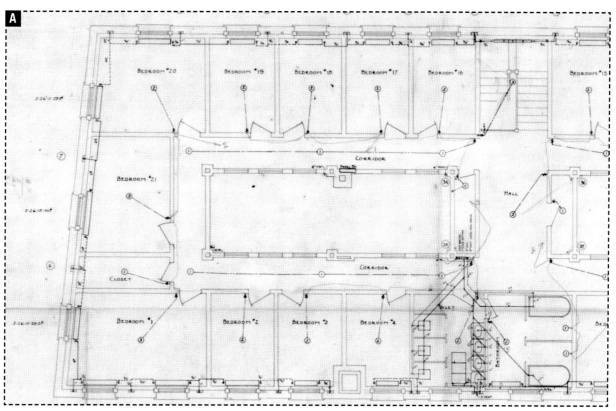

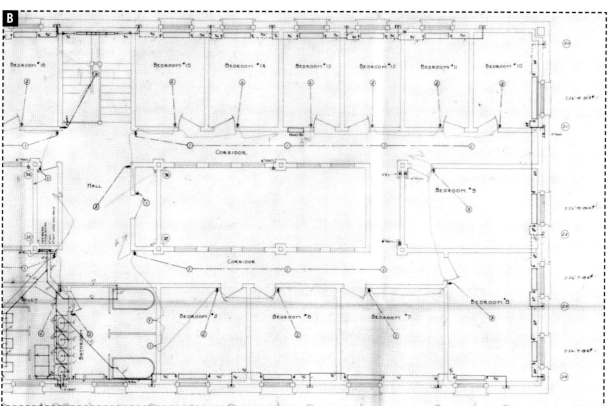

fed would have been much higher in Montreal, where the live-in cook worked full-time.

By the mid-1920s, the Montreal building had the reputation of being for detention only, though the immigration branch regularly reassured clergy, social workers, and transportation companies that shelter for newcomers remained available there. Confusion arose because the CPR also offered overnight accommodations in adjacent Windsor Station for colonist-class travellers awaiting connections. That company also maintained a large dormitory for Chinese labourers travelling in bond.[110]

Meanwhile, throughout its life the Montreal building continued to be used mainly as a detention facility, and its condition continued to deteriorate due to lack of maintenance. As Roberts explains, for immigration-branch officials in Ottawa, "a penny spent on a deport was a penny wasted." It was one thing to cure desirable immigrants arriving at the ports of Quebec City or Halifax; it was quite another to provide medical or merely humane care for undesirables on their way out of the country. Almost from the start, the plumbing was deficient: toilets backed up, or were plugged by wrathful detainees; pipes leaked regularly, damaging floors and ceilings. Broken windows and other small repairs took months to accomplish. In the wards and surgery, Public Works refused to pay for cleaning and disinfection on par with how a hospital would be maintained. During the First World War, most of the building was turned over for the internment of enemy aliens and prisoners of war en route to camps. This use came with attendant wear and tear, plus security modifications, including the removal of the doors from toilet stalls. The Internment Operations Branch did not bother to come around and have the rooms fixed up until two years after the end of hostilities. By the mid-1920s, indeed, continual repairs were required, and the building was "dirty and dilapidated" and "a dismal place to

work" according to Roberts.[111] Not so long after the ribbon-cutting event, the facility had become a great disappointment.

Although Roberts explores in great detail the work conditions and quarrels of staff in the Montreal detention building, immigrants did not write about their time spent there. We are forced to infer their experiences: the neglect and overcrowding of the facility; their fear, anger, or disillusionment; the heady mixture of criminals, public charges, political activists, the sick and the well. What were the experiences and emotions of a thirteen-year-old girl, travelling alone in 1919, and kept in the Montreal building until her father could be contacted in Alberta? A local volunteer lodged a formal complaint about the situation, raising the spectre of diseased, immoral, or insane women corrupting this young lady. The Montreal staff denied that she had been exposed to anything untoward, avowing that prostitutes and others with venereal diseases were kept in isolation cells. However, given the shared lavatories, corridors, stairs, and dining and recreation spaces in the institution, she must have had some surprising interactions with detainees.[112] A further sense of the immigrant experience is provided by the Montreal doctor, who wrote to Ottawa only a few months into the new building's operation, begging for improvements: "I beg to inform you that there are in our Detention Hospital this morning 49 men. Of these twelve are insane; six have tuberculosis; one has diabetes; and the rest are nearly all criminals; many of whom are dangerous characters. Many of these people have been here several weeks, and owing to the close confinement are on the border of mutiny, and I am afraid the guards may be attacked." But having made the capital investment in the new facility, the Dominion government was unsympathetic to calls for increased staff or immediate renovations. Ottawa responded by telling the doctor to mind his own business: the Montreal agent was in charge and would handle all future communications with head office. This favoured agent unapologetically referred to the detainees as "our prisoners."[113]

Once again, the "prisoners" voted with their feet, by fleeing. In fact, many more escaped in Montreal than in Victoria and Vancouver combined, probably because Montreal was their last stop prior to being sent away from their loved ones, property, or business enterprises in Canada, whereas the west-coast sites were the first stops for immigrants aspiring to enter the country. The first escape from the brand-new Montreal building occurred less than two months into its operation, when a deserting sailor jumped from an unprotected first-floor window "to the ground ten feet below." Four more deports absconded out a window one month later, despite the wire screen protecting it; the doctor pointed out that the cheap padlocks securing the screens to the building "could be pried open with a strong pencil or toothbrush handle." As usual, the Department of Public Works and the architects it hired had no real concept of, or experience with, prison design. Six months after the building opened, the Montreal doctor itemized each escape to that point: there had been ten separate incidents, with a total of twenty-two escapees, including one "insane" who had absconded four times. Seven of these had been recaptured within a few days, including the only two female fugitives.[114] Presumably the others were never found. The Montreal staff refused to take the blame, though, given the building's deficiencies as carceral space.

Escapes continued throughout the history of the building's use as an immigration station. The creativity of detainees, desperate to elude the final step of repatriation, knew no bounds. One fled through the coal chute, and another through the unprotected window in the basement laundry; a criminal being deported due to a manslaughter conviction slipped into the medical isolation wards and went out the lavatory window. Four climbed out over the top of the wire screens on the verandas before these were finally replaced with more prison-like iron bars early in 1918. The same renovation saw the windows of all detention rooms covered with iron bars let into the brickwork. This still did not solve the problem of breakouts. Within days of their installation, some of the new window bars were "cut from the outside" by the "accomplices" of a detained "pimp … suspected of being a white slaver." This operation took place in the gap between the immigration building and the carriage works, a "passageway which is narrow and dark and which is now used by undesirables for various purposes." For years, requests to wall off this alley fell on deaf ears (Figure 5.33).[115]

Escapes could take on a certain romantic flair. One British man experienced a picaresque journey that culminated in his surprising 1928 escape from the Montreal detention building. Deported by US authorities from Portland, Oregon, he was placed on a German steamship, which proceeded down the west coast and eventually up the east coast, with a scheduled stop in Saint John prior to crossing the Atlantic. In a Saint John hospital, he underwent emergency surgery for appendicitis, his ship departing in the meantime. It being mid-summer, there were few transatlantic passenger vessels going via Saint John. After a brief recovery in the immigration building there, he was transferred to the Montreal facility, where, as a deport, he could receive post-operative care. When he arrived, "he could hardly walk and was still all bandaged up," so he was lodged in the ward next to the doctor's examining room. But less than two days later, according to the Montreal agent, "it was discovered that this man had succeeded in getting through the transom into the corridor, and again through the transom into the medical office, where he succeeded in making his escape through the window by using a sheet tied to the radiator and letting himself down to the ground." Before absconding, the man took the time to write a courteous note to the Montreal staff, which he left on his bedside home to my folks who are aged and dependent on me." Unlike many escapees who wanted to remain in North America, this gentleman snuck out of the building in order to effect more efficiently his own deportation. And, he noted, he was "saving the Government expense" in doing so.[116]

Another tale gleaned from government correspondence is that of a French immigrant who fled for the love of a woman in 1931. Along with a detained German denied entry at the US border, the agent reported, "the two men have escaped by sawing two iron bars in a window in one of the rooms connected with the Men's Dormitory on the fourth floor, and by using about twelve blankets tied together to form a rope … sliding down to the alley" by the carriage works. The Frenchman left not one, but two, notes: one to staff and one to his lover, both written in his native language. "Gentlemen," he addressed the guards and agent, "If I have left this place, it is your fault – for keeping me in jail when … I have done nothing wrong in Canada." His simple goal had been "to start a new life" after three years in the French army, because in Montreal there was a "woman whom I love." In case the escape went awry, he wrote: "Dear Maggie – If I die it will be for you … Adieu." The response of the authorities was to try and use the name of his *amour* to track him down, "but inquiries made at the address of this woman show that she also has disappeared." Hopefully, the two lovers lived happily ever after. During the inquiry about this escape, it came to light that one of the night guards was in the habit of slipping out to the corner tavern to take a beer while on shift. He claimed that "beer does not affect him," and besides, no one had ever given him specific instructions *not* to imbibe on duty.[117] These rather intimate narratives of escaping detainees remind us that a range of real emotions motivated the spatial practices of immigrants. Their ingenuity in discovering routes and egress through immigration architecture was the physical manifestation of an ongoing negotiation

5.33 A view of the narrow gap between the Montreal immigrant detention building and the carriage works on the left. Part of the enclosed veranda is visible in the right foreground.

table: "I hope you will pardon me for taking leave from here, but … I can't stand being locked up, and no idea when I'm to be sent home. Well I know I can get a ship either here or Quebec, for I'm well acquainted with the shipping game … I want to get among the intents of government officials, the design decisions of architects, the actions of civil servants, the negligence of hapless guards, and the needs and desires of the immigrants themselves.

The bars on the windows and the verandas were sawn through on a regular basis for more than a decade, by which time the local agent was complaining of the "soft iron" they were made from. Ironically, though, it was not the litany of escapes that finally prompted a retrofit. The bars were spaced widely, and with several sawn through and missing as well, there was too much visibility into the verandas and detention rooms from adjacent buildings and from the residential district to the south of the site. The agent noted in 1928 that "the detained men are very often of very bad character and are annoying neighbours around the yard through indecent exposure." More robust steel screens (Figure 5.34) were finally added to the verandas at this time; in essence, they were privacy screens that still allowed fresh air and light to the

5.34 Barred verandas on the rear elevation of the Montreal immigrant detention building.

detainees. This had not been the first instance of neighbours complaining about the comportment of detainees. In 1920, the manager of the Canadian General Electric factory next door to the east had raised the issue of his female clerks being "openly affronted by some of these degenerates" from the windows of the first-floor detention quarters. In addition, he wrote, "I have personally observed from my own private office" that the yard around the immigration building was used frequently by accomplices to pass up various articles to the inmates. The solution arrived at by local officials was to paint out the panes of glass and to limit how far the double-hung windows could slide up and down.[118]

These various small fixes were constants in the life of the building. As well, functions were shuffled numerous times among the different floors to respond to increased detentions or decreased medical cases. The travelling inspector concluded a long report on the structure in 1931, as Depression-era deportations skyrocketed: "During the past few years a large amount of money has been expended and still the building is unsatisfactory for the purposes for which it is utilized." The division commissioner concurred, providing a historical contrast with the hybrid program of offices, hospital, "housing accommodation," and "temporary detention of a comparatively small number of deports" that was devised by the immigration branch and its architects at the time of construction. "Today the building is used … almost wholly as a detention and clearing house for deports of all classes and conditions, deports being collected practically all over Canada." Both men recommended a new building to replace the dated and ramshackle institution. They were overruled. The Ottawa commissioner argued that the "serious overcrowding and poor service" at Montreal "can only be considered a passing phase of our work." On this letter he later appended a handwritten

note: "Minister not prepared to consider new building at present time."[119] And that was that.

These concerns regarding functionality and congestion at the Montreal building were crystallized by the deportation boom of the early 1930s. All levels of government in Canada tried to solve the problems of the Depression by "shovelling out" the unemployed, the institutionalized, and the politically radical. Among the many tarred with these brushes were recent, or not so recent, immigrant arrivals that the Dominion government wanted to deport. An application for welfare relief in Calgary or hospitalization in Edmonton, or the act of publishing a socialist newspaper in Winnipeg, could see you incarcerated in Montreal, awaiting a transatlantic steamship.[120] In effecting deportations, the immigration branch even seems to have used its network of buildings in a kind of cat-and-mouse game with labour organizations, lawyers, family members, and others attempting to intervene in and prevent a suspect's embarkation. In one notorious case, the Canadian Labour Defense League (CLDL) was told a deportee was being sent to the Montreal immigrant detention building, and then it was told the Saint John pier building. The deportee went to neither facility, being secreted to Halifax, where he stayed in the Pier 21 detention rooms before being shipped out to Europe. The CLDL was unable to locate him in time to launch an appeal.[121]

In the midst of this deportation boom, the condition of government detention facilities – and especially Montreal's – were protested strenuously. A 1932 exposé in the Toronto *Star* described the situation in Montreal: "a dozen families were forced to occupy one large room. There were, beyond some milk bottles, no accommodations in the room. A sheet was erected as a screen, and one end set apart for the men. The beds provided for them, they said, were full of vermin."[122] Internally, immigration officials readily admitted the truth of all the complaints, while emphasizing that "every possible effort is made by the Montreal staff to keep the building clear of vermin" and to segregate the different classes and genders of deportees to ensure that "the mothers and daughters are amply protected." But Ottawa did nothing to provide more-salubrious spaces. The principle had been established in 1931, when the decision was made to continue using the existing building. Wrote the commissioner: "With existing conditions, we shall unquestionably have some complaints from deports, but I believe we can better face this than justify heavy capital expenditure."[123] By this time, we had come a long way from when Dominion government officials feared complaints about reception architecture that immigrants might send home in letters to family and friends, and constructed pier buildings and Prairie immigration halls to circumvent those ill-feelings.

One of those reception buildings had been Pier 21 in Halifax, which now in the 1930s became a holding centre for political and economic deportees awaiting transportation. There the journalist from the Toronto *Star* witnessed twenty-two deportees as they "plodded up the gangplank" of the ship taking them away: "They looked a harmless lot, scarcely meriting the strenuous guard placed over them. As far as could be ascertained, few had criminal records, but … strict censorship had been established over all news of deportees sailing from Halifax … [and] none of them will have an opportunity of telling their story to the outside world." Indeed, no memoirs or oral histories have come down to us from these deportees.

During the Depression, though, sympathetic writers tried to give them a voice and a face, even when they were locked in the "immigration sheds," a term that now came to stand in for arbitrary power. Most notoriously, Pier 21 received national attention in 1932 during the detainment there of the "Halifax 10" – men accused of communism and sedition. The ten were immigrants to Canada, though some had been in the country for twenty years at that point. They had been arrested in May Day raids across western Canada, "seized, kidnapped, spirited away" by night from their homes and communities. These detainees were sent directly to Halifax, to separate them from their local support networks in the west while an immigration-branch board of inquiry determined their deportation cases. The "Halifax 10," like others during the 1930s, were deported for reasons of politics or indigence, sometimes to horrible fates in fascist countries. One of the "10" managed to have a narrative of "his own experience" smuggled out to friends in the CLDL, which published it in multiple venues. Arrested with another man in Sudbury, they were "whisked out of the city … [to] a deserted station," where they were entrained for Montreal in the middle of the night. There, "a few hours were spent in cells, and then to Halifax" and Pier 21. He continues: "Escorted through a maze of corridors, we finally land in the steel-and-concrete detention quarters where we find some of the victims of the Immigration Act, others having yet to come. A guard is always maintained in addition to securely-locked, strong-doors and barred windows." Having learned from the deficiencies of its facility in Montreal, the immigration branch seems to have ensured its detention rooms in Pier 21 were better made.

Photographs of the ten men, "taken under greatest difficulties," and published at the time by *Labor Defender*, lend an eerie aspect to the space (Figure 5.35). The bars on the windows cast shadows across the faces of the men, who seem to be posing in the lavatory of the upper-floor detention area, while the furtive photographer somehow clung to the outside of the structure. A single photo, likely taken by an inmate with a camera passed through the bars, is perhaps the only surviving image of a Dominion government

HOW THEY TREAT DEPORTEES

IVAR JOHNSON: Deported from Vancouver to Sweden because of his working class activity.

Deported!

Deported for activities in the class struggle, Ivar Johnson was visited by the sheriff two days after arrival home. This servant of the master class insisted that Johnson should pay his fare and his keep in Gothenburg, Sweden.

This comrade did not ask for deportation, was not on relief, but was active in the picket lines, in the unemployed demonstrations and selling revolutionary papers on the streets in Vancouver and, as be stated to the immigration authorities when called up for interview, "I never missed a demonstration yet."

We here reproduce his letter:

His Letter:

"I am home and have been here two weeks. The trip as far as to Winnipeg was decent enough, but from there I had different treatment. We did not get anything but beans and fish to eat, and it was rotten. We then decided to go on hunger strike, and did so, and then we got better grub.

"They gave us ham and eggs and fruit and cheese. They kept us in Montreal for two days. Here it was very poor food, and we had to stay in a lousy place. On the train from Montreal we were packed like herrings and they put handcuffs on me and a Finnish worker until we came to Halifax. I said, "Hello," to Zurcher and Kist but did not get an opportunity to speak to them.

"The trip on the sea was tolerable. We were twenty-two deportees and fourteen were beating their way and a few worked their way. In Gothenburg we were kept for two days until I was sent home. Two days after my arrival home the Sheriff came and wanted to collect fare from Vancouver and home and also for those two days in Gothenburg.

"There is no possibilities of getting a job here, for all the work I have seen here is relief work on the most miserable conditions.

"I wish you would send me some papers from Canada. I'll send you some from here. Greetings to all the Comrades.

"Ivar Johnson."

AMNESTY FOR THE 10 HALIFAX PRISONERS!

M. Parker, A. Vaara, J. Stahlberg, S. Worozbet, J. Farkas, D. Holmes, C. Cessinger, J. Sembay, H. Kist and F. Zurcher have now been locked up in the immigration sheds at Halifax for over six months.

Their case is now before the Supreme Court of Canada.

Again we warn the Canadian workers that only mass pressure can free our Halifax comrades and put a stop to deportations.

Demand amnesty for the Halifax prisoners!

DEAD!

As we go to press, Urho Jaaska, unemployed worker of Port Arthur, is dead. A mass funeral has just drawn to a close. Reports from Port Arthur state that he was viciously beaten by police at the unemployed demonstration of October 18, and that he died as a result of his wounds.

Mass protests are being directed to the Port Arthur city council, to Premier Henry and to Minister of Justice Guthrie.

DONATIONS

B.C. District of the C.L.D.L. has sent in the following sums as donations for the Defender during the last two months. We urge other districts to take note;

Vancouver	$4.85
Port Haney	10.00
Prince Rupert	5.00
Savona	5.00
Vancouver	1.00
N. Westminster,	1.00
Prince George	2.00
Vancouver	2.00
Vancouver	2.00
Prince George	1.00
Vancouver	2.17
Vancouver	3.25

HALIFAX: These pictures, taken under greatest difficulties, show the Halifax Immigration Detention Sheds, where M. Parker, A. Vaara, J. Stahlberg, S. Worozbet, J. Farkas, D. Holmes, C. Cessinger, J. Sembay, H. Kist and F. urcher have been locked up for over six months. In the photos can be discerned some of these comrades.

immigration-branch detention room in this era.[124] It appears little different from any dormitory, with iron bedsteads, and a bench and table around which the men are gathered – except that the backlighting and unstudied postures of the subjects suggest a hasty and surreptitious composition.

Other than the locked doors, the primary difference between a dormitory and a detention space was the direction of travel. The contrasting nature of arrival and departure were captured in an editorial cartoon included in a CLDL broadside. The top panel depicts three upright men, carrying hand luggage and smoking their pipes, confidently descending the gangplank of a CPR steamship; below, the same men, now slumped, with their hands in the pockets of patched trousers, shuffle back up the gangplank on their "way out" of Canada. The captions of the two images juxtapose the "Land of Opportunity" with the "Land of Deportunity."[125]

CONCLUSIONS

As the population of Canada increasingly globalized around the turn of the twentieth century, it seemed desirable to somehow inspect and sort new arrivals at the border. Pier buildings were renovated and newly constructed on both coasts to effect these examinations. Hospitals were erected, for treating those who were ill but still admissible; rejects were also detained in these same institutions. But border inspection had its limitations. Immigration-branch officials recognized that some "undesirables" would get through, only to be identified as such after being in the country for some years. An increasing number of detentions and deportations during the first four decades of the century resulted in the need for infrastructure to serve this purpose. Partly, this need was satis-

fied within existing reception buildings. But a special architecture of immigrant detention was also developed, often co-located in facilities that incorporated bureaucratic offices and file storage, medical wards, and non-carceral dormitories.

The mix of government offices with immigrant accommodations in the same structure may seem odd, and certainly produced some uncomfortable interactions. However, this mixing participated in a long tradition dating back to the quarantine stations and pier buildings of the nineteenth century. In that earlier era, though, the detention of immigrants on both coasts was largely limited to quarantine events, and it was understood that these were temporary delays on a linear journey to land or employment in Canada. With the ascendance of inspection and deportation, the experiences of some immigrants were characterized by return journeys, after varied lengths of sojourn. For others, such as Asian immigrants, or those rounded up for investigation, detention could be a more-or-less long-term deviation from their life paths. For those released – and perhaps also for those who escaped – their detention was less a punishment than a disciplining. As Fiona Alice Miller argues, deportation "was a system of moral regulation," which helped produce citizens by its demonstration of what could happen to those who deviated from the norms of Canadian society.[126] During this disciplinary experience, they were forced to prove their identities, their health, and their worth to the country.

Historian Donald Avery contends that, by 1920, the immigration branch "had now evolved from a recruitment agency to a security service."[127] Its architecture followed suit, even if, as we have seen in this chapter, it was not always that secure, and not everyone in the branch was comfortable with the changes. On the one hand, recurring escapes made officials worry that the locks on the doors were merely "a show of security" – even when they were installed by the same contractor that had built

5.35 (opposite) Smuggled photographs of the "Halifax 10" taken while they were detained in Pier 21, published in *Labor Defender*, 1932.

Montreal's Bordeaux Prison. On the other hand, immigration agents were concerned to remove the "iron bars" from the corridors and install them in more subtle locations, so that detainees would not "get the impression that they are being put in jail."[128] Regardless, the immigrants perceived the buildings in Victoria, Vancouver, and Montreal – and the hospitals in other ports – as little other than prisons. Sadly, our story of immigration architecture, which began optimistically with attempts to shelter and care for the welfare of indigent travellers, ends with stories of locked cells, barred windows, terrible living conditions, and return journeys. The Toronto *Star* journalist provides a conclusive contrast from their visit to Pier 21 in Halifax:

Strangely enough, with deportees sailing out of the country on one ship, new settlers were arriving on another … The new arrivals were given a great reception … There was hot tea and sandwiches for the mother, milk for the children.

The babies were bathed and looked after by the volunteer workers. There was a Christmas tree in the long shed for them and all the children went away laden with toys. Canada welcomed them …

And as they marched out of the shed to the waiting train which would bear them westward, the procession of twenty-two guarded deportees climbed the long ramp to the wharf and went on board … There were no gifts for these children. No cups of tea for the mothers and no extra scarves or mittens for them. They had that greeting on their arrival in Canada some years ago, and no notice was taken of their departure.

EPILOGUE

Late-nineteenth- and early-twentieth-century immigration architecture on the piers and the Prairies hosted prototypical social-welfare institutions designed and built to make Canada a more welcoming immigrant destination. Meanwhile, with quarantine and detention facilities, other building types were developed to help Canada be more discerning about the immigrants it received. As symbols of an activist government, the success of these architectural projects was partial and short-lived. Pier buildings were a fleeting, though memorable, life landmark for migrants. Prairie immigration halls, often the first public buildings in a community, were among the first to be discarded, as immigrant waves subsided and towns developed their own community and ethnic support structures. Immigrant experiences of quarantine stations and detention facilities may have been of longer duration, and more emotionally scarring, but in the view of policy-makers and civil servants these were essential landmarks establishing sovereignty over the boundaries of the polity. The present study establishes a context in which these largely forgotten Canadian government buildings, as well as the experiences and practices of migrants within them, can be taken seriously, marking significant moments in the history of the country and the world.

Canadian immigration architecture helped establish the role of the state in forming new citizens according to its imperatives: English-speaking, hardworking, healthy, and willing and able to inhabit the wide-open agricultural spaces of Canada's frontier regions. In establishing a federal presence in the lives of immigrants in transit (and sometimes after), immigration buildings often made favourable impressions on new Canadians, though they were not institutions designed to forge obedience or assimilation. At best, government officials and other interested parties, such as religious groups, could only effect an assimilation-in-passing, as immigrants paused for several hours, days, or weeks inside Dominion government facilities. This process was begun with English-language pamphlets and dictionaries, and packets of Kellogg's cereals, distributed by the nuns and other social-service workers greeting newcomers in the port buildings of Quebec City, Saint John, and Halifax. It continued through to desks at the Winnipeg immigration complex, staffed by student missionaries from J.S. Woodsworth's Methodist congregation. But it was the government itself that had the most opportunities to achieve assimilation-in-passing, as its agents and officials advised and steered immigrants at every stop across a network of immigration architecture that emanated from east-coast ports. By contrast, no such network spread out from Canada's west coast. The Asian migrants arriving there were not deemed to be immigrants or settlers, and the Dominion government had no interest in providing them with services or ensuring their allegiance to the country.

While both the intent and the success of such social and political projects were necessarily indeterminate, the immigration buildings were physical markers distributed across Canada to remind immigrants and other publics that they were in a country that esteemed certain social mores, cultural characteristics, and everyday behaviours. By the layout of space in immigration architecture, the government sent messages about its vision of Canadian society; for instance, its ambition to sort and segregate immigrants as desirable and undesirable, as British and foreign, as single men and women and families, represented the racial and domestic hierarchies thought necessary to nation-building. However, as we have seen to a great extent in the preceding chapters, contingencies on the ground meant that the labels on architectural plans were followed inconsistently in practice. The Dominion government lacked the vertical integration to monitor or control what went on in each remote immigration hall – or even at its buildings in the major cities of central Canada and the coasts. Still, as a network of buildings intended to support the social welfare of (at least some) future citizens, Canada's immigration architecture began to distinguish it as a nation, in both a competitive global market for immigrants and in the everyday life of local communities.

The chapters of the book end in the early 1930s, because the nature of immigrant reception and control changes after that period. A significant gap in both immigration and deportation marked the years of the late 1930s and the 1940s. Depression and then war reduced or eliminated the incentives and the physical possibility of migrating to or from Canada. But not all the immigration buildings sat idle in this period. The pier buildings were always useful to the government any time that large numbers of people had to be moved through the ports, and they had been mobilized for troop movements as early as the Boer War. Extant immigration buildings would be pressed into service once more during the Second World War. My own father passed through Halifax's Pier 21 in 1943

and, thankfully, on his way back from the European theatre in 1945 – not as an immigrant, but as an Air Force man.

Some of the remaining immigration buildings were of use again immediately after the war, even before organized transportation of displaced persons and others began. In 1948, over three hundred Estonian asylum seekers, who had escaped Soviet subjugation and crossed the Atlantic in a rickety ship, spent several months in Pier 21 and the immigrant detention hospital in Halifax. The mayor and other Haligonians organized Christmas parties for the Estonian children, with the ship's captain playing Santa to dole out donated gifts, candy, and fruit. As one reporter described the event, "a loudspeaker on a police car played carols. The children were scrubbed clean and dressed in spotless frocks and suits."[1] These stories of the Estonians add a layer of spatial practices, with domesticity woven into the industrial and governmental architecture of Pier 21.

Nonetheless, when scheduled migrant arrivals recommenced after 1950, there had been many transformations to the network of immigration architecture. The quarantine stations were all closed or closing, most of their infrastructure abandoned or put to new uses. The Prairie immigration halls were long gone, except those of a more substantial model found in cities such as Winnipeg and Edmonton. Immigrant detention hospitals were relics of an earlier era; medical inspection and treatment now occurred abroad, prior to departure, with doctors sanctioned by the Canadian government. The liberalization of federal immigration policy during the 1960s largely eliminated the need for the detention practices in effect at the notorious government buildings in Victoria, Vancouver, and Montreal. Deportations became more rare, and Canadian borders slowly opened to migrants from all over the world. Only a handful of buildings remained in operation, and their days were numbered. The network of reception infrastructure became fully irrelevant with the rise of commercial air travel.

All immigration buildings were shuttered by the early 1970s, and few have survived demolition. In that decade, Grosse-Île was recognized for its national historical significance; with many of the original buildings extant, Parks Canada began to manage it as a historic site in the 1990s. Meanwhile, the William Head quarantine station was transformed – perhaps easily and appropriately – into a minimum-security federal penitentiary at the end of the 1950s. At least two of the later Prairie immigration halls, built during the 1920s, continue in use as different kinds of social housing. For its part, Pier 21 closed as an immigration facility in 1971. The building was occupied for other purposes during the next twenty years or so, when a community organization leased it with the intention of creating a museum commemorating the historic function of the space. The operations were taken over by the federal government in 2011, which formalized the institution as the Canadian Museum of Immigration at Pier 21. From the beginning, one of the strengths of the museum has been the oral histories collected by volunteers and staff, who have interviewed hundreds of people who passed through, lived, worked, and served in the building. The museum at Pier 21 has contributed greatly to educating the public about the stories of Canadian immigration and how they played out in specific spaces.

In the twenty-first century, the history of Canadian immigration architecture from Confederation to the Depression remains relevant in other ways as well. The management of thousands of immigrants arriving in the pier buildings at once forced the Dominion government to develop spatial strategies that would carefully and efficiently conduct people through various examinations in a secure space, secluded from outsiders.

The marshalling of immigrants in queues, the spatial distinction between the steps in the process, the handling of baggage along a separate path through customs: none of these innovations of late-nineteenth- and early-twentieth-century pier buildings would seem surprising to international air travellers today. Similarly, the slightly odd procedures of US pre-clearance that are in place at every Canadian airport with cross-border flights, were established as early as the 1890s in the pier buildings of Quebec and Halifax. Nowadays, entering US territory (or being refused admission) within the architectural space of the Calgary or Vancouver international airports seems somehow appropriate to our virtual and securitized world. In the nineteenth century, though, the Dominion government's decision to allow this encroachment on Canadian soil had been driven more by the commercial viability of homegrown transportation companies, which hoped to compete on routes between Europe, Asia, and US ports of entry, with brief stops alongside Canadian piers.[2]

Detention too has re-emerged as a practice engaged in by the federal government for dealing with suspect or undesirable immigrants. The procedures and spatiality of twenty-first-century detention are eerily analogous to what I have described in the present volume. As criminologist Anna Pratt has argued, what is now called "administrative detention" situates immigrant arrivals and asylum applicants in extralegal spaces – or "zones of exclusion" – where they have few rights. Not considered criminals, these detainees are not subject to reform measures. Instead, as with the deportees languishing in Dominion government detention buildings during the 1910s and 1920s, the aim of incarceration is to control and reject, and not to release into society. And, as in that earlier era, some are detained upon arrival, while others are rounded up after being in the country for a while. Like the Montreal immigrant-detention building described above, for today's detention centres – which often occupy space in airport hotels or purpose-built facilities alongside penitentiaries – proximity to the national border is largely irrelevant. In effect, detainees then and now are kept in liminal space. As Pratt concludes, detentions today are sometimes effected for symbolic purposes, so that the federal government can appear to be protecting Canadian borders.[3] The deterrence of Asian immigration through the medium of the Victoria and Vancouver pier buildings perhaps established the symbolic precedent for this representational gambit.

As this book was nearing completion, we all became concerned with modifying our spatial practices to stem the global coronavirus pandemic of 2020–21. Social distancing would have been impossible for immigrants using the buildings studied in the chapters above, but many of their experiences resonate directly in North America today. Quarantine has become a familiar term to many who never before considered it, let alone experienced it. For Canadians returning home, quarantine has been akin to what was described in Chapter 2 as "the English system," based on a combination of self-isolation and state surveillance, rather than exile to an island station. The overarching premise once again is that travellers are associated with contagion, that there is a healthy inside and a dubious outside.

Though the science has improved since the nineteenth century, public-health problems remain remarkably similar, as do the solutions – protecting a population by controlling individuals' access to spaces of our cities and towns. Inspectors take our temperature before we are permitted to enter certain spaces; we are questioned about our symptoms and our associations with others; and our communication with loved ones is necessarily over long distance rather than in face-to-face reunions. In these ways, we become like nineteenth- and early-twentieth-century immigrants: suspect

newcomers within our own communities and separated from family and friends. During the pandemic, we have all had our mobilities constrained, but, as in earlier times, some have been constrained much more than others. When public-health measures were enacted and borders began to close, many millions of international migrants were in transit. Stranded in airports or along borders, ejected from guest-worker positions, or with their detentions and paperwork prolonged indefinitely, these migrants have been forced to survive across the extranational, infrastructural spaces of global mobility.

Looking back to the previous chapters of this book, it seems that Canada lacks a federal presence in the way of immigration architecture in support of new arrivals. Since the postwar era, immigrant-settlement services have neglected the spatial aspects of reception in favour of social and economic supports, such as language training, cultural orientation, and employment assistance. Only for refugees and asylum seekers is there housing provided, and that is run by social-service agencies.[4] In the future, welfare states with aging resident populations like Canada will have little choice but to do more to attract and welcome young, hardworking families from other places in the world, just as it did in previous centuries. We can study the precedents in this book when we next begin to design architectures of immigrant reception. While the buildings described and analyzed here have mostly disappeared, along with the Dominion government policies that made them, the infrastructures and practices of immigrant reception retain their vital importance in Canada, and globally. Aside from the pandemic year, worldwide migration numbers have continued to grow in recent decades, tripling since 1960. If we can understand how newcomers negotiate the spaces provided by receiving societies, perhaps we can make their transition to new places a little more comfortable.

FIGURES

NOTES

INTRODUCTION

1 A note regarding terminology: the historian of immigration Dirk Hoerder critiques "the North American habit of calling all arrivals 'immigrants,'" which suggests a linear journey from leaving a homeland to assimilation in a new country. This effectively elides the practices and desires of people who plan to sojourn, who move among multiple countries, who do not naturalize. Given the reasoning of the present book, I have tried to use the term "migrant" when referring to the actions, perspectives, and emotions of people arriving in Canada, and have retained the use of "immigrant" when referring to Canadian government programs, attitudes, and architecture, which conceived of them as such. See Hoerder, "*The Transplanted*: International Dimensions," *Social Science History* 12, no. 3 (Autumn, 1988): 255–63.

2 Arthur E. Copping, *The Golden Land: The True Story and Experiences of British Settlers in Canada* (Toronto: Musson; London: Hodder & Stoughton 1911), 35–6.

3 Joseph Oleskow, *Memo about Emigration* (Lvov: Kachkovsky Educational Society, 1895), 4, 6, 10. Quotations from this guidebook are from an unattributed translation that seems to have been commissioned by the Canadian Department of Citizenship and Immigration during the 1950s or 1960s and found in Medicine Hat's Esplanade Archives, John W. Bennett fonds, 2002.01.2874. In the book I have used the currently standard spelling of "Oleskiw." For the significance of cleanliness and hygiene in immigration architecture, see Catherine Boland Erkkila, "American Railways and the Cultural Landscape of Immigration," *Buildings & Landscapes: Journal of the Vernacular Architecture*

Forum 22, no. 1 (2015): 48–50. The standard study of the association of immigrants with contamination in the United States is Alan M. Kraut, *Silent Travelers: Germs, Genes, and the "Immigrant Menace"* (New York: Basic Books, 1994). For Canada, see Jay Dolmage, *Disabled upon Arrival: Eugenics, Immigration, and the Construction of Race and Disability* (Columbus: Ohio State University Press, 2018), 55–6, 71.

4 Ann Laura Stoler, "Tense and Tender Ties: The Politics of Comparison in North American History and (Post) Colonial Studies," in *Haunted by Empire: Geographies of Intimacy in North American History*, ed. Ann Laura Stoler (Durham: Duke University Press, 2006), 25.

5 J.M. Gordon, Inspector of Agencies, Immigration Bureau, to A.M. Burgess, Deputy Minister of the Interior, 24 March 1893, LAC, Department of Interior fonds, RG 76, Immigration Branch, volume 34, file 802, part 1, "Department of Agriculture General Correspondence," microfilm reel C-4693.

6 Henri Lefebvre, *The Production of Space* (Oxford: Blackwell, 1991). For the distinction between strategies and tactics of space, see Michel de Certeau, *The Practice of Everyday Life* (Berkeley: University of California Press, 1984), 122–45. Proposals for exploiting Lefebvre's insights in architectural history are found in Mary McLeod, "Henri Lefebvre's Critique of Everyday Life: An Introduction," in *Architecture of the Everyday*, ed. Steven Harris and Deborah Berke (New York: Princeton Architectural Press, 1997), 9–29; and Dell Upton, "Architecture in Everyday Life," *New Literary History* 33, no. 4 (2002): 707–23.

7 Using material culture, popular images, legal documents that establish precedents of use, and other sources, these scholars have reconstructed

habitual activities and meanings in space. Kenneth A. Breisch and Alison K. Hoagland, *Building Environments: Perspectives in Vernacular Architecture*, Vol. 10 (Knoxville: University of Tennessee Press, 2005); Dianne Harris, *Little White Houses: How the Postwar Home Constructed Race in America* (Minneapolis: University of Minnesota Press, 2013); Bernard Herman, *Town House: Architecture and Material Life in the Early American City, 1780–1830* (Chapel Hill: University of North Carolina Press, 2005); Dell Upton, *Holy Things and Profane: Anglican Parish Churches in Colonial Virginia* (New Haven: Yale University Press, 1997).

8   For studies of deviant practices in space, see Iain Borden, *Skateboarding, Space and the City: Architecture and the Body* (Oxford: Berg, 2001); George Chauncey, *Gay New York: Gender, Urban Culture, and the Makings of the Gay Male World, 1890–1940* (New York: Basic Books, 1994); Nayan Shah, *Contagious Divides: Epidemics and Race in San Francisco's Chinatown* (Berkeley: University of California Press, 2001); Nayan Shah, *Stranger Intimacy: Contesting Race, Sexuality, and the Law in the North American West* (Berkeley: University of California Press, 2011). For biographically based studies of spatial practices, see Dana Arnold and Joanna R. Sofaer, *Biographies and Space: Placing the Subject in Art and Architecture* (London; New York: Routledge, 2008); Jessica Ellen Sewell, *Women and the Everyday City: Public Space in San Francisco, 1890–1915* (Minneapolis: University of Minnesota Press, 2011); Lisa C. Tolbert, *Constructing Townscapes: Space and Society in Antebellum Tennessee* (Chapel Hill: University of North Carolina Press, 1999).

9   Lisa Chilton and Yukari Takai, "East Coast, West Coast: Using Government Files to Study Immigration History," *Histoire Sociale/Social History* 47, no. 96 (2015): 8.

10   Bruce Elliott, David A. Gerber, Suzanne Sinke, eds., *Letters across Borders: The Epistolary Practices of International Migrants* (New York: Palgrave Macmillan, 2006).

11   Dirk Hoerder, *Creating Societies: Immigrant Lives in Canada* (Montreal: McGill-Queen's University Press, 1999), 15. For critiques of Hoerder's privileging of subjective sources, see Sylvia Hahn, et al., "Staking Narrative Claims: A Round Table on *Creating Societies: Immigrant Lives in Canada* by Dirk Hoerder," *Histoire Sociale/Social History* 38, no. 76 (2005): 461–77. A comprehensive discussion of the debate over using "subjective documents" is found in Virginia Yans-McLaughlin, "Metaphors of Self in History: Subjectivity, Oral Narrative, and Immigration Studies," in *Immigration Reconsidered: History, Sociology, and Politics*, ed. Virginia Yans-McLaughlin (New York: Oxford University Press, 1990), 254–90. A vital tradition in North American immigration history has deployed migrants' first-person sources in a variety of ways; see, for example: John W. Bennett and Seena B. Kohl, *Settling the Canadian-American West, 1890–1915: Pioneer Adaptation and Community Building, an Anthropological History* (Lincoln: University of Nebraska Press, 1995); Lisa Chilton, *Agents of Empire: British Female Migration to Canada and Australia, 1860s–1930* (Toronto: University of Toronto Press, 2007); Sheila McManus, *The Line Which Separates: Race, Gender, and the Making of the Alberta-Montana Borderlands* (Edmonton: University of Alberta Press, 2005).

12   Dell Upton, *Another City: Urban Life and Urban Spaces in the New American Republic* (New Haven: Yale University Press, 2008), 14.

13   Sucheng Chan, "European and Asian Immigration into the United States in Comparative Perspective, 1820s to 1920s," in *Immigration Reconsidered: History, Sociology, and Politics*, ed. Virginia Yans-McLaughlin (New York: Oxford University Press, 1990), 61.

14   See, for example: Franca Iacovetta, *Gatekeepers: Reshaping Immigrant Lives in Cold War Canada* (Toronto: Between the Lines, 2006); Vadim Kukushkin, *From Peasants to Labourers: Ukrainian and Belarusan Immigration from the Russian Empire to Canada* (Montreal: McGill-Queen's University Press, 2007); Gerald Tulchinsky, ed., *Immigration in Canada: Historical Perspectives* (Toronto: Copp Clark Longman, 1994); Mariana Valverde, *The Age of Light, Soap, and Water: Moral Reform in English Canada, 1885–1925* (Toronto: McClelland and Stewart, 1991).

15   Significant overviews of immigrant reception include Lisa Chilton, *Receiving Canada's Immigrants: The Work of the State before 1930* (Ottawa:

288

The Canadian Historical Association, 2016); and Robert Vineberg, *Responding to Immigrants' Settlement Needs: The Canadian Experience* (New York: Springer, 2013).

16 Michel Foucault, *Discipline and Punish: The Birth of the Prison* [1975], trans. Alan Sheridan (New York: Random House, 1995); Foucault, *The History of Sexuality*, Vol. 1: *An Introduction*, trans. Robert Hurley (New York: Vintage, 1990). For an architectural interpretation of governmentality, see Aggregate, *Governing by Design: Architecture, Economy, and Politics in the Twentieth Century* (Pittsburgh: University of Pittsburgh Press, 2012).

17 Ann Laura Stoler, "Intimidations of Empire: Predicaments of the Tactile and Unseen," in *Haunted by Empire: Geographies of Intimacy in North American History*, ed. Ann Laura Stoler (Durham: Duke University Press, 2006), 7. The argument that scholars must attend to the sense perceptions and affect of historical actors influenced the composite fiction that opens this Introduction. See the assertion by Joy Parr, "Notes for a More Sensuous History of Twentieth-Century Canada: The Timely, the Tacit, and the Material Body," *Canadian Historical Review* 82, no. 4 (2001): 719–45.

18 Adam McKeown, *Melancholy Order: Asian Migration and the Globalization of Borders* (New York: Columbia University Press, 2008), 3, 7. For analogous transnational studies see Marilyn Lake and Henry Reynolds, *Drawing the Global Colour Line: White Men's Countries and the International Challenge of Racial Equality* (Cambridge: Cambridge University Press, 2008); and Carl Nightingale, *Segregation: A Global History of Divided Cities* (Chicago: University of Chicago Press, 2012). For an overview of scholarly issues in border studies, see David Newman, "The Lines that Continue to Separate Us: Borders in our 'Borderless' World," *Progress in Human Geography* 30, no. 2 (2006): 143–61.

19 Dorothee Schneider, *Crossing Borders: Migration and Citizenship in the Twentieth-Century United States* (Cambridge, MA: Harvard University Press, 2011). See also Donna Gabaccia and Vicki Ruiz, eds., *American Dreaming, Global Realities: Rethinking U.S. Immigration History* (Urbana: University of Illinois Press, 2006); Erika Lee, *At America's Gates: Chinese Immigration during the Exclusion Era, 1882–1943* (Chapel Hill: University of North Carolina Press, 2003); Paul Spickard, ed., *Race and Immigration in the United States: New Histories* (New York: Routledge, 2011).

20 Hoerder, *Creating Societies*, 13–14 and *passim*. Key policy studies that have provided a scaffold for my research include Donald Avery, *Reluctant Host: Canada's Response to Immigrant Workers, 1896–1994* (Toronto: McClelland and Stewart, 1995); Ninette Kelley and Michael Trebilcock, *The Making of the Mosaic: A History of Canadian Immigration Policy*, 2nd ed. (Toronto: University of Toronto Press, 2010); Valerie Knowles, *Strangers at Our Gates: Canadian Immigration and Immigration Policy, 1540–2015*, 4th ed. (Toronto: Dundurn, 2016).

21 A beginning has been made in scattered sources, including Chilton and Takai, "East Coast, West Coast"; Lisa Chilton, "Travelling Colonist: British Emigration and the Construction of Anglo-Canadian Privilege," in *Empire, Migration, and Identity in the British World*, ed. Kent Fedorowich and Andrew S. Thompson (Manchester; New York: Manchester University Press, 2013): 169–91; Dolmage, *Disabled upon Arrival*; Lynda Mannik, *Photography, Memory, and Refugee Identity: The Voyage of the SS Walnut, 1948* (Vancouver: UBC Press, 2013); Henry Yu, "Conceiving a Pacific Canada: Trans-Pacific Migration Networks Within and Without Nations," in *Within and Without the Nation: Canadian History as Transnational History*, ed. Karen Dubinsky, Adele Perry, and Henry Yu (Toronto: University of Toronto Press, 2015), 187–211. For published work on Angel Island, see Erika Lee and Judy Yung, *Angel Island: Immigrant Gateway to America* (New York: Oxford University Press, 2010); and the work of geographer Gareth Hoskins, such as "Materialising Memory at Angel Island Immigration Station, San Francisco," *Environment and Planning A: Economy and Space* 39, no. 2 (2007): 437–55.

22 A few US facilities have been studied for how their spaces served to inscribe power on immigrant bodies; e.g., Jay Dolmage, "Disabled upon Arrival: The Rhetorical Construction of Race and Disability at Ellis Island," *Cultural Critique* 77 (2011): 24–69; Alexandra Minna Stern, "Buildings, Boundaries, and Blood: Medicalization and Nation-Building

on the U.S.-Mexico Border, 1910–1930," *Hispanic American Historical Review* 79, no. 1 (1999): 41–81. The sole book in English to focus exclusively on the connection between architecture and immigration is Stephen Cairns, ed., *Drifting: Architecture and Migrancy* (London: Routledge, 2004); however, it addresses contemporary global issues.

23 An influential early study into institutional typologies was Thomas Markus, *Buildings and Power: Freedom and Control in the Origin of Modern Building Types* (New York: Routledge, 1993). Other key works to influence my approach in this book are Annmarie Adams, *Medicine by Design: The Architect and the Modern Hospital, 1893–1943* (Minneapolis: University of Minnesota Press, 2008); Paula Lupkin, *Manhood Factories: YMCA Architecture and the Making of Modern Urban Culture* (Minneapolis: University of Minnesota Press, 2010); Jeanne Kisacky, *Rise of the Modern Hospital: An Architectural History of Health and Healing, 1870–1940* (Pittsburgh: University of Pittsburgh Press, 2017); Carla Yanni, *The Architecture of Madness: Insane Asylums in the United States* (Minneapolis: University of Minnesota Press, 2007). A separate stream of scholarship emanating mostly from the social sciences, examines the interaction of citizens with bureaucratic space, and offers valuable models for understanding architecture and political institutions. See Murray Edelman, "Space and the Social Order," *Journal of Architectural Education* 32, no. 2 (1978): 2–7; Charles T. Goodsell, *The Social Meaning of Civic Space: Studying Political Authority through Architecture* (Lawrence: University of Kansas Press, 1988); David Monteyne, "Boston City Hall and a History of Reception," *Journal of Architectural Education* 65, no. 1 (2011): 45–62.

24 Catherine Boland Erkkila, "Spaces of Immigration: American Railroad Companies, the Built Environment, and the Immigrant Experience" (PhD diss., Rutgers University, 2013). This dissertation includes comprehensive chapters on immigrant reception in Baltimore, New York, and San Francisco. See also Boland Erkkila, "American Railways and the Cultural Landscape of Immigration," *Buildings & Landscapes: Journal of the Vernacular Architecture Forum* 22, no. 1 (2015): 36–62.

25 For architectural histories of ordinary, non-monumental, or temporary structures, see Daniel M. Abramson, *Obsolescence: An Architectural History* (Chicago: University of Chicago Press, 2016); David Monteyne, *Fallout Shelter: Designing for Civil Defense in the Cold War* (Minneapolis: University of Minnesota Press, 2011); Abigail Van Slyck, *A Manufactured Wilderness: Summer Camps and the Shaping of American Youth, 1890–1960* (Minneapolis: University of Minnesota Press, 2006); and works on housing, such as Peter Ennals and Deryck Holdsworth, *Homeplace: The Making of the Canadian Dwelling over Three Centuries* (Toronto: University of Toronto Press, 1998); or Fred W. Peterson, *Homes in the Heartland: Balloon Frame Farmhouses of the Upper Midwest* (Minneapolis: University of Minnesota Press, 2008).

26 Janet Wright, *Crown Assets: The Architecture of the Department of Public Works, 1867–1967* (Toronto: University of Toronto Press, 1997), 1–6, 14–15; quotation, 27.

27 During the period covered by the present study, the ministries, departments, and branches responsible for immigration to Canada changed numerous times. From 1868 to 1892, immigration was under the Department of Agriculture; from 1892 to 1917, there was an Immigration Branch in the Department of Interior; and then from 1917 to the middle of the 1930s, there was a designated Department of Immigration and Colonization. To further complicate matters, the responsibility for quarantine stations remained with Agriculture after 1892, until transferred to the new Department of Health in 1919. Meanwhile, Chinese immigration was handled by the Department of Trade and Commerce until it was placed under the same umbrella as other immigration in 1911. Regardless, the program of immigration architecture transcends these bureaucratic reshufflings, as it was pursued consistently across five decades, by successive administrations. For example, the 1892 transfer of immigration matters from the Department of Agriculture to that of Interior had little effect on the design or construction of immigration architecture. The history of the different branches is not particularly relevant to this study,

and I have therefore tried to use the term "immigration branch" as a general term across these bureaucratic eras.

28 For Parks Canada heritage studies, which are not easily accessible to the public, see Norman Anick, *Thematic Study: Immigration to Canada, 1814–1914* (Ottawa: Historic Sites and Monuments Board of Canada, 1984); Anick, *Immigration Stations: History and Description* (Ottawa: Historic Sites and Monuments Board of Canada, 1984); Shannon Ricketts, *Immigration Sites on the West Coast, 1840–1940* (Ottawa: Historic Sites and Monuments Board of Canada, 2000); Ivan J. Saunders, *Former Immigration Hall, Edmonton, Alberta* (Ottawa: Historic Sites and Monuments Board of Canada, 1984); André Sévigny, *L'immigration au Canada via le Port de Québec* (Québec: Service Canadien des Parcs, 1988). Also useful are the articles by historian Steve Schwinghamer and others that are posted to the website of the Canadian Museum of Immigration at Pier 21. I have looked at immigration architecture after the period of the present study in David Monteyne, "Pier 21 and the Production of Canadian Immigration," in *The Design of Frontier Spaces: Control and Ambiguity*, ed. Carolyn Loeb and Andreas Luescher (Farnham, UK: Ashgate, 2015), 109–28. Vineberg's policy study, *Responding to Immigrants' Settlement Needs*, includes a brief survey of immigration infrastructure, and he presents an in-depth description of the buildings at one site in Vineberg, "Welcoming Immigrants at the Gateway to Canada's West: Immigration Halls in Winnipeg, 1872–1975," *Manitoba History* 65 (2011): 13–22. The work of Lisa Chilton also takes up immigration facilities to some extent, especially in her "Managing Migrants: Toronto, 1820–1880," *Canadian Historical Review* 92, no. 2 (2011): 231–62.

CHAPTER ONE

1 See, for instance, Thomas Markus, *Buildings and Power: Freedom and Control in the Origin of Modern Building Types* (New York: Routledge, 1993), 48–69; and Dell Upton, "Lancasterian Schools, Republican Citizenship, and the Spatial Imagination in Early Nineteenth-Century America," *Journal of the Society of Architectural Historians* 55, no. 3 (1996): 238–53.

2 These paragraphs are assembled from the detailed accounts of immigration routes in Norman Anick, *Thematic Study: Immigration to Canada, 1814–1914* (Ottawa: Historic Sites and Monuments Board of Canada, 1984), 12, 15, 20–2, 52–8, 77–80; and in the same author's inventory, *Immigration Stations: History and Description* (Ottawa: Historic Sites and Monuments Board of Canada, 1984), 11–12, 16–17. In addition, there are numerous accounts of voyages across the ocean and upcountry in William Loe Smith, *The Pioneers of Old Ontario* (Toronto: George N. Morang, 1923).

3 Geoffrey Bilson, *A Darkened House: Cholera in Nineteenth-Century Canada* (Toronto: University of Toronto Press, 1980), 141; for the sites of the disease's appearance, see 25–6.

4 Anick, *Immigration Stations*, 19–20.

5 Ibid., 13.

6 Anick, *Thematic Study*, 17–18, 22–31.

7 Uncited eyewitness in Edwin C. Guillet, *The Great Migration: The Atlantic Crossing by Sailing-Ship since 1770* (Toronto: Nelson & Sons, 1937), 155.

8 Ibid., 155–6.

9 John and Esther Chantler, "The Cholera Came," in *The Land Newly Found: Eyewitness Accounts of the Canadian Immigrant Experience*, ed. Norman Hillmer and J.L. Granatstein (Toronto: T. Allen Publishers, 2006), 57–60.

10 Initially the British government paid for these agents, then the colonial government did after 1854; Ninette Kelley and Michael Trebilcock, *The Making of the Mosaic: A History of Canadian Immigration Policy*, 2nd ed. (Toronto: University of Toronto Press, 2010), 48–51, 85–6. Detailed description and analysis of the duties of these agents can be found in Lisa Chilton, "Managing Migrants: Toronto, 1820–1880," *Canadian Historical Review* 92, no. 2 (2011): 231–62; Stanley C. Johnson, *A History of Emigration: From the United Kingdom to North America, 1763–1912* (1913; New York: Augustus M. Kelley, 1966), 165–7; and in Norman Macdonald, *Canada: Immigration and Colonization, 1841–1903* (Toronto: Macmillan, 1966), 40–1.

11 His Majesty's Chief Immigration Agent, "Travel Advisory," in Hillmer and Granatstein, eds., *The Land Newly Found*, 63–4.

12 Catherine Parr Traill, Nathalie Cooke, and Fiona Lucas, *Catharine Parr Traill's "The Female Emigrant's Guide": Cooking with a Canadian Classic* (Montreal: McGill-Queen's University Press, 2017), 44.

13 Guillet, *The Great Migration*, 158.

14 Johan Schroder, "Trapped in Quebec," in Hillmer and Granatstein, eds., *The Land Newly Found*, 90. Another Norwegian immigrant on her way to the United States, in a letter to her parents, told of an "English skipper" and some of his sailors who "had been stabbed to death by the rough and ready men of Quebec." In Theodore Christian Blegen, *Land of Their Choice: The Immigrants Write Home* (Minneapolis: University of Minnesota Press, 1955), 116.

15 Chilton, "Managing Migrants," 240–5, 252.

16 Ibid., 235.

17 This was early in the era of Chief Architect Thomas Fuller, who came to the role with significant experience in private practice, as argued by Janet Wright, *Crown Assets: The Architecture of the Department of Public Works, 1867–1967* (Toronto: University of Toronto Press, 1997), 36–50.

18 Kelley and Trebilcock, *The Making of the Mosaic*, 64.

19 Ibid., 78–94.

20 Quotations from "Canadian Immigration" and "The Princess Louise Embankment at Quebec," both *Canadian Illustrated News*, 14 Aug. 1880, 98.

21 "Payne's Draft Report," LAC, Department of Agriculture fonds, RG 17, "Reports 1889," volume 2395, page 167. For the influence of the Turnerian thesis, see also Valerie Knowles, *Strangers at Our Gates: Canadian Immigration and Immigration Policy, 1540–2015*, 4th ed. (Toronto: Dundurn, 2016), 88–9.

22 Other than quarantine stations, and the involvement of State-appointed (but unpaid) commissioners at Castle Garden, all reception work in the United States before the establishment of Ellis Island was commercial or philanthropic, according to Dorothee Schneider, *Crossing Borders: Migration and Citizenship in the Twentieth-Century United States* (Cambridge, MA: Harvard University Press, 2011), 62–9.

23 "Payne's Draft Report," all quotations from pages 149–52, 168. Emphasis in original.

24 Kelley and Trebilcock, *The Making of the Mosaic*, 102, 101. There is a detailed analysis of the competition for immigrants in Macdonald, *Canada: Immigration and Colonization*, 116–20.

25 Canada, Parliament, House of Commons, Debates, 9th Parl., 3rd sess., Vol. 1 (1903), 1125.

26 E. Borlauch [?], "Postage Report," LAC, RG 17, volume 2395, file "Reports 1889."

27 Montreal agent in LAC, RG 17, volume 2395, file "Reports 1889." Cf. the official version in Canada, Parliament, *Sessional Papers, 1890*, Paper no. 6, "Report of the Minister of Agriculture," xxix.

28 Wright, *Crown Assets*, 65.

29 Canada, Parliament, *Sessional Papers, 1890*, Paper no. 6, "Report of the Minister of Agriculture," xxvii–xxviii.

30 Annmarie Adams, *Medicine by Design: The Architect and the Modern Hospital, 1893–1943* (Minneapolis: University of Minnesota Press, 2008), xxi.

31 Joseph Oleskow, *Memo about Emigration* (Lvov: Kachkovsky Educational Society, 1895), 10.

32 J.M. Gordon, Inspector of Agencies, Immigration Bureau, to A.M. Burgess, Deputy Minister of the Interior, 24 March 1893, LAC, Department of Interior fonds, RG 76, Immigration Branch, volume 34, file 802, part 1, "Department of Agriculture General Correspondence," microfilm reel C-4693.

33 Wright, *Crown Assets*, 65.

34 Series of letters, 2–22 March 1893, LAC, Department of Interior fonds, RG 76, Immigration Branch, volume 51, file 355, part 1, "Landing of immigrants at ports," microfilm reel C-4679. Beaver Lines was the shipping company, and letters were received from the East End Immigration Fund, the Self Help Immigration Society, the Tower Hamlets Emigration and Colonisation Fund, and the Women's Protective Immigration Society.

35 Draft of the Royal Proclamation, and internal correspondence justifying the decision, 1893, found in ibid.

36 Vice-President, CPR, to Charles Drinkwater, 18 April 1888, LAC, Department of Interior fonds, RG 76, Immigration Branch, volume 34, file 802,

part 1, "Department of Agriculture General Correspondence," microfilm reel c-4693.

37 "Diaries of Henry Welch," Library and Archives Canada (LAC), Henry Welch and family fonds, 1881–1902, R7550-0-7-E.

38 "Shipload of Immigrants: Over Seventeen Hundred at Halifax," *The Globe*, 1 May 1902, 5, ProQuest Historical Newspapers: The Globe and Mail.

39 Geirfinnur Peterson, "The Narrows Settlement," in *Memory Opens the Door to Yesterday: History as Told by Pioneers of the Central, West-Interlake Area*, ed. Lucy Lindell (Eriksdale, MB: self-published, 1970), 174.

40 Secretary-Treasurer, Harbour Commissioners' Office, Quebec, to Frank Oliver, Minister of the Interior, 6 July 1906, LAC, Department of Interior fonds, RG 76, Immigration Branch, volume 34, file 802, part 2, "Department of Agriculture General Correspondence," microfilm reel c-4694.

41 As told to Eliane Leslau Silverman, *The Last Best West: Women on the Alberta Frontier, 1880–1930*, 2nd ed. (Calgary: Fifth House, 1998), 23.

42 *An Official Handbook of Information Relating to the Dominion of Canada, 1897* (Ottawa: Government Printing Bureau, 1898), 33–4.

43 Departmental correspondence often preserves news clippings of this sort from both port and Prairie towns, such as: "Cleared for Action: The Immigration Building's Ready for Summer's Work," Quebec *Chronicle*, 21 Apr. 1894, in LAC, Department of Interior fonds, RG 76, Immigration Branch, volume 34, file 802, part 1, "Department of Agriculture General Correspondence," microfilm reel c-4693. A survey of newspapers from an earlier period confirms this tradition of reporting; see Merna Foster, "Through the Eyes of Immigrants: An Analysis of Diaries and Letters of Immigrants Arriving at Grosse-Ile and the Port of Quebec, 1832–1842" (Master's thesis, Université Laval, 1991), 99.

44 Quotation from Maria Adamowska, as told to Andriy Nahachewsky, Maryna Chernyavska, and Larisa Sembaliuk Cheladyn, *Journey to Canada* (Edmonton: Kule Folklore Centre, 2017), 15. Cf. Vera Lysenko, *Men in Sheepskin Coats: A Study in Assimilation* (Toronto: Ryerson, 1947).

45 A. Akerlindh, Dominion Immigration Agent, Quebec, to A.M. Burgess, Deputy Minister of Interior, 14 July 1892; plus various letters between Quebec and Ottawa, 8 Feb. to 8 Apr. 1893, LAC, Department of Interior fonds, RG 76, Immigration Branch, volume 34, file 802, part 1, "Department of Agriculture General Correspondence," microfilm reel c-4693.

46 Letters and telegrams between Quebec and Ottawa, 21–26 Apr. 1899, LAC, Department of Interior fonds, RG 76, Immigration Branch, volume 34, file 802, part 2, "Department of Agriculture General Correspondence," microfilm reel c-4694.

47 C.E. Ussher, General Passenger Agent, CPR, Montreal to W.D. Scott, Superintendent of Immigration, Ottawa, 19 June 1903. There are dozens of letters about fencing. Examples include: James A. Smart, Deputy Minister of Immigration, to A. Gobeil, Deputy Minister of Public Works, 9 June 1904; and [Signatory illegible], to Chairman, Quebec Harbour Commissioners, 12 July 1905. All of these from LAC, Department of Interior fonds, RG 76, Immigration Branch, volume 34, file 802, part 2, "Department of Agriculture General Correspondence," microfilm reels c-4693 and c-4694.

48 J.F. Peachy, Public Works architect, Quebec, to Thomas Fuller, Chief Architect, Ottawa, 5 Aug. 1890, LAC, Department of Interior fonds, RG 76, Immigration Branch, volume 34, file 802, part 1, "Department of Agriculture General Correspondence," microfilm reel c-4693. With the opening of the 1887 building, the old one built circa 1880 became a dedicated baggage shed. A large middle section of this building was removed in 1898 to permit the laying of railroad tracks, and the two remaining parts survived as baggage sheds until 1906 and 1910, respectively.

49 Secretary, Department of Public Works, to W.D. Scott, Superintendent of Immigration, Department of the Interior, 13 March 1903; Frank Pedley, Superintendent of Immigration, to Secretary, Department of Public Works, 7 Dec. 1901; and P. Doyle, Immigration Agent, Quebec, to Secretary, Department of the Interior, 16 June 1897; all in LAC, Department of Interior fonds, RG 76, Immigration Branch, volume 34, file 802, part 1,

"Department of Agriculture General Correspondence," microfilm reel c-4693.

50 Oleskow, *Memo about Emigration*, 4.

51 *Official Handbook, 1897*, 30, 31.

52 LAC, RG 17, volume 2395, file "Reports 1889."

53 Lisa Chilton, *Agents of Empire: British Female Migration to Canada and Australia, 1860s–1930* (Toronto: University of Toronto Press, 2007), 98.

54 Carl Zetterman, Dairy Inspector, to Alfred Akerlindh, Dominion Immigration Agent, 5 Nov. 1894, LAC, Department of Interior fonds, RG 76, Immigration Branch, volume 34, file 802, part 1, "Department of Agriculture General Correspondence," microfilm reel c-4693. Chilton notes of the Toronto immigration depot that requests for return stays often were unsuccessful, but also documents some long-term stays; "Managing Migrants," 247–50.

55 George Hannah, H. & A. Allan, Montreal, to W.D. Scott, Superintendent of Immigration, Ottawa, 21 April 1905, LAC, Department of Interior fonds, RG 76, Immigration Branch, volume 34, file 802, part 2, "Department of Agriculture General Correspondence," microfilm reel c-4694.

56 Madame du Tremblay, [Assistant] Matron, Emigration Hall, Quebec, to Frank Pedley, Superintendent of Immigration, Ottawa, 1 Dec. 1901, LAC, Department of Interior fonds, RG 76, Immigration Branch, volume 34, file 802, part 1, "Department of Agriculture General Correspondence," microfilm reel c-4693.

57 For details and analysis of the personas and roles of the immigration matrons and assistant matrons, see Barbara Roberts, "Ladies, Women, and the State: Managing Female Immigration, 1880–1920," in *Community Organization and the Canadian State*, ed. Roxana Ng, Gillian Walker, and Jake Muller (Toronto: Garamond, 1990), 108–30.

58 Dr J.P. Lavoie, Dominion Immigration Agent, Quebec, to W.D. Scott, Superintendent of Immigration, Ottawa, 12 Dec. 1911 and 20 Dec. 1911; cf. the tersely-worded telegram from Scott to Lavoie, 13 Dec. 1911: "Have you closed building as directed? If not, why not? Answer." All in LAC, Department of Interior fonds, RG 76, Immigration Branch, volume 34, file 802, part 2, "Department

of Agriculture General Correspondence," microfilm reel c-4694.

59 Dirk Hoerder, *Creating Societies: Immigrant Lives in Canada* (Montreal: McGill-Queen's University Press, 1999), 34. In recent years, historians of the United States have been highly critical of the "Ellis Island myth"; see the enlightening analysis in Anna Pegler-Gordon, "Debating the Racial Turn in U.S. Ethnic and Immigration History," *Journal of American Ethnic History* 36, no. 2 (2017): 40–53; and Paul Spickard, *Almost All Aliens: Immigration, Race, and Colonialism in American History and Identity* (New York: Routledge, 2007).

60 Michel Foucault, "Of Other Spaces," *Diacritics* 16 (1986): 22–7; Jay Dolmage, "Disabled upon Arrival: The Rhetorical Construction of Disability and Race at Ellis Island," *Cultural Critique* 77 (2011): 24–69.

61 David Monteyne, "Pier 21 and the Production of Canadian Immigration" in *The Design of Frontier Spaces: Control and Ambiguity*, ed. Carolyn Loeb and Andreas Luescher (Farnham, UK: Ashgate, 2015), 109–28.

CHAPTER TWO

1 Catherine Parr Strickland Traill, *The Backwoods of Canada* [1836], ed. Michael A. Peterman (Ottawa: Carleton University Press, 1997), 13–20.

2 Geoffrey Bilson, "'Muscles and Health': Health and the Canadian Immigrant, 1867–1906," in *Health, Disease, and Medicine: Essays in Canadian History*, ed. Charles G. Roland (Toronto: Hannah Institute for the History of Medicine, 1984), 399. As Bilson notes, until the early twentieth century, there was no selection process for immigration; all immigrants were presumed admissible to Canadian territories, so quarantine was a delay, but not a rejection. The one exception to admissibility was the unemployable immigrant without family support, figured as a potential "public charge," who the quarantine superintendent could report to the customs agent.

3 Immigration officials in the United States shared similar perceptions of the qualities of different classes of passengers. Their assumptions

regarding the better health of first-class travellers held as late as the 1920s, according to Amy L. Fairchild, *Science at the Borders: Immigrant Medical Inspection and the Shaping of the Modern Industrial Labor Force* (Baltimore: Johns Hopkins University Press, 2003), 123–29 and 328n7. See also Howard Markel and Alexandra Minna Stern, "Which Face? Whose Nation? Immigration, Public Health, and the Construction of Disease at America's Ports and Borders, 1891–1928," *American Behavioral Scientist* 42, no. 9 (1999): 1314–31.

4 Alison Bashford, "Maritime Quarantine: Linking Old World and New World Histories," in *Quarantine: Local and Global Histories*, ed. Alison Bashford (London: Palgrave 2016), 6.

5 Krista Maglen, "In This Miserable Spot Called Quarantine: The Healthy and Unhealthy in Nineteenth Century Australian and Pacific Quarantine Stations," *Science in Context* 19, no. 3 (2006), 320.

6 Krista Maglen, *The English System: Quarantine, Immigration, and the Making of a Port Sanitary Zone* (Manchester: Manchester University Press, 2014), 24; for a survey of the debates over quarantine policy and practice, 30–3. In Britain, critiques of quarantine began in earnest during the epidemic of 1832; Traill likely would have been aware of these debates when she published her letters (originally written home to her mother) in 1836.

7 Geoffrey Bilson, "Dr Frederick Montizambert (1843–1929): Canada's First Director General of Public Health," *Medical History* 29, no. 4 (1985): 390–3.

8 Krista Maglen, "A World Apart: Geography, Australian Quarantine and the Mother Country," *Journal of the History of Medicine and Allied Sciences* 60, no. 2 (2005): 196–217.

9 Alison Bashford, "At the Border: Contagion, Immigration, Nation," *Australian Historical Studies* 33, no. 120 (2002): 344–58; the collected chapters in Bashford, ed., *Quarantine*; Maglen, *The English System*; Markel and Minna Stern, "Which Face? Whose Nation?"; Alexandra Minna Stern, "Buildings, Boundaries, and Blood: Medicalization and Nation-Building on the US-Mexico Border, 1910–1930," *Hispanic American Historical Review* 79, no. 1 (1999): 41–81.

10 The major quarantine sites in Canada have all had their popular historians, whom I draw upon below. For Grosse-Île, see Marianna O'Gallagher, *Grosse Ile: Gateway to Canada, 1832–1937* (Sainte-Foy: Carraig Books, 1984); for William Head, Peter Johnson, *Quarantined: Life and Death at William Head Station, 1872–1959* (Nanoose Bay: Heritage House Publishing, 2013); for Lawlor's Island in Halifax harbour, Ian Cameron, *Quarantine, What Is Old Is New: Halifax and the Lawlor's Island Quarantine Station, 1866–1938* (Halifax: New World Publishing, 2007); and for Partridge Island in Saint John there are several books by Harold E. Wright, including *Partridge Island: A Gateway to North America* (Saint John, NB: Partridge Island and Harbour Heritage, 1995).

11 John Joseph Heagerty, *Four Centuries of Medical History in Canada and a Sketch of the Medical History of Newfoundland* (Toronto: Macmillan, 1928), 116.

12 Geoffrey Bilson, *A Darkened House: Cholera in Nineteenth-Century Canada* (Toronto: University of Toronto Press, 1980), 13.

13 Ibid., 41, 58–66; and Heagerty, *Four Centuries of Medical History*, 180.

14 Robert Vineberg, *Responding to Immigrants' Settlement Needs: The Canadian Experience* (New York: Springer, 2013), 2–4. For a comparable description of the interactions between local service providers and quarantined or sick travellers, see Maglen, "In This Miserable Spot Called Quarantine," 325–6.

15 Bilson, *A Darkened House*, 8.

16 André Sévigny, "La Grosse Île: Quarantaine et immigration à Québec (1832–1937)," *Les Cahiers des dix* 47 (1992): 160–1.

17 Told to William Loe Smith, *The Pioneers of Old Ontario* (Toronto: George N. Morang, 1923), 330.

18 Heagerty, *Four Centuries of Medical History*, 181; Montreal health committee report quoted, 197.

19 Henry Deaves, "Grosse Île, 1831," in *The Land Newly Found: Eyewitness Accounts of the Canadian Immigrant Experience*, ed. Norman Hillmer and J.L. Granatstein (Toronto: T. Allen Publishers, 2006), 55–6. The date given in this collection is 1831, but there were no facilities on Grosse-Île in that year, so 1832 is likely the year of Captain Deaves's letter.

20 I was unable to access the original diary of Benjamin Freure, held at the Toronto Public Library, but it is quoted extensively in the excellent thesis by Merna Foster, "Through the Eyes of Immigrants: An Analysis of Diaries and Letters of Immigrants Arriving at Grosse-Ile and the Port of Quebec, 1832–1842" (Master's thesis, Université Laval, 1991), 83, 88.

21 Quotations from ibid., 59–60, 69, 94. For graffiti at other immigration stations, see, for instance, Alison Bashford and Peter Hobbins, "Rewriting Quarantine: Pacific History at Australia's Edge," *Australian Historical Studies* 46, no. 3 (2015): 392–409; and H.M. Lai, Genny Lim, and Judy Yung, *Island Poetry and History of Chinese Immigrants on Angel Island, 1910–1940* (Seattle: University of Washington Press, 1991).

22 Susanna Moodie, *Roughing It in the Bush; or, Life in Canada* [1852], Carl Ballstadt, ed. (Ottawa: Carleton University Press, 1988), 17.

23 Ibid., 15, 20, 21, 23.

24 Heagerty, *Four Centuries of Medical History*, 117–21.

25 Sévigny, "La Grosse Île," 161.

26 Cecil Woodham-Smith, *The Great Hunger: Ireland, 1845–1849* (New York: Harper and Row, 1962), 230–5.

27 Paragraphs summarized from Sévigny, "La Grosse Île," 161–3; Woodham-Smith, *The Great Hunger*, 218–27, 236–7. From 1832 to 1847, a little more than four thousand immigrants were hospitalized on Grosse-Île, according to the tally of Foster, "Through the Eyes of Immigrants." For the transfer of Grosse-Île to civilian authority in 1842, see Charles A. Mitchell, "Events Leading up to the Establishment of the Grosse Ile Quarantine Station," *Medical Services Journal Canada* (December 1967), 1441.

28 Smith, *Pioneers of Old Ontario*, 208–9. Note that this immigrant incorrectly identifies hospital isolation as "quarantine."

29 Edwin C. Guillet, *The Great Migration: The Atlantic Crossing by Sailing-Ship since 1770* (Toronto: Nelson and Sons, 1937), 152.

30 Jim Whalen, "'Allmost as Bad as Ireland': Saint John, 1847," *Archivaria* 10 (Summer 1980): 86–7. See also Norman Anick, *Thematic Study: Immigration to Canada, 1814–1914* (Ottawa: Historic Sites and Monuments Board of Canada, 1984), 37–41, 94–7. According to Anick, quarantine stations also appeared in 1847 on islands off the Maritime harbours of St Andrews and Miramichi.

31 Guillet, *The Great Migration*, 152.

32 Whalen, "'Allmost as Bad as Ireland,'" 86, 91.

33 Robert Whyte, *The Ocean Plague; or, A Voyage to Quebec in an Irish Emigrant Vessel Embracing a Quarantine at Grosse Isle in 1847: With Notes Illustrative of the Ship-pestilence of That Fatal Year* (Boston: Coolidge and Wiley, 1848), 85.

34 Ibid., 84.

35 Ibid., 85–6.

36 Ibid., 91–2. For the nineteenth-century fear of hospitals as places to contract further infections and to die, see Jeanne Kisacky, *Rise of the Modern Hospital: An Architectural History of Health and Healing, 1870–1940* (Pittsburgh: University of Pittsburgh Press, 2017), 3, 13–14, 78–9.

37 Maglen, *The English System*, 31.

38 Guillet, *The Great Migration*, 147.

39 Immigrant narrative discussed in Theodore Christian Blegen, *Land of Their Choice: The Immigrants Write Home* (Minneapolis: University of Minnesota Press, 1955), 110–11.

40 Bilson, *A Darkened House*, 114–19.

41 Sévigny, "La Grosse Île," 163; Anick, *Thematic Study*, 105–6.

42 Sévigny, "La Grosse Île," 166–7.

43 Bruce Curtis, "Social Investment in Medical Forms: The 1866 Cholera Scare and Beyond," *Canadian Historical Review* 81, no. 3 (2000): 360–8. Only about 1,300 immigrants were hospitalized on Grosse-Île during the navigation seasons from 1865 to 1868, and only a few perished there.

44 Janet Wright, *Crown Assets: The Architecture of the Department of Public Works, 1867–1967* (Toronto: University of Toronto Press, 1997), 27.

45 Ibid., 29.

46 Bilson, *A Darkened House*, 177.

47 Bilson, "Dr Frederick Montizambert," 389–90; Anick, *Thematic Study*, 109.

48 Quoted in Bilson, "Muscles and Health," 400.

49 Ninette Kelley and Michael Trebilcock, *The Making of the Mosaic: A History of Canadian Immigration Policy*, 2nd ed. (Toronto: University of Toronto Press, 2010), 85, 492n82.

50 For example, in 1889 only thirty-two immigrants were admitted to hospital on Grosse-Île out of about fifty thousand inspected. There were no admittances to quarantine hospitals at Partridge and Lawlor's islands, nor at the minor stations in Chatham, Pictou, Sydney, and Charlottetown. There was one case of diphtheria admitted at Port Hawkesbury. See Frederick Montizambert, "Quarantine Service Report," Library and Archives Canada (LAC), RG 17, volume 2395, file "Reports 1889."

51 Bilson, *A Darkened House*, 154; and Bilson, "Muscles and Health," 400–3.

52 "Defenceless," Victoria *Daily Colonist*, 17 Sept. 1892. The saga of the smallpox scare, and the conditions at Albert Head, are chronicled in numerous articles in that newspaper, e.g., on 21, 24, and 30 July 1892, and 13 Sept. 1892. See also Johnson, *Quarantined*, 48–60.

53 "Getting Ready for Occupancy," Victoria *Daily Colonist*, 29 Aug. 1893; and "A First-Class Station," Victoria *Daily Colonist*, 1 Sept. 1893.

54 M. Sutherland, "Vancouver Agency Report," LAC, RG 17, volume 2395, file "Reports 1889."

55 The provenance and program of this building are described in Wright, *Crown Assets*, 29–31.

56 Kisacky, *Rise of the Modern Hospital*, 31–5, 101–3, 115–17.

57 Annmarie Adams, *Medicine by Design: The Architect and the Modern Hospital, 1893–1943* (Minneapolis: University of Minnesota Press, 2008), 10, 14.

58 For an excellent discussion of germ theory and its architectural effects, or lack thereof, see Kisacky, *Rise of the Modern Hospital*, 79–91, 106–7.

59 Montizambert, "Quarantine Service Report," LAC, RG 17, volume 2395.

60 Sévigny, "La Grosse Île," 174; Wright, *Crown Assets*, 64.

61 Vera Velichkina, "Quarantine Island," in *The Land Newly Found: Eyewitness Accounts of the Canadian Immigrant Experience*, ed. Norman Hillmer and J.L. Granatstein (Toronto: Thomas Allen Publishers, 2006), 103–4.

62 S.L. Tolstoy, *Sergej Tolstoy and the Doukhobors: A Journey to Canada: Diary and Correspondence*, ed. Andrew Donskov, John Woodsworth, and T.G. Nikiforova (Ottawa: Slavic Research Group at the University of Ottawa, 1998), quotations on 306, 310–11, 313, 358, 361–2. See also Ian Cameron, "Sergey Tolstoy and the Doukhobors: The Halifax Quarantine," *Canadian Medical Association Journal* 174, no. 11 (2006): 1600–2.

63 Dr A.T. Watt, "Annual Report, 1897," LAC, Department of Health and Welfare fonds, RG 29, "Quarantine, Immigration, Medical and Sick Sailors' Services, 1867–1957," volume 753A, file "Book Giving Brief History of William Head." Note that this file, though entitled a "brief history," merely comprises the William Head medical superintendent's annual reports from 1897 to 1932.

64 Kisacky, *Rise of the Modern Hospital*, 88–9; see also 107–10, 120–22; and for a discussion of design parameters for nineteenth-century isolation wards, 70–2, 156–7.

65 Watt, "Annual Report, 1897," LAC, RG 29, volume 753A, file "Book Giving Brief History of William Head."

66 Watt, "Annual Report, 1903," in ibid.

67 Watt, "Annual Report, 1897," in ibid.

68 Ibid.

69 "A Protest from a Quarantine Passenger of the 'Empress of China,'" Victoria *Daily Colonist*, 30 April 1897.

70 Superintendent, CPR, to T.G. Shaughnessy, Vice-President, CPR, 19 May 1897, LAC, Department of Health and Welfare fonds, RG 29, "Quarantine Division, 1893–1930," volume 767, file 412-10-1, "Quarantine Station, William Head (Victoria) British Columbia, General," part 1.

71 Watt, "Annual Report, 1904," LAC, RG 29, volume 753A, file "Book Giving Brief History of William Head." Asian immigrants detained at the previous Albert Head quarantine station had also suffered maltreatment; see Johnson, *Quarantined*, 76–7.

72 Kay Anderson, *Vancouver's Chinatown: Racial Discourse in Canada, 1875–1980* (Montreal: McGill-Queen's University Press, 1991); Marilyn Lake and Henry Reynolds, *Drawing the Global Colour Line: White Men's Countries and the International Challenge of Racial Equality* (Cambridge: Cambridge University Press, 2008); Carl Nightingale, *Segregation: A Global History of Divided Cities* (Chicago: University of Chicago Press, 2012); and especially Nayan Shah, *Contagious Divides:*

Epidemics and Race in San Francisco's Chinatown (Berkeley: University of California Press, 2001).

73 Maglen, "In This Miserable Spot Called Quarantine," 326–7.

74 Wright, *Crown Assets*, 104.

75 "A First-Class Station," Victoria *Daily Colonist*, 1 Sept. 1893.

76 Wright, *Crown Assets*, 64.

77 Superintendent, CPR, to T.G. Shaughnessy, Vice President, CPR, 19 May 1897, LAC, Department of Health and Welfare fonds, RG 29, "Quarantine Division, 1893–1930," volume 767, file 412-10-1, "Quarantine Station, William Head (Victoria) British Columbia, General," part 1.

78 Johnson, *Quarantined*, 119–20.

79 Dr H. Rundle Nelson, "Annual Report, 1916," LAC, RG 29, volume 753A, file "Book Giving Brief History of William Head." Even this new kitchen was insufficient during the mass movements of Chinese workers on their way to war-torn Europe the following year; see Dan Black, *Harry Livingstone's Forgotten Men: Canadians and the Chinese Labour Corps in the First World War* (Toronto: James Lorimer, 2019), 277.

80 Velichkina, "Quarantine Island," 101–4.

81 Ibid., 105.

82 Tolstoy, *Sergej Tolstoy and the Doukhobors*, 306–9.

83 "The Eastern Quarantine," Victoria *Daily Colonist*, 27 May 1893.

84 Johnson, *Quarantined*, 129.

85 "Happiness at William Head," Victoria *Daily Colonist*, 15 Sept. 1900, 7.

86 Nellie McGowan and Harold E. Wright. *The Diary of Nellie McGowan, Partridge Island Quarantine Station, 1902* (Saint John, NB: Partridge Island Research Project, 1984), quotations from 16–17, 21, 24, 35.

87 Johnson, *Quarantined*, 169–70. For his book, Johnson interviewed numerous people who grew up at the William Head station during the 1920s and 1930s, and their recollections share similar senses of space and practices with stories from the earlier period of this study; see 172–93.

88 Jeanette Vekeman Masson, *A Grandmother Remembers Grosse-Île*, trans. Johanne L. Massé (Sainte-Foy: Carraig, 1989), 86. For previous passages and quotations, respectively: ambulance, 79; chatting through the fence, 81; frozen firewood, 108; the story of the protesting immigrants, 84–6. Although Vekeman Masson's in many ways appears to have been a typical rural childhood, her family received certain privileges from the Dominion government: free firewood, transportation, and an annual pilgrimage to Sainte-Anne-de-Beaupré.

89 "The Quarantine Station," Victoria *Daily Colonist*, 5 Feb. 1902.

90 Linda M. Ambrose, "Quarantine in Question: The 1913 Investigation at William Head, BC," *Canadian Bulletin of Medical History/Bulletin canadien d'histoire de la medicine* 22, no. 1 (2005): 145–6; cf. Johnson, *Quarantined*, 131–46.

91 "Annual Report, 1913," LAC, RG 29, volume 753A, file "Book Giving Brief History of William Head."

92 Ambrose, "Quarantine in Question," 147.

93 Johnson, *Quarantined*, 144–5.

94 Nelson, "Annual Report, 1915," LAC, RG 29, volume 753A, file "Book Giving Brief History of William Head."

95 Sévigny, "La Grosse Île," 182.

96 Wright, *Crown Assets*, 100.

97 Sévigny, "La Grosse Île," 183–4.

98 Ibid., 184–90.

99 Canada, Parliament, House of Commons, Debates, 14th Parl., 4th sess., vol. 4 (1925), 3612–13.

100 Johnson, *Quarantined*, 222–7. For the golf course, see Katie DeRosa, "William Head Prison to Get Shorter Fence," Victoria *Times Colonist*, 13 Dec. 2017.

101 Peter H. Bryce, Chief Medical Officer, to W.D. Scott, Superintendent of Immigration, 4 Nov. 1911, LAC, Department of Interior fonds, RG 76, volume 587, file 823247, "Immigration Building, Prince Rupert, BC," microfilm reel C-10659.

102 Alison Bashford and Carolyn Strange, "Isolation and Exclusion in the Modern World: An Introductory Essay," in *Isolation: Places and Practices of Exclusion* (London: Routledge, 2003), 4.

103 Foster, "Through the Eyes of Immigrants," 74.

CHAPTER THREE

1 Secretary, Dept. of Agriculture to William Hespeler, 19 April 1881; Library and Archives Canada (LAC), Dept. of Agriculture, RG17, "Letterbooks," volume 2318, file 489.

2 Valerie Knowles, *Strangers at Our Gates: Canadian Immigration and Immigration Policy, 1540–2006* (Toronto: Dundurn Press, 2007), see chapter 5, "The Sifton Years." See also D.J. Hall, *Clifford Sifton*, Vol. 2: *A Lonely Eminence, 1901–1929* (Vancouver: University of British Columbia Press, 1985), especially 64–5 for a description of the key players in the immigration bureaucracy.

3 For the effect of the National Policy, and then that of Sifton's endeavours to promote immigration, see Ninette Kelley and Michael Trebilcock, *The Making of the Mosaic: A History of Canadian Immigration Policy*, 2nd ed. (Toronto: University of Toronto Press, 2010), 62–6, 118–34; for Sifton, see as well Jaroslav Petryshyn, *Peasants in the Promised Land: Canada and the Ukrainians, 1891–1914* (Toronto: Lorimer, 1985), 19–21. Dirk Hoerder discusses competing nationalisms in *Creating Societies: Immigrant Lives in Canada* (Montreal: McGill-Queen's University Press, 1999), 10–12.

4 E.g., J. Obed Smith, Commissioner of Immigration, Winnipeg, to Frank Pedley, Superintendent of Immigration, 1 Mar. 1902, LAC, Department of the Interior fonds, RG 76, volume 14, file 116, part 1. This nineteen-page letter reports on immigrant accommodations across the Prairie provinces, and refers several times to the "class" of immigrants for whom the buildings were intended. In addition, the phrase "canvas accommodation" is used in this report to describe the situation in Estevan.

5 Dell Upton, "Architectural History or Landscape History?" *Journal of Architectural Education* 44, no. 4 (Aug. 1991): 195–9.

6 Norman Anick, *Thematic Study: Immigration to Canada, 1814–1914* (Ottawa: Historic Sites and Monuments Board of Canada, 1984), 115, 123.

7 Lisa Chilton, "Managing Migrants: Toronto, 1820–1880," *Canadian Historical Review* 92, no. 2 (2011): 244.

8 For example, plans and details of the London and Emerson buildings are to be found at: S. Peters & Son, "Emigrant Building, London, Ontario"; and Thomas Hooper, "Proposed plan of an immigrant shed to be erected at Emerson," LAC, Maps and technical drawings from Public Works Canada correspondence, 1860–1879, RG11M 923004, items 1384-6 and 1343.

9 Both quoted in Lucille Campey, *Ignored but Not Forgotten: Canada's English Immigrants* (Toronto: Dundurn Press, 2014), 246–7.

10 "Manitoba Affairs: Immigration," *The Globe*, 4 June 1872, 2, ProQuest Historical Newspapers: The Globe and Mail. This editorial recommends that the Dominion government supply "fifty or a hundred tents" to "supplement" the proposed shed, and even to loan to homesteaders while they were building the first shelters on their own land. It was almost two years later when the Department of Public Works first established a resident architect in Winnipeg to oversee the construction of several other small public buildings, according to Janet Wright, *Crown Assets: The Architecture of the Department of Public Works, 1867–1967* (Toronto: University of Toronto Press, 1997), 23, 32–4.

11 Quoted in the description of the 1872–73 sheds by Robert Vineberg, "Welcoming Immigrants at the Gateway to Canada's West: Immigration Halls in Winnipeg, 1872–1975," *Manitoba History* 65 (2011): 14–15.

12 Vineberg, "Welcoming Immigrants," 15–17. As he explains, the 1881 Winnipeg hall was used for only one season before being sold to the Winnipeg General Hospital for emergency use; at that time in the city there were only so many structures large enough to serve as patient wards. A new hall was built during the 1882 season, and lasted about five years before burning to the ground.

13 Dirk Hoerder, *Creating Societies: Immigrant Lives in Canada* (Montreal: McGill-Queen's University Press, 1999), 190.

14 Theo Burrows, Member of the Provincial Parliament, Winnipeg, to J.A. Smart, Deputy Minister, Ottawa, 6 Mar. 1897, LAC, Department of the Interior fonds, RG 76, volume 146, file 34560.

15 Kelley and Trebilcock, *The Making of the Mosaic*; for homesteading policy, 69–71; for group migration, 73–8.

16 Saskatchewan Homesteading Experiences collection, LAC, R2206-0-2-E, see 218–26, 247–8, 329–30, 554, 659–72.

17 Regular reports can be found in "Immigration Buildings – General," LAC, Department of the Interior fonds, RG 76, volume 14, file 116, part 1. For the reference to "canvas accommodation," see

J. Obed Smith, Commissioner of Immigration, Winnipeg, to Frank Pedley, Superintendent of Immigration, Ottawa, 28 April 1902, LAC, Department of the Interior fonds, RG 76, volume 194, file 75436.

18 Correspondence from local agents, plus annual reports from the immigration branch, which are included in Dominion government *Sessional Papers* for the presiding department at the time, give statistics on numbers and average length of stays.

19 Arthur E. Copping, *The Golden Land: The True Story and Experiences of British Settlers in Canada* (Toronto: Musson; London: Hodder and Stoughton, 1911), 33.

20 Canada, Parliament, House of Commons, Debates, 7th Parl., 1st sess., vol. 3 (1891), 6251.

21 J. Obed Smith, Commissioner of Immigration, Winnipeg, to W.D. Scott, Superintendent of Immigration, Ottawa, 15 June 1903, LAC, Department of the Interior fonds, RG 76, volume 14, file 116, part 2.

22 Robert Vineberg, "Two Centuries of Immigration to North America," in *Immigrant Experiences in North America: Understanding Settlement and Integration*, ed. John Shields and Harald Bauder (Toronto: Canadian Scholars' Press, 2015), 42–4. For a discussion of railroad and settlement hotels in the United States, see A.K. Sandoval-Strausz, *Hotel: An American History* (New Haven and London: Yale University Press, 2007), 92–9.

23 "Payne's Draft Report," LAC, Department of Agriculture fonds, RG 17, "Reports 1889," volume 2395, page 168.

24 J.A. Smart, Deputy Minister, Ottawa, to J. Obed Smith, Commissioner of Immigration, Winnipeg, 10 Apr. 1902, LAC, Department of the Interior fonds, RG 76, volume 14, file 116, part 1.

25 Canadian Pacific Railway Company, *Farming and Ranching in the Canadian North-West: General Account of Manitoba and the North West Territories* [Montreal: The Railway, 1888], 19; Glenbow Museum Library and Archives.

26 John C. Lehr, "Governmental Coercion in the Settlement of Ukrainian Immigrants in Western Canada," in *Immigration and Settlement, 1870–1939*, ed. Gregory P. Marchildon (Regina: University of Regina; Canadian Plains Research Center, 2009), 270–5.

27 Martin Louis Kovacs, *Esterhazy and the Early Hungarian Immigration to Canada: A Study Based upon the Esterhazy Immigration Pamphlet* (Regina: University of Regina, Canadian Plains Research Center, 1974), 24, 29n44.

28 Campey, *Ignored but Not Forgotten*, 119–21. See also Kelley and Trebilcock, *The Making of the Mosaic*, 79–82. According to Lisa Chilton, "concerns about the poor quality of British immigrants … featured regularly in official correspondence." See her "Travelling Colonist: British Emigration and the Construction of Anglo-Canadian Privilege," in *Empire, Migration and Identity in the British World*, ed. Kent Fedorowich and Andrew S. Thompson (Manchester; New York: Manchester University Press, 2013), 173.

29 Saskatchewan Homesteading Experiences collection, LAC, R2206-0-2-E, see page 249. An 1886 editorial in the Regina newspaper decried the continuing necessity of the town paying for tents to house new arrivals; see Wright, *Crown Assets*, 65.

30 Charles E. Kennedy, *Craik's Golden Jubilee Story* [Craik, SK: Craik Agricultural Society, 1955], 15–16.

31 Davidson and District Historical Society, *Prairie Tapestry: Davidson, Girvin and District* [Davidson, SK: The Society, 1983], 24, 57.

32 Joseph Oleskow, *Memo about Emigration* (Lvov: Kachkovsky Educational Society, 1895), 18–19, John W. Bennett fonds, 2002.01.2874, Esplanade Archives, Medicine Hat.

33 Sandoval-Strausz, *Hotel*, emphasizes the particular American context that produced the modern hotel, including the access of diverse classes of citizen, and the consideration of the hotel as a space of civic engagement in US cities. See 64–7; 231–62.

34 "Quiet at Immigration Hall," Edmonton *Bulletin*, 15 December 1909, 1; Peel's Prairie Provinces, University of Alberta.

35 J. Obed Smith, Commissioner of Immigration, Winnipeg, to Frank Pedley, Superintendent of Immigration, Ottawa, 1 March 1902, LAC, Department of the Interior fonds, RG 76, volume 14, file 116, part 1, file 193156, "Halbrite."

36 Frank Oliver, Member of Parliament, to Sir William Mulock, Acting Minister of Interior, 8 April 1903 LAC, Department of the Interior fonds, RG 76, volume 14, file 116, part 1, file 253572.

37 Canada, Parliament, House of Commons, Debates, 7th Parl., 1st sess., vol. 3 (1891), 6251. Compared to the balloon framing of the earlier immigration halls, platform framing was cheaper and faster to build; see David Monteyne, "Framing the American Dream," *Journal of Architectural Education* 58, no. 1 (2004): 24–33.

38 I am exceedingly grateful to Gareth Evans, Heritage Designations Advisor, Ministry of Parks, Culture and Sport, Regina, who compiled for me the data from financial statements referring to Prairie immigration halls that he had access to in his office. The data were originally published in the *Report from the Minister of Public Works on the Works under His Control* between 1883 and 1930. All subsequent references to the costs of construction for Prairie immigration halls draw on his compilation.

39 I have drawn on descriptions of Dominion government immigration buildings that appeared in the annual reports published in parliamentary *Sessional Papers*, and were compiled painstakingly by Norman Anick, *Immigration Stations: History and Description* (Ottawa: Historic Sites and Monuments Board of Canada, 1984).

40 J. Obed Smith, Commissioner of Immigration, Winnipeg, to W.D. Scott, Superintendent of Immigration, Ottawa, 6 Jan. 1904, LAC, Department of the Interior fonds, RG 76, volume 146, file 34560.

41 J. Obed Smith, Commissioner of Immigration, Winnipeg, to W.D. Scott, Superintendent of Immigration, Ottawa, 1 Sept. 1905, LAC, Department of the Interior fonds, RG 76, volume 682, file 531, part 2.

42 Robert Vineberg, *Responding to Immigrants' Settlement Needs: The Canadian Experience* (New York: Springer, 2013), 70.

43 It should be noted that "white" ethnicities were typically considered separate races in the nineteenth century. I somewhat anachronistically use the term ethnicity to refer to the European immigrants of various origins who were generally welcomed on Canada's east coast, and in time might gain access to the privileges of "whiteness." This allows us to distinguish these immigrants from clearly racialized Asian arrivals on the west coast, discussed in chapter 5. See also below, 303n71.

44 Charles Herbert, Immigration Officer, Calgary, to A.M. Burgess, Deputy Minister of Interior, Ottawa, 21 April 1896, LAC, Department of the Interior fonds, RG 76, volume 20, file 180, part 1.

45 J. Obed Smith, Commissioner of Immigration, Winnipeg, to Frank Pedley, Superintendent of Immigration, Ottawa, 20 June 1902, LAC, Department of the Interior fonds, RG 76, volume 20, file 180, part 1. See Wright, *Crown Assets*, for indication of the "central Canadian focus" of the Department of Public Works, 65 and passim; and for the "cheaply constructed" quality of the first generation of Prairie immigration halls, 30.

46 R.A. Ruttan, Dominion Lands Agent, Edmonton, to Commissioner of Immigration , Winnipeg, 10 Jan. 1901; Frank Pedley, Superintendent of Immigration, Ottawa, to Thomas Bennett, Immigration Agent, South Edmonton [Strathcona], 20 June 1899; both in LAC, Department of the Interior fonds, RG 76, volume 24, file 531, part 2.

47 R.C. Desrochers, Assistant Secretary, Department of Public Works, Ottawa, to Superintendent of Immigration, Ottawa, 16 June 1904, LAC, Department of the Interior fonds, RG 76, volume 36, file 817, part 1. Inventories recorded at the immigration halls on the occasion of immigration's transfer from the Department of Agriculture to that of Interior in 1892 indicate that all the halls had similar collections of furniture and cooking utensils, plus wash tubs, tools (such as axes, coal-scuttles, and brooms), miscellaneous office supplies, out-of-date provincial directories, and wall maps of Canada; see numerous letters from June 1892 in LAC, Department of the Interior fonds, RG 76, volume 14, file 92, "Immigration Buildings – General."

48 J. Obed Smith, Commissioner of Immigration, Winnipeg, to Frank Pedley, Superintendent of Immigration, Ottawa, 24 Feb. 1902; E.H. Taylor, Winnipeg, to W.T. McCreary, Commissioner of

Immigration , Winnipeg, 28 April 1900; J.M. Gordon, Dominion Lands Inspector, Regina, to Commissioner of Dominion Lands, Winnipeg, 23 March 1895; all in LAC, Department of the Interior fonds, RG 76, volume 104, file 16343, part 1 [C-4767].

49 John T. Stemshorn, Immigration Agent, Regina, to G.H. Campbell, General Immigration Agent, Winnipeg, 12 Feb. 1892, LAC, Department of the Interior fonds, RG 76, volume 36, file 817, part 1.

50 C.V. Speers, Brandon, to W.D. Scott, Superintendent of Immigration, Ottawa, 25 Mar. 1905, LAC, Department of the Interior fonds, RG 76, volume 14, file 116, part 2.

51 "Immigration Matters," Calgary Herald, 13 July 1892; Senator James Lougheed, Calgary, to T.M. Daly, Minister of the Interior, 17 April 1893; Amos Rowe, Dominion Lands Agent, Calgary, to Commissioner of Dominion Lands, Winnipeg, 14 Sept. 1892, all in LAC, Department of the Interior fonds, RG 76, volume 20, file 180, part 1.

52 Charles Herbert, Immigration Officer, Calgary, to A.M. Burgess, Deputy Minister of Interior, Ottawa, 21 April 1896, LAC, Department of the Interior fonds, RG 76, volume 20, file 180, part 1.

53 Annmarie Adams, Medicine by Design: The Architect and the Modern Hospital, 1893–1943 (Minneapolis: University of Minnesota Press, 2008), xx. For the nineteenth-century use of Georgian-style architecture in Canada as an expression of personal and political power, see Harold Kalman, A History of Canadian Architecture, Vol. 1 (Toronto: Oxford University Press, 1994), 122–40. Although Kalman demonstrates that, for prominent homes and public buildings, the Georgian style had largely been superseded by other architectural revivals during the period under examination here, it is evident that the forms and their associated meanings continued to be useful to the Chief Architect's Branch in certain situations, such as in the construction of the new town of Dawson in 1901, described by Kalman, A History of Canadian Architecture, Vol. 2, 691–4. By way of contrast, in Shannon Ricketts, Jacqueline Hucker, and Leslie Maitland, A Guide to Canadian Architectural Styles (Peterborough: Broadview Press, 2004), 47–52, the authors refer to a vernacular or "native

classicism," rather than a continuation of the Georgian aesthetic.

54 Thomas Markus, Buildings and Power: Freedom and Control in the Origin of Modern Building Types (New York: Routledge, 1993); see also above, 290n23.

55 Compelling scholarship on the residential and industrial schools has begun to appear in recent years: Geoffrey Carr, "'House of No Spirit': An Architectural History of the Indian Residential School in British Columbia" (PhD dissertation, University of British Columbia, 2011); Sarah De Leeuw, "Intimate Colonialisms: The Material and Experienced Places of British Columbia's Residential Schools," Canadian Geographer 51, no. 3 (2007): 339–59; Magdalena Milosz, "Instruments as Evidence: An Archive of the Architecture of Assimilation," Journal of the Society for the Study of Architecture in Canada 41, no. 2 (2016): 3–10. See also Wright, Crown Assets, 59–61.

56 Paula Lupkin, Manhood Factories: YMCA Architecture and the Making of Modern Urban Culture (Minneapolis: University of Minnesota Press, 2010). On settlement homes and similar schemes, see Dolores Hayden, The Grand Domestic Revolution: A History of Feminist Designs for American Homes, Neighborhoods, and Cities (Boston: MIT Press, 1982), 151–70; and Deborah E.B. Weiner, Architecture and Social Reform in Late-Victorian London (Manchester: Manchester University Press, 1994). On vocational schools, Shannon Murray, "Making a Model Metropolis: Boosterism, Reform, and Urban Design in Minneapolis, 1880–1920" (PhD dissertation, University of Calgary, 2015), 110–65. The Foucauldian notion of biopower, in which social and political relations take the form of an agreement, or contract, between governments and the governed, informs my conceptualization of assimilation-in-passing; see Michel Foucault, The History of Sexuality, Vol. 1: An Introduction, trans. by Robert Hurley (New York: Vintage, 1990).

57 Lisa Chilton, Receiving Canada's Immigrants: The Work of the State before 1930 (Ottawa: Canadian Historical Association, 2016), 3.

58 Jean Bruce, The Last Best West (Toronto: Fitzhenry and Whiteside, 1976), 60; the source for these regulations is not cited in Bruce's book.

59 J. Obed Smith, Commissioner of Immigration, Winnipeg, to W.D. Scott, Superintendent of Immigration, Ottawa, 15 July 1907, LAC, Department of the Interior fonds, RG 76, volume 19, file 179, part 5.

60 R.A. Ruttan, Dominion Lands Agent, Edmonton, to Secretary, Department of Interior, Ottawa, 20 Nov. 1895, LAC, Department of the Interior fonds, RG 76, volume 24, file 531, part 1.

61 Sandoval-Strausz, *Hotel*, 143–61; quotations, 12, 143.

62 Eric H. Monkkonen, *Police in Urban America, 1860–1920* (Cambridge: Cambridge University Press, 1981), 86–7.

63 Todd DePastino, *Citizen Hobo: How a Century of Homelessness Shaped America* (Chicago: University of Chicago Press, 2005), 132; cf. Monkkonen, *Police in Urban America*, 106–9.

64 Michael B. Katz, *In the Shadow of the Poorhouse: A Social History of Welfare in America* (New York: Basic Books, 1986), 28–9. The story was similar in the Canadian context; see Alvin Finkel, *Social Policy and Practice in Canada: A History* (Waterloo: Wilfrid Laurier University Press, 2006), 67–70.

65 Chilton, "Managing Migrants," 248.

66 Katz, *In the Shadow of the Poorhouse*, 26–35. For the early history of nineteenth-century workhouses, see Markus, *Buildings and Power*, 141–6.

67 "Notes from the Capital: Immigration," *The Globe*, 17 Nov. 1891, 4, ProQuest Historical Newspapers: The Globe and Mail.

68 J.B. Morin, St. Albert [AB], to J.A. Smart, Deputy Minister, Ottawa, 2 Apr. 1898; and extract "Cut from Father Morin's Annual Report," 3 Mar. 1899; both in LAC, Department of the Interior fonds, RG 76, volume 24, file 531, part 2.

69 J.M. Gordon, Inspector, Office of Inspector of Agencies, to Commissioner of Dominion Lands, Winnipeg, 6 Apr. 1895 and 27 June 1894; both in LAC, Department of the Interior fonds, RG 76, volume 24, file 531, part 1.

70 Edmund W. Bradwin, *The Bunkhouse Man: A Study of Work and Pay in the Camps of Canada, 1903–1914* (Toronto: University of Toronto Press, 1972), 104–5; previous quotation, 92. In her "Introduction" to this edition, sociologist Jean Burnet argues for these camps as "a characteristic Canadian phenomenon," vii. See also Hoerder, *Creating Societies*, 148–50, for reference to life in the bunkhouses. The precedent for the nineteenth-century bunkhouse, the "camboose shanty," is described in Kalman, *A History of Canadian Architecture*, Vol. 1, 230–1.

71 Sheila McManus, *The Line which Separates: Race, Gender, and the Making of the Alberta-Montana Borderlands* (Edmonton: University of Alberta Press, 2005), 168–9. For histories of the mixing of race and class in the perception of immigrants, see Donna Gabaccia, "The 'Yellow Peril' and the 'Chinese of Europe': Global Perspectives on Race and Labor, 1815–1930," in *Migrations, Migration History, History: Old Paradigms and New Perspectives*, ed. Jan Lucassen and Leo Lucassen (Bern: Peter Lang, 1997), 177–96. United States historians have analyzed the ways in which race was reconceptualized as more immigrants arrived, with the definitions of, and access to, whiteness changing as the demographics of immigration changed; see Matthew Frye Jacobson, *Whiteness of a Different Color: European Immigrants and the Alchemy of Race* (Cambridge, MA: Harvard University Press, 1998); David R. Roediger, *The Wages of Whiteness: Race and the Making of the American Working Class* (New York: Verso Books, 1999).

72 Chilton, "Travelling Colonist," 171.

73 J. Obed Smith, Commissioner of Immigration, Winnipeg, to J.A. Smart, Deputy Minister, Ottawa, 9 Apr. 1902 and 9 June 1903 [Regina], LAC, Department of the Interior fonds, RG 76: respectively, volume 14, file 116, part 1; and volume 36, file 817, part 1. The 1903 letter was in response to similar sentiments expressed in a letter from the local member of parliament, complaining to Smart about the condition of the immigration hall.

74 W.F. McCreary, Commissioner of Immigration, Winnipeg, to Secretary, Department of Interior, Ottawa, 5 Mar. 1898, LAC, Department of the Interior fonds, RG 76, volume 146, file 34560.

75 R.A. Ruttan, Dominion Lands Agent, Edmonton, to W.F. McCreary, Commissioner of Immigration, Winnipeg, 17 Feb. 1899; and J. Obed Smith, Commissioner of Immigration, Winnipeg, to

J.A. Smart, Deputy Minister, Ottawa, 23 June 1902; both in LAC, Department of the Interior fonds, RG 76, volume 14, file 116, part 1.

76 R.A. Ruttan, Dominion Lands Agent, Edmonton, to Secretary, Department of Interior, Ottawa, 20 Nov. 1895; LAC, Department of the Interior fonds, RG 76, volume 24, file 531, part 1.

77 A.M. Burgess, Deputy Minister of Interior, Ottawa, to Amos Rowe, Dominion Lands Agent, Calgary, 15 Aug. 1892, LAC, Department of the Interior fonds, RG 76, volume 20, file 180, part 1.

78 J. Pearce, Dominion Lands Agent, Calgary, to Dominion Lands Commissioner, Winnipeg, 27 Mar. 1896; Dominion Lands Commissioner to Pearce, 4 Apr. 1896; Pearce to Charles F. Herbert, Immigration Officer, Calgary, 9 Apr. 1896; and associated extracts of letters from Pearce, 13 Feb. 1896, and the Dominion Lands Commissioner, 4 Mar. 1896; all in LAC, Department of the Interior fonds, RG 76, volume 20, file 180, part 1.

79 S.J. Dunning, Sergeant, NWMP, Red Deer, to The Officer Commanding, NWMP, Fort Saskatchewan, 27 Aug. 1894; and J.M. Gordon, Inspector, Department of Interior, New Westminster, to The Commissioner of Dominion Lands, Winnipeg, 17 July 1894, both in LAC, Royal Canadian Mounted Police fonds, RG18, volume 97, file 605.

80 C.W. Sutter, Immigration Agent, Edmonton, to W.F. McCreary, Commissioner of Immigration, Winnipeg, 21 Apr. 1899, LAC, Department of the Interior fonds, RG 76, volume 14, file 116, part 1; and Sutter to McCreary, 20 Feb. 1900; Sutter to McCreary, 18 Apr. 1900; in LAC, Department of the Interior fonds, RG 76, volume 24, file 531, part 1.

81 C.W. Sutter, Immigration Agent, Edmonton, to J. Obed Smith, Commissioner of Immigration, Winnipeg, 24 Apr. 1905, and accompanying testimonials, in the order quoted, from: W.P. Perree, Jas. Geo. Parkes, Harry E. Reedman, 29 Mar. 1905; J.E. Vance and Mrs Malica Vance, 28 Mar. 1905; G.W. Ribchester, 3 Apr. 1905; E. Hammond and Mrs Hammond, 30 Mar. 1905; and W.W. and Mrs Larison, 28 Mar. 1905; all in LAC, Department of the Interior fonds, RG 76, volume 682, file 531, part 2.

82 Petro Zvarych, *Memoirs*, trans. William Kostash (Edmonton: Ukrainian Pioneers' Association of Alberta, 1999), vol. 1, 105.

83 John Keaschuk, "Keaschuk Family," in *Norquay Nostalgia* (Norquay, SK: Book Committee, 1982), 81–2.

84 Sylvia Edstrom and Florence Lundstrom, *Memoirs of the Edberg Pioneers* (Edmonton: Douglas Printing, 1955), 95.

85 Simon Belkin, *Through Narrow Gates: A Review of Jewish Immigration, Colonization, and Immigrant Aid Work in Canada (1840–1940)* (Montreal: Canadian Jewish Congress, 1966), 30–2. It seems that the group stayed briefly at the new 1882 immigration hall, before being transferred to the older one for a longer stay; see excerpts from contemporary Manitoba *Free Press* reports included in *The Land Newly Found: Eyewitness Accounts of the Canadian Immigrant Experience*, ed. Norman Hillmer and J.L. Granatstein (Toronto: Thomas Allen Publishers, 2006), 98–100.

86 Quoted in Campey, *Ignored but Not Forgotten*, 115.

87 George Jenkins, interview by Mae Laidlaw, April 1954, Oral history 2008-2-025 67A, transcript, Esplanade Archives, Medicine Hat.

88 "The Story of Mariia Eurchuk," in William A. Czumer, *Recollections about the Life of the First Ukrainian Settlers in Canada*, trans. Louis T. Laychuk (Edmonton: Canadian Institute of Ukrainian Studies, 1981), 44–5. The distance downriver from Edmonton to Victoria Settlement is about 190 kilometres.

89 Gladys M. Rowell, "Memories of an English Settler," *Alberta History* 29, no. 2 (1981): 14.

90 Zvarych, *Memoirs*, 103.

91 Petryshyn, *Peasants in the Promised Land*, 64. Note that "gray-back" is an archaic term for louse.

92 Secretary, Department of Interior, Ottawa, to Dominion Lands Agent, Edmonton, 10 Aug. 1894, LAC, Department of the Interior fonds, RG 76, volume 24, file 531, part 1.

93 Canada, Parliament, House of Commons, Debates, 9th Parl., 1st sess., vol. 1 (1901), 2898–2903.

94 C. Stemshorn, "Report of the Immigration Officer at Regina," in Canada, Parliament, *Sessional Papers*,

1901, Paper no. 25, "Report of the Minister of Interior," 144.

95 S.L. Tolstoy, *Sergej Tolstoy and the Doukhobors: A Journey to Canada: Diary and Correspondence*, ed. Andrew Donskov, John Woodsworth, and T.G. Nikiforova (Ottawa: Slavic Research Group at the University of Ottawa, 1998), 321. A detailed account of the government's use of the East Selkirk roundhouse as an immigration shed is found at "Canadian Pacific Roundhouse at East Selkirk Converted into the Immigration Building," redrivernorthheritage.com/immigration-from-eastern-europe. Accessed 3 Mar. 2019.

96 Vera Lysenko, *Men in Sheepskin Coats: A Study in Assimilation* (Toronto: Ryerson, 1947), 35.

97 Lehr, "Governmental Coercion," 270–9; quotations on 270, 274. These interactions are well reported in the literature of Ukrainian immigration cited elsewhere in this chapter.

98 Geirfinnur Peterson, "The Narrows Settlement," in *Memory Opens the Door to Yesterday: History as Told by Pioneers of the Central, West-Interlake Area*, ed. Lucy Lindell (Eriksdale, MB: Geirfinnur Peterson [self-published], 1970), 174.

99 Quoted in Lehr, "Governmental Coercion," 274. See also James MacGregor, *Vilni Zemli (Free Lands): The Ukrainian Settlement of Alberta* (Toronto: McClelland and Stewart, 1969), 93; Petryshyn, *Peasants in the Promised Land*, 64–5.

100 Quoted in Petryshyn, *Peasants in the Promised Land*, 63.

101 Laura Goodman Salverson, *Confessions of an Immigrant's Daughter* (Toronto: Ryerson Press, 1939); quoted in Hoerder, *Creating Societies*, 125.

102 Hoerder, *Creating Societies*, 121.

103 "Immigrants Gone North," Calgary *Weekly Herald*, 23 May 1888, 8; Peel's Prairie Provinces, University of Alberta.

104 Zvarych, *Memoirs*, 110. This term for the immigration hall also shows up in Michael Ewanchuk, *Pioneer Profiles: Ukrainian Settlers in Manitoba* (Winnipeg: M. Ewanchuk [self-published], 1981), 66.

105 A.E. Snyder, Inspector, North-West Mounted Police, Edmonton, to The Officer Commanding, "G" Division, North West Mounted Police, 29 Oct.

1894, LAC, Department of the Interior fonds, RG 76, volume 24, file 531, part 1. The immigration branch seems to have accepted the opinion of the NWMP inspector, as the complaining Strathcona agent was in the midst of being sacked anyway for neglecting to maintain cleanliness and order at the immigration hall.

106 MacGregor, *Vilni Zemli (Free Lands)*, 145–6.

107 Lehr, "Governmental Coercion," 271. See also Vladimir J. Kaye, and Frances Swyripa, "Settlement and Colonization," in *A Heritage in Transition: Essays in the History of Ukrainians in Canada*, ed. Manoly R. Lupul (Toronto: McClelland and Stewart, 1982), 43–4; and MacGregor, *Vilni Zemli (Free Lands)*, 104–5.

108 Tom Monto and Randy Lawrence, *Old Strathcona before the Great Depression* (Edmonton: Crang, 2008), 161.

109 Brandon *Mail*, 2 Apr. 1885, 8; Peel's Prairie Provinces, University of Alberta.

110 Extensive correspondence from 1894 to 1905 traces the history of government uses of the Qu'Appelle immigration hall, see LAC, Department of the Interior fonds, RG 76, volume 681, file 95.

111 "Accommodation for Immigrants Wanted," Calgary *Weekly Herald*, 3 Apr. 1889, 4; "Changes in the Immigration Building," Calgary *Daily Herald*, 22 July 1890; and "The immigration Building," Calgary *Daily Herald*, 16 Sep 1890.

112 Hoerder, *Creating Societies*, 173–4.

113 Ed Gould, *All Hell for a Basement: Medicine Hat, 1883–1983* (Medicine Hat: The City, 1981), 27.

114 Various correspondence in Royal Canadian Mounted Police fonds, LAC, RG18, volume 1222, files 292-1891. See also "Home & Gossip" section, Qu'Appelle *Progress*, 29 Jan. 1886, 6, and 23 Nov. 1888, 8; Peel's Prairie Provinces, University of Alberta.

115 Ian McWilliams, "Saskatchewan Town Hall Opera Houses and Community Performance (ca. 1883–1913)" (Ph.D. dissertation, University of Regina, 2014), 135; for entertainments, 78–9; for religious uses of the hall, 125–36.

116 Kalman, *A History of Canadian Architecture*, Vol. 2, 560–2. Marc de Caraffe, et al., *Town Halls of Canada: A Collection of Essays on Pre-1930 Town Hall*

Buildings (Ottawa: Environment Canada-Parks, 1987).

117 J. Doolittle, Clerk, Municipality of South Qu'Appelle, to Secretary, Department of Interior, Ottawa, 17 Apr. 1894, LAC, Department of the Interior fonds, RG 76, volume 681, file 95.

118 McWilliams, "Saskatchewan Town Hall Opera Houses," 88–93; McWilliams also offers a sophisticated analysis of the politics of gender (95–125) and race (137–59) in the staging of events at the immigration hall.

119 A.A. den Otter, *The Philosophy of Railways: The Transcontinental Railway Idea in British North America* (Toronto: University of Toronto Press, 1997), 216.

120 Hoerder, *Creating Societies*, 126.

121 Ibid., 196.

122 Alvin Finkel, "The State of Writing on the Canadian Welfare State: What's Class Got to Do with It?" *Labour/Le Travail* 54 (2004): 157; see also Finkel, *Social Policy and Practice*, 65–93; and Elisabeth Wallace, "The Origin of the Social Welfare State in Canada, 1867–1900," *Canadian Journal of Economics and Political Science* 16, no. 3 (1950): 383–93.

123 C.W. Sutter, Immigration Agent, Edmonton, to W.F. McCreary, Commissioner of Immigration, Winnipeg, 17 May 1899, LAC, Department of the Interior fonds, RG 76, volume 14, file 116, part 1.

CHAPTER FOUR

1 J.S. Woodsworth, *Strangers within Our Gates; or, Coming Canadians* (Toronto: University of Toronto Press, 1972), 35–8; previous quotation, 32. Woodsworth's eugenics-inflected racism has been well-rehearsed, most recently by Jay Dolmage, *Disabled upon Arrival: Eugenics, Immigration, and the Construction of Race and Disability* (Columbus: Ohio State University Press, 2018), 61–6.

2 Gerald Friesen, *The Canadian Prairies: A History* (Toronto: University of Toronto Press, 1987), 245–50; Ninette Kelley and Michael Trebilcock, *The Making of the Mosaic: A History of Canadian Immigration Policy.* (Toronto: University of Toronto Press, 1998), 113–15, 167–9.

3 John C. Lehr, "Peopling the Prairies with Ukrainians," in *Immigration in Canada: Historical Perspectives*, ed. Gerald Tulchinsky (Toronto: Copp Clark Longman, 1994), 188. For a further description of the government system for matching immigrants with needful employers in the first decade of the twentieth century, see Stanley C. Johnson, *A History of Emigration: From the United Kingdom to North America, 1763–1912* (1913; New York: Augustus M. Kelley, 1966), 168–9. The phrase referring to Sifton's "chain of officialdom" is from Jean Bruce, *The Last Best West* (Toronto: Fitzhenry and Whiteside, 1976), 6.

4 E.g., Thomas Gelley, Commissioner of Immigration, Winnipeg, to E.E. Wilson, Immigration Agent, Edmonton, 19 Mar. 1920, Library and Archives Canada (LAC), Department of the Interior fonds, RG 76, volume 613, file 907988, part 1. For the Regina bridges, see "Report of the Commissioner of Immigration, J. Obed Smith to Superintendent of Immigration," in Canada, Parliament, *Sessional Papers, 1905*, Paper no. 25, "Report of the Minister of Interior," 76. For the Dauphin episode, see J. Obed Smith, Commissioner of Immigration, Winnipeg, to James A. Smart, Deputy Minister of the Interior, Ottawa, 23 June 1902, LAC, Department of the Interior fonds, RG 76, volume 14, file 116, part 1.

5 "Report of the Commissioner of Immigration, J. Obed Smith to Superintendent of Immigration," in Canada, Parliament, *Sessional Papers, 1907*, Paper no. 25, "Report of the Minister of Interior," 84.

6 The Ottawa commissioner at the time, Frank Pedley, provided to the House of Commons in 1901 a thorough description of the networked operations of immigrant reception, see Canada, Parliament, House of Commons, Committees, 9th Parl., 1st sess. (1901), Appendix No. 1, "The Immigration and Colonization of 1900," 284.

7 "A Visit to Quebec's Immigration Buildings," Quebec *Morning Chronicle*, 27 Apr. 1910. The article explains that the *Chronicle* was known broadly to be critical of "the apathy that exists in some quarters, detrimental to the progress of the city," but it had been a "sincere gratification" to see that Dominion

government immigration officials, civil servants whom the paper may have expected to share that apathy, in actuality were "well up in their work." The Quebec pier building was over twenty years old and built to handle less than half of the immigrant arrivals of the 1910s.

8 "100,000 of Our Farmers Are Coaxed to Canada Yearly," *New York Times (1857–1922)*, 24 Sept. 1911, SM4, ProQuest Historical Newspapers.

9 Alvin Finkel, *Social Policy and Practice in Canada: A History* (Waterloo: Wilfrid Laurier University Press, 2006); see chapter 4, "Early Canada: Continuity and Change, 1867–1914." Michael B. Katz, *In the Shadow of the Poorhouse: A Social History of Welfare in America* (New York: Basic Books, 1986), traces a similar story.

10 Woodsworth, *Strangers within Our Gates*, 270.

11 Alfred Chandler, *The Visible Hand: The Managerial Revolution in American Business* (Cambridge, MA: Belknap Press 1977); JoAnne Yates, *Control through Communication: The Rise of System in American Management* (Baltimore: Johns Hopkins University Press, 1989).

12 S.L. Tolstoy, *Sergej Tolstoy and the Doukhobors: A Journey to Canada: Diary and Correspondence*, ed. Andrew Donskov, John Woodsworth, and T.G. Nikiforova (Ottawa: Slavic Research Group at the University of Ottawa, 1998), 323–4.

13 T.W. Fuller, Assistant Chief Architect, Department of Public Works, Ottawa, to Jas. M. Stevenson, Resident Architect, Calgary, 29 Sept. 1921; and Stevenson to R.C. Wright, Chief Architect, Ottawa; both in LAC, Department of Public Works fonds, RG 11, registry 3, volume 3341, file 2466.

14 Canada, Parliament, House of Commons, Committees, 9th Parl., 1st sess. (1901), Appendix No. 1, "The Immigration and Colonization of 1900," 288.

15 Canada, Parliament, House of Commons, Debates, 9th Parl., 2nd sess., vol. 1 (1902), 980–2.

16 Florence Hamilton Randall, "How Settlers Are Treated in Winnipeg," Manitoba *Free Press* magazine section, 31 Aug. 1907, 23.

17 Canada, Parliament, House of Commons, Committees, 9th Parl., 1st sess. (1901), Appendix No. 1, "The Immigration and Colonization of 1900," 280.

18 Adam McKeown, *Melancholy Order: Asian Migration and the Globalization of Borders* (New York: Columbia University Press, 2008), 12. For the development of vertical-file technology and filing systems in this period, see Yates, *Control through Communication*, 56–63.

19 Janet Wright, *Crown Assets: The Architecture of the Department of Public Works, 1867–1967* (Toronto: University of Toronto Press, 1997), 97.

20 Canada, Parliament, House of Commons, Debates, 9th Parl., 2nd sess., vol. 1 (1902), 833–4.

21 Canada, Parliament, House of Commons, Debates, 9th Parl., 3rd sess., vol. 6 (1903), 13126–7.

22 "Saskatchewan Homesteading Experiences, 1870–1926" (1926), LAC, MG30-C16, page 704; spelling as in original.

23 Canada, Parliament, House of Commons, Debates, 9th Parl., 3rd sess., vol. 1 (1903): Boyd, 1119–21; Roche, 1122–3; McCreary, 1123–6; Mulock, 1129–30; Borden, 1132. See also "Sleep on Floor of Waiting Room," Winnipeg *Telegram*, 4 Apr. 1903.

24 Frank Oliver, MP, to Sir Wm. Mulock, Acting Minister of Interior, Ottawa, 8 Apr. 1903, LAC, Department of the Interior fonds, RG 76, volume 14, file 116, part 1.

25 Detroit *Evening News*, 9 Apr. 1903; clipping in LAC, Department of the Interior fonds, RG 76, volume 14, file 116, part 1. See also *Edmonton Bulletin*, 27 Mar. 1903; Ottawa *Citizen*, 7 Apr. 1903.

26 W.J. White, Canadian Government Agency, St Paul, to W.D. Scott, Superintendent of Immigration, Ottawa, 10 Apr. 1903; J. Obed Smith, Commissioner of Immigration, Winnipeg, to Scott, 11 Apr.; telegram, Smith to James A. Smart, Deputy Minister, Ottawa, 8 Apr.; Smart to Smith, 9 Apr.; all in LAC, Department of the Interior fonds, RG 76, volume 14, file 116, part 1.

27 James A. Smart, Deputy Minister, Ottawa, to J. Obed Smith, Commissioner of Immigration, Winnipeg, 9 Apr. 1903; Smith to Smart, 13 April; Smith to Sir William Mulock, Acting Minister of Interior, Ottawa, 15 Apr.; Smith to Smart, 20 Apr. 1903; all in LAC, Department of the Interior fonds, RG 76, volume 14, file 116, part 1.

28 J. Obed Smith, Commissioner of Immigration, Winnipeg, to W.D. Scott, Superintendent of

Immigration, Ottawa, 3 July and 23 June 1903, LAC, Department of the Interior fonds, RG 76, volume 14, file 116, part 2.

29 Canada, Parliament, House of Commons, Debates, 9th Parl., 3rd sess., vol. 6 (1903), 13127.

30 The process of arranging land, moving the old buildings, and getting the new hall built are described with gusto in Robert Vineberg, "Welcoming Immigrants at the Gateway to Canada's West: Immigration Halls in Winnipeg, 1872–1975." *Manitoba History*, 65 (2011): 16–17. He quotes the deputy minister's advice, the original letter being: James A. Smart, Deputy Minister, to Clifford Sifton, Minister of Interior, Ottawa, 1 Dec. 1902, LAC, Department of the Interior fonds, RG 76, volume 18, file 179, part 2.

31 Wright, *Crown Assets*, 100. See also Harold Kalman, *A History of Canadian Architecture*, Vol. 1 (Toronto: Oxford University Press, 1994), 546–8, 577–9. Cf. Alastair Service, *Edwardian Architecture: A Handbook to Building Design in Britain, 1890–1914* (London: Thames and Hudson, 1977).

32 Arthur E. Copping, *The Golden Land: The True Story and Experiences of British Settlers in Canada* (Toronto: Musson; London: Hodder and Stoughton, 1911), 28, 34–6.

33 "Memoir of Anthony Brocklehurst," [n.d.], LAC, MG30/C-256.

34 Randall, "How Settlers Are Treated in Winnipeg," 17, 23. Randall was a journalist, poet, and the mother of Canadian author Dorothy Livesay.

35 Ibid. Smith confirmed that the post office for "foreigners" in the 1890 immigration hall was meant to circumvent "their crowding the General Post Office in the City"; J. Obed Smith, Commissioner of Immigration, Winnipeg, to W.D. Scott, Superintendent of Immigration, Ottawa, 6 Apr. 1907, LAC, Department of the Interior fonds, RG 76, volume 19, file 179, part 5.

36 Randall, "How Settlers Are Treated in Winnipeg," 17, 23.

37 "100,000 of Our Farmers Are Coaxed to Canada Yearly," SM4.

38 "Bruce Walker, Autocrat of Canada's Immigrants," *New York Times (1857–1922)*, 15 Oct. 1911, SM4, ProQuest Historical Newspapers.

39 Quoted: "At the Immigration Hall," 19 July 1909, 8; and "More Settlers at Immigration Hall," 14 Mar. 1907, 6. Other examples: "The Monthly Returns," 2 Mar. 1911, 3; "Scarlet Fever Prevalent," 14 May 1912, 1; "Month's Statistics Show Development," 3 Dec. 1912, 8; all in *Edmonton Bulletin*; Peel's Prairie Provinces, University of Alberta.

40 "At the Immigration Hall," *Edmonton Bulletin*, 10 July 1909, 8; "From the Landing," Edmonton *Capital*, 14 Sept. 1910, 1; Peel's Prairie Provinces, University of Alberta.

41 Joseph E. Wilder, *Read All about It: Reminiscences of an Immigrant Newsboy* (Winnipeg: Peguis, 1978), 54–5.

42 "Took to the Fire Escape," *Edmonton Bulletin*, 8 Aug. 1911, 10; "Welsh Man Arrested as Lunatic," Gleichen *Call*, 17 Feb. 1910, 7; Peel's Prairie Provinces, University of Alberta.

43 J. Obed Smith, Commissioner of Immigration, Winnipeg, to J.A. Smart, Deputy Minister, Ottawa, 23 June 1902, in LAC, Department of the Interior fonds, RG 76, volume 14, file 116, part 1. See also, in the "Immigration Hall" pamphlet file at the Moose Jaw Public Library, updates on the "Board of Trade" from Moose Jaw *Times* for 1 Feb. 1901; 4 Apr. 1902; 25 Apr. 1902.

44 "New Public Building," 26 Mar. 1909; "Immigration Hall," 14 May 1909; "Discussions at Board of Trade," 25 Aug. 1911; all in Moose Jaw *Times*. See Canada, Parliament, House of Commons, Debates, 12th Parl., 2nd sess., vol. 6b (1913), 11200.

45 W.T.R. Preston, Commissioner of Immigration, London, to W.D. Scott, Superintendent of Immigration, Ottawa, 28 Feb. 1905; followed by letters from the board, the association, and the MP during the next month; all in LAC, Department of the Interior fonds, RG 76, volume 682, file 531, part 2.

46 J. Bruce Walker, Commissioner of Immigration, Winnipeg, to W.D. Scott, Superintendent of Immigration, Ottawa, 15 May 1914, LAC, Department of the Interior fonds, RG 76, volume 24, file 531, part 5.

47 "Government Left Out the Stoves," 20 Nov. 1906; "Another Bungle at the New Immigration Hall," 3 Apr. 1907; both in Edmonton *Journal*. See also J. Obed Smith, Commissioner of Immigration,

Winnipeg, to W.D. Scott, Superintendent of Immigration, Ottawa, 4 Jan. 1906; Memorandum, Scott to Frank Oliver, Minister of Interior, 28 Jan. 1907. All these news clippings and correspondence are collected in LAC, Department of the Interior fonds, RG 76, volume 682, file 531, part 2.

48 J. Bruce Walker, Commissioner of Immigration, Winnipeg, to W.D. Scott, Superintendent of Immigration, Ottawa, 21 June 1910; J.A. Irvine, Secretary, The Calgary Liberal Association, to Frank Oliver, Minister of Interior, 9 Oct. 1909; H.E. Gillis, City Clerk, Calgary, to Oliver, 25 Feb. 1909; all in LAC, Department of the Interior fonds, RG 76, volume 682, file 180, part 3. For the announcement, see "New Immigration Hall to be Built," Calgary *Daily Herald*, 17 June 1910, 3.

49 J. Bruce Walker, Commissioner of Immigration, Winnipeg, to W.D. Scott, Superintendent of Immigration, Ottawa, 13 and 14 Oct. 1910; F.A. Davis, Canitary [*sic*] Inspector, Calgary, to J. Winn, Immigration Agent, Calgary, 9 Sept. 1910; Winn to Walker, 27 Aug. 1910; all in LAC, Department of the Interior fonds, RG 76, volume 682, file 180, part 3. See also "City May Close Immigr'n Hall," Calgary *News*, 12 Sept. 1910.

50 Kalman, *A History of Canadian Architecture*, Vol. 2, 544; Wright, *Crown Assets*, 14, 17.

51 "Immigration Building Wrecked Was Calgary Discharge Depot," Vancouver *Daily Sun*, 6 Jan. 1917.

52 James A. Smart, Deputy Minister, Ottawa, to D. Ewart, Chief Architect, Public Works Department, Ottawa, 13 June 1904; LAC, Department of the Interior fonds, RG 76, volume 14, file 116, part 2. The hall in Nominingue was actually preceded by an identical building in Peribonca.

53 See E.J. Lemaire, Private Secretary, Prime Minister's Office, to Scott, 25 Feb. 1908; C.B. Major, MP for Labelle, to Sir Wilfrid Laurier, Prime Minister, Ottawa, 24 Feb. 1908; J.M. Arnault, Secrétaire-délégué, La Chambre Syndicale d'Initiative de Nominingue, to Charles R. Devlin, Ministre de la Colonisation, des Mines, et Pêcheries Pour la Province de Quebec, 8 Feb. 1908; Henri Bourassa, to Oliver, 18 July 1905; all in LAC, Department of the Interior fonds, RG 76, volume 356, file 403856.

54 Memorandum, W.D. Scott, Superintendent of Immigration, Ottawa, to Frank Oliver, Minister of

the Interior, Ottawa, 31 Mar. 1909, LAC, Department of the Interior fonds, RG 76, volume 356, file 403856. On more than one occasion, the Dominion government's operation of an immigration hall in Nominingue was ridiculed in the House, first when an appropriation was requested for the repairs and renovations itemized by the caretaker; see Canada, Parliament, House of Commons, Debates, 11th Parl., 2nd sess., vol. 1 (1909), 959–63. Also, Canada, Parliament, House of Commons, Debates, 11th Parl., 3rd sess., vol. 1 (1911), 1884–5.

55 Various correspondence in "Nominingue, P.Q. – Immigration Bldg. – Site and Construction," LAC, Department of Public Works fonds, RG 11, registry 3, volume 3534, file 3396-2.

56 Herbert Johnston, T.I.I. [Travelling Immigration Inspector], Calgary, to Robert Rogers, Minister of the Interior, Ottawa, 23 Sept. 1912; LAC, Department of the Interior fonds, RG 76, volume 682, file 180, part 4.

57 Thomas Gelley, Division Commissioner, Winnipeg, to The Commissioner, Department of Immigration and Colonization, Ottawa, 24 Sept. 1930, LAC, Department of the Interior fonds, RG 76, volume 613, file 907988, part 3.

58 W.D. Scott, Superintendent of Immigration, Ottawa, to J. Bruce Walker, Commissioner of Immigration, Winnipeg, 9 Jan. 1914. White with green trim had been the chosen colours of the immigration halls for several years, but became "regulation" at this same moment; see Walker to Scott, 29 July 1915. Both of these in LAC, Department of the Interior fonds, RG 76, volume 14, file 116, part 3.

59 "Regulations to Be Observed at the Dominion Government Immigration Buildings (Western District)," [n.d., c. 1919], LAC, Department of the Interior fonds, RG 76, volume 14, file 116, part 4.

60 "Report of the Commissioner of Immigration, J. Bruce Walker to Superintendent of Immigration," in Canada, Parliament, *Sessional Papers, 1913*, Paper no. 25, "Report of the Minister of Interior," 94. As far as I know, this is the only occasion that the term "Prairie immigration hall," which I have adopted in this book, was used in official sources.

61 C.V. Speers, Brandon, to W.D. Scott, Superintendent of Immigration, Ottawa, 25 Mar. 1905, LAC,

Department of the Interior fonds, RG 76, volume 14, file 116, part 2.

62 Telegram, J. Obed Smith, Commissioner of Immigration, Winnipeg, to W.D. Scott, Superintendent of Immigration, Ottawa, 28 Aug. 1907, LAC, Department of the Interior fonds, RG 76, volume 19, file 179, part 5.

63 Mrs John C. Kerr, Caretaker, Spirit River, to Charles Sellers, Resident Architect, Department of Public Works, Calgary, 2 Sept. 1941, LAC, Department of Public Works fonds, RG 11, registry 3, volume 3347, file 7631.

64 Thomas Gelley, Division Commissioner, Winnipeg, to A.L. Jolliffe, Commissioner of Immigration, Ottawa, 2 Jan. 1929; J.T. Thorson, Member of Parliament, Ottawa, to Robert Forke, Minister of Immigration, 27 Oct. 1928; LAC, Department of the Interior fonds, RG 76, volume 20, file 179, part 11.

65 R.A.S., A Canadian Citizen, Edmonton, to Robert Forke, Minister of Immigration, 8 June 1928, LAC, Department of the Interior fonds, RG 76, volume 25, file 531, part 7.

66 Elizabeth Byrtus, interviewed by V. Kowalchuk, 12 Mar. 1986, Alice B. Donahue Library and Archives, Athabasca.

67 Albert Eskra, "A Difficult Life," in *Memoirs of Polish Immigrants in Canada*, ed. Benedykt Heydenkorn (Toronto: Canadian-Polish Research, 1979), 63–6.

68 Florence Roberts, "Early Memories, 1917–1919," Alice B. Donahue Library and Archives, Athabasca, 99.15, quotations from pages 13–16, 80.

69 Ibid., 112.

70 The records of these alternative uses of the immigration halls are found in LAC, Department of Public Works fonds, RG 11, registry 3.

71 M.A. Cross, Caretaker, Yorkton, to Resident Architect, P.W. Dept. [Public Works Department], Saskatoon, 30 Mar. 1942, LAC, Department of Public Works fonds, RG 11, registry 3, volume 3548, file 2717.

72 Donald Luxton and Associates, *Town of Peace River: Municipal Heritage Inventory Project, 2010–2013* (2013), 78–80.

73 J. Bruce Walker, Commissioner of Immigration, Winnipeg, to W.D. Scott, Superintendent of Immigration, Ottawa, 24 July 1917, LAC, Department

of the Interior fonds, RG 76, volume 14, file 116, part 4.

74 Winnipeg No. 2 also served as a military detention centre during the war. The various uses and renovations of the Winnipeg halls in this period are described in Vineberg, "Welcoming Immigrants," 18.

75 *Canada* (Montreal: Canadian Pacific Railway [1923]), 12. Collection of the Canadian Centre for Architecture, Montreal.

76 Kelley and Trebilcock, *The Making of the Mosaic*, 192–202; quotations, 193. For the Railways Agreement, see also Donald Avery, *Reluctant Host: Canada's Response to Immigrant Workers, 1896–1994* (Toronto: McClelland and Stewart, 1995), 82–113.

77 Immigrant experiences of this coercion are shared in Dirk Hoerder, *Creating Societies: Immigrant Lives in Canada* (Montreal: McGill-Queen's University Press, 1999), 240–1.

78 M.V. Burnham, Supervisor, Women's Branch, Ottawa, to A.L. Jolliffe, [Commissioner of Immigration, Ottawa], 27 June 1927, LAC, Department of the Interior fonds, RG 76, volume 20, file 179, part 11. This criticism of the management of the Edmonton hall came one year before the complaint of the concerned citizen noted above. For the history of the Women's Division, see Rebecca Mancuso, "Work 'Only a Woman Can Do': The Women's Division of the Canadian Department of Immigration and Colonization, 1919–1937," *American Review of Canadian Studies* 35, no. 4 (Winter 2005): 593–620.

79 F.C. Blair, Secretary of Immigration, Ottawa, to Thomas Gelley, Commissioner of Immigration, Winnipeg, 18 June 1923, LAC, Department of the Interior fonds, RG 76, volume 19, file 179, part 10. An excellent analysis of the imperative to prevent the exposure of single female immigrants to social mixing is provided in Lisa Chilton, "Travelling Colonist: British Emigration and the Construction of Anglo-Canadian Privilege," in *Empire, Migration and Identity in the British World*, ed. Kent Fedorowich and Andrew S. Thompson (Manchester; New York: Manchester University Press, 2013), 169–70, 179–84.

80 Thomas Gelley, Division Commissioner, Winnipeg, to A.L. Jolliffe, Commissioner of Immigration, Ottawa, 29 Sept. 1928 and 8 Mar. 1929,

LAC, Department of the Interior fonds, RG 76, volume 20, file 179, part 11. The complaints and explanations of them offered by the immigration branch are reviewed in "A Reflection on Canada," *The Globe*, 29 Mar. 1929, 4, ProQuest Historical Newspapers: The Globe and Mail. For an historical analysis, see W.J.C. Cherwinski, "'Misfits,' 'Malingerers,' and 'Malcontents': The British Harvester Movement of 1928," in *The Developing West: Essays on Canadian History in Honour of Lewis H. Thomas*, ed. Lewis H. Thomas and John Elgin Foster (Edmonton: University of Alberta Press, 1983), 271–301.

81 Ernest Y. Hague, Chief Health Inspector, and Alex Officer, Tenement Inspector, "Report of an inspection made this date of the Immigration Hall (No. 1), Meade Street. Dominion Government of Canada, Owners," 5 Sept. 1923, LAC, Department of the Interior fonds, RG 76, volume 19, file 179, part 10.

82 The reconfiguration of space was not necessary on the top floor, where the inner bedrooms were lit by a large skylight. See F.C. Blair, Assistant Deputy Minister, Department of Immigration and Colonization, Ottawa, to W.G. Egan, Deputy Minister, 12 Jan. 1925, LAC, Department of the Interior fonds, RG 76, volume 20, file 179, part 11. Previous quotation: Thomas Gelley, Division Commissioner, Winnipeg, to [W.W.] Cory, Acting Deputy Minister, Ottawa, 10 Feb. 1921, LAC, Department of the Interior fonds, RG 76, volume 19, file 179, part 9.

83 Wright, *Crown Assets*, 151–68. See also the heritage designation statements for the Edmonton building: Darryl Cariou, "Immigration Hall: Summary of Architectural and Historical Significance" (2003), Edmonton City Archives, EA-495-61; and Ivan J. Saunders, *Former Immigration Hall, Edmonton, Alberta* (Ottawa: Historic Sites and Monuments Board of Canada, 1984), who includes a useful comparison of the three late-1920s immigration halls with other public buildings under construction at the time, 363–5.

84 Acting Deputy Minister, Department of Immigration and Colonization, Ottawa, to J.B. Hunter, Deputy Minister of Public Works, 27 Oct. 1928; previous quotations, A.L. Jolliffe, Commissioner of Immigration, Ottawa, to [W.J.] Egan, Deputy Minister, Department of Immigration and Colonization, 24 Nov. 1927; Jolliffe to Egan, 17 Sept. 1927; all in LAC, Department of the Interior fonds, RG 76, volume 25, file 531, part 7.

85 All three previous quotations, including the lengthy excerpt of the Prince Albert Health Officer's 1923 report, are drawn from A.L. Jolliffe, Commissioner of Immigration, Ottawa, to W.J. Egan, Deputy Minister, Department of Immigration and Colonization, 21 July 1926, LAC, Department of the Interior fonds, RG 76, volume 104, file 16343, part 5. Local lobbying was undertaken under the auspices of the Sons of England Benefit Society.

86 [A.L. Jolliffe], Commissioner of Immigration, Ottawa, to Thomas Gelley, Division Commissioner, Winnipeg, 24 Jan. 1927, LAC, Department of the Interior fonds, RG 76, volume 104, file 16343, part 5.

87 Thomas Gelley, Division Commissioner, Winnipeg, to A.L. Jolliffe, Commissioner of Immigration, Ottawa, 11 Feb. 1927, LAC, Department of the Interior fonds, RG 76, volume 104, file 16343, part 5.

88 W.W. Robertson, Division Boundary Inspector, Department of Immigration and Colonization, Edmonton, to Thomas Gelley, Division Commissioner, Winnipeg, 15 Oct. 1930, LAC, Department of the Interior fonds, RG 76, volume 25, file 531, part 7.

89 Canada, Parliament, House of Commons, Debates, 16th Parl., 2nd sess., vol. 3 (1928), 2717–18.

90 Thomas Gelley, Division Commissioner, Winnipeg, to A.L. Jolliffe, Commissioner of Immigration, Ottawa, 28 Dec. 1929, LAC, Department of the Interior fonds, RG 76, volume 25, file 531, part 7.

91 [A.L. Jolliffe], Commissioner of Immigration, Ottawa, to [F.C.] Blair, Assistant Deputy Minister, Department of Immigration and Colonization, Ottawa, 5 Nov. 1929, LAC, Department of the Interior fonds, RG 76, volume 613, file 907988, part 3.

92 Canada, Parliament, House of Commons, Debates, 16th Parl., 3rd sess., vol. 3 (1929), 2933.

93 Randall, "How Settlers Are Treated in Winnipeg," 17.

94 Canada, Parliament, House of Commons, Debates, 15th Parl., 1st sess., vol. 1 (1926), 571–2.

95 Finkel, *Social Policy and Practice in Canada*, 82–4, 94–106.

CHAPTER FIVE

1 Canada, Parliament, House of Commons, Debates, 8th Parl., 4th sess., vol. 3 (1899), 8563, 8567–8. For Sifton's reluctance to impose further impediments to entry, see Ninette Kelley and Michael Trebilcock, *The Making of the Mosaic: A History of Canadian Immigration Policy* (Toronto: University of Toronto Press, 1998), 123.

2 Alan Sears, "Immigration Controls as Social Policy: The Case of Canadian Medical Inspection, 1900–1920," *Studies in Political Economy* 33 (Autumn 1990): 96. See also Robert Vineberg, "Healthy Enough to Get In: The Evolution of Canadian Immigration Policy Related to Immigrant Health," *International Migration and Integration* 16 (2015): 284–5.

3 Canada, Parliament, House of Commons, Debates, 9th Parl., 3rd sess., vol. 6 (1903), Appendix 2, "The Immigration and Settlement of 1902," 6–8. See also Geoffrey Bilson, "'Muscles and Health': Health and the Canadian Immigrant, 1867–1906," in *Health, Disease, and Medicine: Essays in Canadian History*, ed. Charles G. Roland (Toronto: Hannah Institute for the History of Medicine, 1984), 399.

4 Barbara Roberts, "Doctors and Deports: The Role of the Medical Profession in Canadian Deportation, 1900–20," *Canadian Ethnic Studies* 18, no. 3 (1986): 18.

5 Stanley C. Johnson, *A History of Emigration: From the United Kingdom to North America, 1763–1912* (1913; New York: Augustus M. Kelley, 1966), 162.

6 While Canadian line-inspection procedures await their historian, the corresponding line inspection of immigrants at Ellis Island is described by Amy L. Fairchild, *Science at the Borders: Immigrant Medical Inspection and the Shaping of the Modern Industrial Labor Force* (Baltimore: Johns Hopkins University Press, 2003), 86–95; she also details inspection procedures at the other borders of the United States, including Pacific ports, 132–50. See also Howard Markel and Alexandra Minna Stern, "Which Face? Whose Nation? Immigration, Public Health, and the Construction of Disease at America's Ports and Borders, 1891–1928," *American Behavioral Scientist* 42, no. 9 (1999): 1317–18.

7 Jack Cameron, to his mother, 27 Aug. 1905, Cameron Family fonds, M177, file 7, Glenbow Archives.

8 See, for example, Dr P.H. Bryce, Chief Medical Officer, to Dr Arthur Potvin, Medical Inspector, Quebec, 30 Aug. 1904, plus further correspondence in LAC, Department of Interior fonds, RG 76, Immigration Branch, volume 21, file 355, part 1.

9 Arthur E. Copping, *The Golden Land: The True Story and Experiences of British Settlers in Canada* (Toronto: Musson; London: Hodder and Stoughton 1911), 15–16.

10 See, for instance, two articles in *The Public Health Journal*: J.D. Pagé, "The Medical Inspection of Immigrants on Shipboard," 3, no. 1 (Jan. 1912): 25–8; and Charles A. Bailey, "The Medical Inspection of Immigrants," 3, no. 8 (Aug. 1912): 433–9. Bailey was the United States medical inspector stationed in Quebec City, while Pagé was the Dominion government chief medical officer in that port, and superintendent of the Savard Park immigrant detention hospital.

11 Roberts, "Doctors and Deports," 20; Cf. Sears, "Immigration Controls as Social Policy," 96–8; and Jay Dolmage, *Disabled upon Arrival: Eugenics, Immigration, and the Construction of Race and Disability* (Columbus: Ohio State University Press, 2018), 53–71. A keen political interpretation of trachoma inspection is offered in Krista Maglen, *The English System: Quarantine, Immigration, and the Making of a Port Sanitary Zone* (Manchester: Manchester University Press, 2014), 148–52.

12 Canada, Parliament, House of Commons, Debates, 10th Parl., 3rd sess., vol. 3 (1907), 6235. The different groups arguing for stricter immigration restrictions are enumerated in Kelley and Trebilcock, *The Making of the Mosaic*, 118, 135–8; see also Bilson, "Muscles and Health," 402.

13 This represents the overall argument of Donald Avery, *Reluctant Host: Canada's Response to Immigrant Workers, 1896–1994* (Toronto: McClelland and Stewart, 1995). Cf. Kelley and Trebilcock,

The Making of the Mosaic, 141–5. The immigration doctors, as well as other eugenics-inspired restrictionists, remained largely "unaware of the corporate interest in importing these 'inferior' labourers," notes Roberts, "Doctors and Deports," 20.

14 M.E. Stortroen, *Immigrant in Porcupine* (Cobalt, ON: Highway Book Shop, 1977), 7–8.

15 Roberts, "Doctors and Deports," 30.

16 Kelley and Trebilcock, *The Making of the Mosaic*, 115–16; the Acts and their implications are described, 138–41.

17 An English Traveller, "In Steerage," in *The Land Newly Found: Eyewitness Accounts of the Canadian Immigrant Experience*, ed. Norman Hillmer and J.L. Granatstein (Toronto: Thomas Allen Publishers, 2006), 141–3. The change in tone of interactions between officials and immigrants in Dominion government pier buildings is noted in Bilson, "Muscles and Health," 399–400; and in Sears, "Immigration Controls as Social Policy," 100–3.

18 Quotations from James A. Smart, Deputy Minister of the Interior, to Clifford Sifton, Minister of the Interior, Ottawa, 30 June 1903; and Smart to P. Doyle, Immigration Agent, Québec, 13 Apr. 1903; Doyle to Smart, 15 Jan. 1903; all in LAC, Department of Interior fonds, RG 76, Immigration Branch, volume 34, file 802, part 2, microfilm reel C-4693.

19 Roberts, "Doctors and Deports," 19–21; quotation, 19.

20 "Report of Chief Medical Officer, P.H. Bryce," in Canada, Parliament, *Sessional Papers, 1909*, Paper no. 25, "Report of the Minister of Interior," 115.

21 J.B. Pagé, Medical Superintendent, Detention Hospital, Quebec, to W.D. Scott, Superintendent of Immigration, Ottawa, 6 July 1907; LAC, Department of Interior fonds, RG 76, Immigration Branch, volume 308, file 284188, part 3, microfilm reel C-7858.

22 "Extract from a Report made by Dr P.A. Bryce and Dr L. Catellier, re Accommodation for Immigrants" [Nov. 1903]; LAC, Department of Interior fonds, RG 76, Immigration Branch, volume 308, file 284188, part 1, microfilm reel C-7858.

23 For the flooring issues, see Dr M. Chisholm, Medical Superintendent, Govt. Detention Hospital, Halifax, to W.D. Scott, Superintendent of Immigration, Ottawa, 7 Oct. 1909; Scott to Chisholm, 11 Oct. 1909; F.J. Macnamara, Montreal Doloment Company, to Scott, 12 Oct. 1909; all in LAC, Department of Interior fonds, RG 76, Immigration Branch, volume 313, file 298870, part 4. Hospital design and hygienic building materials are discussed further in chapter 2, above. Blueprints of the Savard Park immigrant detention hospital in Quebec City are found at LAC, F/350/Quebec/1921. Note that, although Bryce went to Saint John in 1904 and 1905 to find a site for a third immigrant detention hospital, he was unsuccessful. That port never received purpose-built facilities until a new pier building was constructed in 1920–21, which included detention space. There was significant local protest raised against the detention house when it was located in an old hotel from 1907 to 1911; from that point it was accommodated in the old pier building. See W.W. Cory, Deputy Minister, to Robert Rogers, Minister of the Interior, Ottawa, 12 Oct. 1911; and T.B. Willans, Travelling Immigration Inspector, St John, to W.D. Scott, Superintendent of Immigration, Ottawa, 2 Dec. 1911; both in LAC, Department of Interior fonds, RG 76, Immigration Branch, volume 310, file 291267, part 2, microfilm reel C-7861.

24 Dr M. Chisholm, Medical Superintendent, Govt. Detention Hospital, Halifax, to W.D. Scott, Superintendent of Immigration, Ottawa, 3 July 1909, LAC, Department of Interior fonds, RG 76, Immigration Branch, volume 313, file 298870, part 4.

25 Dr P.H. Bryce, Chief Medical Officer, to W.D. Scott, Superintendent of Immigration, Ottawa, 6 Feb. 1908, LAC, Department of Interior fonds, RG 76, Immigration Branch, volume 313, file 298870, part 3.

26 W.D. Scott, Superintendent of Immigration, Ottawa, to Secretary, Department of Public Works, 13 Oct, 1913; L.M. Fortier [Chief Clerk], to Scott, 17 Sept. 1913; Dr P.H. Bryce, Chief Medical Officer, to Scott, 1 Feb. 1912; Dr M. Chisholm, Medical Superintendent, Govt. Detention Hospital, Halifax, to W.D. Scott, 12 Nov. 1910; all in LAC, Department of Interior fonds, RG 76, Immigration Branch, volume 313, file 298870, part 4. For

the increase in civil detention cases, see Roberts, "Doctors and Deports," 22–3.

27 Dr M. Chisholm, Medical Superintendent, Govt. Detention Hospital, Halifax, to W.D. Scott, Superintendent of Immigration, Ottawa, 12 Nov. 1910; Chisholm to Dr P.H. Bryce, Chief Medical Officer, Ottawa, 10 Jan. 1910; both in LAC, Department of Interior fonds, RG 76, Immigration Branch, volume 313, file 298870, part 4.

28 "Immigration Sheds at Quebec Were Built for Traffic of Twenty Years Ago" [no source recorded], 9 July 1907; clipping in LAC, Department of Interior fonds, RG 76, Immigration Branch, volume 34, file 802, part 3, microfilm reel c-4694.

29 W.D. Scott, Superintendent of Immigration, Ottawa, to W.W. Cory, Deputy Minister, 9 May and 10 May, and 20 Nov. 1911; Scott to Frank Oliver, Minister of Interior, 28 Apr. 1911; Scott to Sir Wilfrid Laurier, Prime Minister, 9 Aug. 1911; Laurier to Scott, 1 June 1909; P. Doyle, Immigrant Agent, Quebec, to L.M. Fortier [Chief Clerk], 21 Sept. 1906; all in LAC, Department of Interior fonds, RG 76, Immigration Branch, volume 34, file 802, parts 3–7, microfilm reels c-4694 and c-10683.

30 W.D. Scott, Superintendent of Immigration, Ottawa, to [J.G.] Mitchell, Deputy Minister, 23 Apr. 1914; Scott to Buskard [?], 13 Aug. 1912; William Stitt, General Passenger Agent, Canadian Pacific Railway, to Scott, 21 Apr. 1914; all in LAC, Department of Interior fonds, RG 76, Immigration Branch, volume 34, file 802, parts 8 and 11, microfilm reel c-10683.

31 Telegram, J.D. Pagé, Medical Superintendent, Quebec, to W.D. Scott, Superintendent of Immigration, Ottawa, 7 July 1913; Pagé to Scott, 17 June 1913; both in LAC, Department of Interior fonds, RG 76, Immigration Branch, volume 34, file 802, part 9, microfilm reel c-10683.

32 Because Pier 21 survives as the Canadian Museum of Immigration, there is a considerable secondary literature describing the building, its layout and use, and some of the experiences of immigrants and staff. The Oral History Collection in the museum's research centre comprises hundreds of interviews to support this historical work. Since most of these interviews reflect experiences that occurred after the Second World War, they fall outside the present study; however, see my article which deploys some of them, David Monteyne, "Pier 21 and the Production of Canadian Immigration," in *The Design of Frontier Spaces: Control and Ambiguity*, ed. Carolyn Loeb and Andreas Luescher (Farnham, UK: Ashgate, 2015): 109–28. In addition, readers may consult Dolmage, *Disabled upon Arrival*; Trudy Duivenvoorden Mitic and J.P. LeBlanc, *Pier 21: The Gateway that Changed Canada* (Halifax: Nimbus Publishing, 2011); and articles by Steve Schwinghamer and others on the museum web page: https://pier21.ca/research/immigration-history.

33 Canada, Parliament, *Sessional Papers, 1921*, Paper no. 18, "Report of the Department of Immigration," 26.

34 S.L. Cullen, "New Canadian Immigration Terminal," *Agricultural and Industrial Progress in Canada* 3, no. 4 (Apr. 1921): 73–4.

35 W.R. Little, Commissioner of Immigration, to Mr Black, Deputy Minister, 19 Jan. 1922, LAC, Department of Interior fonds, RG 76, Immigration Branch, volume 21, file 355, part 2. After the First World War, the commissioner seems to have replaced the superintendent role in the Ottawa office.

36 W.R. Little, Commissioner of Immigration, to Mr Black, Deputy Minister, 27 Jan. 1922; Little to J.E. Featherston, 7 Feb. 1922; both in LAC, Department of Interior fonds, RG 76, Immigration Branch, volume 21, file 355, part 2. The anti-Semitism of Canadian immigration officials is detailed in Irving Abella and Harold Troper, *None Is Too Many: Canada and the Jews of Europe, 1933–1948* (Toronto: Key Porter, 2000).

37 Simon Belkin, *Through Narrow Gates: A Review of Jewish Immigration, Colonization, and Immigrant Aid Work in Canada (1840–1940)* (Montreal: Canadian Jewish Congress, 1966), 107–9; for the racism of the Saint John assistant immigration agent, see 105–6; for the technicalities of the Immigration Acts by which officials attempted to reject Jewish immigrants, 102–4, 124–5. Belkin argues that the federal election of 1921 resulted in the softening of the immigration branch's stance toward Jewish refugees, as mass deportations would put the government in an "embarrassing position," 126.

38 Albert O. Lee account in Milly Charon, ed., *Between Two Worlds: The Canadian Immigrant Experience* (Montreal: Nu-Age 1988), 38; Sybil Johnson, *The Way We Were: A Memoir* (Thunder Bay, ON: Rainbow, 1999), 20–3; Ken Collins, *Oatmeal and Eaton's Catalog* (Dryden, ON: Alex Wilson [1982]), 15.

39 "Washed Ashore," in Herman Ganzevoort, ed. and trans., *The Last Illusion: Letters from Dutch Immigrants in the "Land of Opportunity," 1924–1930* (Calgary: University of Calgary Press, 1999), 136.

40 John Leigh Walters, *A Very Capable Life: The Autobiography of Zarah Petri* (Edmonton: Athabasca University Press, 2009), 76–80.

41 John H. Amyot, Minister of Health, speaking to public-health officials in 1925; quoted in Robert Menzies, "Governing Mentalities: The Deportation of Insane and Feebleminded Immigrants out of British Columbia from Confederation to World War II," *Canadian Journal of Law and Society* 13, no. 2 (Fall 1998): 167.

42 Canada, Parliament, House of Commons, Debates, 9th Parl., 3rd sess., vol. 6 (1903), Appendix 2, "The Immigration and Settlement of 1902," 6.

43 For Asian immigration and the Chinese Immigration Act, see Arnold J. Meagher, *The Coolie Trade: The Traffic in Chinese Labourers to Latin America, 1847–1874* (Bloomington, IN: Xlibris Corporation, 2008); Harry Con and Edgar Wickberg, *From China to Canada* (Toronto: McClelland and Stewart, 1982); Patricia Roy, *A White Man's Province: British Columbia Politicians and Chinese and Japanese Immigrants, 1858–1914* (Vancouver: University of British Columbia Press, 1989); Jin Tan and Patricia E. Roy, *The Chinese in Canada* (Ottawa: Canadian Historical Association, 1985).

44 G.L. Milne, Medical Inspector, Victoria, to P.H. Bryce, Chief Medical Officer, Ottawa, 15 June and 6 July 1905; LAC, Department of Interior fonds, RG 76, Immigration Branch, volume 352, file 381766, part 1.

45 P.H. Bryce, Chief Medical Officer, Ottawa, to G.L. Milne, Medical Inspector, Victoria, 22 June 1905; Bryce to Robert McPherson, Member of Parliament, Ottawa, 12 May 1906; both in LAC, Department of Interior fonds, RG 76, Immigration Branch, volume 352, file 381766, part 1. And A.S. Munro, Immigration Agent, Vancouver, to

Bryce, 26 Apr. 1906; LAC, Department of Interior fonds, RG 76, Immigration Branch, volume 328, file 318652, part 1. Prior to 1892 there had been Prairie-type immigration halls in both Victoria (1871–92) and Vancouver (1890–92), but these were closed when the Department of Interior assumed responsibility for immigration in that year, and focused its programming on the reception and support of agriculturalists for the Prairie provinces.

46 Yukari Takai, "Navigating Transpacific Passages: Steamship Companies, State Regulators, and Transshipment of Japanese in the Early-Twentieth-Century Pacific Northwest," *Journal of American Ethnic History* 30, no. 3 (2011): 8–16; Erika Lee, *At America's Gates: Chinese Immigration during the Exclusion Era, 1882–1943* (Chapel Hill: University of North Carolina Press, 2003), 137–41, 157–60.

47 Adam McKeown, "How the Box Became Black: Brokers and the Creation of the Free Migrant," *Pacific Affairs* 85, no. 1 (2012): 35.

48 Lisa Rose Mar, *Brokering Belonging: Chinese in Canada's Exclusion Era, 1885–1945* (Toronto: University of Toronto Press, 2010), 24; previous quotation, 18.

49 Cheng Tianfang, *Oriental Immigration in Canada* (Shanghai: Commercial Press, 1931), 78. Other more industrial ports, such as Union Bay and Nanaimo, had no oversight of immigrants and were popular entry points for illegal immigrants and contraband.

50 For the impact of the inquiry, see Mar, *Brokering Belonging*, 40–6.

51 Patricia E. Roy, "British Columbia's Fear of Asians, 1900–1950," *Social History – Histoire sociale* 13, no. 25 (May 1980): 162. For a detailed description of the 1907 Vancouver riot, see W. Peter Ward, *White Canada Forever: Popular Attitudes and Public Policy toward Orientals in British Columbia*, 3rd ed. (Montreal: McGill-Queen's University Press, 2002), 53–76.

52 G.L. Milne, Medical Inspector, Victoria, to P.H. Bryce, Chief Medical Officer, Ottawa, 20 July 1906; annotation by W.W. Cory on Bryce to Cory, Deputy Minister, Ottawa, 9 May 1906; Milne to Bryce, 22 Apr. 1905; Cory to W.D. Scott, Superintendent

of Immigration, Ottawa, 6 Apr. 1906; all in LAC, Department of Interior fonds, RG 76, Immigration Branch, volume 352, file 381766, part 1.

53 P.H. Bryce, Chief Medical Officer, Ottawa, to G.L. Milne, Medical Inspector, Victoria, 26 Oct. 1906; in LAC, Department of Interior fonds, RG 76, Immigration Branch, volume 352, file 381766, part 1. See also "Wants Detention Shed," Victoria *Daily Times*, 17 Oct. 1906.

54 "New Immigration Building for Here," Victoria *Daily Times*, 5 Feb. 1907.

55 Warwick Anderson, "Excremental Colonialism: Public Health and the Poetics of Pollution," *Critical Inquiry* 21, no. 3 (1995): 640–69; Nayan Shah, *Contagious Divides: Epidemics and Race in San Francisco's Chinatown* (Berkeley: University of California Press, 2001). The doctors' design is discussed in numerous letters: J. Obed Smith, Commissioner of Immigration, Winnipeg, to W.D. Scott, Superintendent of Immigration, Ottawa, 9 Feb. 1907; G.L. Milne, Medical Inspector and Immigration Agent, Victoria, to Scott, 26 Apr. 1907; Milne to P.H. Bryce, Chief Medical Officer, Ottawa, 4 Mar. 1907; Milne to Scott, 18 Sept. 1909; Milne to Scott, 8 Dec. 1906; all in LAC, Department of Interior fonds, RG 76, Immigration Branch, volume 352, file 381766, parts 1 and 2.

56 Untitled news clipping from *The Week, A British Columba Review* (Victoria), 19 Mar. 1910; in LAC, Department of Interior fonds, RG 76, Immigration Branch, volume 352, file 381766, part 2.

57 Adam McKeown, *Melancholy Order: Asian Migration and the Globalization of Borders* (New York: Columbia University Press, 2008), 198–9, 206–10.

58 Canada, Parliament, House of Commons, Debates, 10th Parl., 4th sess., vol. 6 (1908), 10874–83.

59 "Detention Shed Badly Needed," 24 June 1908, and "Work Progressing on Immigration Building," 25 June 1908; both Victoria *Daily Times*; and "Immigration Building at … Victoria," Vancouver *World*, 20 June 1908; both archived in LAC, Department of Interior fonds, RG 76, Immigration Branch, volume 352, file 381766, part 2.

60 Canada, Parliament, House of Commons, Debates, 11th Parl., 1st sess., vol. 2 (1909), 2084–9. It is noteworthy that Templeman lost in the election of 1908; he served in the federal government for twenty years, and in the cabinet for ten, without ever winning an open election.

61 "Helping Hand to Immigrants," news clipping from unknown source, 4 Sept. 1912; S.N. Reid, Dominion Immigration Agent, Victoria, to A.L. Jolliffe, Commissioner of Immigration, Vancouver, 12 Feb. 1921; and "Must Use City Cells," Victoria *Daily Colonist*, 28 Oct. 1909; all in LAC, Department of Interior fonds, RG 76, Immigration Branch, volume 352, file 381766, parts 2 and 3.

62 Canada, Parliament, House of Commons, Debates, 11th Parl., 3rd sess., vol. 2 (1910), 2187.

63 Con and Wickberg, *From China to Canada*, 157.

64 Geo. N. LaFarge, Local Manager, Blue Funnel Lines, Vancouver, to W.D. Scott, Superintendent and Chief Controller of Chinese Immigration, Ottawa, 20 Feb. 1913; LAC, Department of Interior fonds, RG 76, Immigration Branch, volume 351, file 379496, part 3.

65 W.D. Scott, Superintendent of Immigration, Ottawa, to G.P. Baldwin, City Comptroller, Vancouver, 11 Nov. 1907; Jaraknath Das, Secretary, Hindusthani Association, Vancouver, to Scott, 21 Sept. 1907; Annie L. Skinner, President, Traveler's Aid Society of the YWCA, Vancouver, to His Worship the Mayor and Aldermen, Vancouver, 5 Oct. 1907; all in LAC, Department of Interior fonds, RG 76, Immigration Branch, volume 36, file 804.

66 Peter Bryce, Chief Medical Officer, to W.D. Scott, Superintendent of Immigration, Ottawa, "Report on Vancouver Detention Hospital," 4 Nov. 1911; LAC, Department of Interior fonds, RG 76, Immigration Branch, volume 351, file 379496, part 3.

67 Malcolm R.J. Reid, Dominion Immigration Agent and Inspector, Vancouver, to W.W. Cory, Deputy Minister, Ottawa, 26 Nov. 1914; LAC, Department of Interior fonds, RG 76, Immigration Branch, volume 351, file 379496, part 4.

68 Norman Buchignani, Doreen M. Indra, and Ram Srivastava, *Continuous Journey: A Social History of South Asians in Canada* (Toronto: McClelland and Stewart, 1985), 55–9. For a description of the situation from 1907–08, the institution of the continuous-journey Order, and South Asian attempts to challenge it on the basis of British-subject status, see 18–25.

69 Malcolm R.J. Reid, Dominion Immigration Agent, Vancouver, to Dr. F.T. Underhill, Vancouver [with copy to W.D. Scott, Superintendent of Immigration, Ottawa], 23 Dec. 1913; Scott to Reid, 26 Dec. 1913; D. Ewart, Chief Architect, Public Works, Canada, to Scott, 18 Dec. 1913; LAC, Department of Interior fonds, RG 76, Immigration Branch, volume 351, file 379496, part 4. The same language was used to announce the call for tenders in "Immigration Sheds," Vancouver *Province*, 25 Nov. 1913.

70 The brief shift away from in-house design is described in Janet Wright, *Crown Assets: The Architecture of the Department of Public Works, 1867–1967* (Toronto: University of Toronto Press, 1997), 85–93.

71 "The New Detention Building, Vancouver," *Western Call*, 23 Sept. 1914. Other publications of the rendering include "The New Immigration Detention Shed," Vancouver *News-Advertiser*, 1 Jan. 1914; and, quoted above, "Fine Building for Immigration Branch," Vancouver *Province*, 20 Jan. 1914; news clippings all in LAC, Department of Interior fonds, RG 76, Immigration Branch, volume 351, file 379496, part 4. For the local politics in which the building was conceived and constructed, see Julie Gilmour, "H.H. Stevens and the Chinese: The Transition to Conservative Government and the Management of Controls on Chinese Immigration to Canada, 1900–1914," *Journal of American-East Asian Relations* 20, nos. 2–3 (2013): 179–82; for the involvement of Stevens in the *Komagata Maru* incident, see 187–8. By the following decade, the Native Sons of British Columbia adopted an explicitly anti-Asian stance, emboldened by the restrictive Chinese Immigration Act of 1923; during these years, Stevens – born in Great Britain and therefore ineligible for membership in the organization – kept in close contact with the leader of the Native Sons. I am indebted to historian Forrest Pass for clarifying these relationships in correspondence with me, 19 Aug. 2019. See Forrest D. Pass, "'The Wondrous Story and Traditions of the Country': The Native Sons of British Columbia and the Role of Myth in the Formation of an Urban Middle Class," *BC Studies* 151 (2006): 3–38.

72 Canada, Parliament, *Sessional Papers, 1915*, Paper no. 19, "Report of the Chief Architect," 63. The cost of the Quebec City pier building was between $250,000 and $300,000.

73 Memorandum, A.L. Jolliffe, Commissioner of Immigration, Vancouver, to W.W. Cory, Deputy Minister, Ottawa, 9 Dec. 1920; LAC, Department of Interior fonds, RG 76, Immigration Branch, volume 351, file 379496, part 8.

74 A.L. Jolliffe, Commissioner of Immigration, Vancouver, to W.D. Scott, Superintendent of Immigration, Ottawa, 10 Nov. 1916.

75 Ward, *Oriental Missions*, 49–50. The story of the Brandon bride is in Alison Marshall, *Cultivating Connections: The Making of Chinese Prairie Canada* (Vancouver: UBC Press, 2014), 141–2. Another arriving bride mentioned her stay in Vancouver's immigration "jail" for a month in 1918; see Chinese Canadian National Council, *Jin Guo – Voices of Chinese Canadian Women* (Toronto: Women's Press, 1992), 101.

76 N. Lascelles Ward, *Oriental Missions in British Columbia* ([London]: Society for the Propagation of the Gospel in Foreign Parts, 1925), 51–2.

77 Quoted in Con and Wickberg, *From China to Canada*, 154.

78 Jack Lee, quoted in Paul Yee, *Saltwater City: An Illustrated History of the Chinese in Vancouver* (Vancouver: Douglas and McIntyre, 2006), 53.

79 A.L. Jolliffe, Dominion Immigration Agent, Vancouver, to W.D. Scott, Superintendent of Immigration, Ottawa, 5 May 1916 and 14 Apr. 1916; both in LAC, Department of Interior fonds, RG 76, Immigration Branch, volume 351, file 379496, part 6.

80 A.L. Jolliffe, Commissioner of Immigration, Vancouver, to [F.C. Blair], Secretary of Immigration, Ottawa, 19 Jan. 1922; both in LAC, Department of Interior fonds, RG 76, Immigration Branch, volume 351, file 379496, part 8.

81 Canada, Parliament, House of Commons, Debates, 14th Parl., 2nd sess., vol. 2 (1923), 1446. The same questioner also raised the issue of recent escapes from the building by Japanese detainees.

82 A.L. Jolliffe, Commissioner of Immigration, Vancouver, to [F.C. Blair], Secretary of Immigration, Ottawa, 5 Feb. 1920; LAC, Department of Interior

fonds, RG 76, Immigration Branch, volume 351, file 379496, part 7. Percy Reid, [Assistant Chief Controller of Chinese Immigration, Ottawa], to Jolliffe, 29 July 1922; LAC, Department of Interior fonds, RG 76, Immigration Branch, volume 352, file 381766, part 3.

83 David Chuen-Yan Lai, "A 'Prison' for Chinese Immigrants," *The Asianadian* 2, no. 4 (Spring 1980): 16–19. For comparable writings from the same period, recorded at the United States immigration station in San Francisco, see H. Mark Lai, Genny Lim, and Judy Yung, *Island: Poetry and History of Chinese Immigrants on Angel Island, 1910–1940* (Seattle: University of Washington Press, 1991).

84 Dan Black, *Harry Livingstone's Forgotten Men: Canadians and the Chinese Labour Corps in the First World War* (Toronto: James Lorimer, 2019), 257–8, 291–302, 438–9.

85 Belkin, *Through Narrow Gates*, 104. For the changeable relation of North American Jews to whiteness, see Matthew Frye Jacobson, *Whiteness of a Different Color: European Immigrants and the Alchemy of Race* (Cambridge, MA: Harvard University Press, 1998).

86 A.L. Jolliffe, Commissioner of Immigration, Vancouver, to [F.C. Blair], Secretary of Immigration, Ottawa, 16 July 1921; John L. Burbrick [?], Inspector in Charge, United States Immigration Service, Vancouver, to Jolliffe, 12 July 1921; both in LAC, Department of Interior fonds, RG 76, Immigration Branch, volume 351, file 379496, part 8. The provisions of the 1921 Emergency Quota Law were extended by the United States Immigration Act of 1924.

87 Yoshy was investigated by the police numerous times during his career with the immigration branch, and was consistently protected by officials such as A.L. Jolliffe; see James D. Cameron, "Canada's Struggle with Illegal Entry on Its West Coast: The Case of Fred Yoshy and Japanese Migrants before the Second World War," *BC Studies* 146 (2005): 37–62. For Victoria, see "Kuwabara: He Greeted the New Immigrants," in Ann-Lee Switzer and Gordon Switzer, *Gateway to Promise: Canada's First Japanese Community* (Victoria: Ti-Jean Press, 2012), 272–3.

88 A.L. Jolliffe, Commissioner of Immigration, Vancouver, to [F.C. Blair], Secretary of Immigration, Ottawa, 5 Feb. 1920, to Deputy Minister of Immigration and Colonization, 1 Aug. 1919; S.N. Reid, Dominion Immigration Agent, Victoria, to Jolliffe, 12 Feb. 1921; G.L. Milne, Medical Inspector, Victoria, to Dr. D.A. Clark, Assistant Deputy Minister, Department of Health, Ottawa, 18 Jan. 1921; all in LAC, Department of Interior fonds, RG 76, Immigration Branch, volume 352, file 381766, part 3.

89 Roy, "British Columbia's Fear of Asians."

90 [A.L. Jolliffe], Commissioner of Immigration, Ottawa, to Percy Reid, Division Commissioner of Immigration, Vancouver, 19 July 1924; A.E. Skinner, Acting Division Commissioner of Immigration, Vancouver, to Commissioner of Immigration, Ottawa, 27 June 1925; Jolliffe, Division Commissioner of Immigration, Vancouver, to [F.C. Blair], Secretary of Immigration, Ottawa, 19 July 1920; W.D. Scott, Superintendent of Immigration, Ottawa, to D. Ewart, Chief Architect, Department of Public Works, 21 Jan. 1914; G.L. Milne, Immigration Agent, Victoria, to Scott, 4 Feb. 1913; Milne to Scott, 9 Feb. 1912; all in LAC, Department of Interior fonds, RG 76, Immigration Branch, volume 352, file 381766, parts 2 and 3.

91 A.L. Jolliffe, Commissioner of Immigration, Vancouver, to [F.C. Blair], Secretary of Immigration, Ottawa, 6 Mar. 1923; Jolliffe to Blair, 23 and 21 Sept. 1920; Jolliffe, Dominion Immigration Agent, Vancouver, to W.D. Scott, Superintendent of Immigration, Ottawa, 20 Mar. 1918; Jolliffe to Scott, 11 Apr. 1917; Jolliffe to William Henderson, Resident Architect, Public Works Department, Victoria, 7 Mar. 1916; all in LAC, Department of Interior fonds, RG 76, Immigration Branch, volume 351, file 379496, parts 6, 7, and 8.

92 Canada, Parliament, House of Commons, Debates, 14th Parl., 2nd sess., vol. 2 (1923), 1446.

93 Rebecca Ginsburg, "Escaping through a Black Landscape," in *Cabin, Quarter, Plantation: Architecture and Landscapes of North American Slavery*, ed. Clifton Ellis and Rebecca Ginsburg (New Haven: Yale University Press, 2010), 52. The Dominion

government's Penitentiaries Branch developed its own in-house design expertise, so the Chief Architect's Branch was not involved in prison design from the 1890s to the 1960s; Wright, *Crown Assets*, 24–6.

94   McKeown, *Melancholy Order*, 18. Global urban historian Carl Nightingale has argued that anti-Asian immigration restriction attempted to achieve the racial segregation seen in Chinatowns at a trans-Pacific scale; Carl Nightingale, *Segregation: A Global History of Divided Cities* (Chicago: University of Chicago Press, 2012), 154–7.

95   Norman Anick, *Thematic Study: Immigration to Canada, 1814–1914* (Ottawa: Historic Sites and Monuments Board of Canada, 1984), 172–6.

96   P.H. Bryce, Chief Medical Officer, Ottawa, to Clifford Sifton [Minister of Interior], Ottawa, 10 Sept. 1904; A.D. Stewart, Medical Inspector, Montreal, to Bryce, 2 Sept. 1904; Stewart to Bryce, 28 Mar. 1904; all in LAC, Department of Interior fonds, RG 76, Immigration Branch, volume 315, file 305241, part 1.

97   A.D. Stewart, Medical Inspector, Montreal, to W.D. Scott, Superintendent of Immigration, Ottawa, 13 Mar. 1909 and 16 June 1908; Stewart to P.H. Bryce, Chief Medical Officer, Ottawa, 21 May 1908; Stewart to Scott, 29 May 1911 and 30 Dec. 1910; all in LAC, Department of Interior fonds, RG 76, Immigration Branch, volume 315, file 305241, parts 2, 3, and 4.

98   "Cunning Swindlers Fleece Many Foreign Immigrants," Montreal *Standard*, 19 Oct. 1907; P.H. Bryce, Chief Medical Officer, to W.W. Cory, Deputy Minister, Ottawa, 14 Oct. 1907; both in LAC, Department of Interior fonds, RG 76, Immigration Branch, volume 315, file 305241, part 2.

99   Roberts, *Whence They Came*, 54–8. See also Kelley and Trebilcock, *The Making of the Mosaic*, 159–61; and Menzies, "Governing Mentalities."

100 Roberts, *Whence They Came*, 65; in general, see 58–88. In effect, all European deportees from the western provinces were collected in Winnipeg first before being sent to Montreal; all left from Montreal when the St Lawrence River was open to navigation, and from Halifax during the winter months; see also Roberts, "Doctors and Deports," 22–3; and Shin Imai, "Deportation in the Depression," *Queen's Law Journal* 66 (1981): 87.

101 George Ross, Chief Superintendent, Post Office Department, to [Thomas Chase-Casgrain], Postmaster General, Ottawa, 25 Apr. 1916; LAC, Department of the Interior fonds, RG 76, volume 18, file 179, part 7. The immigration branch deputy minister at the time, and the target of this sarcasm, was W.W. Cory.

102 Only one was deported in the end; Roberts, *Whence They Came*, 88–95.

103 Fiona Alice Miller, "Making Citizens, Banishing Immigrants: The Discipline of Deportation Investigations, 1908–1913," *Left History* 7, no. 1 (2000): 73; statistics, 64. Her statistics are based on examination of immigration-branch reports in Dominion government *Sessional Papers*.

104 E. Blake Robertson, Assistant Superintendent of Immigration, Ottawa, to W.D. Scott, Superintendent of Immigration, Ottawa, 3 Jan. 1910; Scott to D. Ewart, Chief Architect, Department of Public Works, 24 Jan. 1913; Ross & Macdonald, [Architects, Montreal], to Ewart, 20 Jan. 1913; LAC, Department of Interior fonds, RG 76, Immigration Branch, volume 315, file 305241, parts 3 and 4. It should be noted that the name of the architectural firm changed from Ross & MacFarlane to Ross & Macdonald (due to the retirement of MacFarlane) during the design process for this building, and this is reflected on the legends of the drawings reproduced herein.

105 Roberts, "Doctors and Deports," 24.

106 Herbert B. Ames, Member of Parliament, to W.D. Scott, Superintendent of Immigration, Ottawa, 4 Feb. 1913; Scott to Ames, 11 Feb. 1913. The changes play out in subsequent correspondence: W.W. Cory, Deputy Minister, to Scott, 29 Apr. 1913; Scott to Cory, 3 May 1913; Scott to D. Ewart, Chief Architect, Department of Public Works, 24 June 1913. The Montreal doctor contended that, for convenience, better lighting, and security, the hospital and detention rooms should be the ones situated on the upper floors of the structure; however, it was too late to change the plans of the

ground and first floor, which had been designed for those uses; see A.D. Stewart, Medical Inspector, Montreal, to Scott, 7 May 1913. All correspondence in LAC, Department of Interior fonds, RG 76, Immigration Branch, volume 315, file 305241, parts 4 and 5. It should be noted that the member of parliament, Sir Herbert Ames was well known for his sociological study of the immigrant neighbourhoods that nestled below the site of the new immigration building; see Ames, *The City Below the Hill: The Slums of Montreal, 1897* (Toronto: University of Toronto Press, 1972).

107 W.D. Scott, Superintendent of Immigration, to D. Ewart, Chief Architect, Department of Public Works, Ottawa, 16 Apr. 1914; Scott to John Hoolahan, Dominion Immigration Agent, Montreal, 8 Apr. 1914; Herbert B. Ames, Member of Parliament, to Scott, 11 Dec. 1913; LAC, Department of Interior fonds, RG 76, Immigration Branch, volume 315, file 305241, parts 5 and 6.

108 John Hoolahan, Dominion Immigration Agent, Montreal, to W.D. Scott, Superintendent of Immigration, Ottawa, 1 May and 13 May 1914; LAC, Department of Interior fonds, RG 76, Immigration Branch, volume 315, file 305241, part 6.

109 Canada, Parliament, *Sessional Papers*, "Report of the Department of Immigration": *1923*, Paper no. 13, 45; *1924*, Paper no. 13, 39; *1926*, Paper no. 94, 57; *1928*, Paper no. 14, 95. For these four years in Winnipeg, 113,092 meals were fed to deportees. It was first proposed to take over the third floor of the Montreal building for detention purposes in late July 1914.

110 "Montreal as an Immigration Centre," Wetaskiwin *Times*, 22 Dec. 1921, 5; Peel's Prairie Provinces, University of Alberta. See also the discussion of complaints concerning the lack of accommodation in Montreal by a local immigration chaplain: A. Regimbal, Dominion Immigration Agent, Montreal, to Commissioner of Immigration, Ottawa, 13 Dec. 1923; Assistant Deputy Minister to [W.J.] Egan, Deputy Minister for Immigration, Ottawa, 11 Feb. 1924; LAC, Department of Interior fonds, RG 76, Immigration Branch, volume 668, file C1599, part 1.

111 Roberts, "Doctors and Deports," 30; previous quotation, 24. Other problems with the building recounted in the voluminous correspondence of LAC, Department of Interior fonds, RG 76, Immigration Branch, volume 315, file 305241, parts 6 to 10; and in L.N. Beard, Acting Dominion Immigration Agent, Montreal, to Commissioner of Immigration, Ottawa, 11 Aug. 1923; LAC, Department of Interior fonds, RG 76, Immigration Branch, volume 668, file C1599, part 1.

112 Helen R.Y. Reid, Convener of Auxiliary, [Montreal], to Dr [J.] Pagé, Dominion Immigration Agent, Quebec, 1 Oct. 1919; and T.B. Willans, Travelling Immigration Inspector, to W.R. Little, Commissioner of Immigration, Ottawa, 10 Oct. 1919; LAC, Department of Interior fonds, RG 76, Immigration Branch, volume 317, file 305241, part 10.

113 A.D. Stewart, Medical Superintendent, Montreal, to [W.D. Scott], Superintendent of Immigration, Ottawa, 27 July 1914; John Hoolahan, Dominion Immigration Agent, Montreal, to Scott, 28 July 1914; Scott to Stewart, 31 July 1914; LAC, Department of Interior fonds, RG 76, Immigration Branch, volume 315, file 305241, part 7.

114 A.D. Stewart, Medical Superintendent, Montreal, to John Hoolahan, Dominion Immigration Agent, Montreal, 6 Nov. 1914; Stewart to [W.D. Scott], Superintendent of Immigration, Ottawa, 18 July 1914; Stewart to Scott, 23 June 1914; LAC, Department of Interior fonds, RG 76, Immigration Branch, volume 315, file 305241, part 7.

115 W.D. Scott, Superintendent of Immigration, to P.S. Gregory, Architect in Charge of Maintenance, Department of Public Works, Ottawa, 9 Jan. 1918; A. Regimbal, Dominion Immigration Agent, Montreal, to Scott, 3 Aug. and 25 April 1917; Scott to Gregory, 5 Sept. 1917; Scott to E.L. Horwood, Chief Architect, Department of Public Works, Ottawa, 9 Dec. 1915; LAC, Department of Interior fonds, RG 76, Immigration Branch, volume 315, file 305241, parts 8 and 9. Note that escapes from the Montreal building continued after the period of the present study, at least into the 1940s; see the file "Escapes from detention, Montreal, Quebec,

1924–1947," LAC, Department of Interior fonds, RG 76, Immigration Branch, volume 602, file 882029.

116 E.C. Moquin, Dominion Immigration Agent, Montreal, to J.S. Fraser, Division Commissioner of Immigration, Ottawa, 3 Aug. 1928; LAC, Department of Interior fonds, RG 76, Immigration Branch, volume 602, file 882029.

117 J.M. Langlais, Dominion Immigration Agent, Montreal, to J.S. Fraser, Eastern Division Commissioner, Ottawa, 21 July 1931, with attachments; LAC, Department of Interior fonds, RG 76, Immigration Branch, volume 602, file 882029. The Montreal agent recently had been replaced due to his alcoholism, which may have allowed for the guard's tavern habit. At this moment, the new agent also arranged for an electric light to be placed in the narrow lane between buildings on the west, an improvement first requested by another predecessor eleven years earlier.

118 F.C. Blair, Secretary, Department of Immigration and Colonization, to P.S. Gregory, Architect in Charge of Maintenance, Department of Public Works, Ottawa, 3 Dec. 1920; Manager, Canadian General Electric Company Limited, Montreal, to [J.A.] Calder, Minister of Interior, 29 Nov. 1920; LAC, Department of Interior fonds, RG 76, Immigration Branch, volume 317, file 305241, part 10. And for the "indecent exposure," see E.C. Moquin, Dominion Immigration Agent, Montreal, to J.S. Fraser, Division Commissioner of Immigration, Ottawa, 5 Apr. 1928; in LAC, Department of Interior fonds, RG 76, Immigration Branch, volume 668, file C1599, part 2.

119 A.L. Jolliffe, Commissioner of Immigration, Ottawa, to [W.J.] Egan, Deputy Minister for Immigration, 22 Aug. 1931; and notation, 16 Sept. 1931; J.S. Fraser, Division Commissioner of Immigration, Ottawa, to Jolliffe, 31 July 1931; T.B. Willans, Travelling Immigration Inspector, Ottawa, to Fraser, 24 July 1931; all in LAC, Department of Interior fonds, RG 76, Immigration Branch, volume 668, file C1599, part 2.

120 Roberts, *Whence They Came*, 127–89; quotation, 164.

121 Dennis Molinaro, "'A Species of Treason?': Deportation and Nation-Building in the Case of Tomo Čačić, 1931–1934," *Canadian Historical Review* 91, no. 1 (2010): 81.

122 "Accept New Settlers on One Hand, Throw out Deportees with Other," Toronto *Star*, 19 Dec. 1932, 19; this article is quoted again in subsequent paragraphs.

123 A.L. Jolliffe, Commissioner of Immigration, Ottawa, to [W.J.] Egan, Deputy Minister for Immigration, 22 Aug. 1931; J.S. Fraser, Division Commissioner, to Jolliffe, 4 Jan. 1932, which addresses the newspaper exposé; LAC, Department of Interior fonds, RG 76, Immigration Branch, volume 668, file C1599, part 2.

124 Although see the fascinating account of photographs taken by refugees detained at Pier 21 after the Second World War: Lynda Mannik, *Photography, Memory, and Refugee Identity: The Voyage of the SS* Walnut, *1948* (Vancouver: UBC Press, 2013).

125 All quotations in the previous three paragraphs from Oscar Ryan, *Deported!* (Toronto: CLDL, 1932), 3–4, 9–10; and from "How They Treat Deportees," *Labor Defender* (Nov. 1932): 6. Other periodicals also strove to individualize the stories of deportees, as in the editorial, "Murder by Proxy," *Canadian Forum* 14 (Feb. 1934): 165. For the history of these deportations, see Kelley and Trebilcock, *The Making of the Mosaic*, 246–8; Roberts, *Whence They Came*, 135–41; and the theoretical and biographical work of Dennis Molinaro, "'Citizens of the World': Law, Deportation, and the *Homo Sacer*, 1932–1934," *Canadian Ethnic Studies* 47, no. 3 (2015): 143–61.

126 Miller, "Making Citizens, Banishing Immigrants," 64. Cf. Dolmage, *Disabled upon Arrival*, 56–7, who argues that Canadian immigration-inspection procedures "had an indelible rhetorical effect"; and Molinaro, "'A Species of Treason," 62, 78.

127 Avery, *Reluctant Host*, 79.

128 E.C. Moquin, Dominion Immigration Agent, Montreal, to J.S. Fraser, Division Commissioner of Immigration, Ottawa, 12 Oct. 1925; in LAC, Department of Interior fonds, RG 76, Immigration

Branch, volume 668, file C1599, part 1. L.N. Beard, Principal Clerk, Department of Immigration and Colonization, Montreal, to Fraser, 17 June 1927; and Fraser to Moquin, 4 July 1927; in LAC, Department of Interior fonds, RG 76, Immigration Branch, volume 602, file 882029.

EPILOGUE

1 Joann Saarnit and other Estonians, found in Milly Charon, ed., *Between Two Worlds: The Canadian Immigrant Experience* (Montreal: Nu-Age, 1988), 70–1. See also Lynda Mannik, *Photography, Memory and Refugee Identity: The Voyage of the SS Walnut, 1948* (Vancouver: UBC Press, 2013); and David Monteyne, "Pier 21 and the Production of Canadian Immigration," in *The Design of Frontier Spaces: Control and Ambiguity*, ed. Carolyn Loeb and Andreas Luescher (Farnham, UK: Ashgate, 2015), 109–28.

2 Harry H. Hiller, "Airports as Borderlands: American Preclearance and Transitional Spaces in Canada," *Journal of Borderlands Studies* 25, nos. 3–4 (2010): 19–30. Hiller situates the origin of US pre-clearance in the 1950s, but the present study shows that it was established much earlier.

3 Anna Pratt, *Securing Borders: Detention and Deportation in Canada* (Vancouver: University of British Columbia Press, 2005), 23–52. See also the compelling analysis of the Laval Immigration Holding Centre outside Montreal, in Ella den Elzen, "Between Borders and Bodies: Revealing the Architectures of Immigration Detention," *Journal of Architectural Education* 74, no. 2 (2020): 288–98.

4 Robert Vineberg, *Responding to Immigrants' Settlement Needs: The Canadian Experience* (New York: Springer, 2013), 19–33, 39–48.

INDEX

House of Commons, 90, 154, 156, 207, 233, 256; debates over immigration buildings, 156–9, 161, 201–2

Hudson's Bay Company, 100

immigrant aid societies, 42, 243, 279, 282; in immigration buildings, 153, 218, 222, 228

immigrant detention hospitals, 8, 16, 90, 237; as building type, 204–6, 211–16, 259–60; design of, 260–1, 265, 319n106; ethnic segregation in, 215, 239, 261, 265; local interest in, 261, 273–4; mixing of sick and well in, 215–17, 258, 265–6, 270, 274–5; need for, 210–11; security concerns in, 216–17, 255–6; security features, 204, 212–13, 237–8, 252, 265–8, 271–3; sex segregation in, 215, 265; vermin in, 257, 274–5. *See also* Halifax; Montreal; Quebec City; Victoria

immigrant reception, 7–8, 11, 103, 147–8, 280–2; corruption in, 234–6, 255; infrastructure, 24, 94–100, 128; modernization of, 149–55, 203–4. *See also* Dominion government

immigrants: as burdens on towns, 20–2, 133; as category, 54, 233–4, 287n1; children, 33, 35, 85–6, 231, 252–3; control of, 12, 19, 22–4, 46, 54–5, 125–8, 191–2, 198, 206; desirable, 6, 8, 75, 94, 169, 207; families, 26, 191; hospitalization of, 206–7, 210, 215–16; lack of shelter for, 21–3, 93, 234; letters home, 28–9, 157, 275; protection of, 22–4, 44–5, 54, 104–5, 114, 193, 202, 258–9; recruitment of, 26, 93–4, 105–6; as spectacle, 44, 75, 138, 143; undesirable, 15–16, 69, 106, 149, 169, 277; women, 5–6, 38, 48, 135–6, 144, 191–2, 251–2. *See also specific places of origin*

immigrant sheds, pre-Confederation, 20–3, 55–6, 60

Immigration Acts: of 1869, 66, 207; of 1906, 151, 209, 259; of 1910, 151, 209, 242, 259–60; amendment of 1902, 207. *See also* Chinese Immigration Act

immigration agents (in immigration halls), 93, 100–1, 164–5, 270–1; independence from Ottawa, 103–4, 131–2, 152; interactions with immigrants, 133–4, 137, 163–4, 187–8; monitoring immigrants, 105, 114, 125, 168, 187, 198–9

immigration agents (at pier buildings), 18, 35, 48, 209–10, 222, 229–30

immigration agents (pre-Confederation), 22, 291n10

immigration branch, 13, 184, 218, 290n27; and Chinese Immigration Act, 236, 245; managerial revolution in, 150, 153–5, 195, 250; operations, 93, 101–2, 132,

259–60, 274; paperwork, 154–5, 184, 250, 259; Women's Division, 191

immigration buildings: cost of, 242, 249, 317n72; ethnic segregation in, 222, 250; length of stay allowed, 48, 103–4, 108, 184; local interest in, 44–6, 135, 141–7; modernization of, 155, 193, 195; security of, 45–7; seasonal use of, 38, 49, 98, 108; social mixing in, 140–2, 191; space for clergy in, 218, 230; vandalism of, 185, 192, 252–4. *See also* immigrant detention hospitals; immigrant sheds; immigration halls; pier buildings; quarantine stations; Vancouver

immigration commissioner (western), 101, 103–4, 164. *See also* Gelley, Thomas; McCreary, William; Smith, J. Obed; Walker, J. Bruce

immigration halls, 3, 93, 147–8, 237, 261, 268, 279–80, 309n60; as building type, 122, 125, 193, 195; colour of, 124, 183, 187; as community amenities, 94, 142–7; conversion to alternate uses, 144–7, 175, 189–90, 193, 201; cost of, 114, 116, 120, 201; design of, 98–9, 108–25, 180–4, 192–3, 195, 198; electric light in, 123–4, 173–4, 181, 183; ethnic segregation in, 93, 122, 128–31, 156, 159–61, 195–8; family rooms, 116–19, 129–30; as institutions, 125–34, 142; local interest in, 170–2, 174, 186; migrant experiences in, 107, 134–42, 166–8, 185–8, 192–3; numbers of guests, 102–3, 191, 202; reasons to stay at, 103–6, 131–2; rules governing stays at, 126, 131, 184, 187; sex segregation in, 111–16, 122, 128–30, 167, 192, 198; siting, 100, 111–12, 142, 159; standard design of 1908, 170–2, 180–4, 186, 190, 195, 198; towns lobbying for, 172–5, 193–5; vermin in, 135, 137–8. *See also specific locations*

immigration officials. *See* Dominion government: immigration officials; immigration branch; matrons

immigration policy: post-Confederation (*see* Dominion government: immigration policy; National Policy); pre-Confederation, 19–20

immigration sheds. *See* pier buildings

Indian Residential Schools, 125

inspection of immigrants, 8, 68–9, 103, 169, 204, 250, 277; procedures for, 220–1, 229–32; spaces for, 34, 207–8, 218, 220–4. *See also* civil inspection of immigrants; medical inspection of immigrants

institutional buildings, architecture of, 12, 125–31, 134, 288n23

Irish immigration, 21, 58–9

Japanese immigrants, 236, 242, 254–6
Jewish immigrants (from Russia), 135, 230, 314n37

Kisacky, Jeanne, 71, 76
kitchens, 5, 82–3, 136, 166–8, 187, 268; Chinese kitchens, 82–3, 234, 242, 250

language: as distinguisher of class, 129–31; English, 129, 139, 279; for signage in immigration buildings, 32, 73, 131, 187
laundry rooms, 5, 166–7
Lawlor's Island (NS) quarantine station, 66, 74–5, 84
Lefebvre, Henri, 8–10, 287n6
Lehr, John, 105, 139, 151
London (ON), 98, 108

Maglen, Krista, 54–5, 64, 80
matrons, government-appointed: at immigration halls, 101, 133, 136, 185–6, 191; lodgings of, 33, 38, 49, 222; at pier buildings, 28–9, 48
McCreary, William: as member of Parliament, 28, 138–9, 156–7, 159, 161; as western commissioner of immigration, 28, 130, 137, 141, 153–4
McKeown, Adam, 12, 155, 235, 257
medical inspection of immigrants, 204–9, 233–4, 257, 280
miasma theory, 64, 66–7, 71, 142
migrants: expedient shelter for, 21–2, 101–2; experiences of immigration buildings (*see specific locations*); gratitude for immigration buildings, 133–4, 139; journeys of, 19–22, 42, 95, 136–7; mobility of, 12; stories of, as sources, 9–10, 14–16, 288n11
Miller, Fiona Alice, 260, 277
Montizambert, Frederick (medical superintendent of quarantine), 68, 70–5
Montreal: as eastern hub for deportation, 258, 260, 274; immigrant detention hospital, 204–6, 256, 260–74, 277–8; immigration shed of 1870, 95–8, 257; lack of immigration buildings, 29, 257–9; migrant experiences in, 257–8, 270–4; pre-Confederation immigration buildings, 21; rented immigration buildings, 257–8
Moodie, Susanna, 58–9, 64
Moose Jaw (SK), 172
Mulock, William (MP), 157–60
municipal lodging houses, 127

National Policy, 93–4, 147
New York City: Castle Garden immigration station, 27–8; Ellis Island immigration station, 12–13, 50, 60, 153, 208; quarantine stations, 28, 71
New York Times, 153–4, 168
Nominingue (QC), 179–80
North Battleford (SK), 193–4
North-West Mounted Police, 132, 143–6, 192
North-West Rebellion, 144

Oleskiw, Joseph, 6, 48, 107, 287n3
Oliver, Frank (MP and minister of interior), 108, 121, 151, 173, 218

Partridge Island (NB) quarantine stations, 56, 60–2, 84–5, 90
pier buildings (for immigration), 3, 14–16, 50, 207, 279–81; detention spaces in, 222, 229; sex segregation in, 37–8, 128, 192, 222; spaces for inspection in, 207–8, 210, 221–4, 229. *See also* Halifax; Quebec City; Saint John
Pointe-Lévy (QC), 42, 55
police lodging, 127, 131
Prairie immigration halls. *See* immigration halls
Prince Albert (SK), 195, 201; immigration hall of 1892, 114, 123; immigration hall of 1911, 186, 194–5; immigration hall of 1928, 193, 195–8, 201–2
Prince Rupert (BC) quarantine station, 91
public health, 20, 24, 90, 206–7, 217, 282; relation to quarantine, 55, 68–9, 92

Qu'Appelle (SK), 108–14, 144–7
quarantine: critiques of, 51–4, 92, 295n6; differences between east and west coast, 79–82; inspection, 56, 65–6, 68–9, 207, 234, 257; length of, 53, 72; mixing of sick and healthy, 51, 55–6; as performance, 65, 68, 75, 90; procedures, 51–4, 57–60, 74–5, 85, 282; regulations, 56, 66, 68. *See also* disinfection
quarantine stations, 3, 8, 14, 53–5, 90, 277, 280; medical superintendents, 66, 68, 76, 84–5; migrant experiences of, 80, 84, 87; modernization of, 55, 66, 69–72; staff, 84–7. *See also* Grosse-Île quarantine station; Lawlor's Island quarantine station; Partridge Island quarantine stations; William Head quarantine station
Quebec (province), 175, 179–80, 211